APOCALYPSE ROAD

REVELATION FOR THE FINAL GENERATION

Bill Salus

The Author of Revelation Road

First printing: 2017

Prophecy Depot Publishing
P.O. Box 5612
La Quinta, CA 92248
Customer Service: 714-376-5487
www.prophecydepotministries.net

ISBN: 978-0-9887260-9-3

Cover by Matthew Salhus
Interior by Mark Conn

Printed in the United States of America

APOCALYPSE ROAD

Revelation for the Final Generation

Bill Salus

Acknowledgements

Heartfelt thanks to my wife, children, grandchildren and friends who inspired me to write this book. A further debt of gratitude is extended to Bob and Lynette Holmes, Brad Myers, Ladd Holton, Scott Bueling, the Gaskin's, the Peterson's and all those below who in one way or another, through prayer, encouragement, support, research, or otherwise, genuinely blessed this book.

Contents
The Novel

Introduction 15

Recap of Revelation Road (Reviewing Book One of this Series) 18

Chapter 1   The Message Left Behind 22

Chapter 2   Rabbis Warn of the Future Russian Invasion 28

Chapter 3   The European Union Consoles Israel 33

Chapter 4   The EU Condemnation and Vatican Consecration
of Russia 37

Chapter 5   144,000 Jewish Evangelists 41

Chapter 6   Hooked in the Jaws – Russia Covets Israeli Contracts
with the West .48

Chapter 7   Jews Flee Israel as the Russian Invasion Begins 51

Chapter 8   The Antichrist and the Coming Global Religion 64

Chapter 9   The Collapse of the Russian Coalition 78

Chapter 10   Letter to the Saints Left Behind 84

Chapter 11   The Queen of Heaven Appears Globally 89

Chapter 12   The Harlot Rides the Beast to Peace and Prosperity 94

Chapter 13   Israel Cleanses the Holy Land 98

Chapter 14   Doomsday Conference Erupts Into Deadly Chaos 104

Chapter 15   Jews Return Home as Rumors of Nuclear Wars Abound . 113

Chapter 16   The Vatican Global Council Meeting 125

Chapter 17   Millions Witness Eucharistic Miracles from Rome 138

Chapter 18   Two Witnesses Prepare for the Tribulational Period . . . 146

Chapter 19   The Encounter between Satan and his Seed 150

Contents
The Post-Rapture /
Pre-Tribulation Thesis

Topics Covered:

The Post-Rapture / Pre-Tribulation Thesis 156

1   Introduction to the Post-Rapture / Pre-Tribulation Thesis 157

2   What Will the World Look Like Shortly After the Rapture? 160

3   The Revealing of the Antichrist 161

4   The Church is in Heaven Before the Antichrist is Revealed on Earth 162

5   The Revealing of the Antichrist is Being Restrained 164

6   The Mystery of Lawlessness and the Lawless One 165

7   The Antichrist's Rise to Political Power Takes Time 167

8   The Two Parties of the False Covenant 168

9   The Post-Rapture / Pre-Trib Timing of the First Five Seals 170

10   First Seal: The White Horseman of the Apocalypse 170

11   Second Seal: The Fiery Red Horseman of the Apocalypse 171

12   Third Seal: The Black Horseman of the Apocalypse 172

13   Fourth Seal: The Pale Horsemen of the Apocalypse 173

14   Who are Death and Hades? 174

15   Is Islam the Fourth Horsemen of the Apocalypse? 176

16   Is Islam the Harlot World Religion? 177

17 Who are Death and Hades Killing? 179

18 Fifth Seal: The Martyrs of the Apocalypse 179

19 The Two Killing Crusades that Martyr Christians After
the Rapture 180

20 How Do the Fifth Seal Saints Get Saved? 181

21 The Three Periods of Post Rapture Christian Martyrdom 184

22 Why is the Roman Catholic Church Cast into the
Great Tribulation? 186

23 How Will God Kill the Children of Thyatira? 191

24 The Main Obsessions of the Blessed Mother 192

25 Satan's Plan to Influence Mankind Through the Harlot 193

26 Salvation Comes Through the Roman Catholic Church 194

27 The False Covenant of Death in Agreement with Sheol 201

28 What is the True Content of the False Covenant? 205

29 The Two Deadly Phases of the Overflowing Scourge 210

30 Phase One of the Overflowing Scourge – Isaiah 28:15 210

31 Phase Two of the Overflowing Scourge – Isaiah 28:18 211

32 Summary of the Two Phased Overflowing Scourge 212

Contents
Companion's Commentary

Introduction to The Companion's Commentary 216

Chapter 1 — The Message Left Behind **218**
   Topics Covered   What is the Post-Rapture /
                          Pre-Tribulation Gap Period? 218
                          How Long is the Post-Rapture /
                          Pre-trib Gap Period?. 219
                          Why the Gap Period Takes Time? 220
                          Identifying the Final Generation 222
                          The Post Rapture People Categories 222
                          Why Should a Believer Care About
                          Those Left Behind? 224

Chapter 2 — Rabbis Warn of the Future Russian Invasion **225**
   Topics Covered   Ezekiel 38: The Ezekiel 38 Battle Belongs
                          to the Lord 225
                          Ezekiel 38: The Glory Belongs to the Lord .226
                          Is Ezekiel 38 a Church Age Prophecy? . . .229
                          Topics related to the Timing of Ezekiel 38 . .230

Chapter 3 — The European Union Consoles Israel **234**
   Topics Covered   The EU and the Revived Roman Empire . .234
                          The Coming Greater, Safer and
                          Wealthier Israel 236
                          Russia's evil plan against Israel in
                          Ezekiel 38:10. 239
                          The Decline of the USA and UK 240
                          The Biblical Indictment of America 241

Chapter 4 — The EU Condemnation and Vatican
              Consecration of Russia **250**
   Topics Covered   The Four Final Religions after the Rapture .252

Chapter 5 — 144,000 Jewish Evangelists **257**
Topics Covered   People Get Saved After the Rapture 258
Is Receiving Christ a Now or Never
Proposition Before the Rapture? 259

Chapter 6 — Hooked in the Jaws – Russia Covets Israeli
Contracts with the West **269**
Topics Covered   The Roles of the USA and UK in Ezekiel 38 .270

Chapter 7 — Jews Flee Israel as the Russian Invasion Begins **278**
Topics Covered   The Gog of Magog Invasion from
the Israeli Perspective 278
Does the Israel of Ezekiel 38 Exist Now? . .280
What are the conditions in Israel before
the Gog of Magog invasion? 282
The Mysterious Message Concealed in
the Names of the 144,000 Witnesses 284
Are the 144,000 Witnesses Virgins? 288

Chapter 8 — The Antichrist and the Coming Global Religion **292**

Chapter 9 — The Collapse of the Russian Coalition **293**
Topics Covered   What are the conditions in Israel during
the Ezekiel 38 invasion? 293
What are the conditions in Israel in the
aftermath of Ezekiel 38? 295

Chapter 10 — Letter to the Saints Left Behind **298**

Chapter 11 — The Queen of Heaven Appears Globally **299**
Topics Covered   Is the Catholic "Virgin Mary" the Mary
of the Bible? 300
What is the End Game of the Marian
Apparitions? 303
Will there be more apparitions of Mary
to come? 306
Will Future Apparitions of Mary Facilitate
the World Religion of Revelation 17? 308
The Marian Apparitions Connection with
Ezekiel 38 314

Chapter 12 — The Harlot Rides the Beast to Peace and Prosperity. . 316
Topics Covered   The Supremacy of the Eucharist from
the Catholic Perspective. 316

Chapter 13 — Israel Cleanses the Holy Land 321
Topics Covered   Is the Valley of Hamon Gog in Jordan? . . .321
Did Jesus Instruct Jews to Flee from
The Antichrist into Jordan? 323

Chapter 14 — Doomsday Conference Erupts Into Deadly Chaos . . . 327
Topics Covered   Who is the Woman Drunk with the Blood
of the Saints? 328
Why Did the Apostle John Marvel at
the Harlot?. 329
What is the Blood of the Saints? 331

Chapter 15 — Jews Return Home as Rumors of Nuclear Wars Abound. 334
Topics Covered   Jews Continue to Return to Israel. 334
Brief Overview of the Storyline 335

Chapter 16 — The Vatican Global Council Meeting. 337
Topics Covered   The Problems with Vatican Council
Meetings. 337
The Importance of the Zeitoun Marian
Apparition 341
The Future Pope Receives
Unprecedented Power. 342

Chapter 17 - Millions Witness Eucharistic Miracles from Rome. . . .344
Topics Covered   Past Eucharistic Miracles Encourage
That More Will Follow 344
The Blessed Mother's Obsession with
Russia and World Peace. 348

Chapter 18 — Two Witnesses Prepare for the Tribulational Period . . 351
Topics Covered   Who Are The Two Witnesses?. 351
The Two Witnesses Are The Lord's
Rebuttal To The False Covenant. 355

Chapter 19 — The Encounter between Satan and his Seed 360
Topics Covered   Introduction to the Antichrist 360

Appendices

Appendix 1 — The Sinners Salvation Prayer 366

Appendix 2 — The Tribulation Saints 375

Appendix 3 — The Seven Letters to the Churches 380

Appendix 4 — The Marian Apparitions Connection with Ezekiel 38 383

Appendix 5 — The Apocalypse Road Timeline 389

Endnotes 393

Character List

(Includes some cast and crew from Revelation Road)[1]

The Thompson Family

Lisa Thompson	Wife of Thomas, daughter-in-law of George and Martha, and Tyler and Jami's mother, Tovia's sister, Bella's and Jaxon's aunt, Naomi's daughter
Jami Thompson	Tyler's sister, granddaughter of George and Martha
Grandma Naomi	Lisa's and Tovia's mother, Jami's, Bella's and Jaxon's grandmother
Tovia	Lisa's brother, Jami's uncle, Amber's husband, Bella's and Jaxon's father
Amber	Tovia's wife, Jami's aunt, Lisa's sister-in-law, Bella's and Jaxon's mother
Bella	Tovia's and Amber's daughter, Lisa's niece, Jami's cousin
Jaxon	Tovia's and Amber's son, Lisa's nephew, Jami's cousin
George Thompson	Tyler and Jami's grandfather, Martha's husband, retired Four-Star General
Martha Thompson	(a.k.a. Mimi), Tyler and Jami's grandmother
Tyler Thompson	(a.k.a. Ty), grandson of George and Martha, son of Thomas
Thomas Thompson	Son of George and Martha, Tyler and Jami's mother

Friends and Associates of the Thompson Family

Robert Rassmussen	(a.k.a. Razz), best friend of George Thompson, respected eschatologist
Nathaniel Severs	Razz' best friend, President of UGIC
Jim Linton	Respected eschatologist and Bible prophecy teacher

Religious Leaders

Joseph Levin	Chief Rabbi of Israel's Chief Rabbinate Council

Aaron Edelstein	Rabbi of Israel's Chief Rabbinate Council
Vincente Romano	The Pope
Gabriel Vitalia	Senior Catholic Cardinal
Arturo Amanti	Former Catholic Bishop
Patrick Dolan	Former Catholic Archbishop
Ladd Bitterman	Protestant Pastor
Brad Walters	Protestant Pastor
Gary Hanah	Protestant Pastor

Political and Military

United States
Harold Redding	United States President
John Bachlin	Former United States President
Paul Jordan	Lieutenant, the Watch Commander of Phoenix PD

Israel
Moshe Kaufman	Prime Minister
Jacob Barak	Chief military commander of the Israel Defense Forces
Avi Fleishman	Minister of the Interior

European Union
| Hans Vandenberg | European Union President |

Russia and China
Vladimir Ziroski	(a.k.a. Mad Vlad) Russian President
Sergei Primakov	Russian Prime Minister
Anatoly Tarasov	Russian Ambassador to the United Nations
Hu Jintao	China's President

Middle East (Arabs and Persians)
| Muktada Zakiri | Iranian President |
| Ayatollah Khomani | Spiritual leader of Iran |

Introduction
(How to Read This Book)

*A*pocalypse Road, Revelation for the Final Generation, is the second volume of an end time's Bible prophecies book series. The first book was entitled, *Revelation Road, Hope Beyond the Horizon*, and a recap of that book follows this introduction. This book series undertakes the difficult task of identifying, explaining and chronologically ordering the prophetic events between now and the Second Coming of Jesus Christ.

Apocalypse Road is a story about a family living in the final generation. Without warning, they are forced to face a series of powerful episodes that are guaranteed to change their lives forever. All Lisa Thompson wanted was to get back on track with her life in Israel after her husband and son vanished with the millions of Christians, but a Middle East war of epic biblical proportion postponed her plans indefinitely.

Now Lisa and her daughter Jami must prepare for the coming apocalypse. They have been thrust into the treacherous Post-Rapture / Pre-Tribulation time-period. This vastly unexplored gap of time follows the Rapture of the Christian Church, but precedes the coming seven-year Tribulational Period. It spans an unspecified length of time that will likely last for several years.

The Rapture is when Christ comes in the clouds to miraculously snatch up His believers, the Church, into heaven. This event is imminent, fulfilled in an instant and guaranteed to catch the world by surprise. This means that the Rapture is about to happen, or may have already happened, by the time you read this book. The primary Rapture verses are in John 14:1-6, 1 Corinthians 15:50-55 and 1 Thessalonians 4:15-18. The Rapture was the tear-dropping conclusion of the *Revelation Road* book.

More than a novel

Although *Apocalypse Road* begins as a novel, it concludes with a customized, non-fiction commentary section. The *Companion's Commentary* provides "biblical believability" to the adventurous scenarios depicted inside this novel. Additionally, it adds credence to the characters and their interactions, as well as veracity to the text. This format was chosen to share pertinent, timely information with the broadest possible audience.

This dual approach enables the readers to engage intimately with the novel. They can compose their own scripts inside the story line, as it progresses. This is possible because the characters are easy to relate to, and the prophetic scenarios depicted could occur during the reading of the book.

For instance, one episode describes a massive Middle East invasion of Israel that is spearheaded by a Russian led coalition. Many Israelis and some international tourists inevitably find themselves stranded in the Holy Land because the invasion restricts their ability to flee. About three million tourist travel to Israel each year, which averages out to be approximately eight-thousand on any given day. However, the average length of time a tourist stays in Israel is around eight days, which means when this predicted event happens over sixty-thousand travelers could be trapped in Israel for the duration of this war.

The above scene is more than a mere author creation. The threat of Middle East war is a realistic scenario that residents inside Israel grapple with almost daily. National defense drills are conducted frequently to prepare Israelis for a potential multi-front war. If a would-be traveler gets caught in this crossfire, while reading that chapter, they inescapably would become part of the story, and automatically become cast among the characters.

Note from the Author

It is my sincere hope that you read both the novel and the corresponding chapter-by-chapter commentaries. They can be read at the same time, or back to back; the book was designed so that either portion could be read and understood independently. The majority of comments from those who have read *Revelation Road*, is that they preferred reading the novel first and the commentary afterward.

I chose this unique fiction / non-fiction crossover style of writing to impart timely information to as many readers as possible. The Bible speaks volumes about these uncertain times. Inside its pages lie the secrets to successful living in these last days.

Prophecy is invaluable predictive information given to us by a loving God, with 100% accuracy. In addition to equipping us for the days in which we live, prophecy authenticates God's sovereignty, spares human lives, and ultimately saves lost souls. The primary goal of prophecy is to *inform us*, rather than *impress us*. God is not someone with too much *time on His hands*; He is the one who holds all *time in His hands*. This enables Him to share and declare the end from the beginning. His plan is to *pronounce hope*, rather than *announce harm*. However, He won't *denounce truth* when He foreknows it's about to overtake the world.

How God knows what He knows, only He knows. But, we can be thankful that He does, and that He is willing to share His knowledge with us.

"God so loves us that he wants us to know what's headed our way. And, in turn, our natural response should be to worship him for caring."

Best Reading Regards,

Bill Salus

Recap of Revelation Road
Reviewing Book One of This Series

*R*evelation Road, Hope Beyond the Horizon, was the first book of this end times series. Several powerful biblical predictions happened inside that storyline. The fulfillment of these ancient prophecies set the stage for the powerful events that are described in Apocalypse Road.

In *Revelation Road*, Israel won an epic war against their surrounding Arab enemies. This was the fulfillment of the prophetic war described in Psalm 83. This military victory enabled the tiny Jewish state to expand its borders, improve its national security and increase its economic prosperity. Thus, the Israel described in *Apocalypse Road* is far greater, safer and wealthier than it presently is.

Additionally, the destruction of Damascus predicted in Isaiah 17 took place in the *Revelation Road* storyline. The downing of Damascus coupled with the IDF conquest over their Arab foes created a war torn Middle East that produced multitudes of Arab refugees and prisoners of war. This predicament further fueled the anger of Muslims throughout the world toward the Jews.

Meanwhile, as the Middle East descended into uncontrollable turmoil, other powerful events were happening across the globe. One overwhelming episode was an apparition of Mary that was broadcast on satellite TV and watched throughout much of the world. This supernatural appearance of the "Blessed Mother" served as a precursor to the coming one world "Harlot" religion of Revelation 17. This coming global religion known as, "MYSTERY, BABYLON THE GREAT, THE MOTHER OF HARLOTS AND OF THE ABOMINATIONS OF THE EARTH," receives considerable attention inside of *Apocalypse Road.*

Another dramatic world event took place in America. A multi-pronged terrorist attack occurred that dwarfed the magnitude of the topping of the twin towers on September 11, 2001. Three major league ball parks were targeted by terrorist all at the same time. Bombs exploded in two of them, while the third attack was averted in the nick of time.

Lastly, the Rapture happened in *Revelation Road*. Millions of Christians worldwide suddenly vanished without warnings or explanations. Several of the key characters in *Revelation Road* were among those who disappeared. However, not everyone in the story was raptured, some were left behind. They are the stars of *Apocalypse Road*. These individuals have lost their loved ones and find themselves nervously facing an uncertain future. The plot thickens in Apocalypse Road as the prophecies continue to unfold in rapid succession. Each event triggers a bigger more devastating event in its aftermath.

Below is some of the book trailer and back-cover text from *Revelation Road*, which helps to segue from that book to this one. The *Revelation Road* book trailer is available to watch on YouTube by searching *Revelation Road book trailer by Bill Salus*, or by going to this site: https://www.youtube.com/watch?v=3SOaB7Dahrs

You are invited to a one-of-a- kind reading experience. Enjoy a thrilling novel and a biblical commentary ripped from today's headlines at the same time. The modern world has been thrust into chaos and uncertainty. Iran's nuclear threat; the burgeoning Arab Spring, the toppling of long-ruling Mideast despots and the power vacuum left in the wake.

Modern dangers? Yes, but calamities foretold in the Bible thousands of years ago. Revelation Road explains the events occurring on our darkening horizon and their Biblical significance. George and Mimi Thompson believe their grandson Tyler lives in the final generation. Lovingly, they prepare him for life after the destruction of Damascus, the strategic strike of Iran's nuclear sites, the final Arab-Israeli war, nuclear terrorism in America, and the coming world religion and global government.

All young Tyler wanted was a chance to join his sister at Eastside Middle School in the fall, but the budding Arab Spring mushroomed into an apocalyptic summer, disrupting his plans. Middle East war and nuclear terror in America turned Tyler's world upside down.

Experience the End Times through the eyes of the Thompson family, and discover how their gripping story uncovers the silver lining of hope against the backdrop of global gloom and doom... Their family tale could soon become your reality!

*Enjoy Apocalypse Road...*The opening scene begins with Lisa, her daughter Jami and their dear friend Nathan Severs all seated together in Lisa's home in Bet Shemesh, Israel. They are preparing to watch the important DVD that had been left behind by Lisa's husband Thomas. Since the video was produced by a Christian and was about Bible prophecy, Lisa, who was Jewish and not a believer in Jesus Christ, had ignored her husband's prior pleadings to watch it. However, now that Thomas and her son Tyler had been Raptured, her and Jami longed to view the video's content.

APOCALYPSE ROAD

Novel

Chapter 1
The Message Left Behind

Turning the television volume up, Lisa spoke urgently to her daughter. "Jami, wait a moment before inserting dad's DVD," she said. "Let's watch this breaking news alert!"

Lisa and Jami Thompson had been preparing to watch an important end times video in their home with their friend Nathan Severs, when their plans were abruptly interrupted by the news that Russia had recently launched several missiles into northern Israel. Seated together on the living room sofa, they listened intently as the newscaster announced,

> "This just in: three Russian Kalibr missiles have been fired at Israel from the Black Sea. Although two were successfully intercepted by Iron Dome defense systems, the third has struck in the center of Haifa."

Gasping, Lisa shrieked, "Your uncle Tovia lives in the heart of Haifa. I hope he's OK!"

Placing his arm around Lisa's shoulders, Nathan said, "Don't panic. Let's hear more."

> "Serious casualties are being reported," the newscaster continued.

"My brother's hurt; I have a gut feeling that Tovia has been hurt!" Lisa cried.

Grabbing her mother's cell phone from the coffee table, Jami shoved it at her. "Mother hurry! Call Uncle Tovia right now!"

Handing Lisa his handkerchief, Nathan consoled, "Try to calm yourselves, girls. Let's get the details before jumping to conclusions."

Unable to contain her emotions, Lisa leaped off the sofa, and raced into the parlor to call her brother, while Nathan and Jami listened to the newscaster conclude:

> "It's being reported that Russian President Vladimir Ziroski is giving Israel 24 hours to comply with his recently imposed economic demands, or face a full-scale invasion from his coalition forces. The Russian President declared that the recent missile attack was merely a warning of catastrophic events to come if Israel continues to export its energy resources abroad at unacceptably low prices!"

Terrified, Jami turned to Nathan, asking, "Mr. Severs, does this mean that Israel is going to war with Russia?"

Nathan nodded sadly. "I fear so dear," he replied, "but not just Russia."

"What do you mean?" Jami asked.

"Russia has joined forces with several Muslim countries that include Iran, Turkey, and Libya," he explained.

Rejoining them, Lisa clasped her hands together anxiously. "All the phone lines are busy, and I can't get through to Tovia," she said. "What else did the reporter say?"

"It's not good, Lisa," Nathan replied. "Russia has issued an ultimatum to your government that they must comply with all coalition requests or face all-out war."

Watching her mother sink to the sofa, an anguished Jami cried out, "Not again, Mother! We just fought with the Arabs. Why can't all these Muslim countries leave Israel alone?"

Realizing she needed to be strong for her daughter, Lisa embraced her sobbing teen-ager.

Shaking his head, Nathan said, "It's highly doubtful that Israel will comply with Russia's demands."

Rocking her daughter in her arms, Lisa objected, "What choice does Israel have? Winning a war against the Arab confederacy was one thing, but Russia's coalition is far more powerful."

Nathan clarified, "Russia's commands are only a smokescreen to their true intent. They are determined to wage war against Israel!

"No!" Lisa insisted. "We can comply with Russia's requests and avert

"Not according to your Uncle Razz," Nathan replied.

With the mention of Razz's name, Jami's ears perked up. "What about uncle Razz?" she asked.

Razz, short for Robert Rasmussen, had been Nathan's longtime friend. He had also been Jami's grandfather's best friend. Because of his close relationship with her grandfather, Jami thought of him as her uncle. Razz, along with her grandparents, George and Martha Thompson, her dad, Thomas, and brother, Tyler, had all disappeared instantly with millions of other Christians a few months prior. The mere mention of Razz's name evoked fond memories of Jami's departed loved ones.

Nathan replied, "Razz warned me before he … left us… that Russia would form a predominately Muslim coalition to plunder Israel. He called it the Gog of Magog invasion, and said the event was described in Ezekiel 38. If he was correct, Russia's demands are only the start of far worse things to come."

Lisa rolled her eyes toward Jami, silently imploring Nathan to temper his statement. "That's very interesting, Nathan," she said, "but Israel must concede to the coalition demands."

"Don't you understand, Lisa?" Nathan argued. "Capitulating to Russia's requests would be national suicide. It would only serve to fortify Russia's intent to destroy Israel. Mad Vlad Ziroski would quickly coordinate its coalition members to wage war against the Jewish state. Don't you recognize that Russia's ultimatum is no ultimatum at all? They will wage war against the Jews no matter what your government decides."

Jami sat back and tugged on Lisa's sleeve. "Mother, let's watch Dad's video right now!" she begged. "Maybe Mr. Severs is right. Maybe the Bible predicted what's occurring between Russia and Israel presently, and the video can help us understand what's going on."

Lisa sighed, "You could be right. Your father did say that this DVD contains revelations about what will happen to Israel in the future."

The Message Left Behind

Having recently become a Jewish believer in Jesus, Jami was no longer fearful of watching the apocalyptic video left behind by her father Thomas. While waiting for the DVD to boot up, she propped up the picture on the coffee table of her dad and brother Tyler that they had purposely inserted in the video case prior to their heavenly departure.

"Dad would be proud of us, Mother," Jami said.

Nodding, Lisa replied, "I'm sure he would. After resisting Christianity for so long, we're about to watch the video we were so afraid of."

"Welcome. I'm your host, Jim Linton," the narrator began. *"What you are about to watch is a chronological ordering of powerful last days events. The Bible, the only holy book with a proven track record of accurately predicting future events, provides invaluable insights intended to navigate mankind through these treacherous end times. As you watch this program, I fear that you may be living out some of its content."*

With that introduction, the trio scooted to the edge of the sofa, devoting their undivided attention to the remainder of the DVD. They were astounded to hear the host begin his predictions with the Arab-Israeli war of Psalm 83, which they had just lived through. The fact that the DVD had been produced before the war added additional credibility to the remaining content. Linton suggested that this war would trigger a period of worldwide sorrows.

"After this climactic concluding Arab-Israeli war, powerful prophecies begin to unfold with greater intensity and frequency, like the birth pains of a mother in labor."

Tears swelled from their eyes as eschatologist Linton proceeded to forecast the worldwide disappearance of Christians.

"If not before the Psalm 83 war, probably shortly afterwards, Jesus Christ will come in the twinkling of an eye to catch up His followers into the clouds in an event commonly called the Rapture."

Lisa paused the program. "If only we had watched this DVD beforehand! We would all be in heaven right now with our family!" she wept.

Taking the remote control gently from her hand, Jami soothed, "Mother, you have to let the guilt go, once-and-for-all. There is no way of telling if this video would have convinced us that Christ was the Messiah. Our Jewish heritage inhibited us from accepting what Dad was trying to teach us."

Nathan, himself a recent Gentile convert, confirmed; "Jami's right Lisa. What might have been is water under the bridge. At least now we can learn what the Bible says about our future."

Jami added, "It's going to be up to us to convince Grandma Naomi, Uncle Tovia, and the rest of our family in Israel that Jesus is the Messiah."

Lisa sighed. "Assuming they're still alive," she whispered,

Nestling in and taking notes, the three of them gleaned all the information they could from the video. Future prophetic events discussed in the DVD included:

1. The mystery of "Babylon the Great," the coming world religion of Revelation 17,

2. The future global government,

3. The cashless society of the one-world banking system,

4. The impending world leader called the Antichrist,

5. The coming strong delusion intended to deceive humankind,

6. The false covenant confirmed by the Antichrist with Israel,

7. Daniel's "Seventieth Week," also called the Tribulation Period,

8. The post-rapture / pre-tribulation gap prophecies,

9. The construction of the third Jewish temple,

10. The "Abomination of Desolation" occurring inside the third Jewish temple,

11. The evangelizing ministry of the 144,000 Jews for Jesus,

12. The twenty-one judgments of the book of Revelation,

13. The ten-kingdom break-up of the global government,

14. The "Patience of the Saints" prophecies,

15. The coming Christian martyrdom,

16. The Armageddon campaign of the Antichrist,

17. The False Prophet,

18. The "Mark of the Beast" and the identity of the number "666,"

19. The faithful Jewish remnant of the tribulation,

20. The war in heaven between Michael the archangel and Satan,

21. The casting out of Satan and his fallen angels from heaven to torment the earth,

22. The Second Coming of Christ,

23. The millennial Messianic Kingdom period.

These and many more prophecies were explored in Linton's comprehensive end times production. However, the one event they kept pausing the video to discuss was the Russian-Iranian invasion, foretold in Ezekiel 38, which was unfolding before their very eyes.

Fortunately, the host went into elaborate detail about this prophecy. The little audience was relieved to hear that Jehovah had promised to supernaturally defeat the Ezekiel invaders, and to show His power on behalf of Israel in the process.

When they were finished watching the video, Nathan gathered the girls into his arms and said, "Girls, we need to come to grips with the fact, that this is the FINAL GENERATION. From this point forward, life won't be easy. But, we have the Lord and we have each other. I have made some preparations for us. We can do this, don't give up hope."

Chapter 2
Rabbis Warn
of the Future
Russian Invasion

"Gentlemen," said the haggard Israeli Prime Minister, "as we speak, Russia's coalition is launching missiles into Northern Israel, and mobilizing to wipe us off the map!" Moshe Kaufman pounded a fist onto the table top to emphasize his distress.

The private audience, composed of members of Israel's Chief Rabbinate Council, listened in horror as Kaufman relayed that Russian President Vladimir Ziroski and his Iranian counterpart, Ayatollah Khomani, had issued the command to attack the Jewish state in retaliation for the recent Arab-Israeli war.

Chief Rabbi Joseph Levin spoke out, "Mr. Prime Minister, you stand corrected. It is not the Israelis, but the invaders who will be wiped out, according to the prophet Ezekiel!"

The esteemed Rabbi's confident statement garnered the unanimous support of his half-dozen peers, prompting Rabbi Aaron Edelstein to quote Ezekiel 39:8: *"Surely it is coming, and it shall be done."*

Rabbi Levin nodded approvingly.

"Well," said Rabbi Edelstein, "preparations to cleanse the land of the soon to be dead Russian invaders should be made in advance."

Prime Minister Kaufman had considered it politically expedient to convene this council meeting because in the aftermath of the IDF victory over the Arabs, the political landscape of Israel was becoming vastly more religious. The Chief Rabbinate Council was gaining an enormous amount of clout among the populous, because Rabbi Levin had pointed out the prophecies that had been fulfilled, with great specificity, in the Arab – Israeli war. They explained that the destruction of Damascus was a direct fulfillment of Isaiah 17, and the annexation of Jordan a fulfillment of Jeremiah 49:1-6.

Rabbi Joseph Levin's ability to interpret such prophecies elevated his rabbinical status to an unprecedented level, so much so that there was a saying circulating throughout the land: "If Rabbi Levin proclaimed it, then Jehovah has declared it to be so!"

Prime Minister Kaufman's eyebrows rose with the prophetic utterances of the Rabbis. Skeptically, Kaufman retorted, "Certainly you don't expect me to entrust Israel's national security to the teachings of ancient Hebrew texts! These may have been excellent teaching for their time, but they don't apply to our present circumstances!"

Ignoring Kaufman's comment, Rabbi Edelstein quoted further from the book of Ezekiel:

> *"It will come to pass in that day that I will give Gog a burial place there in Israel, the valley of those who pass by east of the sea; and it will obstruct travelers, because there they will bury Gog and all his multitude. Therefore they will call it the Valley of Hamon Gog. For seven months the house of Israel will be burying them, in order to cleanse the land. Indeed all the people of the land will be burying, and they will gain renown for it on the day that I am glorified,"* says the Lord GOD. *"They will set apart men regularly employed, with the help of a search party, to pass through the land and bury those bodies remaining on the ground, in order to cleanse it. At the end of seven months they will make a search. The search party will pass through the land; and when anyone sees a man's bone, he shall set up a marker by it, till the buriers have buried it in the Valley of Hamon Gog. The name of the city will also be Hamonah. Thus they shall cleanse the land."*
> (Ezekiel 39:11-16, NKJV)

Prime Minister Kaufman scoffed, "What Valley of Hamon Gog and city of Hamonah? That's *Hamo-nonsense*. There is no such place in Israel. Esteemed Rabbis, with all due respect, you put too much stock in the ancient prophecies. We must first defeat the Russians before we can bury them!"

Raising his right hand high in the air, Rabbi Levin jumped to his feet and declared, "The prophecy does not predict any IDF military engagement.

NOVEL

We presiding here today all concur. It is the official position of the Chief Rabbinate Council of Israel that Ezekiel's prophecies regarding Gog are to be interpreted literally! Russia's coalition is presently assembling to invade the Jewish state. They will come like an unstoppable storm, and cover the land of Israel with a cloud of jet fighters. *Hashem*...He is the power that will wage war against them supernaturally and singlehandedly. The IDF will bury the invaders, not fight them. It has been written with great specificity, and it shall be fulfilled as foretold. All glory for the victory is to be reserved for Jehovah, the Holy One in Israel!"

At the conclusion of Rabbi Levin's announcement, the other Rabbis called out, "Hear! Hear!" and pounded the table with their fists.

Angrily, Kaufman replied, "The IDF is exceedingly great, and our only defense against Russia's forces. They have proven their fighting skills against the Arabs. The Rabbinate Council admitted this when it declared Psalm 83 had been fulfilled through their recent victory in *"Operation Israeli Freedom.""*

"We still stand behind our Psalm 83 proclamation," insisted Rabbi Levin, to the unanimous vocal approval of the council members presiding alongside.

"Then why do you oppose my plan to mobilize the IDF against Russia's coalition?" Kaufman asked.

Rabbi Edelstein countered, "Why do you pick-and-choose what prophecies to base your executive decisions upon?"

Offended, the Prime Minister barked, "Be reasonable, Rabbis! Israel's existence is at stake! Are you insinuating that, at this crucial juncture, I should whimsically govern my people?"

Rabbi Edelstein shook his head. "Our interpretation of Psalm 83 you do not question, but our interpretation of Ezekiel 38 and 39 you discard. Where is the logic behind your reasoning?"

In frustration, Kaufman issued his final response: "There is no time for philosophical debate with you people. You may have accurately assessed the prophecies of Psalm 83 *after* our IDF victory, but Russia presents a far more formidable coalition. Pray your interpretations are correct, but I must rely on our IDF commanders rather than your scholarly advice in this matter. Israel faces an unprecedented existential threat and the margin for error is too great for rabbinical deliberation. Israelis must take matters into their own hands, and you all had better hope that your ancient prophecies are, indeed, correct!"

Ezekiel's Exceedingly Great Army Prepares to Fight Again

Meanwhile, IDF chief of staff General Jacob Barak had begun a massive mobilization of Israel's air, land, and naval forces. They had been preparing for a face-off with Russia's coalition ever since the consortium placed its unreasonable demands upon the Jewish state and blockaded the vital waterways against Israel a few months prior. The rapid IDF mobilization, coupled with the outcry of the United Nations, had temporarily deterred the Russian invasion.

In a closed-door meeting with the general, a few hours after the Rabbinate conference, Prime Minister Kaufman inquired, "How much longer will the Russians stall their attack?"

Barak insisted, "Not for long. They won't wait for the militaries of the western nations to recover from the disappearances of some of their soldiers to ally alongside us. America is already hastily refilling their ranks in anticipation of this imminent invasion. The western world fears what Ziroski and his cohorts are capable of if they eliminate Israel. There is no doubt that the Russian coalition is poised to strike while the iron is hot!"

Exasperated, Kaufman sighed, "We can no longer rely on the Americans since their Christians have unexplainably vanished. Their military is fragmented and presently all their interim government can do is protest Russian intentions from the sidelines. Western armies will take too long to regroup, and they may never fully recover. We will have to fight the *Ezekiel invaders* singlehandedly like we fought against the Arabs."

"The *Ezekiel invaders*," General Barak echoed. "Don't tell me you have adopted the Rabbis antiquated beliefs!"

Kaufman reluctantly responded, "They were right when they identified Op Israeli Freedom with Psalm 83."

Grasping the prime minister's shoulder, the general argued, "The verdict is still out on their statement about that prophecy. Besides, they didn't predict the war in advance. They only issued their rabbinical interpretation after the fact."

"In this go-round, this is not the case," Kaufman responded. "Their official interpretation is out in front of this pending invasion. They have instructed me to have you and your IDF forces stand down in this battle. According to their understanding of Ezekiel's prophecy, Hashem alone will do our fighting for us."

"Preposterous!" Barak huffed. "Surely you can't take them seriously! Do you expect our countrymen to shout "Shalom" while their women and children are being ravished by the Russians and their enjoining Muslim hordes?"

Kaufman gritted his teeth and shook his head. "You are right, General! We must defend our country! Position all our forces immediately, and brace for the Mother of all Middle East Wars!"

Chapter 3
The European Union Consoles Israel

Alone in his office, after his critical meetings with the Rabbinate Council and IDF commander, Prime Minister Kaufman was exhausted. He barely possessed enough energy to tidy up his desk and head home to Tamar, his wife of fifty-four years. Before he could retrieve his overcoat from the office rack, he had to field an after-hours phone call from European Union President Hans Vandenberg.

"Prime Minister Kaufman, thank you for accepting my call at this late hour," came the troubled voice through the handset.

"No hour is too late to speak with you, Mr. President," replied Kaufman.

Hans Vandenberg was a charismatic politician, rapidly emerging onto the world stage as one of its premier leaders. His support toward Israel during the recent Arab – Israeli war had elevated him to the top of the nation's list of allies. Moreover, Vandenberg's ability to stave off the collapse of the Eurozone in the aftermath of that war, by forming a "stability union" amongst the strongest pocket of European countries, had helped him get elected as the President of the EU Parliament.

Hans Vandenberg, not one to beat around the bush, dived directly into the point of his call: "Moshe, I want you to know that the European Union is vehemently opposed to Russia's recent threats against your country. As you know, the proper confederation of EU nations has formally opposed all of the coalition's demands imposed upon Israel, and we have called an emergency meeting, scheduled for tomorrow, to formulate an official EU response to Russia's recent attack upon Haifa."

Encouraged by what he was hearing, Prime Minister Kaufman got his second wind from the grueling day. "President Vandenberg," he enthused, "thank you for your support! I have been conducting key meetings throughout the day with Israel's military and religious leaders, and I assure you that Russia's aggression will be met with an expeditious and decisive response from Israel."

"I expected nothing less; such great courage is characteristic of Israel," commended Vandenberg.

"However," Kaufman continued. "As you can appreciate, the Russian Confederation is far too formidable for the IDF to fight single-handedly. Their demands against Israel, and the missile attack upon Haifa, are unwarranted, and it is impossible for Israel to comply with their unreasonable requests. No sovereign nation possessing legal littoral rights over its ports and waterways, and that operates in full compliance with established international commercial law, like Israel does, should be dictated to by another nation as to how to conduct its commerce. The western world should be outraged by Russia's preposterous demands and unruly behavior!"

Vandenberg agreed. "Prime Minister Kaufman, you are absolutely correct! President Ziroski's coalition gravely concerns the EU. At our emergency meeting we intend to raise all the legal issues and their geo-political ramifications, in an attempt to gain international support for Israel's cause in this matter. I assure you that Russia and its coalition will be ostracized from the global community for their unwarranted aggression if it persists."

Concerned about the potential lack of effectiveness of such a stance, Prime Minister Kaufmann replied, "It is important to Israel that military pacts are made between the EU and the Jewish state. Without such pacts in place, Russia will remain unwavering in its aggression toward my country."

President Vandenberg answered diplomatically, "I intend to bring this important point up at the meeting tomorrow. But I am convinced that strong international resolve should impose sufficient pressure upon the coalition to bring about at least a temporary cessation of aggression. Moshe, we have to get Russia to sit down at the table with us; otherwise, we risk World War III!"

Sensing uncharacteristic political cowardice on Vandenberg's part, Kaufman sternly replied, "With all due respect, sir, I strongly disagree! Russia and its coalition covet Israel's newfound prosperity, and mere political pressure is insufficient. They are committed against us militarily, hoping to confiscate our recently discovered bounties of oil and natural gas, and they want the spoil from the Arab war!"

Vandenberg concurred. "Yes, Prime Minister, the EU intends to condemn this aggression promptly, and in the harshest of terms!"

"But, harsh EU rhetoric is not the solution to the problem!" Kaufman insisted. "It should be obvious to the world that Russia intends to seize control of our primary natural energy resources. If successful, they could monopolize energy exports and become the dominant world power! Their current aspirations are not only an existential threat to Israel, but severely problematic for the EU and the West as well. They don't want to negotiate with the western world...they want to *rule* the *whole* world! And they are convinced that Israel is the primary obstacle standing in their way." Taking a deep breath, he tried to calm his racing pulse. "I can appreciate your concerns Mr. President, but war may not be avoidable in this instance!"

Backpedaling slightly, Vandenberg pleaded, "Be reasonable, Mr. Prime Minister! Western armies, especially the USA and UK, are still in a state of disarray, from the massive unexplained disappearances. But Russia's coalition, comprised mainly of Muslim countries, experienced very few disappearances, leaving their armies virtually intact. Moreover, the Muslim populations residing inside Europe are mostly supportive of the Russian coalition, and are crowding our streets in large numbers in protests against Israel."

"*You* be reasonable!" retorted Kaufman. "Who can negotiate with mad Vlad Ziroski and his cohort Khomani? In these unreasonable times, only Israel provides the voice of reason. The Jews are trying to get world markets back on track, but the Russian coalition intends to block our every move. The only way to quiet Muslim protests is to put Europeans back to work, and that's what Israel proposes to do with our commerce campaign."

Sensing Kaufman's frustration Vandenberg patronized, "I understand, Moshe. These are troubling times for you and your people, and we want to partner commercially with Israel. Believe me the EU is on Israel's side in this matter, but this is not the only important issue the EU is grappling with presently. In light of the recent Mideast war with the Arabs, unexplained disappearances, and the supernatural sighting of the Virgin Mary at St. Peter's Square, the EU is doing all it can to resurrect order. We must give diplomacy a chance! This world cannot absorb another major Mideast war! I believe we can engage in diplomacy with President Ziroski and get him to back down."

Realizing that President Vandenberg, the consummate politician, might actually abandon Israel on behalf of "diplomacy," the Israeli Prime Minister declared, "President Vandenberg, the days of negotiations have departed! The western world is reeling and Islam is spiraling out of control worldwide! If that's not enough, the Pope is predicting that the Virgin Mary will win the world to Catholicism! The EU appears to be subtly endorsing this position, so where does that leave my people?"

Vandenberg cleared his throat. "This is not yet the official EU position," he said. "We are presently conducting roundtable discussions with the Pope and the Holy See. Until those meetings are concluded, the EU remains undecided on this matter."

Kaufman drew his handkerchief and blotted the sweat from his brow while commenting, "At the same time that you have your conversations with the Vatican, the Rabbinic Council of Israel is advocating that the temple be rebuilt and the Law of Moses officially reinstated as the constitution of the Jewish state. The nations have gone insane!"

Hearing only silence on the phone line, the prime minister continued, "Ziroski dances to an entirely different drummer than you and I. He is a Communist atheist! As far as he is concerned, the Jewish Jehovah, apparitions of Mary, and Muslim al-Mahdi are all figments of human imagination. To him, they are useful mechanisms that enable him to achieve world dominance. While the western world attempts to restore order, Mad Vlad tips his missiles with nuclear warheads. There is no negotiating with this madman. The sooner the world realizes this, the better! In fact, it is my firm belief that the reason the Russian missile sent into Haifa was non- nuclear, was because Ziroski merely wanted to send your people a warning. The next time Israel may not be so lucky!"

Recognizing that Kaufman wanted more than the EU was prepared to offer, President Vandenberg concluded, "Prime Minister Kaufman, you have clearly articulated Israel's needs, and I will voice your concerns to my ministers at our cabinet meeting tomorrow. I don't believe it is realistic to expect the EU or the west to offer military support to Israel until all political options have been exhausted. The EU will undoubtedly advise that Israel put a moratorium on annexing more Arab lands, and temporarily abandon all plans to construct a Jewish temple. These issues are not constructive to the peace process, and will inhibit our ability to negotiate with Muslim factions inside the Russian coalition."

"As you will, President Vandenberg," Kaufman conceded. "But the EU does the free world a great disservice by failing to recognize that war with Russia is the inevitable option. You surely understand that it will be impossible for me to get full support from the Knesset for such moratoriums."

Chapter 4
The EU Condemnation and Vatican Consecration of Russia

I t was a dismal day in Brussels when the cabinet members assembled at the EU consulate for their emergency meeting. Thunderous clouds accompanied by severe rains caused airport delays for several dignitaries arriving from neighboring nations. So loud were the thunder-clapped skies, that it seemed as though the high heavens had heard about the meeting and voiced divine disapproval.

In addition to the EU member-states, representatives from the United Nations, UK and the Vatican City State, were also in attendance.

President Vandenberg began the meeting by announcing that he had conducted phone conversations with President Moshe Kaufman of Israel, President Harold Redding of America, and President Hu Jintao of China. President Redding had been the US Vice President at the time of the rapture, when President John Bachlin vanished, leaving Redding as his successor.

"As you know, grave events are escalating again in the Middle East," began Vandenberg. "Israel fears war with Russia and its coalition is imminent, and the United States agrees. I informed both Prime Minister Kaufman, and President Redding, that the EU favors diplomacy rather than war to resolve this dangerous impasse."

Those in attendance nodded and murmured their approval of his stated position.

Vandenberg continued, "I expressed to our Israeli and American friends our harshest disapproval of Russia and its coalition, and reminded them that the EU stands firmly by Israel's side in this matter. I told both leaders that we would do everything in our power, short of offering military assistance, to influence the Russian coalition to refrain from further attacks against the Jewish state. It was important to issue this disclaimer in order to alert both countries that any retaliatory military responses against Russia would be at their own risk, and not supported by the EU."

Cardinal Gabriel Vitalia, representing the Vatican, questioned, "What was the response of China's president Hu Jintao to Russia's formation of a Muslim coalition and recent aggression against Israel?"

Vandenberg reluctantly responded, "President Jintao was neutral. He said his country opts to stay out of this matter, and refuses to issue or endorse any official responses concerning the present Middle East conflict. Frankly, he said China was upset with the Israeli occupation of Arab lands after their recent war victory, and equally disturbed by Russia's formation of a Muslim coalition that is obviously planning to seize control of Israel's gas and oil resources. He said China would wait for current Middle East events to play out, to see which direction the balance of power shifts, before determining his country's course of action."

"That's it?" A high ranking female member from the Italian delegation asked.

Nodding "yes," Vandenberg confirmed, "Not surprisingly, that was President Jintao's response."

"Moreover," he continued, "On your desks, you will find my suggestion for the official EU statement condemning Russia's actions, for your collective review and approval. It outlines the steps the EU and its allies are prepared to take in the event Russian aggression persists. This statement harshly condemns the aggression, but also encourages the Russian confederation to come to the negotiating table. This is why no mention of military consequence has been included in the EU statement. In light of volatile world events, the EU must be careful not to alienate Israel, Russia or the Muslim nations."

Voicing disapproval, UK Prime Minister Tony Brown stood up and stated, "The international community needs to send Russia a strong military warning that it will not tolerate its aggression! It is blatantly obvious that Russia plans to steal Israel's prosperity. They cannot be allowed to get away with such scandalous behavior!"

President Vandenberg raised his right hand, rebuffing his British colleague. Looking sternly into Brown's eyes the EU president stated, "Excuse me, Honorable Prime Minister, but you can't even control Muslim protests in London, let alone engage in a world war with Russia,

Turkey, Iran, and the others! Since Brexit, your country's voice is less influential than it was when it was an EU member, and like America's military, Her Majesty's British forces are in a state of disarray from the disappearances. This is not the time for any of us, especially the UK, to abandon diplomacy. We must carefully calculate the consequences of our actions as the leader of the international community. What if Russia wars against Israel and wins? Then what? Do you want the UK to be the coalition's next target?"

Infuriated, the British Prime Minister stormed out of the meeting, setting the stage for what turned out to be a dictatorial conclusion. Vandenberg managed to keep the podium to himself, and in so doing shut out all dissenting voices; only Cardinal Vitalia was given the opportunity to share the platform. Vandenberg had been forewarned that Pope Vicente Romano was about to make an important announcement to the faithful, and that it was imperative that the EU be informed of his pending declaration.

The Vatican spokesman made it clear that the Pope thoroughly disapproved of EU military intervention on the behalf of Israel. Cardinal Vitalia declared, "Pope Vicente is certain that the recent glorious appearance of the Blessed Mother Mary over St. Peter's Square, and the messages imparted through her visionaries, signal that a time of worldwide peace is forthcoming."

These comments opened the door for Vandenberg to say, "Cardinal Vitalia, it has been brought to my attention that the Pope is about to make an important announcement to the faithful. Can you reveal the content of his forthcoming statement?"

Seizing the opportunity, Cardinal Vitalia continued, "Pope Romano wanted me to remind all of you that the apparition of Our Lady of Fatima in 1917 had a message about Russia. [2] Our Lady prophesied that Russia will be the scourge of all nations, but she promised that if the Holy Father along with the Bishops of the world would consecrate Russia to her Immaculate Heart, then a period of peace will be granted to the world. I have been given direct authority by the Holy See to inform you that the prophecies of Our Lady serve as a direct warning to all of you. We are not to battle this confederacy with weapons, but with prayer to the Blessed Virgin Mary. Russia is not to be politically or militarily provoked, but rather to be spiritually consecrated. Pope Romano is feeling a sense of urgency to fulfill the wishes of Our Lady at Fatima in this matter. He plans on consecrating Russia to her Immaculate Heart soon. However today, shortly after the adjournment of this very EU assembly, Pope Romano will infallibly declare a new Marian dogma naming Mary as Co-Redemptrix, Mediatrix of all graces and Advocate. You are all hereby given advance knowledge of these announcements as of today."

Gasps arose from the audience. "Why now? What are the broader implications of this dogma," they asked among themselves?

Without hesitation, the Cardinal concluded, "Advance knowledge of Pope Romano's intention was given to you today in order to ensure that the EU adopts only a non-violent course of action regarding the Russian Confederation. The EU must not provoke the Russian bear to awaken any further out from its Cold War slumber. The EU must pursue the path of peace, and wait upon the Blessed Mother to reconcile the world to her Immaculate Heart."

With these words still echoing in the chamber, Vandenberg declared that the path of diplomacy would be the EU's official position. They would support Israel only up to the point that such support did not provoke Russian aggression. The Pope's pending announcement would draw a line in the Middle East sand, and would seal the EU's decision.

As promised, later that same day Pope Romano consecrated Russia to Mary and declared the Virgin Mary is Co-Redemptrix, Mediatrix of all graces and Advocate for the People of God. Moreover, the EU announced its official statement condemning Russia for boycotting and attacking Israel, but posing no retaliatory threat to the coalition.

Chapter 5
144,000 Jewish Evangelists

It was about noon the day after the Russian missile attack in Haifa, when the phone rang, "Hello, Thompson residence," Lisa answered.

"Tovia and his family are all safe!" Naomi exclaimed.

Lisa had just risen from a restless sleep when her mother sounded the good news. She had slept in far later than normal because Jami, Nathan Severs and she had stayed up deep into the wee hours of the night, repeatedly replaying the end times DVD.

Excitedly Lisa responded, "That's fantastic news! Did you talk to Tovia? I haven't been able to get through to him."

"Yes," Naomi confirmed. "Tovia called and said that he and the children made it into the neighborhood bomb shelter moments before the strike. Apparently, the missile exploded several miles away, not causing any damage to their home."

Hearing her mother's voice, Jami entered the room, rubbing sleep from her eyes. "What is it, Mother?" she asked. "What's going on?"

Cradling the receiver next to her heart, Lisa said, "Tovia and your cousins are fine! They weren't near the blast!"

"Is that Grandma Naomi?" Jami asked.

"It is," Lisa replied. "Grandma Naomi just got off the phone with your uncle. Go get ready for school. I will fill you in on what happened after I hang up."

"School," Jami grumbled. "I don't think schools are even going to be open after what Russia did."

"Hold on a moment, Mother," Lisa spoke into the phone.

Covering the mouthpiece, Lisa said, "Jami, go check out your school's website and find out if school is cancelled, while I finish talking to your grandmother, I don't want you to miss school. We have to go about our normal lives."

"Normal lives?" Jami echoed, "How can you say that after watching dad's DVD all night?"

Lisa shushed her daughter and said, "Just do what I say."

Turning her undivided attention back to her mother, it was only a few seconds into the conversation, when Naomi's disposition changed from excitement to concern. "Tovia said something very unsettling to me," she complained.

"What do you mean? What did he say? Lisa asked.

Naomi elaborated, "Tovia and the family were in the bomb shelter with some of those Jesus Jews, you know the ones that supposedly number 144,000 and parade around Israel claiming to be spoken of in the Christian Bible."

Lisa replied, "Yes, I'm very familiar with them. Some people are calling them the *Royal Jews from the Twelve Tribes of Israel,* and they are predicted in the Bible. What are they saying?"

Naomi gasped, "Oh my goodness! Don't tell me you believe them, too!"

Realizing she had shocked her Jewish mother by her comment, she tried to shift the subject back to Tovia. "Go on, Mother. Tell me what Tovia said."

Naomi composed herself and commented, "Fine, but don't tell me you are falling for these Jesus royal nut-cakes."

Waiting in vain to hear Lisa respond, Naomi grumbled, "I don't like this, Lisa. Your lack of response troubles me. So, okay then, apparently, the Jesus Freaks had the *chutzpa* to say that the prophet Ezekiel predicted the Russian confederacy in ancient times. They warned Tovia that there is a massive invasion coming, and that he and all of his family should leave Israel, already! Can you believe the nerve?"

To Lisa's surprise, Jami, who had been listening in on the receiver, inquired, "Did they say there could be Israeli casualties?"

Dumbfounded that Jami was overhearing, Naomi was silent.

"Jami!" Lisa cried, "You shouldn't be hearing this!"

"Maybe we should all leave," Jami wept.

To Naomi's astonishment, Lisa did not correct the girl. "Where would we go?" Lisa replied. "And how would be get there? Flights out of Israel are undoubtedly selling out as we speak!"

"Have you lost your mind?" Naomi blurted out. "Didn't you just tell Jami that Israelis have to live normal lives? What's gotten into you? What are you NOT TELLING me?"

Lisa confirmed, "Ezekiel did predict this war!"

"*Oy Vey*," gasped Naomi, clapping the palm of her free hand to her forehead. "When did you start reading the Bible? I don't know whether to be proud of you, or furious!"

"Mother," Lisa began, "I was up all last night…watching Thomas' Christian video."

Lisa had no more than spoken the word's "Christian video" before Naomi held the phone in front of her face and began shouting what Lisa took to be Hebrew expletives."

"Stop cussing, Mother!" Lisa cried. "Let me continue!"

Putting the receiver to her ear, Naomi replied, "I'm not cussing! You should know your Hebrew better, so you would understand my words. I am saying this can't be happening! My own daughter turning into a Jesus Jew! My heart is breaking! But who should care?"

"Mother, please," Lisa begged. "Just let me speak."

"I don't know if I can bear to hear what you say!" Naomi fretted.

"Mother, you don't have to believe me, or the Jesus Jews. Just turn on the morning news."

Naomi echoed back, "The morning news? Stop evading my question!"

"It's all over the news!" Lisa replied. "Before you called, Rabbi Joseph Levin of the Chief Rabbinate Council warned that the Ezekiel prophecy could be coming, and that Israelis should prepare for the possibility of another major war."

"Chief Rabbi Levin said that?" Naomi marveled.

"Yes, your *favorite* Rabbi!" Lisa answered, feeling somewhat vindicated.

Naomi muttered, "Hold on. Let me turn on the TV."

As Naomi began to pick up the television remote, she caught herself and said, "Wait a minute, Lisa. You still haven't answered my question. Are you, or are you NOT, telling me that you believe in…Jesus?" The last word caught on her stubborn tongue.

Lisa took a calming breath and replied. "Mother, just watch the news, then do me a favor and read Ezekiel, chapters 38 and 39. Then come over to my house so we can discuss this, face-to-face."

Silence ensued, broken only by a series of deep breaths on Naomi's end.

"Mother, are you still there?" Lisa worried.

"Yes, Lisa, I'm still with you," Naomi begrudgingly confirmed. "Close to fainting, I am. But who should care? I am beside myself! I don't know what to say, already."

Lovingly Lisa replied, "Mother, that's why I want to meet with you. We are living in incredibly treacherous times. As the family matriarch, you need to help us make enormous decisions about how to face the days ahead."

Lisa's diplomacy was intended to soothe Naomi, but the woman only commented, *"Oy Vey!* Now my Christian daughter is a prophetess, would you believe?"

Lisa sighed, "Please, Mother; set aside your prejudice long enough to see what's happening in the world right now. Things have gone absolutely crazy since the Christians vanished, and Israel defeated the Arabs! Even Rabbi Levin is searching ancient Hebrew prophecies for answers."

The mention, again, of Naomi's "favorite" rabbi was hard to fight.

"Very well, Lisa, I will see if I can find your father's Tanakh[3] in his library, and read about Ezekiel's war."

After talking with her mother, Lisa began to phone her brother Tovia, when Jami stopped her in mid-dial. "Mom, as I suspected, there's no school today."

Caught by surprise Lisa stammered, "Oh, uh, alright honey, then go have some breakfast."

Feeling somewhat put-off, Jami asked, "Wait! What did Grandma say? Was she open to talking about dad's DVD?"

"No, she's extremely troubled that I've become a Christian," Lisa answered.

Jami's mouth dropped open. "Oh, no!" she snickered. "You're in big trouble now!"

Lisa smiled. "You'd better brace yourself," she warned, "I invited your grandmother over to talk about things."

Jami perked up as she said, "I'm going to organize my notes from Dad's DVD, in case we can convince Grandma to watch the video."

"Good idea, honey," agreed Lisa.

Scrambling to get his phone, Tovia answered, "Hello, Tovia speaking." "It's me, Lisa," his sister replied.

"Hi, Sis! I got off the phone with mother a few minutes ago, letting her know we were all OK."

"I know," Lisa replied. "She called me right after. How did things happen yesterday with the missile attack?"

"It was dreadfully scary," Tovia began. "It was more frightening than the Hezbollah conflict in 2006, and our recent war with the Arabs."

"In what way?" asked Lisa.

"For starters, we didn't know if these missiles were equipped with nuclear warheads," Tovia explained, "and second, we were entirely ambushed, having only a moment's notice to gather the kids and rush to the shelter."

Lisa sighed, "I'm so sorry, Tovia. It must have been horrific for you and the children."

Tovia replied, "I'm so proud of the way Amber rounded up Isabella and her baby brother Jaxon, while I grabbed our gas masks and bug-out bags. After the last war, we are prepared for almost anything."

"Tell me more," Lisa requested. "What was it like inside the shelter? Mother said you spoke with some of the Jews claiming to be from the 144,000 of the Bible."

"Are you referring to the so-called Royal Jews of the Twelve Tribes?" asked Tovia.

"Yes," Lisa confirmed, "Mother said they suggested that you should leave Israel because Russia is going to wage a massive war against us."

"Yes, wow!" said Tovia. "These two guys were incredible. They were the only ones in our shelter with laptops. I couldn't believe how prepared they were. By the time we all got there they were picking up Internet Wi-Fi news about events above ground in Haifa. They were also communicating with other Jesus Jews, finding out if other cities in Israel had come under attack. We were blessed that they kept us apprised of what was transpiring on the outside."

Putting her phone on speaker at maximum volume, she gestured to Jami to come listen. "What else did they say?" Lisa inquired. "Did they actually call themselves the Royal Jews from the Twelve Tribes of Israel?"

"No," Tovia laughed. "They said that was a label the Rabbinate Council had come up with to mock their claims of being the 144,000 Hebrew witnesses of the Christian Bible."

"So, they did claim to be spoken about in the Bible?" Lisa asked.

"Yes, they did," said Tovia. "Lisa, these guys were very smart, and extremely kind. There were about forty of us in the shelter with them, and by the time they were done quoting from the Tanakh and their Christian Bible, they had most of us convinced that they really were who they claimed to be."

Tovia confessed, "Sis, I have to be honest with you: Amber, the kids, and I were so impressed with these two men, that we, along with about a dozen others in the shelter, received Jesus as our Lord and Savior."

Tovia was stunned to hear both Lisa and Jami cry out, "Hallelujah!"

"What's up?" Tovia laughed. "Am I picking up room noise, or did someone just say 'hallelujah'?"

"Yes," Lisa responded. "Jami and I are elated by this news! We both received Jesus yesterday, also!

Tovia was delighted to hear about their conversions. "Does Mother know?" he asked.

"Yes and no," said Lisa. "I'm pretty sure she realizes this from our conversation, which happened right after you spoke with her. She is supposed to come over to our house today to discuss Ezekiel's prophecy about Russia."

Tovia was overwhelmed. "Wow!" he cried out. "This is all happening so suddenly! I don't know what to say!"

"Don't worry about mother," Lisa replied. "Jami and I know what to say to her when she arrives. Fortunately, Thomas left behind a DVD that outlines end times events, including the Psalm 38 prophecy."

Tovia corrected her, "Don't you mean Ezekiel 38?"

Jami jumped into the conversation and confirmed, "Yes, Uncle, Mother keeps confusing Psalm 83 with Ezekiel 38. Both events were on the video."

"I understand the confusion," acknowledged Tovia. "Are you sure you know what to say to mother about Jesus, Ezekiel, and the 144,000 Jews?"

Lisa replied, "Well, we wish you were here to help explain things, but we will do our best. Also, do you remember Robert Rasmussen…we use to call him Razz? He was my father-in-law's best friend."

"Vaguely," Tovia said.

"Razz was raptured with Thomas, Tyler, and the other Christians, but before he left he willed his sizeable portfolio to us. His dear friend and financial advisor, Nathaniel Severs, delivered the good news to us personally. Nathan got saved recently also, and he was the one who led Jami and me in a prayer to receive Jesus Christ. I am going to ask Nathan to be with us when Mother arrives. He knows more about these matters than we do."

Tovia was delighted to hear this, but cautioned, "I told Mom that we received Jesus when we were in the shelter, and she immediately resisted the news. If she struggles with what you tell her, I advise that you try to locate one of these 144,000 witnesses in your area to assist you. Apparently, they have a special anointing for leading Jews to accept Jesus as their Messiah. I know that the Holy Spirit used Gershom and Simeon to convince Amber, me, and the children about Jesus. I doubt that we would have converted if they weren't in the shelter with us yesterday."

"That's good advice." Lisa agreed.

"I know there are some in town," Jami chimed in, "because my girlfriend Amy said she saw some Yeshiva students hassling two of them by the high school the other day. I will contact her to see if she knows where to find them."

"I think that would be a great idea," Tovia said.

Lisa heaved a sigh. "Jami and I are delighted that you are all safe," she said. "Oh, by the way, I forgot to ask...are you planning to leave Israel temporarily like the witnesses advised?"

"We're talking about it," said Tovia. "Right now we are researching where we would go, and watching the news for breaking events. Please call me after you speak to Mother and we will know more. If the topic comes up, tell Mom that we are seriously considering taking the advice of the two witnesses in the shelter."

"Will do," promised Lisa. "We will sign off for now and call you after we talk to Mom."

"Please do," Tovia said. "I will anxiously await your call. Remember to have your gas masks and other preparations in order in case another Russian attack comes upon Israel and you have to rush to your local bomb shelter."

"We are prepared for anything, Brother," Lisa assured him. "We love you. Give Amber and the kids a hug from us."

Chapter 6
Hooked in the Jaws - Russia Covets Israeli Contracts with the West

"**I**srael to Export Gas and Oil to the West," read the top front page headline of the *Moscow Times*. The article reported that Israel had signed multi-billion dollar contracts with America and the UK to export significant quantities of natural gas and crude oil directly to them. Furthermore, the article said:

> "In addition to The UK and US, Israel is also courting the EU for natural gas and oil export contracts."

Israeli Prime Minister Moshe Kaufman was quoted as saying,

> "'The EU is also Israel's strong ally and should be rewarded for imposing stiff demands against the Russian coalition. Presently, Israel can supply the EU with an abundance of natural gas and oil resources, which minimizes the need for European reliance upon Russia and Iran for these critical commodities.'"

Having advance knowledge of the outcome of the EU general assembly meeting, Prime Minister Kaufman had spoken out of turn in telling the press about EU sanctions against Russia. The presumptuous announcement galled the Russian president. Slamming his newspaper down on his desk, Vladimir Ziroski shouted at his councilors, "What EU demands? These were only rumors until now. Have any of you heard the details about these "stiff demands" Kaufman is alluding to?

Calming himself, Ziroski continued, "So be it! It doesn't matter what the EU plans. Israel has sealed its own coffin with these western contracts. Mother Russia refuses to compete with the Jews! The time has come to defeat and plunder the Jewish state!"

These egregious comments stunned his cabinet members, including Prime Minister Sergei Primakov, and UN Ambassador Anatoly Tarasov. Mad Vlad Ziroski had just convened his cabinet to discuss a potential future invasion of Israel, when his secretary side-swiped him with the *Moscow Times* and suggested that he read the troubling headline and related article first.

"What western contracts?" Prime Minister Primakov asked.

Thrusting the newspaper across the desk, Ziroski snarled, "Israel plans to export oil and gas to the west!"

Ambassador Tarasov, who had recently attempted to dissuade the EU from considering sanctions said, "Those western traitors! Their ambassadors all promised me that they would not execute those export contracts with Israel without Russia's consent."

"If they want an official response, I'll give them an official response!" Ziroski retorted. "War with Israel, that's Russia's official response!"

Motioning toward his secretary, Mad Vlad ordered, "As soon as this meeting adjourns get Ayatollah Khomani on the phone!"

Prime Minister Primakov, already in trouble with Ziroski for the missing suitcase nuclear weapons that terrorists used to strike American ballparks, patronizingly said, "I vote 'yes' on that Mr. President. This way you can accomplish two important feats at once: dispossess Israel of its energy resources, making the EU solely reliant upon us; and eliminate any threat of sanctions against us. We shall become the superpower that determines the future of the world!"

Ziroski confirmed, "Precisely! My thoughts exactly!"

Mad Vlad informed his cabinet that Russia was fast-forwarding coalition plans to launch a massive attack against the Jewish state, beginning with the northernmost parts of Israel.

Ziroski pledged, "Our confederacy will not allow Israel any further export access through the surrounding regional waterways. Iran will close off the Strait of Hormuz, and our other coalition commanders will police the Mediterranean and Red Seas."

Ambassador Tarasov objected "In light of today's headlines, these maritime measures will undoubtedly upset the Americans and the British."

Pounding his desk, Mad Vlad declared, "The Americans and British have the Russian bear in an uproar! Their armies are weakened and disoriented due to the disappearances. They are no match for our coalition forces and weapons. Our troops have not vanished into thin air like many of theirs. They will protest our invasion from the sidelines, but they won't draw us into a multi-front war. If they do, we will take the battle into their lands. The same applies to the EU. They have Muslim insurgents causing severe unrest internally. If the EU decides to come against us, they will have to fight with the Muslims from within and without!"

Russia Commands Iran to Attack Israel

As the last of Ziroski's cabinet departed, his secretary handed him the phone.

"President Ziroski, I was expecting your call," announced Iran's supreme leader, the Ayatollah Khomani.

Mad Vlad replied, "So you have also read the reports about Israel's contracts with the west?"

The Khomani declared, "Indeed, I have already told President Muktada Zakiri to prepare his commanders for battle! He is awaiting my final order. IRGC generals are probably already coordinating attack details with your generals."

"Prime Minister Primakov is communicating with our military Chief of Staff as we speak," Ziroski boasted.

"Israel has defiantly crossed our final red line in the Middle East sand," the Ayatollah proclaimed. "We Muslims rejoice to send the Jews to their appointment in Jahannam."[4]

President Ziroski smiled. "So be it Supreme Ayatollah!" he agreed. "The Jews will have their rendezvous with death. Assemble your forces for battle. Muslim world leaders await your command."

Chapter 7
Jews Flee Israel as the Russian Invasion Begins

Rushing to the nearby bomb-shelter, Naomi stumbled and fell to the ground, spraining an ankle. Grasping her leg in agony, she moaned. Fortunately, this round of sirens in Jerusalem turned out to be a false alarm, allowing Naomi time to calm herself down and slowly get up to test her footing. As she limped back toward home, she called Lisa on her cell phone.

"Hello, Thompson residence," Lisa answered.

"Honey," Naomi sadly said, "I'm sorry to say that I won't be able to come over this afternoon."

"Oh Mother, not again! It's critical that we watch that DVD. It explains what the Bible says Russia is about to do to Israel!"

Naomi apologized. "I know this makes two afternoons in a row that I have cancelled, but I have a legitimate reason today. My excuse yesterday may have been lame, but..." she shuddered. "...Speaking of 'lame,' I think I just sprained my ankle racing to the bomb shelter. I think the Thirty-mile drive to your home in Bet Shemesh will aggravate the sprain. *Oy Vey!* All these sirens and trips to shelters are wearing me out. I'm so stressed I hardly sleep anymore."

"Are you going to be okay"? Lisa asked.

"Yes, of course," Naomi replied. "I'm almost home and plan to ice down the swelling. I'm sure I will be able to get around better after I nurse the ankle a bit."

"I'm going to grab Jami and Nathan Severs, and head to your house. I'll bring the DVD with me," Lisa insisted.

"No, no, no," Naomi argued. "Don't bother! That won't be necessary. I'm not up for it today. Let me rest my ankle and my mind, and I will see how I feel in the morning."

"The morning may be too late!" Lisa responded, "Did you get a chance to read Ezekiel 38, like you promised?"

"Comments like that are not helping me to calm down," Naomi rebuffed. "And, no, I didn't get a chance to comb through the Ezekiel predictions. I was going to start reading the verses when the sirens started sounding. Let me take the rest of the day to rest my ankle and study his writings. I have your father's Tanakh sitting beside my reading chair."

Conceding to her mother's wishes, Lisa replied, "Alright, Mother, but promise me you *will* read Ezekiel 38, and that you will call me if you have any questions. If you need me to come over to nurse your ankle sprain, I will. But, tomorrow we must for sure meet to discuss what's taking place between Israel and Russia. I spoke with Tovia, and he said that he, Amber, Bella, and Jaxon may leave Israel until the Russian threat subsides."

"*Oy Vey!*" Naomi cried. "I'm losing my mind with you kids. I can't tell your father that you are all Christians! This is not the time for Jews to become Christians! This is the time for Jews to be Jews!"

Forfeiting another phone fight, Lisa consented, "Okay, Mother. Have it your way for now, but as you will see on the news, time *is* of the utmost essence."

Hanging up, Lisa greeted Nathan Severs at the front door. He had come in response to Lisa's request that he be present to talk to Naomi about Ezekiel 38 and the other prophecies on the DVD.

"Greetings, Lisa," said Nathan. "Thanks for inviting me over. Is your mother here yet?"

Reluctantly, Lisa replied, "No, she hurt herself while fleeing to the bomb shelter. She may have sprained her ankle. She wants to rest and nurse it for the rest of the day. She won't be coming over after all."

Handing Lisa a bag of sandwiches and desserts from her favorite neighborhood deli, Nathan said, "I am sorry to hear that. I brought along these goodies to pave the way for our discussion. You told me how much she loves to eat Kosher foods."

Lisa gratefully received the treats. "Please, come in," she welcomed him. "I assure you that these delicious morsels won't go to waste."

Nathan took off his coat and followed Lisa to the kitchen, "This is the second time your mother has stood us up," he said. "I appreciate that an ankle sprain is a serious issue, but we are running out of time to warn her about the impending Russian invasion."

Lisa moaned, "I know, Nathan! I am beside myself concerning her indifference. I sincerely believe that the DVD will lead her to Christ like it did for Jami and me." Moving into the parlor while Lisa prepared the food, Nathan saw Jami watching the breaking news. "What's going on now?" he asked.

"Not good," Jami anguished. "They're showing satellite shots of troops assembling in Russia, Iran, and Turkey and a couple of other countries that are Russia's allies. These must be the hordes of Gog that the DVD spoke about. The newscaster says that Israelis should brace for an im-immena, um, I can't say the word, but it means like for an immediate attack."

"You mean an 'imminent' attack," Nathan offered.

"Yes, that's the word he used." Jami agreed.

"Lisa, hurry up! You'd better get in here right away," Nathan hollered toward the kitchen.

Scurrying into the parlor, Lisa asked, "What now?"

"Ezekiel 38 seems to be setting up quicker than we thought," Nathan alerted.

Hand-in-hand the trio sat on the sofa's edge as Israel Network News (INN) issued an alarming alert:

> *We are getting reports from credible Israeli military sources that a massive deployment of Russian, Turkish, and Iranian troops is underway. These reports indicate that the Syrian port city of Tartus, due north of Israel, is their rendezvous destination. Only about 150 miles lies between Tartus and Haifa. As we have been reporting over the past few weeks, Russia, in cooperation with Turkey, has sent large quantities of missiles, tank and heavy artillery into Tartus. Furthermore, our sources warn that the IDF is expeditiously mobilizing for war, and that Israelis should prepare immediately for an imminent large-scale attack from Russia and its coalition.*

Frantic, Jami cried, "Didn't Dad's DVD say that Ezekiel talked about Russia attacking from the 'uttermost parts of the north'?"

"Yep, that sounds correct" Nathan replied.

"Mother what are we going to do?" Jami implored.

"I don't know." Lisa said, tears in her eyes. "I don't have the answers. This is all too overwhelming for me."

As the two girls wept together, Nathan stood up and took charge. "We have to get out of here," he ordered. "I have an escape plan prepared. I have kept my private plane and personal pilot on ready standby, just in case things began to escalate."

Startled, Lisa stammered, "Right now? Leave now?"

Pulling her to her feet, Nathan insisted, "We three are getting out of here *right now,* before Russia attacks!"

White-faced, Jami croaked, "But, how, where, when, what are you talking about?"

Nathan went for his jacket, calling over his shoulder, "You told me what the two Jesus Jews said to Tovia. They warned that people might need to flee, scat, vamoose, get out of Dodge."

"B-but," Lisa resisted, "we can't just pick-up and leave!"

"Oh yes we can, and we will!" Nathan commanded, grabbing the girls' coats from the hall closet." If you don't, I'm going to pick you both up over my shoulders and strap you into the plane personally! It's not safe for any of us to be in Israel right now. The video said Israel wins the war, but it didn't promise zero Israeli casualties!"

Lisa balked. "What about my mother?" she groaned.

Nathan stopped short, hands on hips. "Look girls," he barked, "I have a private twin engine Cessna jet gassed and ready to go. It will seat up to a dozen passengers with ample luggage space. It is already in a berth by the airport runway. That makes room for you two girls, my pilot, me, your parents and several of your family members. I have made arrangements for us to travel to my villa in Rome. If you have more people, we might have time to make a second flight."

Nathan Severs had paid cash for this home in Rome prior to moving to Israel, in preparation for just such a time as this. He still owned his mansion in America, and was in the process of purchasing additional properties located in several other strategic parts of the world, as part of his plan to set up a network of safe-haven locations for Jews coming under persecution. All of this was to honor his personal promise to Christ to become a last days Oskar Schindler of sorts.

Lisa tried to compose herself... "What do we pack? What about my job? I fill an important position for the Ministry of Interior. I can't just pick-up and leave. What would I tell my boss?"

Firmly grabbing her by the shoulders and staring squarely into her eyes, Nathan replied, "Pack some clothes, personal photos, and banking and portfolio information. Keep it light; I have everything else we need:

food, water, gold, and plenty of cash stockpiled in Rome. Regarding your boss, just request a short sabbatical. Tell him you are concerned about a pending Russian invasion and want to move your daughter to safer ground for the time being. Inform him that you will work from your laptop and return after the dust settles. Let him know that you will stay in close contact with him. If he doesn't like it, then don't worry about it. Your uncle Razz bequeathed you a sizeable fortune. You don't have to work another day in your life if you don't want to."

Facing reality, Lisa looked at Jami. "Honey," she said, "Mr. Severs is right. I have to get you out of harm's way and we have to go right now."

"Whoa!" Jami requested. "What about all my BFF's? I don't want them to suffer."

"I understand, honey," Lisa replied, embracing her daughter. "but family first, *best friends forever* are second. If there is time and if they are willing, I'm sure Nathan will do the best he can to help the others."

"Pack your bags and make the calls," Nathan said firmly, "In light of what's transpiring we are definitely leaving before midnight. I'm going to get my gear loaded, contact my housekeeping staff in Italy, and make sure my pilot has the plane readied for several potential flights back and forth to Israel. Call me and let me know who wants to depart with us, and I will be back at 10:00 P.M. to pick all of you up. Remember, the Lord wins this war for Israel according to Ezekiel, so the odds are that you should be able to return home when it's all over. Don't pack the kitchen sink, only the essentials.

Lisa asked, "What if Tovia and his family want to go with us on the first flight? Can we pick them up in Haifa?"

"I hope so" said Nathan. "That's a question for my pilot. He will have to schedule everything through flight control. I need to know as soon as you know about Tovia."

"Certainly," Lisa replied, "I understand. I will call him and my mother right away! Oh, Nathan," she said, looking at him fondly, "thank you so much for being here for us all; you are a life saver!"

Hugging the girls' goodbye, Severs headed home to make preparations for their midnight departure.

Several hours had passed from the time Nathan left Lisa's home, when an urgent call came in.

"Tovia and his family are coming Nathan," Lisa's breathless voice came through. "Can you please inform your pilot to make arrangements with air traffic control to pick them up in Haifa?"

"Arrangements to pick up your brother and his family have already been made," Nathan informed her. "I expected he would want to leave with you, so I had my pilot schedule a flight in advance. Setting this up on such short notice was no easy undertaking, so, please make sure they arrive at the Haifa airport no later than 1:15 A.M."

"Absolutely!" Lisa confirmed. "The family and the two Jesus Jews will arrive on time to leave with you and Jami."

"Me and Jami? And what's this about Jesus Jews?" Nathan balked.

Lisa responded, "I'm not going with you, at least not on the first flight. I can't convince my father and mother or the rest of my family to leave Israel. They think that the US and EU can smooth things over with Russia, and they are accusing me of panicking prematurely. I need another day or two to persuade them. Please take Jami to safety and then come back for me in a few days when I have the other members of my family prepared."

"Yeah?" Nathan quipped. "Well, that's not going to happen, girl!"

"What do you mean?" Lisa argued.

"It's very admirable of you to want to help the family," Nathan replied. "But, you don't have the luxury of a few days. The Russian confederacy has declared war with Israel, and has already given Prime Minister Kaufman a twenty-four-hour ultimatum to surrender unconditionally, or else! We leave now, or we won't leave at all! You'll have to convince the stragglers by phone from Rome, providing subsequent flights are even possible."

A silent interlude passed as Lisa digested the news.

"Okay," Nathan proceeded, "what about these Jesus Jews? What's up with that?"

Grappling with her emotions, Lisa reluctantly explained, "The two gentlemen in the bomb shelter that led my brother and his family to Jesus visited him at his house today. Tovia told them the family was leaving, as they had advised." Lisa took a stuttering breath. "When he told them about your plane, they asked if there might be room for them."

Nathan rolled his eyes. "And...?"

Lisa continued, "My brother called me and I told him I thought there would be enough room on the plane, since I knew Mother and Daddy and the others weren't ready to come." There was a heady pause." I hope I didn't overstep my boundaries, but I believed you would want to help a couple of the Lord's servants."

Nathan cleared his throat, and gave a thoughtful reply. "First let me tell you I'm sorry your parents and siblings are reluctant to leave. If there is any way to return for them down the road, I will personally come back for them all. Second, we should be able to squeeze these two Messianics into the plane, but it's going to be tight. It is probably not a coincidence that they called on Tovia today. Perhaps, they are meant to leave with us. Last, we are still on schedule to pick you and Jami up at 10:00 sharp tonight, so please be ready."

He could hear Lisa's tearful sigh of relief. "Can you contact Tovia and tell him to have everyone ready at the Haifa airport on time?" Nathan directed. "Also, please give me his phone number in case I need to make direct contact with him."

Fleeing for Safety

It was 2:00 A.M. and things were going according to plans. All the passengers and cargo were loaded on board, including the two Jesus Jews, and the plane was ready to take off from Haifa airport. Patiently waiting for the airport tower to grant permission for their departure, they heard the Haifa air raid sirens begin to sound. In a matter of moments, they heard a loud explosion that rocked the plane violently on the runway. Looking through the jet windows they saw a flashing light flaring close by the airport.

"Holy smoke! I think that was a missile explosion!" shouted the pilot. "We need to fly out of here immediately. We can't wait for the traffic tower's permission; we have to take our chances and depart!"

Accustomed to making executive spot decisions, Severs hollered, "Go for it! I don't see any planes arriving or departing. The runway is ours for the taking!"

They safely lifted off and flew into the dangerous skies. The jet was scarcely off the tarmac, when they witnessed several more fiery explosions through the plane's windows. Plumes of smoke were emanating into the charred night skies above Haifa.

Although the two Jesus Jews remained calm, everyone else in the cockpit and cabin were horrified. Amber and Bella began to weep profusely for their hometown family and friends below.

Simeon Abrams, the younger of the two Jesus Jews, startled everyone when he called out, "Don't look down at the destruction; look up for Israel's deliverance. The Lord will make an abrupt end of this battle!"

As they all turned their attention toward the two saintly passengers, Gershom Gold, Simeon's elder clarified, "Simeon speaks correctly. The Lord has prepared a snare for Israel's enemies. Ezekiel declares that the enemies will descend upon Israel from the uttermost parts of the north like a storm, covering the land like a cloud. This process has now begun."

Simeon spoke in turn and declared, "Ages ago the Lord prophesied through Ezekiel in His jealousy and wrath, declaring that when Gog comes against the land of Israel, His fury will show upon His face. This night under the camouflage of darkness, the hordes of Gog will begin their ascent upon the mountains of Israel. A great company will come with their bucklers and shields and they will fill the land with their innumerable troops and spectacular arsenals."

Gershom interjected, "And when they all have arrived and set their arsenals in place, there will be a great earthquake that will shake the entire Holy Land. It will be felt well into the expanded territories Israel recently annexed after their war with the Arabs. Mountain tops will topple and hordes of enemy soldiers will be cast down to their deaths in steep crevices and ravines. The valleys will be filled with the slain hordes of Gog. The magnitude of the event will be an astonishment to all those dwelling upon the face of the earth."

Simeon looked soberly at his companion, "Those that survive will draw their weapons upon each other from fear and panic. They won't know where to launch their missiles. Their rockets will backfire, killing many of their own."

As the two of them took turns speaking, their proclamations became increasingly passionate, the volume of their voices increasing with each declaration. It was as if they were speaking from pulpits in the center of a village announcing the oracles decreed by a powerful king.

Gershom spoke again, raising his right hand for emphasis, "And then the Lord will enter into final judgment with pestilence and bloodshed. He will rain down on Gog and his troops, and on the many peoples who are with him, flooding rain, great hailstones, fire, and brimstone. The carnage will be so widespread that even the birds of the air and the beasts of the earth will have their fill. And the Lord will be magnified in His victory before the watchful eyes of the nations."

Simeon concluded, his tone ominous, "The destruction will extend even to the coastal areas and beyond, as the Lord sends fire from heaven into the enemy's homelands, so that even those who thought they were secure will experience the judgment. The advanced weapons that they have fashioned against Israel will be knocked out of their hands, and Israel will use them as sources of fuel and energy."

Gershom bowed his head, exhausted from the oration, and implored, "Let us pray that the Lord will be merciful to Israel in all of this, and let us invoke the peace of Jerusalem."

Throughout the duration of the flight to Rome, Simeon and Gershom were peppered with questions from Nathan, Lisa, Jami, Tovia, and Amber. Meanwhile, Tovia's children could hardly keep their eyes open, dozing in an out of slumber. Although eight-year-old *Bella* tried to keep up with the adult conversation, both she and her three-year-old curly haired brother Jaxon, succumbed to the need for sleep.

Tovia's wife, beautiful and inquisitive Amber, began the first round of questioning. Amber was a devoted reader of religious writings, and possessed a better than basic understanding of the New Testament. She asked, "What did you both do before you became members of the 144,000 witnesses of the book of Revelation?"

Simeon, at age twenty-nine, closely resembled the American movie star Ryan Gosling. In fact, young Jami asked him, somewhat flirtatiously, if he was any relation to the actor. Shaking his head, Simeon answered, "I was a tour guide in Israel for Christian pilgrims touring the Holy Land. I started giving tours when I was twenty-two years old. I was required to have expertise in both the Old and New Testaments of the Bible for this job. Although I wasn't a believer in Christ at the time, my photographic memory enabled me to nearly memorize the entire New Testament."

Impressed by Simeon's resume, everyone turned toward forty-eight-year-old, short and pudgy Gershom, who announced that he was a Hebrew scholar that had been a professor at Hebrew University of Jerusalem for the past twenty-years. What Gershom, with his round and jovial face, lacked in appearance, he made up for with his deep, eloquent voice. "Unlike Simeon," he said, "I spent most of my time reading, memorizing, and teaching the Tanakh, the Old Testament of the Bible."

Tovia asked, "When you met us in the Haifa bomb shelter you mentioned that most of you travel in pairs. Why is that?"

"We follow the biblical model of discipling," Simeon explained. Examples are given in Matthew 21:1, Mark 14:9 and elsewhere evidencing that Jesus often sent out his disciples in pairs. Moreover, we have come to recognize that the pairs among us have complimentary skill sets that work well in tandem. Take Gershom and myself, for example. Understanding he may lack in the New Testament, I compensate for, and vice versa with the Old Testament, which is his area of expertise."

Amber had her Bible open to Revelation chapter 14, where she read aloud: *"The hundred and forty-four-thousand who were redeemed from the earth. These are the ones who were not defiled with women, for they are virgins."*

Jami blushed, and her mother winked at her. Looking up from the Bible, Amber inquired, "Does this mean that neither of you have been married before, or does it mean that you won't get married from this point forward?"

Young Jami, who was finding it hard to keep her eyes off handsome Simeon, found this question of particular interest, and she leaned in to hear Simeon's response.

Since this question was based on the New Testament, Simeon responded, "That's an excellent question and being an eligible bachelor, one of particular interest to me. Certainly, on the surface it suggests that we are all virgins and in that condition, we can devote 100% of our attention toward serving the Lord. I have looked closely at the original Greek language of the biblical text and I have compared it to the teachings of Paul about married life in 1 Corinthians 7. In some ways, we members of the 144,000 wear the similar shoes of the apostle Paul. Before his Damascus Road experience, which was when he received his calling to serve the Lord, he had unknowingly been prepared for his apostolic ministry beforehand. Paul was an expert on the interpretation of the Law of Moses, which equipped him for his ministry. The 144,000 have also unsuspectingly been prepared in advance for our important call of duty in the end times. In 1 Corinthians 7:6-9, Paul makes an interesting comment after having laid down the groundwork for a successful marriage. He says, *'But I say this as a concession, not as a commandment. For I wish that all men were even as I myself. But each one has his own gift from God, one in this manner and another in that. But I say to the unmarried and to the widows: It is good for them if they remain even as I am; but if they cannot exercise self-control, let them marry. For it is better to marry than to burn with passion.'* I understand that to mean that Paul was unmarried and preferred to carry out his ministry in that capacity."

"What are you saying, that you are never getting married?" Jami blurted out. Then, having embarrassed herself, she sunk back into her seat.

Simeon smiled and wisely dodging her question, he went on: "Amber, you only read part of Revelation 14:4, about the *defiled by woman* and us being *virgins*, would you kindly read the rest of the verse?"

Revisiting the verse, Amber read, *"These are the ones who follow the Lamb wherever He goes. These were redeemed from among men, being* firstfruits to God and to the Lamb."

Now, let me explain the problems I have with simply saying we are virgins. First, the verse implies that women are defiling and that's why we remain as virgins. It's as if we don't want to become contaminated by a woman. That's utter nonsense! God didn't create Eve to defile Adam. In fact, a good woman can serve a vital role in a man's ministry. In my estimation, the apostle Paul didn't remain single out of a fear that he would become corrupted by a woman. He calculated that he could better devote his undivided attention to his calling in an unmarried capacity. He traveled extensively, was often beaten severely, and he spent many of his days impoverished and imprisoned. He recognized that these are not suitable conditions to sustain a healthy and vibrant marriage. This realization alone caused me to look deeper into the true meaning of this verse."

Pausing momentarily, he asked, "Does that make sense so far?"

Jami responded giddishly, "Yes, especially the part about *a good woman can serve a vital role in a man's ministry.*"

Chuckling for a moment, Simeon continued: "I had Amber read the rest of the verse because it emphasizing that we are the ones who follow the *'Lamb wherever He goes.'* This is in stark contrast to, we are the ones who follow the Harlot, wherever she goes. This may be difficult to explain until you learn about the coming global religion, which is represented in Revelation 17 and elsewhere as a harlot. It appears that these verses may teach that the 144,000 witnesses remain chaste solely to the Lord, and are not stained, soiled, or defiled by the coming false world religion represented by the Harlot. One of the distinguishing characteristics of our 144,000 witnesses will definitely be that we will not be defiled by the harlot religion. Or another way of explaining it would be that we are considered virgins because we won't partake of the pagan idolatries that come out of the harlot global religion."

"Oh. I think I understand," Amber muttered, still obviously mystified.

"Wow, that's pretty deep," acknowledged Jami, who was now infatuated with both Simeon's good looks, and obvious intellect. Jami, the Miss Teen Beauty Queen of her old American school, had no idea what Simeon meant, but realized this handsome guy was the full package.

Gershom, sensing Jami's puppy love adoration of his partner, smiled and said, "Amber's question was deep, and deep questions require deep answers." Gershom continued, "Whatever the interpretation will prove to be, it is doubtful that marriage is in the cards for handsome young Simeon. He will be preoccupied serving the Lord."

Tovia took his turn and asked, "How did you both recognize your calling as members of the 144,000 witnesses?"

Gershom decided to answer this question. "What we have been able to ascertain through our communications with the others is that on the day the rapture took place each of us had either a celestial dream or vision. I had a dream, but Simeon had a similar vision. This seems to be universal across the boards. The older among us dreamed dreams, but the younger saw visions."[5]

"What did you dream?" Amber asked.

Gershom elaborated: "First let me say that it appears we all shared miraculously in the same experience. We saw four angels standing at the four corners of the earth. A peaceful calm permeated throughout the entire earth. No wind blew upon the earth, sea, or on any tree. Then we saw another angel ascending from the east, holding a seal in his hand that had been given to him by God. This fifth angel said loudly to the other four angels, *Do not harm the earth, the sea, or the trees till we have sealed the servants of our God on their foreheads*. Then we heard the number One-hundred-and-forty-four-thousand shouted out, after which the names of the twelve Israelite tribes were called out in Hebrew."

"Did it happen that identical way in your vision Simeon?" Jami asked.

"Yes, but there was more," Simeon clarified. "After these things, all 144,000 of us were standing with Christ on Mount Zion. He was clearly recognized by all of us as the Messiah. At that time, we received a seal upon our foreheads, and were given our tribal identities. I found out that my ancestors were from the tribe of Judah, and Gershom discovered that he descended from the tribe of Levi. Then there was a thunderous sound and suddenly we heard harps playing and voices singing. They sang a new song that was specifically sung for us."

Amber asked, "How did you know it was a new song?"

Simeon revealed, "The lyrics were very specific to us. For instance, one stanza announced that we were the undefiled that follow the Lamb of God wherever He goes. Then the chorus declared that we were redeemed as first-fruits to God and to the Lamb. And that there was no deceitfulness coming out from our mouths, or faults counted against us before the throne of God."

Lisa commented, "Wow! That sounds more like a proclamation than a song."

Gershom agreed. "You could say it was both," he confirmed.

Nathan chimed in, "Speaking as a newbie Christian, it is indeed a blessing to learn more from you about Christ, heavenly worship, the importance of our faith, and the coming Bible prophecies. With that said, I am wondering: Does your service to God make you both invincible to the coming dangers predicted in the Bible? And, if you are protected from harm because of your calling, then why did you flee Israel at this time?"

Gershom looked to Simeon and suggested, "Why don't you answer the first question, and I will tackle the second one."

"Certainly," responded Simeon. "First, let me say the honor is ours to be among all of you. The apostle Peter said in his first epistle that a believer's faith is more precious than gold that perishes. Peter added, 'Jesus Christ, whom having not seen you love. Though now you do not see *Him,* yet believing, you rejoice with joy inexpressible and full of glory, receiving the end of your faith—the salvation of *your* souls.'[6] The fact that you all have become born again believers at a time when true Christianity is being severely mocked bodes extremely well for you. To answer your first question, yes, although I prefer the word *protected* over *invincible.* It does appear that the Lord's protection was bestowed upon us during the Mt. Zion experience."

Gershom answered the next question saying, "We are not traveling with you to flee danger in Israel, but to spread the gospel abroad. This is our calling. Simeon and I are clear that we are called to witness to all nations, tribes, peoples, and tongues."[7]

With authority and great command of the scriptures, Gershom Gold and Simeon Abrams answered dozens of questions that night. By the time Nathan's jet landed in Rome, the passengers could comfortably claim that they had completed courses in Christianity and Bible Prophecy 101.

Chapter 8
The Antichrist and the Coming Global Religion

Upon landing safely in Rome, the group established their temporary headquarters in Nathan Severs' luxurious residence near the center of the city. His lavishly decorated, 9500 square foot palatial home made them feel more like tourists than refugees. The mansion came complete with a four-member housekeeping and cooking staff that promptly attended to all the guests' needs.

In short order, events in the Middle East began to resemble the prophetic descriptions given in Ezekiel 38. The Russian invaders were positioned to pounce upon Israel at any moment just as Gershom and Simeon had warned. Everyone in Nathan's house was nestled in and watching news reports with bated breath. They eagerly expected the Lord to deliver Israel in the manner foretold.

Meanwhile, Lisa repeatedly attempted to contact her family in Israel. Overloaded phone lines kept her from establishing communication. Even though she believed that Israel would survive, she feared for her family, and wanted them to flee somewhere safe.

Seated on Nathan's expansive veranda, which overlooked picturesque Vatican City, Simeon Abrams asked, "Nathan, what prompted you to purchase this spacious home with this priceless view? This property would be perfect for a bed and breakfast business. Is that something you were considering at the time of purchase?"

Nathan responded, "No, not necessarily. But you are correct about this home's investment potential. The primary reason for purchasing this property is because I made a commitment to Christ when I recently received Him as my Lord and Savior that I would become an Oskar Schindler type person in the "Tribulational Period." I believe Rome might serve as strategic

NOVEL

escape locations for persecuted Christians and Jews. I hope to someday use this residence as part of an underground network to that end."

Seated alongside them was Tovia, who asked, "What do you mean by persecuted Jews?"

Nathan looked at the Messianics. "I'm no prophecy expert, but I read in Zechariah 13:8, the Antichrist is going to attempt the final genocide of the Jews. Some Gentiles are going to stand up for them in the last days, like Oskar Shindler did during the Nazi era. In Matthew's twenty-fifth chapter, Jesus called them righteous Gentiles and compared them to obedient sheep rather than indignant goats."

Tovia looked toward Simeon and asked, "Do you know anything about this?"

"Yes," Simeon replied. "The prophet Zechariah declared that two-thirds of the Jewish population will be killed in the land of Israel as part of this Antichrist campaign."

Concerned for his unsaved Israeli relatives, Tovia asked, "So what happens to the other one-third that survives? Do they hide out at the Vatican and elsewhere in Rome?"

Nathan responded, "I am uncertain about that. Frankly, I don't know where the surviving Jews will end up, but I do believe that Rome plays a significant role in the end times. I think Scripture is quite clear about that. That's why I decided to prepare a safe house near the Vatican."

Turning to Simeon, Tovia inquired, "Do you know the final destination of this Jewish remnant, according to Bible prophecy?"

"You are right about Rome figuring in Bible Prophecy," the Messianic answered, "but Rome is not the final destination of the faithful Jewish remnant. They end up in ancient Edom according to Isaiah 63 and elsewhere. Edom was located in modern-day Southern Jordan. Just recently, as a result of the IDF victory in the predicted Arab-Israeli war of Psalm 83, Israel annexed this territory as part of its bid for a greater Israel. Presently Edom exists as part of the Jewish state."

Nathan scratched his head and commented, "The end times video Lisa, Jami, and I watched a few days ago made this similar prediction. My close friend Robert Rasmussen was a prophecy expert and he informed me that Rome was a key city in the end times, I bought this property before moving to Israel. Perhaps I purchased this home under misguided assumptions."

Simeon was thoughtful. "Nathan, your house is presently serving a vital function for Jewish refugees," he said. "In fact, apart from you, your pilot, and house staff, the rest of us here are all presently persecuted Jews taking refuge as we await the final fulfillment of Ezekiel 38."

Nathan marveled. "Simeon, you make a good point, but if I am not mistaken, this group isn't the final remnant of Jews that Zechariah predicted would be persecuted by the Antichrist."

Simeon cautioned, "Not yet, anyway."

Simeon's comment caused Tovia to ask, "Are you suggesting that Lisa, Jami, Amber, Isabella, Jaxon, and I will someday be persecuted by the Antichrist?"

Looking Tovia squarely in the eyes, Simeon sympathetically asked, "Do you want my honest answer?"

Taken aback, Tovia gulped. "I…I don't know, now. Then, pondering the staggering possibility, he sighed, "For the sake of my loved ones; please give me the truth."

Simeon replied, "I am not trying to be evasive, but, truthfully, it depends."

"Depends on what?" Tovia urged.

"It depends on your family's ability to survive the dangerous prophecies that come between now and then," Simeon said.

Tovia's face grew pale. "Wh-what should we do in case we face this persecution?" he asked.

"Be informed and obedient," Simeon instructed. "Learn all that you can about this period before it comes. And also, follow Christ's instructions in Matthew 24:15-20 to depart from Israel before the genocidal campaign commences at the midpoint of the Tribulation Period. In these Matthew verses Jesus warned that the Antichrist would enter the third Jewish Temple and fulfill the *abomination of desolation*,' which was spoken of by Daniel the prophet. This pivotal prophecy is when the Antichrist initiates his killing campaign that Zechariah predicted. Gershom and I will familiarize all of you with the pertinent prophetic scriptures before you head back home."

Humbled by Simeon's comments, Nathan confessed, "Now more than ever, I am committed to becoming an end times Oskar Schindler."

Simeon reached out and patted the host's knee. "Nathan, this house can be used for surveillance of future Vatican events, and to safely house persecuted saints, be they Christians or Jews. So, don't fret over the soundness of your investment."

"Please elaborate about the 'persecutions'," Nathan requested.

Simeon sat back and studied Nathan's pensive face. "The Bible speaks about a perilous time called the *Patience of the Saints*," he explained. "This period is characterized by Christian martyrdom, which can include both Jewish and Gentile believers. A related verse in Revelation 14 actually declares; *Blessed are the dead who die in the Lord from now on.* This alludes to the fact that people who become believers after the Rapture will be blessed with their eternal salvation, but for many of them it will come at the cost of a martyr's price. They will need to exhibit patience in their faith until Jesus returns in His Second Coming. After which, Christ will establish His Messianic Kingdom."

Nathan beseeched, "Please tell me how my Rome residence could prove useful at such a time."

Simeon expounded, "The final Jewish genocidal attempt mostly occurs in the last half of the Tribulation period, otherwise known as the Great Tribulation. This final three-and-one-half-year time span will be the worst period of Jewish persecution in history. It will not only be characterized by Jewish persecution, but also many Gentiles will be executed for refusing to take the Mark of the Beast in their right hand or forehead. However, several prophecies occur before the Antichrist attempts to extirpate the Jews and execute those refusing his mark."

Nathan inquired, "In Rome? Does this martyrdom occur nearby?"

Simeon clarified, "No, this round of martyrdom in the Great Tribulation is worldwide, but there is a prior group of last days martyred saints. These persecuted saints appear to be distinct from those I just mentioned, and their executions appear to be associated with a global religion headquartered in Rome. Revelation 17:6 says, '*I saw the woman, drunk with the blood of the saints and with the blood of the martyrs of Jesus.*' Many believe that this woman represents the harlot world religion and, in my estimation, you can see her headquarters at the Vatican from your veranda."

This jaw-dropping statement caused Tovia to ask, "Are you suggesting that my family has to survive the coming pogroms[8] of some harlot religion in addition to the extermination attempts of the Antichrist?"

"I expect that you and your family need to be primarily concerned with the genocidal campaign of the Antichrist. The leadership of Israel will soon participate in a seven-year covenant with the Antichrist that affords Jews residing in Israel temporary safety, a form of pseudo peace. But at the midpoint of the seven years, the Antichrist will go into the Jewish Temple and exalt himself above all gods, then promptly commence his campaign of extermination!"

Nathan pushed his glasses, which had dropped down on his nose, back in place, then referred to his notes: "Simeon, you said that the Harlot is drunk with the blood of the saints and the martyrs of Jesus, but you just suggested that you think Tovia and his family will escape this first blood bath. Why do you believe this?"

"This gets tricky," Simeon admitted. "But Gershom and I believe Revelation 17:6 identifies four primary things: the blood, the woman drunk with the blood, the martyred saints, and the martyrs of Jesus."

Nathan's glasses began to slip back down his nose as he attempted to take more copious notes. "I see," he said. "Don't stop, please interpret the meaning of these four things."

"The woman is clearly the Harlot and I believe she represents the false global religion which will be headquartered in Rome. The latest Catholic dogma, which was executed through papal infallibility, elevated Mary as Co-Redemptrix. The global threat to peace posed by the Russian coalition provoked Pope Romano to exercise papal authority in this matter. The world clamors for peace and the Pope believes that the Blessed Mary will bring in this peace."

"How so?" asked Nathan.

Simeon explained, "With the help of supernatural signs and lying wonders this woman will attempt to unite all religions under the canopy of the Roman Catholic Church. She will also usher in the worship and adoration of Jesus in the Catholic communion wafer."

Nathan was astonished, breaking his pencil lead as he struck his notepad. Turning to Tovia, he gasped, "Do you realize what this implies?"

"I have no idea," Tovia answered.

Pointing to the Vatican, Nathan said, "I watched the Marian apparition that occurred right over yonder from a live feed on TV. I was in an American restaurant, and everyone there was absolutely stupefied. I believe this supernatural event was a game-changer, because it has convinced multitudes in the world that the Roman Catholic Church is really the only true church established by Jesus Christ for all the people. While we watched, millions of Christians disappeared in the rapture without warning. These paranormal episodes have left the whole world in a quandary, susceptible to religious deception.

Simeon agreed, "That's what I sincerely believe is happening. Consider the following; Islam is crumbling and will be essentially decapitated after the Lord defeats the Russian coalition. Christianity, apart from people like us, is apostate because the true believers have been raptured. Once the Jews witness their Jehovah defeat the Russian coalition they will reinstate Judaism and construct the third temple. Most Eastern and New Age religions like Hinduism already embrace female goddesses, so the Catholic Queen of Heaven already fits right into their religious framework. I could go on but you get my drift."

Tovia interjected, "Not really. I can understand how Jews will embrace Judaism nationally after Ezekiel 38 concludes, but why will the others jump on the Marian bandwagon?"

Looking at Simeon, Nathan said, "Allow me?"

Simeon nodded.

Nathan went on: "Tovia, mankind has never been more primed in all of its history to be influenced by the supernatural. Everything that is happening defies scientific logic. Add everything up: first there was the unexplained disappearance of millions. Second a miraculous sighting of Mary was witnessed worldwide at the same time. Third was the improbable victory of tiny Israel over the Arabs. And last but not least, soon the Russian coalition will be destroyed by an earthquake, and fire and brimstone cast down from heaven. When you factor all the above you have a formula for enchantment, for an unearthly figure to mysteriously appear out of nowhere and say, "Look to me. I will usher in true peace, prosperity and a benevolent global transformation. Consecrate your lives to your queen who can comfort and prosper you." And why will they follow her? Because she will perform great signs and wonders and have all the right answers."

With that explanation, Simeon nodded approvingly, and Tovia folded his hands and bowed his head in astonishment.

Pushing his glasses back in place, Nathan reviewed his notes and said, "Simeon, how do you interpret the other three things in the Revelation passage?"

Simeon pondered this and cleared his throat. "Appreciating the aspect of the *blood* is important in that, it was the sacrificial blood of Christ shed upon the cross that saves sinners. But in Revelation 17:6 we see that the woman is drunk with the blood of two groups of saved souls. This is an utter perversion of the true intent of the blood. When Christians take communion they commonly consume a bread wafer and drink a red liquid resembling the blood of Christ, like wine or grape juice. Luke 22:17-20 teaches that the elements of the Passover, the bread and the wine, represented the body and blood of Christ in the crucifixion. When Christians partake of the wafer and the liquid they are to do so in remembrance of Christ's sacrifice for sin. However, in the Catholic Mass the communion wafer and red liquid supposedly become miraculously transformed into the literal body, blood, soul and divinity of Christ. This is commonly referred to as the Eucharist. I believe this Eucharistic Christ becomes the centerpiece of the global religion."

Nathan spoke up, "Please, indulge me. Let me see if I comprehend the gist of what you are suggesting. My notes say that you believe that the Eucharistic Christ of Roman Catholicism could become the theological centerpiece of the harlot world religion. Therefore, the Catholic teachings will dictate that the sacrificial blood of Jesus needs a continuous ceremonial outpouring through the sacrament of the Eucharist of Christ's blood. This implies that the blood of Christ shed upon the cross two-thousand years ago was insufficient. Because if it was sufficient it would not be necessary for it to be poured out time and time again for the sake of one's salvation. Therefore, the salvation of one's soul is only as secure as his or her last partaking of the Eucharist. Does that sound right?"

Simeon nodded in agreement.

Nathan continued, "This implies that the balance of power over the individual soul shifts to whoever controls the authority over the Eucharist. In essence, the Harlot can say, if you want redemption from Hell you must become a member of my Son's True Church and partake of the Holy Eucharist."

Simeon confirmed, "I think you westerners say, 'By Jove,' I think he's got it, or something of the sort. Nathan, one of the problems with elevating the status of Mary to Co-Redemptrix is that she becomes Christ's co-equal in the eyes of the faithful. As such, this empowers her to sway the faithful in the direction she wishes. In other words, whatever the Co-Redemptrix says goes, even if it contradicts the Bible. Concerning the other two things, which were the *blood of the saints*, and *the martyrs of Jesus*, I believe this is another reason to suspect that the present Catholicism of these last days represents the harlot world religion."

"How so?" Asked Nathan.

Simeon added, "The Catholic Church killed many Christians during the inquisitions dating back as far as the 12th century. Some Protestant estimates range from 50 million to 150 million. The estimates are so vague because the numbers are hard to trace and Roman Catholics typically give much smaller numbers. Many of those identified and killed as heretics were true believers. Thus, from a biblical perspective these were true *saints* and their *blood* was shed by the Catholics. Shockingly, in far too many cases they were martyred because of their refusal to embrace the sacrament of the Eucharist. This explanation would account for why the woman of Revelation 17:6, i.e. historical papal Rome, is guilty of being drunk with the *blood of the saints.* However, the *martyrs of Jesus* that follows in that same verse probably represents a different generation of Christians. I suspect these *martyrs* embody the true believers of today! They are those that accept Christ as their Savior after the rapture. The historical precedent for their martyrdom probably finds connection with the past Catholic inquisition period of persecution. If they rebel from the present teachings of the Catholic Church, especially at this critically chaotic point in time, they run the risk of likewise being killed. Thus, with all that said, the prophecy to be on the lookout for next, besides Ezekiel 38, is regarding the coming false religion, which is headquartered in Rome. And this is why, my beloved friend Nathan, your residence in Rome may prove to be an important investment."

Clearly overwhelmed by Simeon's comments, Tovia stood up, stretched and said, "I need a smoke after all that."

Grinning, Nathan commented, "I didn't know you smoked cigarettes."

Tovia soberly replied, "I don't smoke nor drink, but after learning that you and I are apparently identified in Bible prophecy as the *martyrs of Jesus*, I need something to settle my nerves."

After about five minutes of deep contemplation ensued, Nathan broke the silence with a personal experience. "Razz, which is the nickname given to my friend Robert Rasmussen, was speaking about this harlot religion as 'Mystery Babylon' just before he was raptured. Razz and I were watching the Mary apparition – or as he would say the 'Queen of Heaven' apparition - taking place above the Vatican at the time of his departure. Razz was connecting Rome with Mystery Babylon and this harlot system at the time. His disappearance, the apparition, and the Vatican left such an indelible impression on me that day. I guess this is the other reason, in addition to wanting to be like Oskar Schindler in the end times, that I felt drawn to Rome as an important location in the end times."

Simeon explained, "Your friend Razz was correct. There appear to be prophecies concerning this divine demonic feminine that allures a majority of mankind into the global religion. Revelation 17 identifies her as a harlot, but additional possible prophetic references may allude to her as the "Queen of Heaven." But it is Revelation 17:9 and 18 that tips us off that the city of Rome appears to be the central location of her earthly headquarters."

Nathan reflected. "Right," he said. "That adds credence to why the apparition happened at the Vatican on the day of the rapture."

Simeon nodded in agreement.

Dumbfounded Tovia commented, "I'm confused. Does this mean I have a lot of time after the Ezekiel war to prepare for the great tribulation and also witness to my Jewish parents and siblings in Israel, providing they survive the coming invasion?"

Simeon shook his head. "No, there will probably not be a *lot* of time to accomplish this."

"Then, how much time is there until the Antichrist shows up?" Tovia asked.

"The Antichrist is already here," Simeon announced, to the shock of his listeners. "He hasn't been entirely revealed yet, and he won't dominate until the mid-point of the seven-year tribulation period. But, as prophesied, he comes out of the revived Roman Empire, which corresponds with the European Union. Present indications suggest that it could be Hans Vandenberg, the current EU President, because Revelation 6 informs that he arrives on the world scene promptly after the rapture of the Church, as the first horseman of the apocalypse. Developing ties between the new EU President and Pope Romano also indicate that Vandenberg may be the Antichrist because Revelation 17:3 informs that the Harlot uses the Antichrist's political platform as her religious pedestal.

"According to the apostle Paul, in Second Thessalonians, he went on, "the Antichrist rises to power according to the workings of Satan, with all power, signs, and lying wonders. We have not yet witnessed his great signs, but we will in the coming years. According to Daniel 9 and Isaiah 28, he will be recognized when he confirms a covenant between Israel and Death, which Isaiah says is an agreement with Sheol. This means it is a deceptive covenant that originates from the depths of Hell! When we see EU President Vandenberg confirm this covenant with Israel, then we will know beyond a shadow of doubt that he is the Antichrist. We must watch for the confirmation of the false covenant because it could precede the signs and lying wonders as the first clue to the identity of the Antichrist."

Giving Nathan a deer-in-the-headlights look, Tovia scratched his head in bewilderment.

"Nathan, did you know all this?" he gasped.

"No," Nathan admitted. "Now *I* need a smoke! I'm verging on information overload. Which reminds me: I need to record these critical discussions from now on. I'm kicking myself for not recording all along."

Simeon agreed. "Do you have a recorder handy?" he asked.

"Absolutely," Nathan confirmed, rising from his chair. "I have a pocket size digital recorder. I'll go get it."

Returning moments later with his recorder, Nathan set it, along with a mysteriously sealed box, on the table between them.

Bewildered by the heading on Nathan's glass faced box, which read, *"The Post Rapture Survival Kit,"* Simeon inquired, "Where did you get this?"

"It looked important so I grabbed it off the fireplace mantle of my best friend Razz's house," Nathan replied. "I totally forgot that I had it shipped here along with a few other personal items that he left behind. The movers had placed it next to my recorder, so I grabbed it for you guys to see."

"We need to break open the opaque glass now so that we can see what's inside it," exclaimed Tovia!

"Absolutely!" Simeon agreed.

Gesturing his hand to pause, "Wait, let's record the remainder of this conversation while it's still fresh on our minds; then we'll gather everyone together afterward to join us to break open the glass," requested Nathan.

"*Hmm...*Alright," Tovia reluctantly agreed.

Turning on his recorder Nathan assessed, "If I understand you, Simeon, you are suggesting that a global religion based out of the Vatican emerges, followed by the Antichrist's rise to power."

"That's partially correct," Simeon said, "but there will be some overlap period. The simple way to organize end time is as follows: two distinctly different global religions are forthcoming. The first is headed by a queen who will head the Catholic Church; she will have an outward Christian veneer and encourage the worship of the Eucharistic Christ. Although she masquerades as Mary, in reality she is nothing more than a demonic imposter. The second, and last, is the compulsory worship of the Antichrist. The last false religion standing is that of the Antichrist. He will claim to be God and usher in a New Age type of religion – promising his adherents that they too can evolve to some form of a godhood consciousness. Both religious systems are rooted in satanic deception, which means that mankind experiences a double religious jeopardy after the rapture."

NOVEL

Assuming the role of an interviewer, Nathan formatted the discussion so that the information could someday be transmitted through radio, social networks and other media venues.

"What causes the schism between the Vatican-based religion and the geo-political goals of the Antichrist?" he asked.

Amused by Nathan's talk-show approach, Simeon smiled and replied, "The ultimate aim of the Antichrist is to achieve exclusive worldwide worship. This is why the two systems cannot coexist indefinitely. The Antichrist does not want to share the allegiance of humankind with any other religious system or entity. As his religious platform gains credibility, the popularity of the Harlot will become extremely problematic. This is because the harlot religious system will advocate that Jesus Christ mystically indwells the Eucharist. Although this is an unbiblical spiritual deception, it does indirectly identify Christ in a Messianic role. Any allusions to Jesus Christ as the Messiah will be strictly forbidden by the Antichrist. In fact, during the reign of both religious systems, many who come to a genuine faith in Jesus Christ, through our witness or otherwise, will be martyred."

Nathan requested, "Please, tell us more about the fate of the harlot religion."

Simeon elaborated, "After the harlot religious system has overstayed its usefulness, the Antichrist will have it removed from power by ten kings. After which, the worship of the Antichrist will be imposed upon the preponderance of humanity. Revelation 13 teaches that no one will even be able to buy or sell unless they receive a mark that identifies their allegiance to the Antichrist."

Nathan inquired, "Is this the prophecy concerning the Mark of the Beast, and the infamous number 666?"

"Yes," Simeon answered.

Nathan apologized, "I am sorry to be so slow Simeon, but I need more clarification. Please continue speaking about the fate of the harlot system."

"The desolation of the Harlot is prophesied in Revelation 17:16," Simeon explained. "These ten kings will receive their authority from the Antichrist according to Revelation 17:12. Although these ten political leaders are probably alive presently, they are not yet positioned in their places. However, when they come into their respective powers, the prophecy predicts that they will grow to hate the Harlot. From the perspective of these kings, the Harlot's abundant wealth and worldwide religious and political power threatens their autocratic authority. This is probably why they eagerly comply with the Antichrist's wishes to eradicate her system."

As Nathan continued to interview Simeon, Tovia got a burst of energy and began note- taking as quickly as he could scribble.

"What then?" asked Nathan.

Simeon informed, "After the Queen of Heaven is dethroned from power, the Antichrist abruptly promotes his religious agenda to the apparent dismay of three of the ten kings. The Antichrist subdues these three adversaries leaving eight kings.

Nathan corrected, "You mean leaving seven kings remaining, don't you?"

Simeon clarified, "No, eight is the correct number, because the Antichrist becomes the eighth king. He will preside in addition to the seven left from the original ten, but he will become their superior. After the remaining seven experience the manner in which the Antichrist eliminates the other three kings, they will probably fear a similar fate as their comrades, if they do not comply with the Antichrist's final system. Remember that the Antichrist rises to power through supernatural means, which suggests the seven subservient kings are either enamored or intimidated by him."

Tovia motioned to Nathan to hit pause on the recorder, and Nathan obliged.

"All of this could take many years Simeon," Tovia reasoned. "Why do you believe time is so short?"

Turning on the digital device, again, Nathan motioned to Tovia to restate his question.

Tovia cleared his throat, and rephrased the matter: "Simeon, in light of what you describe, it seems like the establishment of these two religious systems could require decades or longer to organize. Why do you think these prophecies are fulfilled in a short time span?"

Simeon explained: "I know it seems that what I am suggesting should take decades to fulfill, but in Matthew 24:8, Jesus stated that end times events happen in rapid succession. He likened it to the birth pains of a woman. When a woman is about to give birth, her contractions become more frequent and intense. From this analogy, we presume this will be the case with end time events. Once they begin, they happen one upon another with increased frequency and intensity."

"I was wondering about those birth pains. I was under the impression that was mainly dealing with the rise of earthquakes in various places in the verse prior," Nathan commented. Opening his Bible to Matthew 24:7, he read "And there will be famines, pestilences, and earthquakes in various places."

Simeon replied, "Nathan, you could be right, but I think it's best to look at the birth pains analogy in the overall context of the second coming of Christ. In other words, as the time of His return decreases, the frequency of calamities and world judgments increases. I base this on the questions the disciples asked in Matthew 24:3. They asked Him, "Tell us, when will these things be? And what *will be* the sign of Your coming, and of the end of the age?"

Nathan inquired, "What about the order and timing of the other prophecies, like the building of the Jewish Temple, the two witnesses in Jerusalem, and Armageddon?"

Simeon expounded, "Very astute, Nathan. There will be many prophecies happening while these world religions are operational. Some will find fulfillment during the harlot religious period, while the others don't occur until the worship of the Antichrist takes place."

Simeon had barely finished his final sentence when Amber, who had been glued to the television for hours, frantically cried out, "Come quickly, Tovia! I think a massive earthquake has struck the Middle East!"

Quickly turning off his recorder, Nathan motioned the trio to hurry up and join the group inside who were watching the breaking news. Razz's mysterious box was again left behind.

The seismic rumblings lasted nearly five minutes and it was apparent that a massive amount of devastation had occurred in the Holy Land.

Gershom, who was watching the television with Amber, wiped his brow with a handkerchief. "That must have been the earthquake Ezekiel predicted against the Russian forces," he reasoned.

In a matter of a few minutes the entire household was watching the devastating images come across the television set. It was far too early to estimate the overall extent of the damage, but according to early indications, the death toll was expected to be in the tens of thousands. Initial reports said the epicenter was north of Israel in Lebanon. The magnitude was registered above 12-plus, exceeding the Richter scale maximum measurement capability.

One seismologist suggested it would be a miracle if any structures remained standing in the most affected areas. Oddly enough though, the quake did not produce a Tsunami in the Mediterranean Sea. One thing was certain: the earthquake was responsible for killing many

Russian coalition troops. This became abundantly evident from helicopter images that displayed hordes of dead soldiers strewn all over the surrounding mountains and ravines. If the earthquake didn't abruptly end the Russian invasion of Israel, it most certainly postponed it until the death and carnage could be addressed.

Gershom announced, "The worst is not over for the coalition invaders. The other calamities we discussed on the flight over here will now occur. It won't be until the world witnesses every sort of bird in the air and beast from the field eating the flesh and drinking the blood of the invaders that the battle-zone will be safe to survey."

Tovia rubbed his arms nervously. "When will it be safe for us to return to Israel?" he asked.

Gershom explained, "Ezekiel 39 informs that manpower will be in great demand in Israel in order to help cleanse the land of the dead and mop-up the mess. I don't suspect it will be much longer until it is safe to return, perhaps a few weeks."

Chapter 9
The Collapse
of the Russian
Coalition

"What you are witnessing on your TV screens is an unexplainable phenomenon; satellite zoom shots show multitudes of vultures hovering in the sky above the warzone, in tandem with a convergence of assorted carnivorous animals on the ground," reported meteorologist Jonathan Levinson of *Israel Network News* (INN).

"Simeon," Lisa asked, "could this be the fulfillment of Ezekiel's bird and beast predictions which you were explaining?"

Tuning up the television volume on the remote, Simeon nodded and put his index finger gently to his lips, requesting silence. "Let's hear the entire report to be certain," he said.

"Our correspondents in the field can only feed us limited information about what is transpiring on the ground," Levinson continued. "Contamination from the coalition's weapons of mass destruction, combined with treacherous weather conditions, is restricting their access into the warzone. We are relying heavily on IDF reports and satellite feeds to find out what is happening on the battlefield. We have Dr. Ori Weizman, a spokesperson from the Israel Zoological Society, in the studio with us. Dr. Weizman, welcome to INN."

"It's my pleasure to be with you, Jonathan," the dignified guest replied.

Levinson was quizzical. "The IDF reports that flocks of birds and hordes of animals are converging upon the fallen coalition troops. Supposedly there is such a multitude of creatures that clear satellite surveillance of the battleground is nearly impossible. Can you explain what is causing this strange phenomenon?"

Weizman shrugged. "I wish I could," he answered, "but there is no precedent for this bizarre behavior to be found anywhere. In the past we have witnessed unexplainable deaths of large flocks of birds, as they fell randomly from the skies, and there have been occurrences of multitudes of fish floating dead upon the ocean's surface; but this episode, we have no history to compare."

Levinson shook his head. "Can you give us an educated guess as to what could be causing this peculiar spectacle?"

"Our best educated guess at the IMS is that the unnatural events occurring in the natural order of creation is provoking these creatures to behave abnormally."

"Could you elaborate on what you mean by that statement?" Levinson asked.

Dr. Weizman rubbed his chin. "The enormous earthquake and its powerful aftershocks have toppled mountaintops and created deep crevasses on the earth's surface. Simultaneous flooding rains, huge hailstones and lightning bursts have convulsed the localized order of things. This alone could impact the behavior of birds and beasts."

Levinson turned to the audience and, in uncharacteristic editorializing, offered, "These unexplainable weather patterns cause one to wonder if the Russian coalition is warring against Israel, or the God of Israel. Whichever is the case; all indicators suggest that Israel is miraculously winning the war." Then, looking at his guest again, he said, "Please continue with your hypothesis about the birds and animals."

Weizman cleared his throat. "Concurrent cataclysmic conditions are sweeping hordes of dead coalition soldiers off mountain slopes and into torrential wadis, creating stockpiles of carrion for the beasts of the earth and the fowls of the air. Chaos and opportunity have spurred into a feeding frenzy, as they have converged upon the fallen human prey. After saying this, he took a handkerchief from his pocket and mopped his brow. "Quite simply, we have never seen anything like this!" he croaked.

"It sounds like a reply of Alfred Hitchcock's horror film, called *The Birds*." It appears as though Hashem has served up some old fashioned fire and brimstone for Israel's enemies."

Scarcely grinning at Levinson's remark, Weizman added, "What we are finding highly unusual is that the vultures and animals are preying upon those upturned from the wadis rather than those remaining on the hilltops and mountainsides."

"Why do you suppose that is?" Levinson questioned.

Dr. Weizman speculated, "It is too soon to tell, because contamination, rain, and hailstorms have prevented IDF teams from deploying deep into the battlefield to make a full assessment. Early reports are that those remaining on the hillsides are contaminated from the coalition's WMD's, which in many cases, backfired against their own forces. If this is the case, somehow the creatures have detected this and avoided preying upon them. It makes no sense at all, but this is the only explanation that we have been able to put forth."

Jonathan Levinson's jaw dropped in astonishment. Then, as though a light had gone on in his head, he deduced, "This would imply that the rushing waters of the wadis are cleansing the contamination from the deceased, making them safe for the birds and animals to eat."

Nodding, Dr. Weizman replied, "What other answer could there be?"

Levinson concluded the interview by reporting that the Israelis had seemingly escaped the natural disasters that had struck the Russian hordes. He drew a comparison to the biblical accounts of the Hebrews miraculously escaping the plagues of Egypt.

Fittingly, he quoted Exodus 9:26 to end his report: *"Only in the land of Goshen, where the children of Israel were, there was no hail."*

"Holy smoke!" Nathan expressed after hearing the news report. "Or should I say holy waters! Did Ezekiel predict rushing waters would decontaminate the Russian invaders?"

Gershom piped up, "Yes and no. Yes, there would be dead soldiers for the birds and animals to devour, but no, he didn't specify how the deceased would become edible.

Handing her father's Bible to Gershom, Jami asked, "Could you read to me what Ezekiel said?"

Opening to Ezekiel 39, Gershom read verse 4:

> *"You shall fall upon the mountains of Israel, you and all your troops and the peoples who are with you; I will give you to birds of prey of every sort and to the beasts of the field to be devoured."*

Then he followed with a supporting scripture in verse 19,

> "And as for you, son of man, thus says the Lord GOD, 'Speak to every sort of bird and to every beast of the field: "Assemble yourselves and come; Gather together from all sides to My sacrificial meal Which I am sacrificing for you, A great sacrificial meal on the mountains of Israel, That you may eat flesh and drink blood."

Amber inquired, "How can there be human sacrifices for animals? Isn't it supposed to be the other way around?"

Gershom marveled at her insight, and responded, "Very astute, Amber. The Mosaic Law did prescribe animal sacrifices for the sins of the people. However, Jesus the Messiah provided the final sacrifice for all sins at the time He was crucified upon the cross. What Ezekiel appears to be proclaiming is a sort of biblical irony: Gog of Magog invaders sought to sacrifice the blood of the Jews, but the Lord intervened on Israel's behalf and turned the invaders' blood into a sacrifice throughout the land."

Simeon Abrams interjected, "Let me elevate everyone's understanding of the magnitude of what is taking place right now with the convergence of all these birds and beasts. As a tour guide in Israel I have been announcing over the past several years how birds and animals have been migrating and populating in Israel unexplainably. For instance, vultures non-indigenous to Israel, like the Griffon vultures that normally breed in mountain crags in southern Europe, north Africa, and Asia, have been colonizing in northern Israel, the Golan Heights, and areas of the Negev desert."[9] Also, Israel is home to several species of carnivorous animals like badgers, cheetahs, jackals, hyenas, leopards, wolves, foxes and more." [10]

Lisa asked the two witnesses, "Does this mean we can all return to Israel soon?"

Gershom consoled, "Yes, it won't be long, but it could be a few more weeks until the IDF quarantines the unsafe areas and restores order throughout the land."

Looking at Nathan, Lisa responded, "Since I work for the Ministry of the Interior, I must get back immediately to assist with the national restoration process. With your permission, Jami and the others can stay behind until the government informs me that it is safe for their return."

Nathan confirmed, "Permission granted; that is what this home in Rome is for. However, not all of us will be returning to Israel with the group."

Puzzled, Lisa asked for clarification.

Gershom interjected, "Simeon and I have asked Nathan to take us to America with him when he goes soon to visit his Unistate Global Investments Corporation (UGIC) headquarters."

Nathan confirmed, "I have been in contact with my staff in the states and they need me to come back to our main office headquarters for some important meetings."

Jami, who had attached herself to Nathan as a father figure, hugged him and worried, "You're not leaving us alone here in Rome are you? I'm only a teen-ager. What if my mother says we can't come back to Israel for several months?"

Nathan, who had never had a daughter of his own, became choked up by her affections and comforted, "No, never Honey! Your mother and I would never let anything happen to you."

Tovia, came close and put his hand firmly upon Jami's shoulder. He motioned to Lisa, Amber, Bella, and Jaxon to huddle together for a group hug, "Jami, as your uncle and the father of your two favorite cousins, I say we are all in this together. None of us will be left alone throughout all of this. From now on we all stick together!"

After Jami's nerves were quieted, Amber asked Gershom, "Why are Simeon and you not returning to Israel with the rest of us? Don't you think your understanding of Bible prophecy is needed in Israel?"

Gershom explained, "We have been summoned by some of the other 144,000 residing in America to come disciple them. They realize who they are, but feel their teaching needs some fine tuning. They informed us that throngs of Americans are responding to their messages of hope in Christ, but they can't keep up with all the questions they are encountering. When Nathan told us he was departing to his corporate office we asked to join him."

"When will you all be leaving?" Lisa asked.

Nathan alerted, "We leave at 3:00 P.M. tomorrow. We will be traveling Air France so as not to tie up my jet, in case you and the others need transportation to and from Israel."

With that announcement, Nathan's chef beckoned everyone into the dining room for a gourmet Italian dinner. Not certain as to how long he would be detained in America, Nathan made certain that his last night with his friends from Israel was festive. No expense was spared on the meal and the assortment of desserts his chef prepared.

When the night was through, everyone had unwound from the stress of the day and was ready for a good night's sleep. Nathan, however, decided to stay up a little longer and search the Internet to see how the news media was reporting on the supernatural defeat of Russia and the large coalition of Muslim nations. He also spent some time visiting some Christian news and blogsites to get their take on this incredible event. To his utter amazement, he was shocked to see that several top Catholic websites were attributing this incredible victory over Russia and its coalition to the intercession of the "Lady of Fatima" and not exclusively to the Lord, Himself, as described in Ezekiel 38 and 39!

One article went on to explain that the consecration of Russia to the Immaculate Heart of Mary by Pope Romano, and the prayers of millions of Catholics worldwide, proves to have led to the miraculous intervention of "Our Lady" in this invasion of Israel.

After reaching the point where he couldn't make any sense of what he was reading on the Catholic websites, he prayed to calm his nerves and quiet his spirit. Then he retired from the overwhelming day.

Chapter 10
Letter to the Saints Left Behind

It was about 8:00 a.m. the next morning when Tovia awoke from his slumber. With cup of coffee in hand, he made his way to the veranda where he saw his sister and niece weeping in Nathan's arms. As he approached them, he felt the crunching of glass beneath his shoes. Looking down, he realized that it was fragments of the opaque glass from the mysterious sealed box. In all of the media mayhem from his motherland the day prior, he had completely forgotten about this curious container.

"Good morning Tovia," greeted Nathan.

Cautiously sidestepping more broken glass Tovia replied, "Good morning. Is it ok if I ask, what's happening here? Why all the early morning emotions?"

"Tovia, when the girls heard that this box that I showed Simeon and you yesterday came from Razz's house, they couldn't wait to break it open to view what was inside," Nathan explained.

Brushing back tears, Lisa handed her brother a folded letter and said, "Here read this. It came out of this *Post Rapture Survival Kit*. We couldn't see what was inside because of the opaque glass on the front so we followed the instructions on the box, which said to, "BREAK THIS GLASS WINDOW IF YOU HAVE BEEN LEFT BEHIND!"

Nathan explained, "Among other things, the contents of this box included a Bible with a couple of letters that were signed by Razz and strategically inserted inside it."

Holding up the first letter, Nathan continued, "This letter concerns the Rapture."

Lifting up another letter in his other hand he said, "This one was in Romans 10 and explains how a person gets saved through receiving

Christ. The letter Lisa gave you was in the book of Revelation, and when the girls read it, they were deeply moved."

Pulling up a chair, Tovia silently read the letter addressed to the Saints of the 5th Seal.

A Personal Message of Hope to the Saints of the 5th Seal

To the Saints of the 5th Seal; greetings in the name of our Lord and Savior, Jesus Christ. He is Risen!

This letter is intended to inform you about your fate and to comfort you therein. As I author this letter of hope to you, you are yet unaware of your future. The good news is that your souls are saved and your brave testimonies adorn the precious passages in the New Testament of the Bible. Read below what the book of Revelation says about you.

> When He (*Jesus Christ*) opened the fifth seal, I saw under the altar the souls of those who had been slain for the word of God and for the testimony which they held. And they cried with a loud voice, saying, "How long, O Lord, holy and true, until You judge and avenge our blood on those who dwell on the earth?" Then a white robe was given to each of them; and it was said to them that they should rest a little while longer, until both *the number of* their fellow servants and their brethren, who would be killed as they *were,* was completed. (Revelation 6:9-11)

Many of you could be among those that will be slain for the word of God and your testimonies as believers in Christ. By the time you understand your placement on the prophetic timeline and the important role you fulfill for the Lord, many Christians will have instantly vanished in a supernatural event called the Rapture. This major promise and miracle of Christ was predicted in John 14:1-5. The details were further explained by the apostle Paul in 1 Corinthians 15:51-55 and 1 Thessalonians 4:15-18. You became a believer after this supernatural spectacle happened.

You now exist in a post Rapture world that is experiencing extremely turbulent times. Soon a charismatic world leader known as the Antichrist will confirm a seven-year covenant between Israel and the governing body that is perpetrating a global agenda, which is contrary to what you realize is the truth. You know that Jesus Christ is the "way, the truth and the life!"

NOVEL

Christ is your Savior and this is your testimony from the word of God. However, your message is unpopular among the masses and you will be caused to count the cost of following Christ. You will rise to the occasion and your courage will inspire many others to follow in your footsteps. These are your *"fellow servants and their brethren"* spoken of above.

Your testimonies, alongside the teachings of 144,000 Jewish evangelists, who are identified in Revelation 7:1-8, will inspire "a great multitude which no one could number, of all nations, tribes, peoples, and tongues." (Revelation 7:9). They will follow your great examples and when you, and your *"fellow servants and their brethren"* arrive together in heaven you all will shout "Salvation belongs to our God who sits on the throne, and to the Lamb!" (Revelation 7:10). At that time the angels along with you and all the rest of us in heaven will worship God saying:

> "Amen! Blessing and glory and wisdom, Thanksgiving and
> honor and power and might, Be to our God forever and
> ever. Amen." (Revelation 7:12)

You ask *"How long, O Lord, holy and true, until You judge and avenge our blood on those who dwell on the earth?"* The response you receive is to *"rest a little while longer."*

After the Rapture there are three periods of Christian martyrdom that follows. You are in the first phase, which occurs after the Rapture, but before the confirmation of the false covenant of Daniel 9:27. You reside in the gap period between these two powerful events. Some of you will survive this gap period, but regardless of whether or not you do, all of your souls are saved. The *"white robe"* alluded to above is the assurance of your eternal salvation.

The Post Rapture – Pre Tribulation gap is an unspecified period of time and this is the reason why you don't know the length of time until your blood will be avenged upon those that dwell upon the earth. Your *"fellow servants and their brethren"* will not ask this question because they will know their placement on the prophetic timeline. They will know this because they will be martyred after the confirmation of the seven-year false covenant. They will be able to calendar the days until the second coming of Christ.

Your *"fellow servants"* are the ones persecuted and martyred in the first three and one-half years of the seven-years of Tribulation. They will be martyred by the same source that presently persecutes you. This is described in Revelation 17:6.

NOVEL

"I saw the woman, drunk with the blood of the saints and
with the blood of the martyrs of Jesus. And when I saw
her, I marveled with great amazement."

You know why the apostle John *"marveled with great amazement."*
You are these *"martyrs of Jesus!"* It is your blood that is stained upon her
hands. You are preaching the true gospel of Christ, the literal interpretation
of the Bible and the valid explanation of the Christian disappearances.
The Harlot is prostituting the word of God for world control and global
gain. She is preaching a counterfeit gospel, a different Jesus.

John says in Revelation 17:4-5 that her sacrament is a *"golden cup
full of abominations and the filthiness of her fornication. And on her
forehead a name was written: MYSTERY, BABYLON THE GREAT, THE
MOTHER OF HARLOTS AND OF THE ABOMINATIONS OF THE EARTH.*
You have received the true Lord, but Satan is using the Virgin Mary as
a demonic imposter, and now your teachings are in direct opposition to
hers.

Because she embodies the overpowering religious system that is
backed by the one world order, you are identified as a dissidents and
marked for martyrdom. She represents part one of the *"overflowing
scourge"* that Isaiah 28:15 identifies. The Antichrist will confirm a
covenant between Israel and her for seven years. Some of you won't be
alive when this happens, but your *"fellow servants and their brethren"*
will witness this marquee event.

The global government will view this religious system as the
temporary opiate of the unruly masses, but they will ultimately dethrone
this violent harlot in Revelation 17:16 when the Antichrist is ready to rise
to ultimate power. This lawless charismatic character will instruct ten
powerful world leaders to desolate this false religious system. This will
occur at the midpoint of the seven years of tribulation.

Then the *brethren of your fellow servants* will face off with the final
three and one-half years of the Tribulation Period. This will be a time
of Great Tribulation and the Antichrist and his False Prophet will be
deceiving mankind to believe in *"the Lie"* described in 2 Thessalonians
2. They will force people to worship the Antichrist, and in order to buy or
sell they must receive a mark on their right hand or on their foreheads.
This is all predicted in Revelation 13. The *brethren of your fellow servants*
will not participate in their system, and they will refuse to take the "Mark
of the Beast." This will cause them great persecution and many will be
martyred like you, the FIFTH SEAL SAINTS.

Be patient in your plight for the Lord, dear saints.

"If anyone has an ear, let him hear. He who leads into captivity shall go into captivity; he who kills with the sword must be killed with the sword. Here is the patience and the faith of the saints." (Revelation 13:9-10)

"Here is the patience of the saints; here are those who keep the commandments of God and the faith of Jesus. Then I heard a voice from heaven saying to me, "Write: 'Blessed are the dead who die in the Lord from now on.'" "Yes," says the Spirit, "that they may rest from their labors, and their works follow them."" (Revelation 14:12-13)

After reading the letter Tovia said, "Wow, I'm going to need Simeon to explain this letter to me."

"Come on Uncle, even I understand it. We all missed the Rapture and now we are going to be martyred for becoming believers," Jami sobbed.

"Wait honey," replied Tovia. "I'm not so sure this letter applies to all of us because we are Jewish believers. Simeon informed me yesterday, right here where we are all seated, that we may be part of a remnant that survives until the return of Jesus Christ."

"Really Uncle, is it true? Are we going to stay alive until Jesus comes back to Israel?" Jami asked.

Biting his tongue, Tovia said, "Well umm... Well, yes that's what Simeon said. Isn't that right Nathan?"

Realizing that Tovia was telling only the partial truth of the matter to comfort Jami, Nathan nodded his head in agreement.

Thinking for a moment, it dawned on Jami that Nathan was not Jewish. Tears began to roll down upon her face again. "Oh no! Nathan," she began.

Before she could finish, Nathan gently put his fingers upon her lips and said, "Jami, don't worry about me. Simeon had some comforting words for us Gentiles also. He said that some of us survive until the return of Christ. The Bible calls us the "Sheep Gentiles." When Jesus returns, He gathers the Jewish remnant and the Sheep Gentiles to be together forever. So, see honey this is encouraging news for all of us."

Chapter 11
The Queen of Heaven Appears Globally

By the time a break in the Mideast storm arrived, it had become abundantly clear to all that the unprecedented poor weather had won the war for Israel. Like many of Israel's ancient victories, it was obvious that their God was behind the scenes making certain that His chosen people survived another Goliath battle.

While the IDF mopped up the battlefield, the world wondered what had happened to the Blessed Mother. Where was the Queen of Heaven when the world needed her most? Pope Romano had made a number of predictive comments in the media that he felt strongly that the Virgin Mary would soon bring a period of peace to the world. He reminded the press on more than one occasion, that in her apparition messages the Blessed Mother had made promises to that effect. What better time than now to prove that she would keep her commitments?

With the clearing of the weather a few days after the Russian coalition was defeated, Lisa was instructed to return to her post with the Ministry of the Interior. She gave a round of hugs to Jami, Tovia, Amber, Bella, and Jaxon, and boarded Nathan's jet for home. As the jet was returning to Israel, Nathan, Gershom, and Simeon were busily conducting their affairs in America.

Meanwhile, Pope Romano prayerfully pleaded, "Blessed Mother, come quickly, the faithful long for your guidance."

As the Pope prayed inside his chamber, an unexplainable luminous figure appeared over the partial ruins of Mecca. It descended downward gracefully until it hovered a few feet above the sacred Kaaba stone. The Saudis had recently reinstated worship around the black megalith, which had narrowly escaped damage during the Arab-Israeli war. As fate would have it, the Russian coalition invasion of Israel and the horrendous weather patterns had coincided with the Muslim month of Ramadan, stranding a multitude of pilgrims inside Islam's holiest city.

Upon witnessing the strange apparition, the worshippers fell prostrate. Within moments the light took a Marian shape that could be seen motioning to a respected Muslim cleric nearby. Spellbound, he rose and walked to the base of the Kaaba. After kissing the black stone, he turned and began shouting a message to the large Muslim crowd,

> "Mary, God has chosen you. He has made you pure and exalted you above all women."[11]

While the crowd began chanting these same words from the cleric, the apparition suddenly disappeared.

By the time word of the sighting reached Vatican City, Pope Romano was receiving the Rock Star treatment from his peers and the press. News of the Pope's dogma of Mary, which elevated her to be Co-Redemptrix, Mediatrix and Advocate, began to spread rapidly to even the remotest parts of the world. Even Muslims, who were in a state of disarray from their two Mideast war defeats, began embracing his teachings.

Subsequently, to worldwide amazement, the apparition of "Mary" made several surprise supernatural appearances at other key world locations repeating her universal message of love, peace, and global unity. In addition, miracles and healings were occurring at these multiple apparition sites, which prompted many conversions to the Catholic Faith.

After Mecca, she arrived in the clear skies above India's Taj Mahal, which rallied many Hindus to her side. Then she visited Zeitoun, Egypt, where she had been previously witnessed by millions during 1968-1971. Doubling back, she made additional appearances at former notable apparition sites in Fatima, (Portugal) Lourdes, (France) and Guadalupe, (Mexico).

Her sightings became so commonplace, that one late night television talk show host humored in his monologue, the "Queen of Heaven appears to have hit the political campaign trail hard in order to recruit some faithful followers. Who travels to caucuses in an RV anymore?

Nowadays you just soar through the heavens with no TSA or other travel restrictions." He further jested, "The Blessed Mother sightings have become so commonplace that the network producers are trying to get her to make a guest appearance on my show."

As a result of her various impactful appearances, multitudes from other religions began streaming into Catholic Churches worldwide. Both new and old members of the "Faithful" began flocking to Rome in anticipation that the Queen might arrive there as well.

And then it happened! Her crowning moment came. She arrived over the Eternal City in all her splendor.

Hovering quietly over Vatican City in what appeared to be brightly lit luminescent figure, she caused an eerie silence to fill the square for about half an hour. Only the prayerful whispers of the multitude penetrated the stillness. Then she revealed herself to the throng assembled beneath.

Her radiant beauty shown so brightly that she could scarcely be looked upon. Her splendor epitomized the essence of serenity. Overwhelming feelings of love, peace, charity, and joy wove together the hearts of the faithful, without a word yet spoken.

No longer able to contain their joy, they began crying out at the top of their lungs, praises to their Queen.

She lifted her hands high toward the heavens and, after several minutes of ecstasy had subsided, she slowly lowered them in front of her in a call for silence.

Meanwhile, Pope Romano and Cardinal Vitalia had made their anticipated appearance on the balcony of the Pope's study. Mimicking his Queen, Pope Romano also lowered his hands in a call for calm.

When not even a whisper could be heard, the majestic woman, suspended high above, turned her full attention toward Pope Vicente Romano. All eyes followed her gaze, and then an enchanting, ethereal voice emanated from the apparition.

Uncharacteristically, the Blessed Mother spoke audibly during the apparition. Her serene voice could be heard throughout the assembly and a local news crew in attendance was able to broadcast her message to its local audience. It so happened that this live program was being watched at Nathan's house at the time of the telecast, which enabled everyone there to hear these words:

> *"Dear Children, thank you for your loyal presence here.*
> *Behold my servant, the Vicar of Christ. He will speak*
> *my words and carry out my earthly instructions. And*

through My Son's Church in Rome, the waters of world peace will flow. This is already happening before your eyes. As I warned in my secret message at Fatima, the day would come when Russia would spread its errors throughout the world, but in the end, my Immaculate Heart would triumph. With the collapse of the Russian invasion, the world has witnessed my supernatural powers. Now I will use those powers for the spread of world peace."[12]

The news camera's shifted their focus to the Pope as a brief pause followed this shocking announcement. Placing his right hand upon his heart, the Pope nodded toward the apparition in solemn approval, which prompted the Queen of Heaven to continue her divine discourse.

"Blessed are the faithful who heed my calls for peace. Therefore, my peace I present to them and I urge the entire world to diligently seek my Son in the Eucharist. The Eucharist can protect you from penalty of mortal sin and provide reparation for your sins against my Immaculate Heart. When you partake of this Holy Sacrament, all will be well with your souls. This is because my Son's holy body and blood is present in the Eucharist. His sacrifice is perpetuated in this holy sacrament. Now my beloved children, the Reformation has ended and you must come to full unity in the faith."

And with those closing words she departed into the blue skies, leaving the cheers and chants of the faithful echoing behind her.

"That counterfeit imposter," Amber shouted from the veranda of Nathan's home in Rome.

"Sssssh, Auntie! You are going to get us in serious trouble with the neighbors outside on the balcony across from us," Jami pleaded.

The entire clan, still residing in Nathan's home in Rome, had been watching the events at the Vatican from the bird's eye view of his veranda.

Lowering his binoculars to his chest, Tovia asked, "Did you hear everything that the apparition said?"

Unable to control her anger, Amber retorted, "We certainly did! We turned the TV up to almost full volume the whole time she spoke. The apparition tried to steal the Lord's thunder by claiming that she interceded in the defeat of the Russian invaders. I heard those words resonate loud and clear," she bellowed at the top of her lungs.

Quickly placing his hand over her mouth, Tovia ordered, "Quiet! Have you gone mad, Wife? Jami's right; we have to be careful. We are treading on dangerous waters by staying here in Rome!"

Amber calmed herself and said "We need to get Gershom and Simeon on the phone immediately to discuss this."

"Please, before you call them, we need to pack our suitcases and board Nathan's jet!" exclaimed Jami. "I'm frightened by all of this; we need to get out of Rome right now!"

Pushing her father's binoculars back up to his eyes, Bella pleaded, "She's right, Daddy! I'm scared! Look! Those Catholics are acting crazy! We need to go home now!"

Tovia reached into his pocket and pulled out his cell phone. "I know Nathan's plane has returned from Israel, so I'll call the pilot to make sure we are clear to leave immediately," he said. "You all go get packed, because once the pilot gives us the thumbs up, we are all getting out of here."

Chapter 12
The Harlot Rides the Beast to Peace and Prosperity

"Holy Father, EU President Hans Vandenberg has requested a private audience with us," Cardinal Vitalia informed his Marian Pope.

"And, where does he propose such a high level meeting should take place?" Pope Romano inquired.

"In Frankfurt," Vitalia replied.

Donning a curious expression, Romano questioned, "Why Frankfurt of all places, and what concerns our charismatic colleague?"

Vitalia explained, "He has meetings throughout the week with the European Central Bank (ECB) to discuss the faltering Eurozone monetary matters. Vandenberg is fretting over a global economic collapse and believes it can be forestalled by capitalizing on the developing fervor for the Queen of Heaven. He is gravely concerned that the fall of the Russian coalition will result in the utter collapse of their respective governments and economies. Moreover, he fears the mop-up of the Middle East warzone will take months, maybe years. Vandenberg wants to tackle these urgent matters promptly, before the flow of energy resources to the world in general, and Europe specifically, is disrupted.

"Vandenberg's concerns are warranted," Pope Romano agreed. "The Israelis have pledged the bulk of their energy exports to the US and the UK, making it difficult for them to meet European needs. It will be up to the EU to garnish these resources from the defeated lands, and for that they will need the Vatican network."

Cardinal Vitalia reluctantly reminded, "Yes, Most Holy Father, but remember that our influence is not as extensive as it once was, since some people who were known to be Catholics seem to have been taken during the worldwide disappearances. In places like America, Mexico, and Brazil, we are still recovering from the loss."

"I disagree," Romano retorted. "Those who disappeared are being replaced by multitudes of new believers. The Catholic Church has never been in a better position than now to lead the world into a millennial period of peace, prosperity, and unity. And, by no means make mention of this in front of President Vandenberg!"

Acquiescing to the Holy Father's wishes, Romano confirmed, "Travel plans to Frankfurt have already been arranged. We depart early tomorrow."

Accompanied by their heavily armed motorcade, the duo arrived safely at the ECB headquarters the next morning. Adorned head-to-toe in lavish priestly garb, they were swiftly escorted into an extravagant secluded office. Indicating a meeting shrouded in secrecy, the tall thick doors were promptly shut behind them.

Graciously cupping and kissing the Pope's right hand, Vandenberg issued his salutation: "Dear Holy Father and my favorite cardinal, thank you both for interrupting your busy schedules, and coming to Frankfurt on such short notice."

Seating themselves across from Vandenberg, with the mammoth conference table between them, Cardinal Vitalia began, "The Holy Father has already been apprised of your concerns, and agrees that time is of the essence to form a unity pact between the EU and the Vatican."

Turning his gaze to Romano, Vandenberg sought confirmation.

Romano nodded and boasted, "The Queen of Heaven's blessings are upon us."

At this acknowledgment, Vandenberg swiftly spoke: "Excellent! I need you to host a Vatican Council meeting immediately in order to unite all the world's religions under the Catholic canopy for our mutual benefit! We will call it "Vatican Global Council." I wish it to be broadcast live throughout the world!"

Protective of his Pope, and provoked by Vandenberg's abrupt dictates, Cardinal Vitalia complained, "We scarcely just arrive as your guests, and immediately you impose your will upon the Holy Father. Excuse yourself for this irreverent behavior!"

NOVEL

Vandenberg took a sharp breath, faked a smile, and calmly apologized, "Yes, you're absolutely right Cardinal Vitalia. How insensitive of me! In my haste I took for granted that his holiness and I were on the same political page. Please forgive my thoughtlessness."

Turning his attention back to Pope Romano, Vandenberg, an expert at using the Socratic method of reasoning, restructured his comment: "Your Holiness, in light of the overwhelming favor shown to you by the Queen of Heaven; how should we implement our pact to unite the world and stave off imminent economic calamity?"

"We are on the same page," the Pope replied, smiling wanly at the Cardinal. "Vatican Global Council hosted in Vatican City is a good start, but I am uncertain of both the logic and the logistics of a hastily held live global broadcast. Such a high-level meeting must be conducted behind closed doors. A shroud of secrecy will whet the world's appetite, and provide time to formulate the official Vatican dogma. Additionally, the Vatican dare not subject Our Lady's authority to an uncensored assembly of snake charmers, New-Age mystics, and Hindus that have more deities than there are days on the calendar. Moreover, achieving the full attention of a global audience requires more than just a single broadcast; it will require a universal awareness of the Blessed Mother's benevolent intentions toward all religions."

Scooting closer to the table's edge, the EU president raised one eyebrow and slyly said, "Fascinating plan. Please tell me more."

"We will invite the foremost leaders from every world religion to Vatican City, especially the influential Protestants and Muslims. I have been in contact with many of them, along with our cardinals and bishops over the past few days, and most of them are already pledging solidarity to the Catholic Church and faithfulness to Our Lady. Her miraculous appearances, and supernatural signs and wonders have persuaded most of them to ally with us. We will convene ecumenically and then, through a global satellite broadcast, highlight some of the historical miracles associated with the Eucharist and the apparitions of our Blessed Mother, along with those presently occurring again through her. This will emphasize the importance of worshipping our Eucharistic Lord in the Blessed Sacrament. We will conclude with a joint statement that most religious leaders have presently pledged allegiance to the will of the Queen, the dogmas of the Catholic Church, and the supremacy of the Eucharist."

Somewhat bewildered, Vandenberg inquired, "'Most' of them? Is dissention developing among the Catholic clergy regarding the Queen, the Church or the Eucharist?"

Realizing he had said too much, Romano reflexively grabbed the large crucifix adorning his necklace, and fumbled for the right response.

The pontiff's awkward silence spoke loudly to Vandenberg's suspicions that discord existed within Roman Catholic ranks. "Rumors are currently circulating," Vandenberg noted, "that some US bishops and cardinals, along with several prominent Protestant ministers, openly advocate the apparition's messages are unbiblical...even demonically inspired. Is there truth to these claims?"

Vitalia quickly interjected, "The Holy Father has matters in America well in hand. Such rumors are unfounded."

"Even Archbishop Patrick Dolan? Is he well in hand, Cardinal Vitalia?" Vandenberg queried dubiously.

"He has been ostracized from the ranks of the clergy by his own choice," Vitalia replied, "No longer are his dissenting views about the disappearances and the apparitions given a platform in our churches."

Unconvinced, Vandenberg predicted, "I foresee this scenario as extremely problematic for the greater good of our goals. More serious measures must be taken by the Vatican to prevent these influential leaders from standing in the way of our global unity plans."

Upset by the challenge, Romano countered, "The former Archbishop and his Protestant cohorts serve no threat whatsoever to our unity plans. We have already put harsh measures in place to counteract their schemes. They will be duly warned that Vatican Global Council will have zero tolerance for their blasphemous teachings. Should they challenge our authority, they will realize there are limitations to my patience!"

With that assurance, the trio adjourned, agreeing to enact their unity plans promptly.

NOVEL

Chapter 13
Israel Cleanses the Holy Land

Mopping up the carnage from the Magog war proved to be no minor undertaking. Hordes of dead and contaminated coalition soldiers lay strewn over vast expanses of Israel. The Israeli government feared a pandemic contagion was inevitable unless a national effort to rid the land of the deceased took place quickly. Wisely, Prime Minister Moshe Kaufman convened with Rabbi Joseph Levin and the Chief Rabbinate Council, seeking support to cleanse the land by whatever methods necessary.

"Rabbi Levin," Kaufman inquired, "disposing of the deceased enemy soldiers expeditiously presents our country with a huge challenge. What does the Torah teach about unclean corpses polluting the holy land? Certainly Moses must have laid down laws regarding catastrophic conditions that threaten the safety and fertility of the land."

Israel's leading religious figure stood before the council and replied, "The Law of Moses is clear on this matter! There is a prescribed process for handling dead bodies, and a ceremonial purification process that must take place. Numbers 19:11-22 and Deuteronomy 21:1-9 determine that the dead must be buried immediately because exposed corpses are a source of contamination. The land must therefore be completely cleansed and purged of all physical and spiritual defilement. Neither the enemies, their encampments, nor any of their belongings can be left to pollute the land!"[13]

"Agreed," Kaufman replied. "There is no way to comb through the fallen hordes to retrieve their personal effects. We are facing a logistical nightmare in dealing with the burial of the dead. We will need to locate a valley suitable to establish the region's largest mass gravesite.

Meanwhile, our military will need to work feverishly to stockpile the enemy's weapons into IDF arsenals. Efforts to accomplish this are...."

Interrupting the Prime Minister in mid-sentence Rabbi Levin informed, "The Rabbinate Council interprets the Torah to teach that all of the enemy's belongings, including their weapons, must be destroyed."

Prime Minister Kaufman pleaded, "Be reasonable, Rabbi. We can agree that the dead must be buried without delay, but the government must be allowed to harness the enemy's weapons to benefit the Israeli people and their military. These high tech weapons are now the property of the Jewish State."

"Reasonable?" repeated Levin. "Israel's victory was accomplished entirely by the hand of Hashem, the Almighty. All aspects of Levitical Law must be followed in this matter."

Kaufman was aghast. "Show me historical precedent for this in the wars fought by our forefathers, I know of none," he quipped. "Surely such a vast arsenal must not be squandered. Besides, no such talk arose in the aftermath of the IDF victory over the Arabs in what you believe was the Psalm 83 war. Why do you make it a point of legal contention now?"

Kaufman's abrupt remarks sent shudders throughout the rabbis assembled in the room. They murmured amongst each other and cast disgruntled glances at the Prime Minister.

Rabbi Aaron Edelstein reasoned that perhaps the government could be convinced to convert the weapons into sources of fuel and energy to serve Israel. Speaking over the murmurs, Edelstein suggested that since the Torah is speaking about unclean open vessels, and not weapons, that the council could accept the weapons conversion.

Growing increasingly impatient, Kaufman questioned. "Do we have a deal?"

The Rabbis spoke amongst themselves for several more minutes before Levin announced, "We concur that the cleansing of the land is of utmost urgency at this time, so we will keep quiet about the government's treatment of the weapons, and its choice of location for the mass graves. However, our silence must not be construed as approval regarding this weapons matter. In the near future we will propose a suitable plan for the disposal of the weapons that we believe will be mutually acceptable to the Israeli government and the demands of the Law."

Kaufman replied, "That works for me. The Rabbinate Council can perform the ceremonial ritual that un-defiles the land, and the government will use the occasion to reach out to Israelis to purge the land from the dead and collect their weapons. The mammoth task before us requires a nationalized effort. The sooner we begin, the sooner your temple can be constructed. Let's put our people to work to accomplish all of this so that we can get this war torn country back on its feet!"

Comfortable that his mission had been accomplished with the chief rabbis, Prime Minister convened the members of the Knesset to inform them of the good news. They heaved a collective sigh of relief that the religious and political communities were united for the good of the nation. During the assembly, Kaufman called upon his minister of the Interior, Avi Fleishman, to orchestrate a national campaign to accomplish the monumental feat of cleansing the land of the deceased.

After returning from the parliament meeting that afternoon, the first order of business for Fleishman was to contact his most trusted staff member, Lisa Thompson. "The Ministry of the Interior has been instructed to unite the country in a nationalized campaign intended to cleanse the land of the dead bodies," he told her. "I am putting you in full charge of this operation. Let me know what staff and resources you will need to accomplish this."

"Why me?' Lisa marveled.

"I can't think of anybody on staff that I trust more than you," Fleishman complimented. "The way you have handled affairs from day one on the job is unparalleled, and especially praiseworthy is your faithful service in the days following the disappearances of your husband and son. I don't know how you held up."

Lisa graciously replied, "Thank you for your trust; it means the world to me. Losing Thomas and Tyler in the rapture was gut wrenching, but…"

Suddenly, Fleishman interrupted. "We will have no more mention of the word 'rapture' inside this government department! I caution you; do not embrace the Christian jargon that some are associating with the vanishings!"

Understanding the centuries-old divide between Christians and Jews firsthand, Lisa diplomatically questioned, "Avi, don't you find it curious that Thomas, Tyler, and all the others unaccounted for were Christians? Isn't this slightly suspicious? Don't you have to admit that there may be some truth to what the so-called 144,000 Jews for Jesus are saying about the rapture?"

Putting his index finger to his lips, Fleishman rebuked, "*Ssssh!* That's the second time you've used the "R" word!" Smiling, Lisa bartered, "Look, Avi, if I roll up my sleeves and get busy with the blueprints of Israel's national unity campaign, then the least you can do is let me believe my family disappeared to a better place. After all, why are the Jews still waiting for the Messiah to show? In light of what just happened, don't you think he would have shown up by now?"

"The rabbis are predicting he will come soon," Avi replied, "now that the Ezekiel prophecy has just been fulfilled."

"Well, I think our dear rabbis need to read Daniel 9, Psalm 22, and Isaiah 53 again," Lisa argued.

"Why's that?" Avi asked.

"Because they evidence that the Messiah already came about 2000 years ago as a sacrifice for our sins," Lisa explained, "in fulfillment of those prophecies and many more."

Lisa, having gotten the last word in edgewise, bid her boss goodbye as his secretary informed him that Prime Minister Kaufman was on the phone. But before answering the call, he looked sternly at Lisa and cautioned, "I'm warning you Thompson, keep your private beliefs to yourself. There is no place for them inside this workplace!"

Exiting back to her corner office, Lisa silently prayed the Serenity Prayer:

> *"God, grant me the serenity to accept the things I cannot change, Courage to change the things I can, and wisdom to know the difference."*

Lisa realized that she had been called to her high level post in the Ministry of the Interior for such a time as this. It reminded her of her favorite female Bible character, Hadassah, later renamed Queen Esther; who had to reveal her Hebrew identity to the Persian King Ahasuerus at the risk of being killed. She thought: *If Esther was willing to die to save the Israelites from Persian genocide, then the least I can do is stand up for Jesus so that Jewish souls can be saved by their Messiah.*

Sitting down at her desk, she humored herself: *How Ironic? Jesus was a Jew. He was one of us. How hard can it be to tell fellow Jews that Jesus is the Jewish Messiah?*

Suddenly Lisa's cell phone vibrated and she noticed that Jami's caller ID was on the lit screen. The phone had been silenced throughout her important morning meetings so she didn't realize that her daughter had left several important messages. Hastily, she answered the phone and greeted, "Hello honey, how are you?"

"I'm upset!" Jami replied. "Why haven't you responded to any of my messages?"

"I'm sorry, dear. I have been in important meetings all morning at work," Lisa apologized.

"I'm at uncle Tovia's and aunt Amber's house," Jami informed. "We had Mr. Severs' pilot fly us home on his private jet because of all that supernatural stuff going on at the Vatican. We arrived in Haifa a few hours ago. This town looks like a war zone and I don't feel safe. Mother, I need you to come get me right away!"

"Calm down, honey. Everything will be alright," Lisa comforted.

Jami began crying. "Mommy I miss you," she wept. "I'm so scared!"

"I will make sure you get home soon, dear," Lisa said. "Please let me speak to your uncle."

"Tovia is out surveying the city," Jami replied, "and checking out if he still has an office to work from. But Aunt Amber is next to me."

"Please put her on the phone."

"Hi Lisa. Jami is quite unnerved right now," said Amber.

Lisa acknowledged, "I know, I need to figure out the best way to get her back home immediately."

"What does your schedule look like today," Amber inquired. "Can you come for her?"

"I just got promoted to chief of staff of the Ministry of Interior," Lisa replied, "and Fleishman wants me to lock myself indoors to draft a national campaign to mop up the Magog war mess. He wants it on his desk yesterday, so there is no way I can get up north to your neck of the woods."

"What do you want me to do?" Amber asked.

Lisa instructed, "Please have Nathan's pilot fly her down to Ben Gurion airport and I'll have her escorted to me in a government vehicle."

"No can do," Amber responded. "Nathan instructed him to fly back to Rome for important business. He departed moments after we arrived home."

"What important business?" Lisa questioned.

"You're asking the wrong person," Amber replied. "Tovia can tell you more. Apparently there is some underground network of former Catholics who are trying to flee from the Vatican to America, or something of the sort. I guess there is an opposition group of left-behind Catholics and Protestants forming in the US."

"Opposition to what?" Lisa asked,

"Again, I'm not the person to ask. It's all Latin to me," Amber quipped. "I can have Tovia call you when he returns."

Lisa sighed, "Amber, for the good of Israel, I need you do to an important favor for me. Please would you consider bringing Jami home to me? It is utterly impossible for me to make the trip to Haifa right now."

"I think that will work," Amber said, "because Tovia wants to witness to his mother about Jesus. He was talking about bringing Jami home and then explaining to Naomi and your father about what the Bible says is happening right now. Frankly, he doesn't think he has a job anymore, after what just happened in Israel. He mentioned that we might have to pack up the family and move closer to all of you."

"I think that's a wonderful idea!" Lisa exclaimed. "It would be such a blessing to have you all near. I'm going to be so busy with this national campaign and I'm sure I can keep you all busy. Besides, my father-in-law's friend Razz left Jami and me more money before he was raptured than we will ever be able to spend in the short time remaining on earth. We will all be taken care of."

Amber confessed, "Lisa you're the best sister-in-law a woman could ever want. I will make sure that Tovia gets Jami home sometime on Monday."

With those words, both Jami and Lisa were comfortable to conclude the call and get prepared to rendezvous on Monday a couple of days after the Sabbath. Jami got back on the phone and said, "Mother, I will be okay those couple of days with my cousins, so don't worry. I know that you are busy at work, but please work through the weekend so we can spend time together. I need a time with you when I get home."

Lisa confirmed, "I will burn the midnight oil. I'll take my work home because the department closes down on the Sabbath. Gershom told me that when Christ fulfilled the law at His first coming, observance of the Sabbath is optional for believers, I'll work all weekend. I love you, Jami! Goodbye 'til Monday."

Chapter 14
Doomsday Conference Erupts Into Deadly Chaos

It was a seasonally sunny Saturday morning· and astonishingly, all seven-thousand seats in the Grand Canyon University Arena in Phoenix, Arizona were filled. The symposium entitled "SOSC - *Save Our Souls Christ*," was a kick-off Christian conference primarily designed as a platform to christen a recently conceived organization. It was hosted by the newly formed religious group called "The Society of Second-Chancers, (SOSC)."

The SOSC had been organized by a remorseful group of religious leaders who realized they had missed out on the Rapture. Even though many of their fellow congregants were caught up to be with Christ in the clouds, these men and women had been left behind. Subsequently, they had all repented and received Christ, being born again into a right relationship with Jesus as their personal Lord and Savior.

The group included former Catholics, Protestants, Evangelicals, and Emergents (*members of the post – modern "Emergent Church"*). Importantly, they realized the biblical significance of the 144,000 Jewish Witnesses, and as such, they offered the select group their unconditional support.

The primary purpose of the SOSC was to broadcast the gospel of Christ to the others left behind, credibly explain the Rapture phenomena, proclaim that Christ was returning to judge unrighteousness and ultimately establish His messianic kingdom. Additionally, their mission was to warn the world about the powerful Bible prophecies that would find fulfillment between the Rapture and Christ's Second Advent. The SOSC leaders realized from scripture that the world would eventually experience the emergence of the

Antichrist, Armageddon, and the seven-year Tribulation Period. Their hope was to work closely with the 144,000 to lead as many people as possible to Christ in the short span of time remaining.

The event title was actually selected to serve as a play on words. In addition to pronouncing that the Lord gives second chances, the SOSC acronym was cleverly chosen to be reminiscent of the World War I and II encoded telegraph message S.O.S.,[14] or in this post-rapture case, Save Our Souls Christ. It signaled that Christ was the Savior; that He gives second chances, and that a spiritual World War was underway for souls.

The SOSC conference was hosted by Unistate Global Investment Corporation (UGIC) based in Scottsdale, Arizona, whose longstanding president was Nathan Severs. Featured on the platform was a panel of six speakers, which included Gershom Gold and Simeon Abrams of the 144,000 Jews for Jesus, Archbishop Dolan, formerly of the Roman Catholic Diocese of Phoenix, and three well known US Protestant pastors, Ladd Bitterman, Brad Walters and Gary Hanah.

The audience included all of the members from the American chapter of the 144,000 Jews for Jesus, scores of former Catholic and Protestant leaders, a handful of Muslim clerics, and thousands of the general public. To the delight of the SOSC, this conference quickly burgeoned into a mega-event before the doors had even opened. This was because the cable and mainstream news media made it a point to live stream portions of the occasion globally through satellite networks. Additionally, all the primary social networks, including Facebook, Twitter, and YouTube were buzzing with blogs and streaming with homemade videos.

As a result, millions worldwide took an interest in this conference. Individuals from diverse nations, tribes, peoples, and tongues were still seeking answers about the Christian disappearances, the apocalyptic Middle East, and the horrendous economic hardships confronting their respective homelands. Many hoped that this conference could make sense out of the chaos that had so quickly turned their lives upside down. Their governments were failing them, their various religions were short on answers and the apparition's messages about peace, love, unity and the Eucharist still required scrutiny. On the chance that the SOSC could bring them hope and answers, they observed the happening in whichever way they could, with bated breath and expectant hearts.

NOVEL

The event program read as follows:

Speakers	Topics
Simeon Abrams	The Confirmation of the False Covenant Causes Tribulation.
Archbishop Dolan	Are the Apparitions Divine or Demonic?
Gershom Gold	Israel is the Woman of Revelation 12, Not the Queen of Heaven!
Ladd Bitterman	The Five Horses and Six Horseman of the Apocalypse.
Brad Walters	Does God Give Second Chances After the Rapture?
Gary Hanah	True Christians; Prepare to Be Martyred.

Meanwhile, as the Phoenix event was getting underway, EU President Hans Vandenberg, who had just been briefed by confidants of the SOSC conference, frantically attempted to make contact with Pope Romano and Cardinal Vitalia…

"Holy Father, President Vandenberg seeks to conduct an emergency conference call with us," informed Cardinal Vitalia.

"Not again!" Pope Romano replied, "What a nuisance he has become!"

Vitalia warned, "Vandenberg is on the line right now and says an urgent matter in America requires our undivided attention."

"Is it about the Arizona conference?" the Pope guessed.

Joining his vicar in front of the big conference call screen and preparing to initiate the call, Vitalia said, "I don't know. Let's find out first hand."

Receiving a visual and audio feed on his end, Vandenberg greeted, "Hello gentlemen. Can you hear me?"

"Loud and clear Mr. President," Vitalia reported. "You're coming in just fine."

Vandenberg spoke directly to his concern: "Are you both aware of this SOSC conference going on as we speak in the US?

While Pope Romano nodded yes, Cardinal Vitalia confirmed, "Absolutely; we have people planted inside the assembly instructed to sabotage the entire event."

"And, how do you plan to accomplish that from your headquarters at the Vatican?" asked Vandenberg.

Pope Romano boasted, "We have a full-proof strategy in place. First, when a speaker says something controversial about the Vatican or the apparition messages, our people will protest loudly to interrupt the flow of the teaching. Second, they will seize the question and answer sessions to ask pointed theological questions the Vatican has prepared that are specifically intended to outsmart and embarrass the panel of experts. These inquiries are intentionally designed to initiate a non-violent ruckus among those we have purposely planted inside the auditorium. We assure you that the SOSC will not conclude successfully, and the blasphemous conference organizers will have serious reservations about ever hosting a similar conference."

Vandenberg echoed, "A non-violent ruckus; I don't care if the parishioners come out DEAD or ALIVE; these meetings cannot continue. Nothing can be allowed in America, or anywhere else in the world, to obstruct our plans for global political and religious governance."

Cardinal Vitalia cautioned, "President Vandenberg, please, the Holy Father encourages patience concerning such matters. You are privy to know that, incredibly, several miraculous signs have been given to him privately during his daily devotions before the Blessed Sacrament that have caused him to believe that there will soon be incomparable Eucharistic miracles occurring on an unprecedented global scale. The Holy Father believes the overwhelming magnitude of these Eucharistic wonders will unite world religions under the umbrella of Roman Catholicism, which will ultimately create the global stability the EU seeks."

Vandenberg clarified, "Patience is not a luxury we presently possess. Let the miracles of the Eucharist come, but we need an alternative plan in place. In light of the turmoil in the Middle East and global economic crisis, Pakistan has its nukes pointed at India, China is ready to overtake Taiwan and Japan, and North Korea is mobilizing troops along the border of South Korea. There is a global power struggle underway. Nations are fearful for their survival. In an instant, and without warning, another nuclear crisis could occur anywhere in the world. We must maintain strict control of global scenarios and do everything in our power to prevent all future religious gatherings like this SOSC conference. If these US dissenters aren't already convinced by the multiple supernatural appearances of the apparition, then there are no guarantees that Eucharistic miracles will persuade them either!"

"We have our boots on the ground," Cardinal Vitalia insisted, "We are prepared to do whatever it takes to disrupt the event proceedings. Our insurgents include many former Muslims who have come on board as a result of the Marian apparitions. Among them are radicals who hate this upstart so-called Christian group, and they appear willing to die for their faith. In fact, they seem to be looking for religious license to go after these guys. From the Vatican's perspective, their fundamentalist Muslim backgrounds could come in handy when dealing with all non-compliant religious and secular groups."

Vandenberg questioned, "What do you mean 'boots on the ground'? Are you suggesting your accomplices inside the auditorium are armed and dangerous?"

"Of course not," Cardinal Vitalia clarified, "All of America is on high alert for terrorism. Nobody is able to smuggle a weapon into the conference."

Pausing for a moment, Cardinal Vitalia requested, "President Vandenberg, please allow Pope Romano to depart to his holy chambers; he has other pressing matters to attend to. Meanwhile, you and I can iron out the details of our mutual concerns."

Staring skeptically into the video camera, Vandenberg consented, "As you wish Holy Father, but remember, there are no guarantees that your expected Eucharistic miracles will transform these troublemakers into faithful Catholics."

Unappreciative of Vandenberg's piercing comments; Pope Romano retreated to his private quarters. Once he had departed, Vitalia explained, "What I was revealing, President Vandenberg, is that I have a peripheral plan in place in the conference parking lot."

"What do you mean by this?" asked Vandenberg.

Donning a smug look, Vitalia confidentially replied, "Let's just say that for many of the SOSC attendees it will be a long and arduous journey back to the safety of their cars, if you get my drift."

Upon hearing this, Vandenberg's concerns were temporarily mollified. He was content being on a need to know basis about the cardinal's contingency plan, and, at least for the present, he had heard enough. "Very well, dear cardinal, I'm adjourning to my office to monitor the live streaming of the SOSC conference." he said, "I entrust this matter to your competent hands."

"Rest assured, we are watching the event here also, and we are in constant communications with our people inside and outside of the event," the cardinal concluded.

Meanwhile, the SOSC conference was underway and the first speaker, Simeon Abrams was nearing the end of his teaching about the true content of the Antichrist's false covenant, when he speculated that one component of the deal would concern itself with Israel's rights to worship freely according to their ancient Mosaic Law. "The Jews will want to construct their temple and reinstate their animal sacrificial system, and they will refuse to participate in the required sacraments of the Vatican-ruled world religion," he proclaimed.

These comments sparked a murmur among many of the Vatican implants imbedded within the crowd. The disturbance was short-lived, but set the tone for what could follow if the subsequent speakers spoke adversely about the resurging Catholic Church. In fact, it prompted the conference host, Nathan Severs, to change the order of the speakers. Brad Walters was moved into the second slot, because the speakers originally scheduled before him were certain to throw daggers at the Vatican's authority and the messages of the apparitions.

Walters taught primarily from 2 Thessalonians in the New Testament, he warned that the Antichrist could be the charismatic EU President, Hans Vandenberg. However, Walters reminded, "Presently, we can't be certain. But we do know that this coming lawless one's rise to power will be characterized by deceptive displays of signs and wonders unimaginable. In my estimation, these supernatural exhibitions could include spectacular UFO sightings and much more. These miracles will probably be far greater than the demonic Marian apparitions the world has been witnessing. These paranormal events will cause many to believe in a counterfeit gospel, or what the Bible calls 'THE LIE.' Moreover, the Antichrist will be the one that confirms the false covenant with Israel, which Simeon Abrams just preached about."

He reserved his closing comments to say, "Even though unrighteous deception will deceive the masses into believing in the counterfeit gospel, multitudes from all nations, tribes, peoples, and tongues will become born again believers, like those recently raptured. God gives second chances; this is what The Society of the Second-Chancers stands for, and now is your opportunity to accept Christ as your Savior. Trust me, I speak to you first-hand about this merciful attribute of God's character. Even though I pastored a mega-church, I never truly became born again through a genuine faith in Christ."

Walter's then gave an altar call and throngs in attendance made their way up the aisles of the arena toward the prayer teams in front of the podium. The Lord multiplied his Church by about four-thousand that day.

The antagonists amongst the crowd were silenced by this overwhelming display of faith. What could they do? They were essentially handcuffed by the pervasive power and grace of Christ that was obviously controlling the moment. They kept quiet and waited for a more opportune time to execute Cardinal Vitalia's sinister plan. And after the short lunch break, that time arrived.

Archbishop Dolan, who was one of the first high ranking Catholic members to depart from Catholicism after the rapture, was called to the podium as the third speaker. He began by saying, "The Lord clearly has end times plans for Israel. Zechariah the prophet tells us that Israel is the apple of God's eye."

These comments moved Vitalia's spies to the edges of their seats. They quickly recognized what the Archbishop was leading up to.

Dolan continued, "Down through the centuries the Roman Catholic Church lorded its Replacement theology over the faithful. The church fathers began to teach that when the Jews rejected Jesus, the Lord rejected the Jews. This paved the way for the Catholic Church to become Israel's replacement, and heir by default to the promises given to Abraham, Isaac, and Jacob. It was a diabolical scheme that even Martin Luther ultimately embraced at the time of the Reformation. Throughout past centuries, the faithful sitting in the pews became inculcated regarding the sacraments and generally failed to realize that the clergy were hijacking the Lord's promises to Israel. They attended the Mass, prayed the Hail Marys, and went to confession faithfully, but usually never questioned the dogmas and papal edicts that followed."

These remarks created a stir amongst the Vatican infiltrators. Murmurs filled the auditorium, like the sound of an approaching swarm of Africanized bees.[15]

Hearing this, the Archbishop raised his voice and pounded the pulpit declaring, "This is why Pope Romano, Pope Benedict, and most of their predecessors erroneously believed that the Catholic Church, led by the

Queen of Heaven, is the mysterious woman of Revelation 12. And, most troubling of all, brothers and sisters, this is why the Vatican appears to be identified in Revelation 17's MYSTERY, BABYLON THE GREAT, THE MOTHER OF HARLOTS AND OF THE ABOMINATIONS OF THE EARTH!"

"Blasphemers, Jew lovers, heretics!" the infiltrators cried out. Many of them began lunging toward the stage, fists held high. The crowd became so unruly that security had to escort the speakers and media camera crews to secluded areas for safety, while simultaneously attempting to restore order. Creating an atmosphere akin to a barroom brawl, the enraged protestors lashed out in every direction. The auditorium was becoming a bloody mess, causing many worshippers to flee for the safety of their cars and charter buses in the parking lot.

Awaiting the masses attempting to flee was an even worse fate, the second wave of protestors. But, this unruly bunch was armed and dangerous. Vitalia's plan B was intended to make a lethal statement to those attending the SOSC event. Several dozen stick-toting radicals, some with concealed weapons, had dispersed unnoticed around the perimeter of the arena parking lot, shortly after the conference began. Upon command they put on bandanas to disguise their identities, brandished their weapons, and set off Molotov cocktails and tear gas to create confusion. In addition to these militants, several hundred more angry activists from the nearby vicinity had arrived unexpectedly to participate in the ruckus. These were locals who had become furious from watching the live streamed Christian messages from the conference. They infiltrated the parking lot to violently protest the event.

Those conference attendees rushing for safety found themselves immediately in harm's way. The flood of worshippers exiting the auditorium made it impossible for those already outside to retreat back indoors. Fists began flailing, sticks began smacking, knives began stabbing. People were frantically huddling behind cars, and many wounded or killed were dropping in the parking lot all around.

A patrol unit promptly radioed for backup: "90L requests assistance for a large unruly crowd at the Grand Canyon University Arena. Hundreds of people are fighting inside the auditorium and the adjacent parking lot. Several thousand more are storming the doors out of the auditorium, attempting to exit into the lot. We have numerous wounded, and possible fatalities occurring. Please dispatch emergency assistance to the entrance and exit sides of the University Arena immediately."

Lieutenant Paul Jordan, the Watch Commander in charge, was offsite when the urgent call came in. Immediately he instructed, "I need all available units, and emergency response teams, equipped with crowd control gear to dispatch to 3300 Camelback Road east of the arena to clear the parking lot. COME NOW! We have a riot on our hands!"

By the time the squads began to arrive, several gun shots had been fired into the crowd from the northern and southern ends of the parking lot. The scene had rapidly degenerated into a battle zone. The rebel ambush was extremely well planned, and when the emergency backup arrived on site, the aggressors discarded their camouflage, hid their weapons under nearby cars, and blended into the crowd. The prevailing hysteria provided cover and a means of escape.

The scene was so chaotic; the police were mostly unable to identify the assailants. The emergency first responders were overwhelmed at the sheer number of casualties on location. They did their best to triage the wounded – while overloaded ambulances and rescue vehicles shuttled the injured to nearby hospitals.

At the end of the day, several hundred wounded were listed, dozens critically, and about thirty were pronounced dead at the scene.

The whole world watched in shock as the assault and the rescue took place, including EU President Hans Vandenberg. With mixed emotions, he approved of Cardinal Vitalia's covert chaotic campaign, but seethed at the news coverage by the mainstream media.

"How dare they report the preposterous rumor that I'm the Antichrist?" He raged inwardly. *"Pastor Walters should be shot for making such an accusation before the eyes of the world!"*

Chapter 15
Jews Return Home as Rumors of Nuclear Wars Abound

After Sunday Mass at St. Peter's Basilica, Pope Romano called Cardinal Vitalia into his office for an urgent confidential meeting.

"Vitalia, I'm appalled at how you let matters get so out of hand at the American conference!" Pope Vicente rebuked.

With a nonchalant shrug, the cardinal snickered, "You know what they say about a mob, Vicente. It has a mind of its own!"

Pope Vicente groaned, "Vitalia, have you no regard for the dead and injured? Bishop Arturo Amanti was in attendance, and is feared to be among the wounded."

Vitalia responded unremorsefully, "Holy Father, with all due respect; please come to terms with the enormity of the present situation. It is past time that you recognize your responsibilities to the unity pact between the Vatican and the EU. The world is on the verge of nuclear war, and the Pakistanis and North Koreans are not standing on the side lines praying Hail Marys, while you plead for miracles. Vandenberg swears that they have their fingers on nuclear triggers as we speak! The miraculous healings and signs and wonders throughout the world thus far are sufficient to justify Vatican authority over all religions!"

Appalled by Vitalia's attitude, Romano reminded, "The Eucharistic miracles will come in God's, not man's time; much in the way the apparitions have appeared at perfect and precise times heretofore."

Rolling his eyes, Vitalia rudely recounted, "The SOSC conference was unruly. You heard how Archbishop Dolan and the other speakers blasphemed against God with their hate speech against the Church and the Blessed Mother. Both he and Bishop Amanti are attempting to lead people away from Catholicism. Even though our numbers grow daily,

NOVEL

this venomous rhetoric is being preached from pulpits, it has gone viral over the Internet, and it is spreading like wildfires throughout the world. It must be stopped! The faithful are looking to you for leadership, and frankly, they are not seeing it! You must take total charge before it's too late!"

"How dare you speak to me in this fashion!" Romano exclaimed.

"Better me," Vitalia warned, "than Hans Vandenberg and his political establishment. We need the EU leader to fully support our global plans. He is obviously not supporting our efforts. He is engrossed in soon becoming the world's most powerful leader, and he will try to accomplish this at the Vatican's expense if we are not careful."

Romano glared at the cardinal. "How do you propose to counteract the SOSC?" he growled.

Donning a more sensitive countenance, Vitalia softed his tone and stated, "It's really quite simple. We can kill two birds with one stone. We can appease the EU president and stop the SOSC at the same time."

Romano clenched his fists. "I don't have time for guessing games, Vitalia! Get to the point!" he spat.

The cardinal lowered his head reverently. "As you wish, my dear Pope." Then, taking a deep breath, he declared, "The time to host Vatican Global Council is now! We cannot put it off any longer, waiting for Eucharistic miracles. We must display solidarity with all world religions in support of the Blessed Mother. Vandenberg will commend you for uniting the faithful, but if you delay, he will grow contemptuous of you."

Romano was stunned. "Enough! Depart from me now! I need to consult with the Blessed Mother!"

Later, during his evening Hail Marys, the Pope prayed feverishly for Eucharistic miracles to commence:

"I urge you Blessed Mother: tell your beloved Son to esteem His holy Eucharist before the eyes of the world. Let signs and wonders draw the world to your Sacred Heart. Come quickly! Nuclear wars and apostates threaten to deter your benevolent plans for this earth. Humanity cries out for love, peace, and unity, but spiritual turmoil runs rampant. How long, my Queen, until you command full unity among the faiths?"

After hours of beseeching, Romano retired, completely exhausted.

Early the following morning, he proceeded to go before the Blessed Sacraments for his daily devotions. While he was there something miraculous occurred, a direct confirmation from Christ, about the significance of the Eucharist.

"*I Am truly present in the consecrated bread and wine,*" revealed the Eucharistic Christ. "*I have provided many miracles in the past and present of my real blood coming forth from the host as evidence to the unbelievers, and even far greater ones are forthcoming!*"

Falling prostrate, Pope Romano replied, "*I know dear Lord, salvation is in the Eucharist. Thank you, this was the word from you that I sought, and now I have it. I will move forward to unite the world with you through your holy Eucharist.*"

Meanwhile, in her home in Bet Shemesh, Israel that following Monday, Lisa was tidying up her home in preparation for Jami's return. Breaking briefly from her housekeeping duties, she called Nathan Severs, in America.

"Hello, Severs speaking," Nathan answered.

"Nathan, how are you?" Lisa asked.

"Lisa? Your caller ID said 'restricted.' How good to hear your voice!"

"Yes indeed it's me," Lisa confirmed. "I'm calling from Israel about an important matter."

"An important matter?" Nathan repeated, "Does it have anything to do with your new role as the architect of Israel's restoration campaign?"

"It does," said, Lisa, humbled. "How did you hear about that?"

"I spoke with Tovia and Jami on Sunday," Nathan answered, "the day after the Phoenix riot. Did you hear about that tragedy?"

"Absolutely," Lisa replied. "The SOSC event was well covered here. The media was outraged to the point of anger against the event and portrayed it as a divisive Christian fundamentalist attempt to proselytize Jews, condemn Catholics, and frighten Israelis with scare tactics. Were you there?" Lisa inquired.

"Oh yes," Nathan revealed, "My company, Unistate Global Investment Corporation, was the main sponsor. I have fifteen stitches in my right arm, as a result!"

NOVEL

"Oh my Lord!" Lisa exclaimed. "What happened? Are you okay?"

"I'm okay," Nathan assured her, "and so are Gershom and Simeon, who were featured speakers at the event. I had the misfortune of being among those that got attacked by the mob. While attempting to bring calm to the outburst, I was overpowered and beaten by several assailants. One of them brandished a long sharp dagger, which he jabbed into my arm."

"You realize," Lisa interrupted, "that the Israeli government frowns upon the SOSC. They fear that they are orchestrating a campaign of hysteria, intended to convert mankind to Christianity."

Nathan clarified, "Well, Lisa, they are true believers working with the 144,000 to preach Jesus, and to warn about the Bible's end times prophecies. The violence was initiated intentionally, by those opposed to the teaching of the true gospel message."

Lisa guessed, "The Catholics?"

"We believe they are primarily responsible," Nathan replied.

"So..." Lisa reflected, "What Simeon and Gershom predicted is already happening. The harlot world religion is beginning to persecute post-rapture believers."

"You're probably right Lisa," Nathan concurred, "but what happened in Phoenix was a mob that metastasized out of control. It is difficult to know the extent of the Vatican's culpability just yet."

"But, Nathan," Lisa reasoned, "You are describing born again believers being martyred for their faith, by supporters of Rome. I can't remember everything Simeon said, but I do remember that the harlot religion would be headquartered in Rome and would be drunk with the blood of the saints, and the MARTYR'S OF JESUS! Remember? He repeated himself about these martyrs, and was convinced they represented people who became believers after the rapture."

Nathan conceded, "Yes, I do remember those words. Well," he sighed, "we *are* living in the last days, Lisa. You and I both know, things will get a whole lot worse before they get better, from this point forward. A brief silence ensued as they both digested the truth. Then Nathan resumed, "Speaking of the last days, Lisa, your new job description is right out of the end times playbook. You are at the helm of fulfilling the cleanup described in Ezekiel 38 and 39."

Lisa nodded. "Yes, I'm aware of that. That's why I'm calling. My boss wants me to formulate a full-proof campaign that orchestrates the immigration of millions of American Jews, with their financial portfolios in hand, to Israel. We need manpower and capital to get this country back on track. I figured that your Unistate Global company could become one of Israel's most trusted American business resources. This would be the perfect way for you to become the Oskar Schindler you long to be!"

Nathan applauded, "Outstanding! UGIC has invested a lot of research and money into plans to help the coming Greater Israel. Your uncle Razz set me on this course. Besides, many American Jews probably compose a sizeable contingent of the faithful who will escape to Petra when the Antichrist attempts a final genocide."

Lisa shivered at the thought, but managed, "I knew I could count on you, Nathan. I'm going to email you contact information of key individuals within the American Jewish Congress, and about thirty other US Jewish organizations. I have to hang up for now, because Jami should be here any moment. I will instruct my secretary to get that list off to you immediately. I expect you will be received with open arms by these agencies. Be discreet about your Christianity, but always on the lookout to share the gospel."

"Lisa, you make me proud," Nathan saluted. Then, quoting the story of Esther, he proclaimed, "The Lord has lifted you up 'for such a time as this.'"

ॐॐ

It was midmorning on that Monday when Lisa peered out her window to see Jami rushing to her doorstep. It seemed forever since she had seen her. Opening the door, Lisa noticed that Tovia, Amber, Bella and Jaxon accompanied her precious teen.

"What a wonderful surprise!" Lisa enthused, exchanging embraces all around. "I didn't expect the whole family! What's the occasion?"

Amber replied, "Remember when we last spoke, I told you Tovia was out checking to see if he still had a job?"

Noting Tovia's sad expression, Lisa groaned, "Don't tell me..."

Tovia confirmed, "I'm officially unemployed, Sis."

"I'm so sorry!" Lisa sympathized.

But Jami broke in, "Wipe off those sad droopy faces, guys! This is all for the best."

"How so?" asked Lisa.

"Mother, you told Auntie Amber about uncle Razz's inheritance. You said the family could come live by us, because you have enough money for everyone! I have already promised that you and I would take Bella to the shopping mall to buy her some Barbie dolls and princess outfits."

At that introduction, Bella grabbed Lisa's hand and snuggled close, "Can we go shopping now, Auntie Lisa?" she pleaded.

Grinning from ear to ear, Lisa said, "Hold your horses, Bella! You all just got here. We need to figure out where your bedroom's going to be before we buy lots of dolls and princess outfits. But, I promise, we will go shopping real soon."

"Me, too?" pleaded young Jaxon. "I need some new toys!

Picking up her handsome little nephew, Lisa assured, "Yes, Jax, you," and kissing his smiling face, "too! When we take Bella shopping, we will take you, too! Your Auntie Lisa wants to spoil both of you. I missed you both so much."

While the adults meandered into the living room, Jami escorted her cousins to her bedroom. Sitting alongside his sister, Tovia told them that his workplace had been leveled from the initial barrage of Russian missiles. "They actually struck in the center of my work complex," he said. "The entire plaza was reduced to rubble. Suffice it to say the company is closed indefinitely."

Grabbing her brother's hand and cupping it in hers, Lisa said, "Not to worry! Jami was right: this is all for the best. I have been promoted to a senior director of the Ministry of Interior, and I will be tripling my staff immediately to accomplish the increased responsibilities I have been given."

"Do you mean...you might have a job for your dear brother?" Tovia marveled.

"Not just a job," Lisa replied. "Your supervisory skills will come in handy. We need a field person to roll up his sleeves and serve as liaison between the I.D.F. and the Ministry of Interior. We are working closely with the military to restore and beautify the country. We are implementing a worldwide campaign to encourage the return of Jews into a safer, greater Israel!"

Tovia rejoiced, "That's outstanding, Lisa! It's good to know that twenty-five years of supervising commercial construction projects can still be put to good use for our country. By the way, Amber shared Romans 8:28 with me before we left Haifa this morning. This verse teaches that all things work together for good for believers. Man-oh-man! That certainly rings true right now. This new job opportunity is music to my ears, and it will be wonderful to work alongside my sister on such an important campaign!"

After intentionally clearing her throat, Amber asked, "What about your dear sister-in-law? Do you have any part time work, or tasking that could be done from a home workstation for a former Sales and Marketing Director?

"Why only part time?" Lisa questioned.

Amber answered, "I still have to be a fulltime mom, and also I want to spend a lot of quality time with your mother, Naomi. I want her to enjoy the company of her grandkids, including Jami. As you know, this time of peace will be short, and I'm hoping to witness to her about Jesus."

Lisa thanked Amber from the bottom of her heart. "I can have my staff customize a workload for you that will fit with your schedule. Your skills will be a great asset. And, there is nothing more important to all of us than to get the rest of our family to receive Christ."

Tovia promised, "Come tomorrow morning I'll look into finding us a home nearby, so that we can all live close to each other. Fortunately, mother is not too far away either, so Amber and the kids can visit her often."

Lisa was ecstatic. "The Lord is so great!" she praised. "He works things together for our good. He has obviously united us in these difficult times to serve Him and help with the restoration of Israel."

They all fellowshipped over hot tea, while in the background from Jami's room, they could hear Bella trying to teach Jaxon the "Jesus Loves Me" song."

"Yes Jeesa wubs me," Jaxon mimicked. "Yes Jeesa wubs me, the Biba tell me so."

"That's so darn cute! Lisa laughed. "I have to get this on video."

As she grabbed her IPhone and headed down the hallway to Jami's room,

Tovia and Amber shadowed close behind, to enjoy the precious moment with her.

A Few Weeks Later...

Everything went well for Tovia's family over the next few weeks. They found a home, moved in, and Tovia began working for the Israeli Ministry of Interior. Even Nathan Severs was making inroads with the American Jewish organizations on Lisa's list. Lisa's campaign to attract Jews from the US to a "safer and greater Israel" was working, and her boss, Avi Fleishman, was ecstatic about the progress.

Surprisingly, tens of thousands of American Jews put their homes on the market, influenced by Lisa's *Aliyah* campaign. Many of them tendered job resignations, and began packing for the Promised Land.

Contributing to this overwhelming response was the fact that the Rapture and Middle East wars had adversely affected US and global stock markets. World-changing events had spiraled the American economy into a tailspin.

Further fueling the Zionistic inclination to leave the US was the fact that anti-Semitism was burgeoning in America. The Rapture had removed Pro-Israel Christian Zionists from the US population, leaving behind many Americans who now blamed Israel's for their economic hardships. Persecution of the Jews was smoldering, threatening to rise to fever pitch inside the US.

Highlighting this growing trend, a prominent Jewish historian said, *"What's occurring inside the United States of America today is reminiscent of the days leading up to the formation of the Nazi regime in Europe."*

On the flipside, the SOSC working alongside the 144,000 Jewish evangelists was proactively spreading the gospel of Jesus Christ far and wide. A harvest field of searching souls was being cultivated by a world filled with chaos, uncertainty, and supernatural events like the Rapture and the Marian apparitions.

The Rapture of the born-again believers became a witnessing tool that the SOSC and company wisely used to further the Good News. The unsolicited publicity associated with the infamous "Doomsday Conference" never subsided. In fact, millions worldwide stayed plugged into the flood of blogs streaming constantly over social networks concerning the SOSC.

A Vatican Conference Call....

"Cardinal Vitalia, I need to confer with you and Pope Romano, immediately," insisted President Vandenberg.

Receiving Vandenberg's call in the video conference room, Vitalia activated the speaker phone and greeted the EU president on the video screen. "I know, we desperately need to communicate," agreed Vitalia. "I have been warning the Pope that the world is on the brink of nuclear wars between Pakistan and India, and North and South Korea."

NOVEL

"And what has been the Pope's response?" Vandenberg asked.

" 'I need to pray to the Blessed Mother for direction,' " quoted Vitalia. "The Pope believes prayer is the solution right now. He tells me to be patient, that the Blessed Mother will work everything out in her perfect timing. He truly believes that she is about to unify all faiths, and usher in world peace. But I have been warning him that the Pakistanis and North Koreans aren't praying Hail Marys. Rather, they are dusting off their nuclear warheads!"

"Look!" Vandenberg responded, "I know how much you love Pope Vicente...we all do, But the time for prayer is over, and the hour for power has arrived. I'm certain the Blessed Mother would approve of us taking matters into our own hands under the present circumstances. There is no peace or solidarity among world faiths. The Vatican underestimated the SOSC and Jews for Jesus movements. These subversive cults are burgeoning and posing a genuine threat to the necessary cohesion between Catholicism and other world religions."

This last statement rankled the Cardinal. "*Rivaling*?" he spat. "With all due respect, dear president, let's not give them more credit than they deserve. Yes, the SOSC is getting a lot of publicity, but they are shooting themselves in the feet by claiming the Blessed Mother's appearances are part of a great satanic deception! Besides, their narrow minded dogmatic teachings are alienating many devotees of other religions and encouraging them to accept our Catholic teachings. Throughout the world, many are converting to Catholicism, and even the Israelis are calling the SOSC a fanatical group of religious zealots!"

Vandenberg quickly responded, "Yes, what about the Israelis? They are brazenly pressing for full Jewish sovereignty over Jerusalem, with the explicit intent of rebuilding their temple on its ancient site. Considering your real estate holdings in Israel, how does the Vatican feel about that? Aren't Catholics and Muslims appalled by Israeli plans to take over the holy city? The Jews will never accept your form of Christianity, and Prime Minister Kaufman made this abundantly clear to me in a recent phone conversation."

"What phone conversation?" asked Pope Romano; who had just entered the room.

"Good day, Your Holiness," Vandenberg greeted. "Prime Minister Kaufman called me yesterday in response to the threats of nuclear exchange between Pakistan and India, which I warned you was coming, and he stated that Israel would not choose sides on this war and didn't want to get drawn into this conflict. He said the Israelis were still recovering from the Arab – Israeli war, and their struggle against the Russian coalition."

Pope Romano replied, "That's understandable, but what did the Prime Minister have to say about the Catholic Church?"

"To be precise," Vandenberg answered, "Kaufman cautioned that your belief in Christ as the Messiah, your worship of Mary, partaking of the Eucharist and subscription to all the other sacraments are all forbidden in the Torah. According to recent rulings of the Chief Rabbinical Council, which is restoring Israel to historical roots dating back to Moses, your religion and theology is idolatrous. In fact, they concur with the SOSC that the apparition's messages are demonic."

Vitalia jumped up, pounded the table, and angrily blurted out, "What do you mean they agree with the SOSC? That's preposterous! They have publicly denounced the SOSC as radical fundamentalists attempting to subvert the world to their religious dogmas. They can't have it both ways!"

The Pope, who had slumped into a chair, tugged on Vitalia's robe, pulling him back to his seat. "Mr. President," he said, "Israel's push to possess all of Jerusalem is as intolerable as the false teachings of the SOSC and the 144,000 witnesses. Although the Vatican cannot intervene in the religious affairs of Israel, we forbid the Jewish State from eradicating our real estate holdings, and religious claims within Jerusalem. Since they have won their war with the Arabs, they will move swiftly to construct their temple, but we must prohibit them from restricting rightful access to our holy sites inside the Old City."

Displeased with the religious direction of the conversation, Vandenberg objected, "I didn't call to incite a holy war between Catholics and Jews. I have more pressing matters to contend with. Pakistan and India are certain to engage in a nuclear conflict very soon. North and South Korea will undoubtedly follow suit. The world at large is in a free fall, with nations coveting each other's land and resources. Global economies are dying on the vine and political leaders believe the quick fix to their financial woes is the acquisition of spoils from another nation. They want to emulate the model set by Israel that plundered surrounding Arab countries. As you know, Russia formed its coalition to capture spoils from Israel. I warned you both that more outbreaks of wars were my worst nightmare scenario, and you failed to use the Vatican network to prevent this from occurring."

Cardinal Vitalia jumped up again, raising both hands in rebuttal. "Whoa, now!" he cried. "Don't go blaming us for all the world's problems. If anything, the Catholic Church is the cure. You are familiar with the messages of the apparition. Planetary peace will come! We have this assurance from the Blessed Mother."

Vandenberg could see that Pope Romano nodded in agreement with his colleague.

These belated self-assurances agitated Vandenberg to no end, prompting him to complain, "What cure? If you had hosted Vatican Global Council by now, you might be qualified to speak about remedy. Your procrastination has allowed the SOSC to beat you to the punch, and the world has plunged back into all-out war!"

Vitalia looked at his Pope and shrugged. "See, dear Pontiff," he snapped. "I told you so."

"What is that supposed to mean?" Vandenberg asked.

Glaring at Vitalia, the Pope answered, "He doesn't mean anything by it. Look, Mr. President, we can still accomplish our mutual goals. You need us to host a unity conference, and we need you to make the Israelis promise not to infringe upon our rights in Jerusalem. You scratch our back, and we will scratch yours. Israel is concerned about restoring their economy and gathering Jews back into the nation, correct?"

Vandenberg nodded affirmatively.

"Israelis want world markets to welcome them, and not world wars to come against them, correct?" Romano asked.

Vandenberg nodded again. "Yes, I'm following you. Now get to your point."

Pope Romano clearly stated his case: "Israelis need peace and safety in order to continue their campaign of getting world Jewry to relocate to the Jewish state. The Vatican assembly can create religious unity, and encourage world peace and love, but the EU must commit to Israel's peace and security. Israelis need assurance that foreign powers have to go through western armies in order to attack the new Jewish state. What if Pakistan wins against India? Won't Israelis fret that they may become their next target? You, Mr. President, must use your position to ensure Israel that they waged their last war when the Russian coalition was defeated."

Vandenberg exclaimed, "This is precisely what I have been conveying to the EU assembly! Western militaries must unite as a global peace-keeping force, to stabilize world governments and economies. The world can no longer tolerate rogue nations attempting to war their way into weaker nations. Vast arsenals are being confiscated by dictatorial regimes, and they are meeting with little to no resistance in the process. This must be stopped immediately!"

Pope Romano concurred, "And, what better means to accomplish this than through a united EU military force? Israel toppled Arab armies, and the Russian coalition has met with its bitter defeat as well. With the stoppage of Russia's evil confederacy, most every Muslim army that has been standing in your way is removed. The hour has come for the Vatican to usher in peace, and for you to conquer any remaining aggressors standing in the way."

Vandenberg sat back, a satisfied smile on his face. "So, we are in agreement. Arrange for your great council and let me muster up military support."

Pope Romano signed off, saying, "Done. We will stay in close contact and keep you apprised of the forthcoming Vatican meeting."

Chapter 16
The Vatican Global Council Meeting

The Announcement of the Meeting

It was a momentous occasion witnessed by thousands assembled in St. Peter's Square. The throngs were experiencing a picture perfect, postcard day, as they watched the church's most elite cardinals and bishops parade into the Sistine Chapel for an emergency assembly. This special session was no ordinary conclave. Since the election of a new Pope was not on the agenda, the crowd and media could only speculate as to the nature of this mysterious meeting. All that was known was what had been provided to the press a few days earlier by Cardinal Vitalia's office.

The press release read that the Pope would convene an emergency ecclesiastical conference at the Vatican. The only reported details were the time, date, and place, and that the top ranking Catholic cardinals and bishops from around the world were required to be in attendance. This shroud of secrecy, coupled with the fact that only the most esteemed Catholic clergy were invited, caused the faithful to flock into Vatican City by the droves to see what the Pope was up to.

Once the elite group was seated inside the chapel, Cardinal Vitalia greeted them: "Welcome, my brothers! His Excellency Pope Vicente Romano has summoned you here today to discuss a world conference that is to be hosted in Vatican City next month. You represent the voice of Roman Catholicism worldwide, and for this reason the Pontiff requests your unconditional cooperation as we attempt to bring all unbelievers to the Catholic Faith through the Immaculate Heart of the Blessed Mother. As you know, this is Our Lady's wish as expressed through her miraculous appearances, both recently, and down through the ages. This was evidenced in the past when our glorious Queen in 1722 dictated to Venerable Mary of Agreda[16] what would take place in the last times. I quote, "Before the Second Coming of Christ, Mary must, more than ever, shine in mercy, might and grace in order to bring unbelievers into the Catholic Faith. The powers of Mary in the last times over demons will be very conspicuous. Mary will extend the reign of Christ over the heathens and Mohammedans, and it will be a time of great joy when Mary, as Mistress and Queen of Hearts is enthroned."[17] The time for total consecration to the Blessed Virgin Mary has now arrived, and it is your collective responsibility to serve the Queen's wishes to the best of your God-given abilities."

With this introduction, the Pope entered the chamber and took his customary seat at the head of the assembly. A reverent silence filled the room as Vitalia ceased speaking long enough for the Pontiff's entry.

Cardinal Vitalia announced, "As you are all aware, people from every world religion have been flocking to Catholic Churches in record numbers, and at an unprecedented pace. Never before throughout history has the world experienced such a spiritual phenomenon. Those desiring to become members of the Catholic Faithful are increasing by tens of thousands every day. The global appearances of the Blessed Virgin, coupled with her compelling messages, have broken down all barriers that once divided dozens of diverse faiths. The Blessed Mother has ushered in a new era, the unity of all humankind. When the world needed her most, our Lady arrived to bless our union with all other religions. The time for human disparity has ended. The message of the Blessed Mother is that we are all, including what remains of Russia, to be consecrated unto her Immaculate Heart. What the world is presently witnessing is the fulfillment of a remarkable prediction made in 1878 by Pope Pius IX, who predicted, *"We expect the Immaculate Virgin and Mother of God, Mary, through her most powerful intercession, will bring it about that our Holy Mother the Catholic Church...will gain an influence from day to day among all nations and in all places, prosper and rule from ocean to ocean, from the great stream to the ends of the earth; that she will enjoy peace and liberty...and there will then be one fold and one shepherd."*"[18]

At that pronouncement, the entire assembly, except the Pope, stood up, applauded and rejoiced. The ovation lasted nearly five minutes, until the Pontiff finally raised both hands for silence. It was as an ecstatic experience, and as the exclusive group sat down, some commented that they were certain they had felt the Blessed Mother's presence in the room.

NOVEL

An eerie silence filled the chapel as the aged Pope hunched over the microphone in front of him. Without referencing the source, he quoted:

"In our time, when day by day mankind is being drawn closer together, and the ties between different peoples are becoming stronger, the Church examines more closely her relationship to non-Christian religions. In her task of promoting unity and love among men, indeed among nations, she considers above all in this declaration what men have in common and what draws them to fellowship."[19]

Pausing, the Pope was interrupted by some murmuring amongst the assembly. Some were whispering, "I've heard these words before." Other's recognized the source and quietly shared this source with others.

Looking up at the cardinals and bishops, Pope Romano spoke: "I'm pleased that some of you recognize that I'm quoting from the Nostra Aetate of Pope Paul VI, given on October 28, 1965. In light of the mass conversions from formerly non-Christian religions that the Church is presently experiencing, these inspired words are truly fitting."

Pope Romano continued to quote Pope Paul's poignant words:

"From ancient times down to the present, there is found among various peoples a certain perception of that hidden power which hovers over the course of things and over the events of human history; at times some indeed have come to the recognition of a Supreme Being, or even of a Father. This perception and recognition penetrates their lives with a profound religious sense... Thus in Hinduism, men contemplate the divine mystery and express it through an inexhaustible abundance of myths and through searching philosophical inquiry. They seek freedom from the anguish of our human condition either through ascetical practices or profound meditation or a flight to God with love and trust. Again, Buddhism, in its various forms, realizes the radical insufficiency of this changeable world; it teaches a way by which men, in a devout and confident spirit, may be able either to acquire the state of perfect liberation, or attain, by their own efforts or through higher help, supreme illumination. Likewise, other religions found everywhere try to counter the restlessness of the human heart, each in its own manner, by proposing "ways," comprising teachings, rules of life, and sacred rites. The Catholic Church rejects nothing that is true and holy in these religions. She regards with sincere reverence those ways of conduct and of life, those precepts and teachings which, though differing in many aspects from the ones she holds and sets forth, nonetheless often reflect a ray of that Truth which enlightens all men."

Pausing again to peer into the gathering, the Pontiff was delighted to see that the entire group was listening intently to his every word. So he continued:

"The Church regards with esteem also the Muslims. They adore the one God, living and subsisting in Himself; merciful and all-powerful, the Creator of heaven and earth, who has spoken to men; they take pains to submit wholeheartedly to even His inscrutable decrees, just as Abraham, with whom the faith of Islam takes pleasure in linking itself, submitted to God. Though they do not acknowledge Jesus as God, they revere Him as a prophet. They also honor Mary, His virgin Mother; at times they even call on her with devotion. In addition, they await the day of judgment when God will render their deserts to all those who have been raised up from the dead. Finally, they value the moral life and worship God especially through prayer, almsgiving and fasting."

Ending the quote at that point, Pope Romano repeated, "Prayer, almsgiving and fasting; qualities that we can all learn from our Muslim brothers and sisters."

Observing from the gestures amongst the conclave that his mild reprimands were taken to heart, he stated his case in his own words:

"All of you have been divinely appointed for such a time as this to follow the commands of the Blessed Virgin Mary, and to receive the multitudes that she is gathering into the open arms and doors of the Catholic Church. Protestants, Hindus, Buddhists, Muslims and other religions throughout the world are blending their faiths with ours, because the Blessed Mother has captivated them all with her overwhelming grace. Her undeniable appearances and accompanying miraculous events at a number of apparition sites, have served to fill all of your churches with new members, and your treasuries with increased tithes and offerings. At a time when world economies are faltering, your churches experience the blessings of prosperity. For this much-appreciated increase, we are forever indebted to the Blessed Mother. Undoubtedly, other world religious leaders are threatened by this unprecedented turn of events."

Pausing momentarily to peer again into the attentive eyes of his audience, Pope Romano instructed,

"Therefore, the time has come for all of you, the esteemed clergy of the Catholic Church, to reach out to all religious leaders and demonstrate that Roman Catholicism embraces the commonalities of their unique faiths. Muslim clerics from Mecca, gurus from Kolkata, witch doctors from Nairobi, and every other influential spiritual leader worldwide are invited to attend the Vatican Global Council. This super summit is designed to arrest their fears, address their concerns, and answer their abundance of questions about the Blessed Virgin Mary, and her inseparable supernatural connection with the Catholic Church."

With those concluding remarks, the conclave stood in applause as Pope Romano adjourned. At the Pontiff's departure, all eyes turned back to Cardinal Vitalia, who had packages of information containing the event details distributed to everyone. The packets included a list of key names of the non-Catholic religious leaders who were invited, and the curriculum of scheduled events. Additionally, media kits with press releases were included that required each Cardinal and Bishop to see to it that the momentous occasion was announced worldwide, and that all mainstream media and social networks covered this Vatican conference.

Upon explaining the importance of the materials inside the information kits, Cardinal Vitalia updated his peers:

"The Pontiff and I have been in close contact with E.U. President Vandenberg, who agrees with us that this conference is of critical importance to catalyze world peace through the ecumenical consecration of the faiths to the Immaculate Heart of the Blessed Mother. Unquestionably, we have the full support of the European Union for this endeavor. Working in tandem with the Vatican, the EU will concurrently be introducing a move towards global governance. This comprehensive plan divides the world into ten distinct regions and takes into consideration the diverse cultural and geo-political needs of each province; including the emerging Jewish state of Israel."

With his mention of Israel, Vitalia could hear some grumbling amongst the audience. Israel's religious leadership had become increasingly vocal in their disdain toward the Catholic idolization of the Virgin Mary. Vitalia raised his hands for calm, and clarified,

"I share in your disgust over Israel's Rabbinate Council's outspoken statements condemning the apparitions of Our Lady and referring to our Catholic devotion to the Virgin Mary as idolatry. But this was to be expected of the Jews. Their rejection of our Lord Jesus Christ rendered their hearts hardened toward His Blessed Mother as well. Presently, they do not recognize her redemptory role in the Lord's divine plan. I counsel you to remember what our beloved apostle Paul wrote about this stiff-necked people centuries ago, from a prison cell right here in Rome. In the book of Romans, chapter 11, verses 25 and 26, he writes:

'For I do not desire, brethren, that you should be ignorant of this mystery, lest you should be wise in your own opinion, that blindness in part has happened to Israel until the fullness of the Gentiles has come in. And so all Israel will be saved...'"

This quote caused the preponderance of the conclave to acquiesce to Cardinal Vitalia's reasoning, which calmed the crowd and enabled him to continue:

"As the apostle forewarned, the Jews are blinded to the significance of the Catholic Church. They still don't recognize that the Catholic Church has become the

NOVEL

"Fulfillment of the Promises" that were given to the Jews by God. But even still, for yet a little while longer, the Catholic Church must be patient with Israel for the time being and allow President Vandenberg time to implement the E.U.'s plan for world peace and safety. Vandenberg has assured the Vatican that he will impress upon the Israeli government the importance of the Catholic Church in the grand scheme of the E.U.'s overall world political plan. President Vandenberg and Israeli Prime Minister Kaufmann are presently discussing a strategic seven-year plan that ensures the Jewish state certain religious, economic, military, and political protections. We cannot interfere with these E.U. efforts."

Shortly after Vitalia's exhortation, the assembly adjourned, returning to their various countries to make preparations for the upcoming Vatican super summit.

The Arrival of the Meeting

The weekend of the Vatican Global Council had finally arrived, and the streets of the ancient city of seven hills were bustling with the throngs that had poured in from the four corners of the earth. The atmosphere resonated melodically with the babbling sounds of diverse languages, and the spectacle had become the multi-cultural event of the millennia.

Spectators included nuns dressed in formal black and white habits, Buddhist monks clothed in customary orange robes, Imams draped in sleek white *dishdashas*, foreign diplomats in expensive Armani suits, Eastern Orthodox priests in well-pressed cassocks, and even gothic attired New Agers who were tattooed from top to toe.

Just outside the venue, reporters from all mainstream media gathered hoping to catch interviews with invited guests, or just maybe even a surprise showing of the Blessed Virgin Mary to supernaturally sanction the star-studded event. So many pre-summit interviews were being conducted, that many of the elitist invitees were having trouble gaining entrance through the Basilica's doors. The Swiss Guard had policed many major Vatican events before, but on this specific occasion, their typical quadrant procedures were vastly ineffective. Fortunately, a few of the newscasters were able to seclude some interviewees from the hustle and bustle, to achieve clear audible answers as to why they had come for this convention.

"I have come at the special request of the Vatican to show my support for the unity of the faiths," said a bishop from the Greek Orthodox Metropolis of San Francisco.

A respected Muslim cleric from Saudi Arabia commented, "The Blessed Mary is highly venerated within Islam, and her appearance in Mecca and elsewhere around the world have convinced me and many of my fellow Imams that the teachings of the Holy Koran can be congruent with those of the Catholic Church. We are certain that Allah is commandeering a global campaign of religious unity that will extend far and wide throughout the world."

An Egyptian Muslim leader, who was standing alongside the Saudi cleric, nodded and added, "We have come to learn about the commonalities between Islam and Catholicism. I was one of the fortunate Egyptians who, along with President Anwar Sadat, witnessed Mary apparitions in Zeitoun, between 1968 and 1971. Although I was merely a teen ager at the time, I now realize that her appearances pointed to a future time when all Muslims and Catholics would join faiths together as brothers and sisters. I have primarily come to learn more about the similarities of our respective religions, in order to break down barriers that stand between us."

The newscaster asked a nearby guru from Kolkata, India, several questions: "Why have you come to the Vatican's super summit? Don't Hindus believe there are multiple gods? Why would you come to an event that will obviously be emphasizing that there is only one God?"

The widely respected sage said;

> "We Hindus can appreciate the divinity of Jesus; this is really no big problem for us. Everyone is on the same pathway to enlightenment. Christ-consciousness is the ultimate state of bliss in Hinduism. We consider Jesus Christ to be another guru that received the "Supreme Personality of Godhead," and the Blessed Mother to be like the "Divine Mother," in our religion. Jesus achieved the highest level of god-consciousness that anyone can strive for; this is undeniable. As far as acknowledging the Blessed Virgin Mary, she is no different than Shakti, Vishnu, Durga, and all the other goddesses Hindus worship. Her apparitions have certainly

qualified her as a goddess like the others. In fact, I spent significant amounts of time with Mother Theresa when she selflessly served in my home city, and we always greeted each other with praises of the Blessed Mother together. It was something that bound us together spiritually."

The overall consensus of the many interviews was that the selected guests primarily came to learn about the commonalities of their faiths with Catholicism, and in most instances to demonstrate their support for religious tolerance among the diverse faiths. Even a delegation of Jewish Rabbis commented that they hoped the outcome would be positive for the dramatic spread of Judaism underway in Israel.

One of the Rabbis commented, "We believe it is important that the other spiritual leaders recognize that Israelis should be free to conduct their political and religious affairs in the manner that they see fit.

Not every newscaster onsite was enamored with the Vatican's super summit. One tabloid reporter, with an established reputation for being controversial, cornered a widely respected cardinal who had arrived late and was racing to get into the Basilica before the ceremonies began. Rudely pushing his microphone into the cardinal's face, the reporter questioned,

"What do you have to say to the millions of skeptics around the world who are concerned that the Catholic Church might be fabricating a religious hoax with all the Mary apparitions that is intended to indoctrinate the masses into religious dependency at a time when world events make humanity most vulnerable?"

Caught off guard by the insulting question, the cardinal frowned at the reporter and, pointing to his watch, said, "I apologize, but, I have no time for interviews. I'm running late for the summit."

But, the reporter was relentless in his pursuit for an official Vatican comment and rephrased the question more directly: "According to some, religion is the opiate of the masses, the crutch of the crippled mind. And it is an established fact that when the world grows darker, Catholics cling to their belief in the Virgin Mary. How can the world be assured that the apparitions are genuine and not some high tech holographic campaign of Catholic deception?"

Pushing back the reporter, as the cardinal headed toward the closing Basilica doors, the security guard reprimanded, "Stand back! The cardinal has already stated that he's running late and has no comment for you!"

Summit Ceremonies Commence

Inside St. Peter's Basilica, the Vatican Global Council was beginning and all the doors were officially shut to all outside spectators, and press and media sources except for Al-Jazeera TV, and the ETWN Global Catholic Television Network. Cardinal Vitalia greeted the attendees, made several brief announcements about the theme of the summit, and then began outlining the event agenda.

> "Welcome! Welcome!" he greeted the crowd. "Those assembled here truly represent the world's foremost religious leaders. Additionally, in attendance are many heads of states. All of you have been invited to the Vatican at this most crucial time in human history to share in the Catholic Church's vision of creating world peace through religious unity. Today Pope Vicente Romano will speak directly to the heart of humankind's present predicament. The pontiff will conclude by conducting the traditional mass, aided by the Catholic clergy amongst you, and you who are not Catholic will have the opportunity to remain as observers. Furthermore, over the course of the next two days you are all invited to the various workshops being presented by several of our leading cardinals and bishops. These meetings are designed to deepen your understanding of Pope Romano's benevolent plan for interfaith unity. So now, without further delay, will you all please rise to honor His Holiness Pope Vicente Romano?"

As those in the packed cathedral stood on their feet, the processional of Pope Romano began. Entering in with his usual entourage, surrounded by altar boys bearing incense, and protected by Swiss Guards, the Pontiff moved along the center aisle, waving his hand and blessing the crowd. *A capella* choirs positioned about the nave sang melodically in Latin, the sound reverberating through the mammoth building like the voices of angelic hosts, until the Pope made his breathtaking ascent to the ornate throne behind his altar.

Once the audience was seated, the Pope began delivering his message in Latin. As he spoke, his words were translated into key languages on big screens, recently installed for this special summit:

"Greetings to you all, my beloved brothers and sisters of the world. The barriers that once existed between all of our diverse cultures, languages, and faiths have been replaced by a greater calling; an irrevocable mission which we all must heed. Mankind, left to its own depraved devices, finally faces the eve of its destruction. Our continued survival necessitates that we must all become more united. Longstanding divisions over race, sexuality and religion must not continue to divide us from one another. Undeniably, the challenges facing our present time make all past problems pale in comparison. Together we stand at the final crossroads: on one side lies death and destruction; on the other exists life and liberation. We have only one reasonable choice: we must collectively tackle humanity's strife headlong together. But how? Which man or woman among us has determined the solution that resolves our numerous conflicts, the potential for nuclear war, economic collapse, plagues and pestilences which currently threaten the continuance of human life?"

Hanging on every profound utterance, the Pope's audience, both inside the Basilica and throughout the television world, sat on the edges of their seats. After a brief pause the Pontiff continued:

"The solution is self-evident, that it is impossible for any created thing to sustain itself indefinitely and function in accordance with its design apart from its eternal source of supply. The timepiece's hour hand cannot turn clockwise when the minute hand spins counter-clockwise. The sun cannot rise in the west and set in the east without fatally altering earth's stability. The moon cannot shine apart from the sun's reflection. And, humankind cannot exist without the divine guidance and blessings of their Creator!"

Pausing to peer directly into the lens of the main television camera, Pope Romano appealed to his worldwide audience:

"Wars cannot exist where love abounds, poverty cannot prosper when charity prevails, darkness hides not where the light shines forth, desperation cowers in the face of hope, and evil has no focus apart from the wickedness in the hearts of men. Many religious leaders throughout time have dogmatically declared exclusive allegiance to the Creator, and in so doing provoked the harshest hatred that humanity can experience. Muslims and Christians have warred, Shiites have killed Sunnis, Hindus have killed Muslims, Christians and Jews have massacred each other. These are history lessons that must not be repeated."

His speech was temporarily interrupted by a minor rolling tremor, lasting about twelve seconds, that was clearly felt by all in attendance. Some gripped the seat backs in front of them, while others jumped to their feet. But Pope Romano was unflinching. Reports soon surfaced outside the closed cathedral doors that a 4.8 earthquake had hit in the heart of Rome. Fortunately, only minor damage was done to a few storefront windows and no injuries were reported, but most assembled inside the Basilica drew a correlation between the quake and the warnings of the Pope.

Believing the minor tremor was a divine sign, Pope Vicente capitalized on the moment, becoming even more authoritative in his tone:

"Again, I ask, who among you can remedy the world's woes and right the course of mankind's misdirection? If there be anyone who can profess, with absolute certainty, that his or her way has the blessings of the Almighty, then please come and take my seat upon this world stage. Which of you has the Blessed Mother singled out as her anointed hand within humanity?"

With those pointed questions, the auditorium lights were instantly dimmed and footage of the apparition's previous Vatican appearance, when she had specifically acknowledged Pope Romano as her "servant," was played on all the big screens.

Dear Children, thank you for your presence here. Behold my servant, the Vicar of Christ. He will speak my words and carry out my earthly instructions.

The Blessed Mother's very words broadcast over the basilica sound system loudly and clearly, as the audience viewed her glorious image on the surrounding screens. Never before seen footage, caught on camera by the Vatican, was being shown, not only to the attendees inside the great hall, but also to the world through ETWN and Al-Jazeera. This film was especially powerful because it captured one of the rare instances that the Blessed Mother had spoken directly to the world without intermediaries. Because she spoke audibly, in her own voice, it seemed a double miracle.

This footage caught the entire event from every angle, because Pope Romano had informed Cardinal Vitalia of a premonition that an apparition might come on that eventful day. As a result, the cardinal had instructed ETWN to position its cameras at strategic locations within St. Peter's Square and surrounding elevated sites.

"Wow! What a trump card!" said EU President Vandenberg, as he watched the footage his office TV. He confided to his closest associate, watching beside him, "I had no idea the Vatican had this surprise up their sleeves. If this broadcast doesn't convince the interfaithers to coalesce with our benevolent global program, then I don't know what will!"

Chapter 17
Millions Witness
Eucharistic Miracles
from Rome

With the big screen showing the never before seen footage of the Marian apparition at the Vatican, it was clear that the full attention of everyone inside the Basilica had been captivated. "What does this all mean?" "What will the Pope expect from us now?" "Can he really unite the faiths and bring world peace?" "Where do we go from here?" These were just a few of the questions on the minds of those in attendance.

As the video ended, the lights were restored in the basilica, and the Pope declared:

> "So, as you see, beloved brothers and sisters, it is not merely my wish, but my obligation, at the personal bequest of the Blessed Mother, to unite all faiths to her Immaculate Heart. Born without sin, she lived free from sin all of her life and was assumed into heaven. I quote these words spoken in the 13th century by the esteemed St. Thomas Aquinas, '*God has entrusted the keys and treasures of Heaven to Mary*.'"[20]

Raising up his voice another decibel the pontiff continued,

> "Indeed, the Queen of Heaven, alone, holds the keys to heaven's benevolent future plan for mankind. The time has arrived for all of you, and the members of your respective religions, to submit your allegiances to her. Our Lady of Fatima, the woman clothed with the sun, has chosen this extraordinary time to reveal herself to the whole world. This is described vividly in the pages of Holy

Scripture in the twelfth chapter of the Apocalypse. Only through your submissions to the Blessed Mother can the peace the world so desperately needs be obtained. She has made the evidence abundantly clear, you have seen it with your own eyes, that the dawn of this blessed new era has arrived. The apparitions, miracles, healings and massive Catholic conversions are a testimony, along with Our Lady's supernatural intervention against Russia and its multinational armies, that the Blessed Mother is preparing the way for world peace."

Taking a momentary pause to shift his focus upon a large Muslim contingency from Mecca that had been intentionally seated in front of him, Pope Romano said,

"Long before Mohammed the prophet of Islam ever lived, St. Peter Chyrsologus, our infamous "Doctor of Homilies" from the fifth-century announced unequivocally that, *"God wills that Mary exact from His goodness peace for the earth, glory for Heaven, life for the dead, and salvation for all who are lost.""*[21]

Lifting his gaze back to the broader audience without interrupting the flow of his homily, he further stated,

"Those nations that persist in waging wars, will face the same undesirable fate as Russia. If rogue states, with their dictatorial leaders, do not cease their spread of evil, they will also be destroyed. Bloodshed and violence are at odds with the sovereign wishes of the Queen of Heaven. But you, the religious leaders of the free world, must not resort to such behavior. United we will stand strong and enable the Blessed Mother's peace to flow through us like a river of life unto the nations. I proclaim to you her sincere promise that, through the guidance of the Catholic Church, all of you can lead the people of every tribe, tongue, and nation into life, liberty, love, and the noble pursuit of world peace and to the salvation of their souls."

Standing up slowly and opening his arms to the crowd and the worldwide audience, Pope Romano issued this benediction,

"Come to her, all my brothers and sisters, come one and all into the open arms of our Blessed Mother, and be fully accepted by her true Church. Do not doubt, but believe when I say that the salvation of every soul can and must be obtained through Our Lady and her Roman Catholic Church. I quote this undeniable truth from Gregory XVI, who presided as our Pope between 1831-1846 A.D., *"It is not possible to worship God truly except in Her; all who are outside Her will not be saved."*[22] Over seven-centuries ago, one of our greatest saints of all times, St. Bonaventure, declared this truth about Our Lady when he admonished, *"No one can enter into Heaven except through Mary, as entering through a gate… He who neglects the service of the Blessed Virgin will die in his sins . . . He who does not invoke thee, O Lady, will never get to Heaven . . . Not only will those from whom Mary turns her countenance not be saved, but there will be no hope of their salvation . . . No one can be saved without the protection of Mary."*[23]

Scanning the room, the television cameras captured the faces of the faithful and the newly convinced, whose countenances clearly displayed adoration and allegiance to the Pope. This scene reinforced before the watchful world that the Pope deserved the titles of the Vicar of Christ and the Chosen One of the Blessed Virgin Mary.

Having spoken his final words, the Pontiff made his way to the altar, where the Eucharistic elements were prepared for him to distribute.

Meanwhile, Cardinal Vitalia extended an invitation to the assembly seated inside the Basilica. "You are all invited to witness the Catholic Faithful assembled among you as they partake of the Holy Mass. Although the ceremony is restricted to them alone, we would like to share this sacred observance with all of you who would like to experience how salvation occurs by the partaking of the Eucharist by our Faithful members of the Catholic Church. You are free to remain inside or depart if you prefer."

Only a handful of skeptics left the cathedral. Among the majority who remained, there appeared to be an anxious expectation that something miraculous would occur.

With the Pontiff in place at the altar, the deacon sang the traditional offering of the sign of peace.[24] The Holy Father turned to the cardinals arrayed to receive the sacrament, and offered them the ritual sign of peace, then all the Catholic people turned to each other and passed the peace among themselves. As this transpired, the big screens flashed: *We offer you the peace that the world cannot offer, but that only Christ can give.*

As the Catholics lined up for the partaking of the Eucharist, the choirs, accompanied by the mammoth pipe organ, began singing the familiar song "Lamb of God, take away the sins of the world."

Afterward, Pope Romano began the proceedings by passing out the first few elements to some of the deacons who had lined up. Alongside were about eighty priests assisting the Pontiff, due to the oversized crowd hoping to receive the Holy Communion. Shortly after the proceedings commenced, the Holy Father, with his golden chalice in hand, slowly made his way to a group of about fifty guests of honor among the faithful, who were to receive the elements of the Eucharist personally from the Pope. These included select cardinals, bishops, nuns, deacons, priests, and a few visionaries.

With his departure to the VIP area, the cameras shifted their coverage to Pope Romano's serving of the Holy Eucharist. The Mass was proceeding smoothly as planned, as both the Pope and the priests were distributing the elements in a coordinated fashion.

But curiously, while performing the Intinction[25] of dipping the wafer into the wine filled golden chalice for a respected female visionary standing before him, the Pope paused. It was as if he instinctively sensed that something mystical was about to occur. Fixing his full focus upon the communicant, the Pontiff extracted the Sacred Wafer and delicately lifted it toward her when suddenly something spectacular occurred!

The Miracle of the Eucharist...

When the consecrated element was only inches away from being inserted into her opened mouth, human blood began to exude out of the wafer and swiftly stream down the Pope's robe and drip to the floor. A few seconds into this miracle the Pope experienced a burning sensation in his hand that caused him to drop the wafer back into the chalice from whence it had been dipped. As he quickly peered down into his cup, he was astonished to see that the communion Host had altered its form into flesh.

By now all eyes and TV cameras in the hall directed their undivided attention to the Eucharistic miracle taking place with the Pope. The big screens in the Basilica were all synchronized and live streaming the supernatural events taking place.

"It's turned into flesh," the Pope enthusiastically exclaimed!

Lifting the golden goblet for all to see, he repeated, "The Holy Host has become the bloody flesh of our Lord!"

At that moment, things took a new turn as the blood in the chalice began spurting upward toward the Cathedral's ceiling causing people nearby to step back. It was as though the ceremonial vessel had tapped into a wellspring and converted into a fountain source for this life sustaining substance. To everyone's surprise, the phenomenon defied gravity as the blood did not splash back down upon the ornate marble floors. Rather, it resembled a radiant red tower of plasma.

Pope Romano ecstatically cried out, "HE IS ALIVE! HE IS RISEN!"

With these words echoing throughout the auditorium, another supernatural metamorphosis took place. The towering lifeblood transformed from red liquid into white light. It slowly began to swirl and spiral upward from the cup and sparkle like a luminescent holograph.

The scene was so surreal, a cameraman filming inside the Basilica blurted out to his TV host nearby, "This only happens in animated movies! Tell me this isn't really happening!"

The TV newscaster enthusiastically replied, "I hope you're catching this on camera. We're capturing a live miracle at the *Vatic...!*"

Before she could complete the word *Vatican*, her mouth dropped open at the sight of a semi-transparent male image floating above her. Appearing to be in his early thirties, he was levitating with his arms stretched wide open as though hanging upon a cross. His visage included a crown of thorns reflecting in the light like a halo and His face, though hard to make out, resembled the one from the Shroud of Turin.

While the Eucharistic Jesus was still suspended in mid-air, the renowned female visionary who had been deprived of her wafer began speaking aloud in Latin. Quickly a microphone was whisked over and held in front of her. Anxiously her voice bellowed throughout the auditorium asking for quiet, the Pope and priests began lifting their hands calling for calm. It wasn't long until the apparition's message was piercing through the deafening silence and being translated upon the screens all about the basilica. These powerful words were displayed,

> *"This is My body that was broken and My blood that was shed for you. They are always present in the Eucharist. I have been troubled with many doubters among you, who*

in the past, have questioned My promise to be present in every Eucharist offering. Who am I, that I would ever fail to fulfill my commitments in this Holy Communion? Am I not the Savior of the world?

There was a momentary pause in the message, which allowed the audience to take a gulp of humble pride. Then, the visionary continued channeling and speaking the Lord's message.

*"Now learn this; In this miracle of the Eucharist, you were privileged to experience My gospel supernaturally through the elements. The wafer is My body in **Death**. It became My blood that ran down My Beloved Pope's robe where it now stains the floor. Likewise, My blood still cries out from Jerusalem where I was crucified. My Vicar's hands burned as I conferred upon him the agony I felt when the nails were hammered into my hands! The blood touching the floor was my **Burial.** The transformation of My blood into the white light is My **Resurrection** and its upward reach to the cathedral ceiling is My **Ascension** into heaven. For, I Am the Resurrection! I alone hold the keys to Heaven and Hell. Redemption is in My Holy Eucharist. It is the Blessed Sacrament that cleanses you from sin and saves your soul!"*

With this interpretation of the miracle, the Pontiff raised up and displayed the chalice before the throngs. As he did, all the Catholic Faithful in attendance folded their hands and fell to their knees in reverence. Then, the audience gasped as the apparition's eyes turned into a flame of fire. The visionary ratcheted up her voice and continued.

"I know your works, love, service, faith, and your patience; and as for your works, the last are more than the first. Nevertheless, I have this against some of you in My Church. You allow the sacrilege of My Holy Eucharist to occur. You tolerate, rather than excommunicate, those among you who boldly deny My Presence in the Eucharist."

With these piercing words, the fiery eyes of the apparition became even brighter and their focus shifted noticeably to several rows filled with affluent Cardinals. The visionary's message paused momentarily in synchronization. As an eerie silence fell upon the audience, it became obvious to everyone that this portion of the message was an admonishment specifically intended for their hearing.

> "Many of My Eucharistic miracles have been proven to be real blood by the scientists. Even in the face of reality and technical proof, there are still many who do not believe in My Real Presence. This denial of My Presence is the worst of insults and a disrespect for My Gift of the Eucharist. This is why those same people, who reject My Presence, do not feel it necessary to confess their sins. Those, who teach against My Real Presence, and put down these miracles, are the real blasphemers. Those, who do not love My Blessed Sacrament, are the lukewarm that I will vomit from My mouth."[26]

Tears started flooding the faces of many Cardinals and Bishops who realized that the Eucharistic Christ was speaking directly to a problem that they were struggling with in their congregations. Some of them beseeched aloud repeatedly to the apparition, "Forgive us. Help us our Lord."

As if to acknowledge approval to their requests, the apparition returned to its original form, and as the visionary presented the Lord's final words, a feeling of peaceful bliss permeated the room.

> *"I speak to all of you here now. I have provided this miracle today so that the world will truly know Who I Am. I Am the universal truth and the Giver of eternal life! I wish for all to have Holy Communion with me. I will continue to come into this world faithfully through the petitions of My anointed priests on the appointed days of obligation, now you come devotedly to Me, all of my children. Greet Me through the doors of My "True Church," entreat Me in the extended embrace of My "Blessed Mother" and meet Me in My Holy Eucharist!"*

About twenty seconds lapsed after these final words before the image disappeared. Immediately, a kaleidoscope of emotions - fear, joy, disbelief, awe - overcame the interfaith assembly. Most of them started transmitting emails and texts to their friends, families and associates worldwide. In a matter of minutes, blogs and social networks began buzzing with posted photos and reports of the Eucharistic miracle.

It wasn't long before a stir of amazement spread outside the basilica throughout St. Peter's Square. Most everyone began praising the Blessed Mother and the Pope, but a few others seriously suspected that charlatanism had occurred. One Protestant contingent embedded in the center of the large crowd started shouting, "This is demonic! Pure idolatry! That's not Jesus!"

The people around them started calling them "heretics" and "blasphemers!" Before the Swiss Guard could get there to arrest the matter, the crowd had pounced on the Protestants dropping them to the ground. Then, they began brutally beating them to a pulp. When paramedics arrived on the scene, three were dead and the other six were rushed to the hospital in critical condition.

Meanwhile, inside the Basilica, the apparition's message remained displayed upon the big screens long after the visionary stopped speaking. The Eucharistic miracle became the top news story throughout the mainstream medias of every country. This widely publicized supernatural event served to validate Roman Catholicism as the premier world religion. It also helped to esteem the Pope as the arbiter of moral values and all spiritual truths.

Chapter 18
Two Witnesses Prepare for the Tribulational Period

I t was the Tuesday evening following the Vatican super summit event, when Lisa received an alarming message on her home answering machine.

She, along with Naomi, Jami, Amber, and little Bella, had just returned from a short girls' vacation at the recently renovated 5-Star Hilton Eilat Queen Sheba Resort. The lavish hotel, located at the northern tip of the Red Sea, had suffered severe structural damage during the Arab-Israeli war, and was having its grand reopening. Due to Lisa's prestigious position in the government, the fivesome had received the VIP treatment throughout their stay. Having just dropped everyone off at their homes, she and Jami proceeded to check their missed messages.

It was a frantic call from Nathan Severs: "Lisa, where are you? Gershom, Simeon, and I came by your house yesterday to warn you of some very troubling developments! We have all returned to Israel, and we have some critical information to share with you and your family! Please, you must call me immediately, and let me know that the two of you are safe."

Instantly, Jami locked onto her mother's arm and cried, "Oh, no, Mother! Not again! What now?"

Patting her daughter's white-knuckled hand, Lisa comforted, "We're home safe, Jami. Calm down and take a deep breath. Look, the pictures are still hung in place, the furniture's not turned upside down, and our house is still standing. It's going to be okay, honey."

Then, more seriously, she admitted, "But something is definitely troubling Uncle Nathan. Perhaps something serious happened while we were away."

Giving her mother a puzzled look, Jami asked, "Didn't you talk to Uncle Nathan about a week before we left on vacation?"

Lisa confirmed, "Yes, but he didn't say anything about coming back to Israel. In fact, when I asked when we might see him again, he said probably not for a while. He said he was making solid inroads with the Jewish organizations in the U.S. I asked him to contact, and promote the return of American Jews to Israel. I was thrilled that he was having so much success with the project, but I felt disheartened that we might not see him anytime soon."

After dead bolting the front door for extra security, the two of them sat down at the kitchen table and Jami proceeded to return Nathan's urgent call. With the speaker phone turned up to maximum volume, they could both hear it ringing repeatedly.

"Come on, Uncle Nathan! Pick up the phone, already!" Jami moaned.

Finally, after what seemed a month of Sabbaths, the girls heard his voice. "Hello, this is Nathan….."

Not realizing that it was only his recording, Jami bellowed, "Uncle Nathan, it's us! We are…."

Disappointment overtook them when they realized it was only his answering machine. Pausing, Lisa quieted herself and waited for his recorded message to play out. At the sound of the beep, Lisa started to let him know they were safe at home. She had scarcely begun leaving her message, however, when suddenly there was a loud rapping upon her front door.

Stunned, the two girls looked into each other's eyes. "What do we do, Mother?" Jami squeaked.

Lisa gingerly hung up the phone, and with a lump in her throat, softly said, "Here's what we do: you go get our two biggest butcher knives, one for each of us, while I peek through the blinds to see who's knocking down the front door."

Grabbing her mother by the arm again, Jami pleaded, "Wait a minute! Don't peek yet! Knives won't do us any good if someone has a gun!"

Shocked, Lisa swept Jami into her arms. Together they shivered, until a familiar voice beyond the door shouted, "Lisa! Jami! Are you in there? Open up! It's me, Nathan."

Instantly, they ran for the door, unlocked it and threw it open.

Standing at the threshold, Uncle Nathan said, "What took you so long? I saw your car in the driveway and heard you both talking in …"

Before he could finish, the girls held him in a group bear hug.

"You'll never know how good it is to see you!" Lisa exclaimed.

"And I missed my two favorite girls so much!" Nathan echoed. "It's great to hug you both again."

Jami pulled away and looked at him with troubled eyes. "So, what did your message mean, 'troubling developments'?"

Caressing their hands, Nathan replied, "I have some good and some bad news. According to Gershom and Simeon, Moses and Elijah have returned to earth and are in Jerusalem about to begin their three and one-half years of ministry. That's the good news!"

Squeezing his hand tightly, Jami agreed, "That's amazing! What a miracle, these are two of our famous Jewish people from the past!"

"Wait a minute," Lisa cautioned. "What's the bad news?"

"That's the 'troubling development'," he responded. "According to Revelation 11, the ministry period of these two witnesses overlaps with the first half of the dreaded 'Tribulational Period.' This means that the final seven-years of tribulation on earth must be rapidly approaching!"

"Not the 'Tribulational Period;' not already," Lisa winced, gasping for breath. "Doesn't the Bible say this is when the Antichrist attempts the final genocide of the Jews? What does that mean for us Jewish believers?"

Teary eyed, Jami pleaded, "Say it's not true Uncle Nathan, there must be a mistake. What about the Israeli national mantra, 'Yad Vashem?' Remember the holocaust is *never* to happen *again!*'"

Blotting back her tears, he said, "These were my exact sentiments to Gershom and Simeon. They warned us that the first half of the tribulation is a time for Israelis to get out of harm's way. This period provides Israel with a short time of peace. They called it a pseudo peace, because it's a false sense of security created by a seven-year treaty that doesn't last; it gets broken at the midpoint."

"*Oh my*,… the treaty…," Lisa mumbled.

"Yes mother, the treaty," Jami echoed. "Out with it, what do you know?"

Collecting herself, Lisa informed, "This treaty is already being negotiated!"

"What?... Are you sure?" Nathan asked.

"Yes," replied Lisa. "Prime Minister Kaufmann and E.U. President Vandenberg have been secretly hashing this out. I caught drift of it from my boss. He let it slip out before we took off on our girl's trip. After catching himself, he swore me to secrecy until the treaty is officially announced."

"Did Fleishman specify the seven year term?" Nathan wondered.

Lisa's eyes closed as her head nodded up and down slowly. Nathan and Jami exchanged glances when suddenly Jami shuddered, "I can't believe this is happening! We return from vacation to this shock! What's next?... How much more bad news can we endure?"

"Girls..., we have to remain calm and be smart about this," Nathan advised. "We must prepare an exit strategy to get you and Tovia's family to safety. I'm thinking we need to go back to my place in Rome."

"What?... No Nathan," Jami rebuffed. "Things are getting really creepy there with all that is happening on the news at the Vatican. Remember, we couldn't leave there fast enough last time!"

"We need to get advice from Gershom and Simeon," Jami pleaded. "They will know what we should do."

Nathan agreed. "I will arrange a meeting with Tovia's family and all of us right away."

Chapter 19

The Encounter between Satan and his Seed

Awaking abruptly to the sound of a thunderous noise, Hans Vandenberg swiftly moved to the side of his bed. Collecting his thoughts, he sensed something unusual in his spirit. "What was that startling noise," he pondered.

He began reflecting upon the dream he had been brusquely awoken from. "There must be a connection," he surmised. *Hmm...let's see. I was in a verdant valley encircled by hordes of soldiers. Oddly, they were arrayed in a wide variety of uniforms. What was that all about, and what was I doing there?*"

"*Think, Hans,*" he whispered patting his cheeks intermittently. "*Why was I there? Yes...*, a white horse, I was sitting atop a magnificent white steed. I was holding an ornate bow in my right hand and wearing a spectacular crown upon my head. When I lifted up the bow, trumpets began bellowing throughout the basin and the armies proceeded to assemble into orderly ranks. They were preparing for war."

"*What war? Come on, try hard to recall Hans,*" he continued. "They were waiting for me to lead the charge somewhere... *I'm drawing a blank... What war...? What valley...? What voice...?*"

Exacerbated, he stood up and began pacing, when suddenly the thunderous noise sounded again startling him in his tracks. The sound resonated powerfully, the house shook and his soul became increasingly restless.

Racing outside, he shouted, "What's happening? Who are you?"

His pleadings were greeted with eerie silence.

Standing in utter disbelief, a gentle breeze enveloped his body.

Something magical about its embrace soothed his spirit. He had never experienced such a sudden shift in emotions.

Turning his gaze toward heaven, his countenance changed. He sensed something surrounding him. Something unexplainable was occurring; it was blissful. He felt powerful, yet peaceful at the same time.

"Divine appointment," said the stranger. "Hans, you have been prepared for such a time as this."

Turning toward the visitor, Vandenberg became intimidated by his appearance. He was tall, towering about twelve feet high. His robe was white, his shoulder length hair was black and an aura illuminated from his visage. Hans collapsed prostrate in astonishment.

Helping him up, the foreigner smiled and said, "There's no need for that."

Dwarfed standing beside him, Hans, the consummate politician, found himself at a loss for words.

"Do you know who I am?" The mystery man asked.

Stupefied, Hans silently nodded no.

"Where I come from, I have many titles," stated the alien. "Prince of the Power of the Air, Angel of Light, god of this Age and King of the Bottomless Pit, just to name a few."

"So, do you claim to be all of the above?" Hans asked.

"I do," he acknowledged. "I claim whatever title and wear whichever crown I must to maintain my throne, which is exalted above all the stars in the universe."

"You have my undivided attention," Hans admitted. "Certainly you possess symmetry like no other, but what proof did you bring to substantiate such bold claims?"

"My thunderous sound alarms you and the stature of my presence humbles you," the newcomer humored. "Do you also seek a sign? Hmm…, let me think, what shall I show you?"

Then suddenly and without warning, Vandenberg was transported to an exceedingly high mountain. Beneath him lay all the kingdoms of the world and their splendor.

The stranger spoke, "All of these are mine! They are subservient to me and I can share them with whomever I please!"

Vandenberg pondered what it would be like to preside over these empires. "Control over economies, the environment and population growth rates. No more reliance upon the Vatican to control the masses. The cessation of diplomatic compromises with self-serving politicians.

Also, an end to negotiating with Israel's unceasing demands for land and security. Finally, the creation of a utopian society."

"What are you thinking?" asked the Angel of Light. "Are you wondering where do I sign to reign over these kingdoms?"

"What world leader in his right mind wouldn't jump at the opportunity?" Vandenberg replied.

Breathing deep, Hans thought, "This can't be real. I must be dreaming."

"Han's, you're probably thinking that this is too good to be true...; *am I right*? Why can't it be true?" the stranger asked. "Millions recently vanished unexplainably, the Russian coalition was vanquished mysteriously, and apparitions have been occurring supernaturally around the globe. The world has evolved into a place where the paranormal is now the new normal. Everything has changed. People are no longer questioning if there is a god, now they are wondering which god to serve. This is where you come in."

"Me?" asked Hans.

"Yes you," he confirmed. "Why do you think you are positioned as one of the world's most prominent politicians in this new era? Do you think it's a coincidence that the E.U. emerges, while America and Russia declines? Think hard Han's! How did you rise to power so easily and unexpectedly? Reflect upon your political career. Finances came in at crucial moments, rivals were eliminated by scandals and the enemies of your past became stricken with illness, or in some cases assassinated. Do you think this was all merely happenstance?"

"What are you saying?" Han's questioned.

"You are the work of my hands," prided the extra-terrestrial. "I have seeded the life on this planet. In ages past, I called upon my minions to make mankind in my image, and you are the cream of the crop. I have coddled you since birth to reign over my realms. The time has come to set this truth in motion."

"How have you coddled me? Where were you in my troubled childhood?" Han's probed.

"When your father beat your mother into a coma, I heard your pleadings and healed her. When your father tried to brutalize you, I prevented it by causing him to have a heart attack. When you were diagnosed with brain tumors, I made them all disappear at the same time. The doctors said it was a miracle. Indeed, it was, it was my miracle for you."

"It was you that night in the hospital, wasn't it?" Han's asked. "I couldn't see you, but I felt your presence touching my head. I knew I was healed in that instant. I felt a great peace come over me. It was like the peace I felt when you breathed upon me this morning."

"Yes, and oh how I so desperately wanted to reveal myself to you then," his companion confirmed. "But, the hour had not come."

With outstretched hand, Han's said, "This must be the hour. This is why you greeted me today and enlightened me as to who you are. Oh, how I have longed for a remedy to cure the world's madness. I put no faith in religious devotion to Mary to right the wrongs of this world. I knew at some point that a true god would have to eliminate the Vatican stronghold upon the masses, but it was politically expedient to come alongside the Pope to restore calm amidst world chaos."

Smiling, the giant said, "The apparitions, miracles and healings were implemented centuries ago to only play a temporary role in preparing the minds of the masses for the ultimate great deception that is coming. Humanity was not ready in the past for the new age about to be revealed now through you my beloved seed."

"What's next, my benevolent father?" Han's asked. "Where do we go from here? I absolutely accept your offer to reign over the realms of this world."

"My son," he said, "You will need to sideline Israel temporarily, while we establish the world into ten districts. These territories will be governed independently by the kings of your choosing. In the near future, you will confirm the seven-year agreement that you are currently negotiating with Israel. During the first half of the agreement, you will establish the ten domains. In the middle of the seven years, you will call upon the ten kings to overpower the Vatican empire, at which time you will confiscate all of its wealth and holdings. Possessing the Vatican treasures and the loyalty from the ten kings, you will become enthroned as the uncontested ruler of this world. I have spoken it, now let it come into existence!"

"Yes, my lord, but what about the Jews?" Han's questioned. "We must do something about those Jews. They will never comply with your benevolent plan for this planet. They will never abandon their Jehovah mindset."

"Every last one of them must be eliminated," said the Angel of Light. "In so doing, we will prove that their Jehovah is the lesser god, in whom no one will ever trust again!"

And so it was that Satan, the Angel of Light, convinced his point man, the Antichrist, to prepare for the new age to come! Stay tuned for Tribulation Road...

NOVEL

APOCALYPSE ROAD

Thesis

Post-Rapture/Pre-Tribulation Thesis

By Bill Salus

The topics covered in this thesis are listed below.

1. Introduction to the Post-Rapture / Pre-Tribulation Thesis

2. What Will the World Look Like Shortly After the Rapture?

3. The Revealing of the Antichrist

4. The Church is in Heaven Before the Antichrist is Revealed on Earth

5. The Revealing of the Antichrist is Being Restrained

6. The Mystery of Lawlessness and the Lawless One

7. The Antichrist's Rise to Political Power Takes Time

8. The Two Parties of the False Covenant

9. The Post-Rapture / Pre-Tribulation Timing of the Five Seals

10. First Seal: The White Horseman of the Apocalypse

11. Second Seal: The Fiery Red Horseman of the Apocalypse

12. Third Seal: The Black Horseman of the Apocalypse

13. Fourth Seal: The Pale Horsemen of the Apocalypse

14. Who are Death and Hades?

15. Is Islam the Fourth Horsemen of the Apocalypse?

16. Is Islam the Harlot World Religion?

17. Who are Death and Hades Killing?

18. Fifth Seal: The Martyrs of the Apocalypse

19. The Two Killing Crusades that Martyr Christians After the Rapture

20. How Do the Fifth Seal Saints Get Saved?

21. The Three Periods of Post Rapture Christian Martyrdom

22. Why is the Roman Catholic Church Cast into the Great Tribulation?

23. How Will God Kill the Children of Thyatira?

24. The Main Obsessions of the Blessed Mother

25. Satan's Plan to Influence Mankind Through the Harlot

26. Salvation Comes Through the Roman Catholic Church

27. The False Covenant of Death in Agreement with Sheol

28. What is the True Content of the False Covenant?

29. The Two Deadly Phases of the Overflowing Scourge

30. Phase One of the Overflowing Scourge – Isaiah 28:15

31. Phase Two of the Overflowing Scourge – Isaiah 28:18

32. Summary of the Two Phased Overflowing Scourge

THESIS

Introduction to the Post-Rapture / Pre-Tribulation Thesis

This thesis is based upon the major premise that a gap of time exists between the Pre-Tribulation Rapture and the seven-year Tribulational Period (Trib-period). The minor premise is that it is not the Rapture, but the confirmation of a covenant by the Antichrist between Israel and some other party that triggers the ticking of the Trib-period. This covenant is identified primarily in Daniel 9:27 and Isaiah 28:15 and 18.

This dissertation is an integral part of the book entitled, "*Apocalypse Road, Revelation for the Final Generation.*" Together, the book and this treatise attempt to accomplish the following;

1. List and chronologically order the potential prophecies that fit into the Post-Rapture / Pre-Trib gap period, which is also referred to in this book and thesis as the "*gap period.*"

2. Determine how long the gap period could be from the clues provided in the prophecies that find fulfillment within this vastly overlooked period.

3.   Set the world stage as it transitions from the Church age, which concludes with the Rapture, into the gap period that follows.

4.   Explore the details, timing and purpose of the Gog of Magog prophecy of Ezekiel 38 and 39, in addition to;

    a. Discover the location of the Valley of Hamon Gog as the burial grounds of the hordes of Gog, (Ezek. 39:11-16),

    b. Reveal the potential connection between the Marian apparitions and Ezekiel 38 (Refer to the appendix called, *The Marian Apparitions Connection with Ezekiel 38*).

5.   Explain why the first five seals of Revelation 6:1-11 probably start during the gap period, but conclude during the Trib-period. This includes;

    a. Introduce the Antichrist as the white horseman of the Apocalypse, (Rev. 6:1-2),

    b. Examine the wars that plague the planet through the fiery red horseman of the Apocalypse, (Rev. 6:3-4),

    c. Warn about the wide scale famines, pestilences, and economic upheavals that occur during the ride of the black horseman of the Apocalypse, (Rev. 6:5-6),

    d. Put a face on the fourth horsemen of Death and Hades of the Apocalypse, (Rev. 6:7-8),

    e. Reveal the identities of the three primary groups of martyred believers after the Rapture, which are the fifth seal saints, their fellow servants and their brethren, (Rev. 6:11).

6.   Identify Roman Catholicism as "Mystery, Babylon The Great, The Mother Of Harlots And Abominations Of The Earth" of Revelation 17:5.

7.   Determine who the two parties are to the seven-year covenant that starts the Trib-period.

8.   Define the *true content* on what is commonly called the *false covenant* of Daniel 9:27, as it pertains to the "overflowing scourge," of Isaiah 28:15 and 18.

9.   Reveal the Lord's hidden message to the 144,000 Witnesses in Revelation 7:1-8.

10. Identify the Two Witnesses of Revelation 11:3-13, and demonstrate how they serve as God's rebuttal to the false covenant.

11. *Most importantly*, the sincerest goal of this timely and unique work is to forewarn and prepare EVERYONE for the SOON ARRIVAL of this treacherous Post-Rapture / Pre-trib gap period!

Many readers will get Raptured as true believers of Jesus Christ before this gap period commences. The good news is that they will not personally face the frightening events that are forthcoming in the gap period. The bad news is that someone they love will!

This work has been specifically designed to stimulate the mind and pulsate the heart of believers, and to invigorate their love for the lost. Careful consideration in that regard has gone into the overall content of this entire composition. If you are concerned about the eternal destiny of an unsaved loved one, then consider *Apocalypse Road* as your invaluable guidebook for these last days. The biblically supported scenarios within this book will embolden you to share the good news about Jesus Christ with the ones you love.

Important Caveats

First, Apocalypse Road contains controversial subject matter. Therefore, DON'T TAKE MY WORD FOR IT, rather do these three things: *First*, read the Bible to ascertain the pertinent details of the prophecies presented in this book; *Second*, read this entire book; *Third*, after reading this book, then read the commentaries of those who disagree with my conclusions to see if their arguments make more sense.

Second, it is important to read this entire book because the scenarios presented within the novel storyline are based upon the conclusions that are explained in this thesis and in the Companion's Commentary. These determinations have been arrived at from uncovering one prophetic principle at a time. Precept upon precept, line upon line, as Isaiah 28:10 alludes to, is how this book was written. The process is likened to the completion of a complex puzzle one piece at a time.

Third, some of the text in this thesis is repeated in various parts of this book. This links the thesis with the related content covered in that

THESIS

chapter. This book attempts to chronologically order forthcoming events, which makes it difficult to confine the explanations of each prophetic topic solely in its own section of commentary.

Lastly, this thesis section presents the most complex text within the entire book. If you are unfamiliar with some of the prophetic topics, please don't let that discourage you from reading the rest of the book. A cover to cover reading should adequately familiarize you with these critically important Bible prophecies.

What Will the World Look Like Shortly After the Rapture?

After the Rapture, humankind will enter a new era. The paranormal will become the new normal, the supernatural will swiftly seem more natural, and what was once considered futuristic rapidly becomes very realistic. This is because the Rapture is a miraculous event and Satan immediately follows it up with powerful lying signs and wonders.

The worldwide disappearances of millions of believers will likely warrant more than a simple scientific explanation. The spiritual and prophetic implications surrounding the event will necessitate a religious response. Satan realizes this and, after the Rapture, he has a campaign filled with supernatural surprises ready to be promptly put in place. According to 2 Thessalonians 2:6-7, nothing after the Rapture will hinder the double religious jeopardy that the Devil has prepared to deceive mankind.

First, the Harlot world religion of Revelation 17 will surface and after it has overextended its usefulness, it becomes desolated by ten kings in Revelation 17:16. This appears to happen at the mid-point of the Trib-period, which means that the reign of this false global religion likely begins during the gap period, but concludes in the middle of the Trib-period. When the Harlot is dethroned, the Antichrist becomes fully enthroned. He hails over the second global system described in Revelation 13. Satan has devised a one-two punch that people left behind won't expect, but many sadly will accept.

In the immediate aftermath of the Rapture, the world will become increasing unruly as lawlessness is predicted to increase. Wars occur as world peace departs as per the opening of the second seal in Revelation 6:3-4. These catastrophic global conditions facilitate the emergence of the "Lawless One," which is another title of the Antichrist. His introduction into the world theater is among the first order of events to occur after the Rapture. This crazed world leader is the White Horseman of the Apocalypse described in the first seal in Rev. 6:1-2.

All the things described in above paragraph closely parallel the predicted events in 2 Thessalonians.

> Do you not remember that when I was still with you I told you these things? And now you know what is restraining, that he may be revealed in his own time. For the mystery of lawlessness is already at work; only He who now restrains (*lawlessness*) *will do so* until He is taken out of the way. And then the lawless one (*Antichrist*) will be revealed, whom the Lord (*Jesus Christ*) will consume with the breath of His mouth and destroy with the brightness of His coming. The coming of the *lawless one* is according to the working of Satan, with all power, signs, and lying wonders, and with all unrighteous deception among those who perish, because they did not receive the love of the truth, that they might be saved. (2 Thessalonians 2:5-10; emphasis added)

Summary: The World Shortly After the Rapture

With the disappearances of believers, the world clock nears midnight. Ancient biblical prophecies, which were intended to be fulfilled in the last days, will begin to roll off their parchments and pound onto the pavement in relatively rapid succession. Each one has the potential to pack a more powerful punch that the one that preceded it.

Many people who were left behind will wonder where the believers went. As they attempt to return to their normal lives, a paranormal reality promises them an uncertain future. Global chaos will be mounting, which will necessitate the formation of a world government to restore international order. The stage will be set for Satan to send his point man, the Antichrist, into the world theater, and that's exactly what he does!

The Revealing of the Antichrist

One of the first things that happens after the Rapture is the revealing of the Antichrist. The consensus among many Bible prophecy experts is that he shows up with the opening of the first seal.

THESIS

Now I saw when the Lamb opened one of the seals; and I heard one of the four living creatures saying with a voice like thunder, "Come and see." And I looked, and behold, a white horse. He who sat on it had a bow; and a crown was given to him, and he went out conquering and to conquer. (Revelation 6:1-2)

There are at least two important questions to ask and address concerning this event.

1. Question: *When is the first seal opened?*
   Answer: Probably in the early stages of the Post-Rapture / Pre-trib gap period.
2. Question: *Does the Trib-period begin when the first seal is opened?*
   Answer: Probably not.

This section explains why the opening of the first seal probably happens in the gap period and does not likely trigger the start of the seven-year Trib-period. These conclusions are supported by the following reasons.

First, the church is pictured in heaven before the first seal is opened, which means that the Rapture has previously occurred. *Second,* the Antichrist's rise to political power takes time. *Third,* the other party to the false covenant of Daniel 9:27 factors into prophecy after the first seal has already been opened. The Trib-period doesn't commence until after this covenant is made between Israel and another party. The role of the Antichrist in this scenario is to confirm this covenant between the two parties.

The Church is in Heaven Before the Antichrist is Revealed on Earth

The Christian Church is residing in heaven before the tribulation period commences. This conclusion is supported by understanding the chronological ordering of chapters two through six in the book of Revelation. Revelation 2 and 3 describe the Church on earth while Revelation 4 and 5 pictures the Church residing in heaven. Revelation 6 introduces the earthly events that occur after the Christian Church has been removed from the earth via the Rapture. The prophecies in Revelation 6 segue into the Trib-period. The details of this ordering are explained below.

Revelation 2 and 3 contain the seven letters to the seven Churches. These letters had multiple applications at the time of their issuance. First, they provided important individualized information for the seven specific Churches that they were addressed to. Second, these letters detailed the distinguishing characteristics that would exist at any given time within various Churches throughout the Church age. Third, they outlined the prophetic future of the Church age. These two chapters portrayed the Church during its existence on earth during the Church age from its inception until its completion. More information on this topic is provided in the Appendix entitled, *"The Seven Letters to the Churches."*

After the Church age is completed, meaning once it is removed from the earth, Revelation 4 begins with the Greek words *"meta tauta,"* which means *"after these things,"* and pictures the Church being raptured into heaven. In other words, after these things pertaining to the Church on earth, it is caught up to heaven in Revelation 4 and 5.

> "After these things (meta tauta) I (the apostle John) looked, and behold, a door standing open in heaven. And the first voice which I heard was like a trumpet speaking with me, saying, "Come up here, [representing the rapture] and I will show you things which must take place after this." (Revelation 4:1, NKJV; emphasis added).

It is commonly taught that the twenty-four elders, who are identified several times in Revelation 4 and 5, represent the Church in heaven. Revelation 5:9 informs that these elders are redeemed by the blood of Christ. Only true believers are qualified to make such a salvation claim. Moreover, these redeemed are *"out of every tribe and tongue and people and nation."* This is an acknowledgement that the twenty-four elders represent the believers saved throughout the world during the Church age.

Quoted below, is how noted Bible prophecy scholar Dr. Arnold Fruchtenbaum interprets the identity of the twenty-four elders

> *"While the text does not clearly state as to what these twenty-four elders refer, there are clues in the text by which their identity can be deduced. First, these elders are clothed with white garments, which throughout the Revelation are symbols of salvation. Celestial beings before the throne of God do not need salvation for they were not lost to begin with. But these elders were at one*

time lost and at some point received salvation as is seen by their wearing of the white garments. The second clue is the fact that they are wearing crowns. These crowns are not diadem crowns worn by those who are royal by nature, which would have been the case had these been celestial beings. These crowns are the stephanos crowns, the crowns of an overcomer; the type of crown given as rewards to the members of the church at the Judgment Seat of Christ. A third clue lies in their very title of elders. Nowhere else in Scripture is this term used to describe celestial or angelic beings. This term is used of humans in positions of authority either in the synagogue or church. Hence, from these three clues, the twenty-four elders must represent the church saints. If this is true, then they provide further evidence for a pre-tribulation Rapture. The church is already in heaven in chapter four and five before the tribulation begins in chapter six."[27]

Sometime after the Church gets caught up into heaven, the events described in Revelation 5 commence. One very significant event that the twenty-four elders witness is the opening of the heavenly scroll by Jesus Christ. This scroll contains the seven seal judgments. The first seal judgment, which is described in Revelation 6:1-2, introduces the Antichrist upon the earth. As per Daniel 9:27, the Antichrist confirms a covenant with Israel for seven years. It is commonly taught that the ratification and implementation of this covenant becomes the starting point of the seven years of the tribulation period.

Therefore, it can be concluded that only when the Church resides in heaven, can it watch Christ open the scroll that contains the seven seal judgments. Until these seal judgments are opened, the Antichrist can't emerge upon the world scene and confirm the seven-year covenant with Israel. As long as the covenant can't be confirmed, the tribulation period can't commence. Simply stated, the Antichrist won't be revealed and the tribulation period can't begin until sometime after the Christian Church has been raptured into heaven.

The Revealing of the Antichrist is Being Restrained

2 Thessalonians 2:5-10, which was previously quoted, pointed out that the "lawless one" can't be revealed until the restrainer is removed.

> For the mystery of lawlessness is already at work; only He (*the one presently restraining lawlessness*) who now restrains *will do so* until He is taken out of the way. And then the lawless one (*the Antichrist*) will be revealed, whom the Lord (*Jesus Christ*) will consume with the breath of His mouth and destroy with the brightness of His (*second*) coming. (2 Thess. 2:7-8; emphasis added)

Some Bible teachers, myself included, correlate the timing of the Rapture with the removal of the restrainer. 2 Thessalonians 2 appears to inform that the Church is Raptured, the restraint of lawlessness is removed, and promptly afterward the Antichrist is revealed. The timing of these events chronologically coincides with the timing of Revelation 4, (the Rapture), Revelation 5, (the presentation of the heavenly scroll) and Revelation 6, (the opening of the seals and the revealing of the Antichrist).

The Mystery of Lawlessness and the Lawless One

There are at least three mysteries exposed in the New Testament that find a Pre-trib fulfillment. One of them happens before the gap period and the other two appear to begin in the gap period. They are the Mysteries of the Rapture, (1 Corinthians 15:51), Lawlessness, (2 Thess. 2:7), and Babylon, (Revelation 17:5, 7). Once the Rapture becomes a reality, the stage is set for the fulfillment of the other two. The "mystery of lawlessness" is presented here because it is relevant to the timing of the revealing of the lawless one.

The Greek word for mystery is *"musterion,"* and it is translated as a mystery or secret doctrine.[28] Lawlessness, also translated as iniquity in some translations, is the Greek word, *"anomia."* It is used 13 times in the New Testament. It is defined as sin in 1 John 3:4. However, the fact that lawlessness is sin is not a mystery. So, the question arises; why did the apostle Paul label lawlessness as a mystery?

The common interpretation of a biblical mystery is that it is something that was not disclosed in the Old Testament, but is now exposed in the New Testament. A mystery in this case is information that is solely privy to God until He makes it known to the public, mostly through the Holy Scriptures. Some mysteries deal with future events. Once the future episode finds fulfillment, it becomes a reality and ceases to be a mystery. It becomes an actuality to the generation that witnesses its fulfillment.

For instance, once the Rapture happens, it can no longer be classified as a mystery because it has become a historical fact.

A summary of what lawlessness is, as per its thirteen usages in the New Testament, is provided below.

Lawlessness is the opposite of righteousness, (2 Corinthians 6:14). It is an integral part of Satan's end time scheme, (2 Thess. 2:1-10). It characterized the condition of the scribes and Pharisees at the time of the first coming of Christ, (Matthew 23: 27-28). Similarly, it becomes implanted into the Kingdom of God prior to the second coming of Christ. Like tares adversely affect the wheat during harvest time, Satan uses lawlessness as a stumbling block to harm the people of God in the last days, (Matt. 13:36-43). When lawlessness goes unrestrained in the end times, it metastasizes into its most cancerous condition, causing the love of many throughout the world to grow cold, (Matt. 24:12). It's only cure is forgiveness through Jesus Christ, (Romans 4:7, Hebrews 10:17).

Lawlessness is so bad that it must be restrained, for the overall good of the Church while it exists upon the earth. The Church is not appointed to experience lawlessness when it spreads throughout the world without further hindrance, and that's why it is Raptured out beforehand. As per 1 Thess. 5:9, the Church is likewise not appointed to the wrath of God, however lawlessness is not poured out by God, rather it is unleashed according to the working of Satan, with all power, signs, and lying wonders, and with all unrighteous deception among those who perish, (2 Thess. 2:9-10; abbreviated).

A lawless world provides the ideal environment through which the seed of Satan can incubate. The seed of Satan is another name for the Antichrist used in Genesis 3:15. Therefore, the lawless one is introduced into the end times equation in the immediate aftermath of the removal of the restraint of lawlessness. With the opening of the first 5 seal judgments, lawlessness no longer remains a mystery, but becomes a global reality. The breakdown goes as follows;

1. The Lawless one is revealed with the opening of the first seal, which evidences that lawlessness is no longer restrained, but is dispersing rapidly throughout the world,

2. This unhindered spread of evil disrupts world peace, giving rise to war(s) as per the second seal,

3. Impoverished conditions plague the planet because of the first two seals, during the third seal,

4.   A global government, which is made up of an unholy Church and State alliance, forms to remedy the dire situation in the fourth seal,

5.   True believers get martyred for their Christian testimonies by the world government, which is perpetrating lawlessness and suppressing the truth about Christ. God allows these believers to die for their faith, because He is no longer restraining lawlessness, like He did during the Church Age. In Revelation 6:11, 13:10 and 14:12, Jesus instructs His Post-Rapture followers to be patient until He physically returns in His second coming.

The Antichrist's Rise to Political Power Takes Time

One of the reasons that the seven-year Trib-period probably doesn't start immediately with the opening of the first seal, is because the Antichrist accomplishes his threefold career in two stages. This topic is covered in the chapter called, "The Encounter between Satan and his Seed." Below is a quote from that chapter.

> "The Antichrist rises to political prominence, military power and religious dominance through a process of two stages. The two stages are apparent in these verses (Rev. 6:1-2) by the usage of the words "conquering and to conquer.""

The dual usage of the word conquer implies that the Antichrist embarks upon a process, which eventually over an unspecified time-period, leads him to his desired destination of becoming the world's political and religious leader.

This conclusion is further supported by Revelation 17:3, 7, which predicts that an unholy alliance will be made between the Harlot world religion and the Antichrist. These verses denote that the Antichrist allows the Harlot to "sit" on him, while he "carries" her to the heights of her position of becoming the predominate world religion. The Antichrist plays a subservient role to the Harlot, until he is ready to exert his dominance over the world. The relationship between the Harlot and the Antichrist is covered in greater detail in several different sections of commentary within this book.

As the Antichrist ascends to the heights of his political career, at some point along the way he earns the respect of Israel and the other party to the false covenant. They entrust him with the important responsibility of "confirming" the covenant between them. It is not until then, that the seven-years of tribulation begins.

The Two Parties of the False Covenant

> "Then he (the Antichrist) shall confirm a covenant with many for one week; (consisting of seven years) But in the middle of the week He shall bring an end to sacrifice and offering. And on the wing of abominations shall be one who makes desolate, Even until the consummation, which is determined, Is poured out on the desolate." (Daniel 9:27; emphasis added)

> "Bill, you can't confirm a dentist appointment unless one has already been made. Similarly, the Antichrist can't confirm a seven-year covenant, unless one already exists."

This is a direct quote from a conversation I had with Bible prophecy expert Jack Kinsella. Jack has since passed on to be with the Lord in March of 2013, but a couple years prior he and I were filming interviews with Jonathan Bernis for the Jewish Voice television show. After the TV shoots, Jack and I had a discussion in my hotel room about the Antichrist's prophesied role in relationship to the false covenant that triggers the Trib-period. That was when Jack made this profound statement to me.

I mention this here to emphasize the important point that the Antichrist merely confirms the false covenant. He may draft up the text of the document and he may even be a party to the treaty, but all the Bible tells us for certain is that he confirms it. This means that something is taking place in the world just prior to the drafting of this document that troubles the Jewish state and warrants Israel's participation in this infamous covenant.

I stated, *"troubles the Jewish state,"* because of what Isaiah says about this covenant. The prophet informs that Israel is concerned about an overflowing scourge that is raging within the world, which has the potential of being harmful to the Jewish state. This concern motivates them to covenant with the party that is perpetrating this overflowing scourge.

"Because you (Israel) have said, "We have made a covenant with death, And with Sheol we are in agreement. When the overflowing scourge passes through, It will not come to us, For we have made lies our refuge, And under falsehood we have hidden ourselves."" (Isaiah 28:15; emphasis added)

What the overflowing scourge might be, when it will occur and who death and Sheol represents, will be discussed later in this thesis. It is simply introduced here to bring to the reader's attention, that until this scourge sweeps through the world, there is no need for the covenant of Daniel 9:27 to exist.

This is important because all parties to the covenant, Israel, the Antichrist, and death and Sheol, must be present in the world theater prior to the commencement of the Trib-period. When will these parties all be in place? Israel is now and the Antichrist will be swiftly after the Rapture, but when does death and Sheol arrive to implement its scourge campaign? Shortly, I will explain why death and Sheol seem to arrive as the fourth horsemen of the apocalypse. If this is the case, then the false covenant does not get confirmed when the first seal is opened.

Summary About the Timing of the Antichrist's Arrival

The Antichrist will be the first horsemen out of the starting gates after the Rapture. Satan will inject his point man, the Lawless One, onto the world stage the instant he is no longer restrained from doing so. This inserts his time of entry onto the prophetic timeline during the Post-Rapture / Pre-trib gap period.

Introducing the Antichrist into the global theater as a first order of events is important for Satan because his well calculated plan to perpetrate widespread lawlessness, via deceptive supernatural means, facilitates the Antichrist's ability to become a conqueror. As the choice mediator of the false covenant between Israel, and death and Sheol, the Antichrist must ascend to his position of political prominence without much delay.

Meanwhile as the Antichrist waits to confirm the false covenant, he forms an unholy Church and State alliance with the Harlot. This marriage of convenience becomes politically expedient for him and his Harlot companion. As I point out shortly, the Harlot may be the other covenanting party.

The Post-Rapture / Pre-Trib Timing
of the First Five Seals

There are no shortages of biblical commentaries that place the timing of the seven seal judgments within the Trib-period. Traditional teachings tend to group most of them together within the first half of this seven-year period. Although I believe the seven seals conclude within the Trib-period, it is possible the first five seals are opened prior, during the Post-Rapture / Pre-trib gap period. This following section will explore the details of the first five seal judgments to uncover the clues about their timing.

First Seal: The White Horseman of the Apocalypse

Now I saw when the Lamb opened one of the seals; and I heard one of the four living creatures saying with a voice like thunder, "Come and see." And I looked, and behold, a white horse. He who sat on it had a bow; and a crown was given to him, and he went out conquering and to conquer. (Revelation 6:1-2)

The White Horseman is commonly taught to be the Antichrist. Since he is the subject of commentary elsewhere within the book, not much about him will be discussed here, other than to note the important things below;

1. *With the introduction of this Lawless One, lawlessness is no longer being restrained.*
   2 Thessalonians 2 informs that until the Rapture happens, the Lord protects His believers on earth by hindering the devastating effects of three things. *First*, is Lawlessness, *Second*, is the Lawless One and *Third*, is strong Satanic deception that is empowered through supernatural signs and lying wonders. The fact that the Antichrist is introduced with the opening of the first seal, means that God is no longer hindering these three things.

2. *One of the required parties involved with the finalization of the false covenant of Isaiah 28:15, 18 and Daniel 9:27 exists on earth.* The false covenant, which initiates the Trib-period upon its finalization, involves at least three parties. The *confirmer*, who is

the Antichrist and the *covenanters*, who are Israel and whoever Death and Hades represents. With the opening of the first seal, at least two of these parties exist on earth. They are Israel and the Antichrist. However, the third party appears to surface subsequently.

3. *The false covenant of Daniel 9:27 can now be confirmed.*
   The political figure that confirms the false covenant between Israel and the other party is the Antichrist. Now that the White Horseman is revealed, the covenant can be confirmed. This doesn't mean the covenant necessarily exists yet, rather it simply implies that from this point forward, when it does exist, it can be confirmed.

4. *The Harlot world religion can form an alliance with the Antichrist.*
   Revelation 17 discloses that the Harlot world religion marries up with the Antichrist in a Church and State union. Once the Antichrist exists on earth, the wedding invitations can go out and this marriage can be consummated.

Second Seal: The Fiery Red Horseman of the Apocalypse

When He opened the second seal, I heard the second living creature saying, "Come and see." Another horse, fiery red, went out. And it was granted to the one who sat on it to take peace from the earth, and that *people* should kill one another; and there was given to him a great sword. (Revelation 6:3-4)

These verses are relatively self-explanatory. The Fiery Red Horseman represents the unavoidable inevitability that when lawlessness spreads without hindrance throughout the world, peace becomes illusive, world wars occur and global chaos results. In biblical typology, *a great sword* alludes *to great war(s).* If the prophetic Middle East wars of Psalm 83 and Ezekiel 38 have not happened prior, they could find fulfillment at this point.

Psalm 83 and Ezekiel 38 are two different prophecies. They both deal with major Middle East Wars. In the commentary of the chapter entitled, "The European Union Consoles Israel," I explain why Psalm 83 precedes

Ezekiel 38, and in the commentary of the chapter called, "Rabbis Warn of the Future Russian Invasion," I provide reasons why Ezekiel 38 happens before the Trib-period. Thus, these two conflicts conclude prior to the Trib-period.

These epic wars waged against Israel involve mostly Muslim countries. Israel's victories in both biblical battles will have a devastating effect on Islam! Presently, there are an estimated 1.6 billion Muslims in the world. Approximately 500 million of them are involved in the wars of Psalm 83 and Ezekiel 38. These are only estimated numbers and not all 500 million Muslims will be killed when these Islamic nations are defeated. However, the important point is that Muslims worldwide will justifiably become concerned about the future of their religion.

In the aftermath of these two prophetic wars it is likely that Islam will begin to decline in numbers and in popularity. Many Muslims will begin to question their faith, especially if Satan begins to prop up Roman Catholicism as the Harlot world religion through supernatural signs and lying wonders, which is the position presented within this book.

I mention this to rebut the relatively new prophetic teachings below, which I believe to be erroneous. In my opinion;

1. Islam WILL NOT be the Harlot world religion, (Mystery Babylon), of Revelation 17,

2. The Antichrist WILL NOT be a Muslim,

3. The false covenant of Daniel 9:27 WILL NOT involve Islam.

Third Seal: The Black Horseman of the Apocalypse

> When He opened the third seal, I heard the third living creature say, "Come and see." So I looked, and behold, a black horse, and he who sat on it had a pair of scales in his hand. And I heard a voice in the midst of the four living creatures saying, "A quart of wheat for a denarius, and three quarts of barley for a denarius; and do not harm the oil and the wine." (Revelation 6:5-6)

The introduction of the Black Horseman signifies that the darkest of times have fallen upon the earth. When great wars happen, severe suffering results. Famines occur as plagues and pestilences spread uncontrollably throughout the warzones. This creates a humanitarian crisis as refugees' surface and become stranded in the affected areas.

THESIS

The fact that the prior horseman wielded a great sword, implies that the global consequences of the second seal wars were catastrophic.

The third seal imposes the enormous burden upon the international community to resolve the disastrous dilemma before it burgeons out of control. It encourages the expeditious formation of a global government to deal with the escalating emergencies, like world starvation and disease control.

Presently, The Office for the Coordination of Humanitarian Affairs, (OCHA), and The Central Emergency Response Fund, (CERF), are among the United Nations agencies in place to deal with international emergencies. Perhaps they will be the organizations called upon to bring relief to the refugees.

Whatever international agency takes responsibility for administering aid to the afflicted, the Black Horseman instructs them to ration the world's food supplies. The price tag for the necessary food staples to survive becomes fixed at two days wages. A denarius was the equivalent of a day's wage when this prophecy was written. One denarius will put a quart of wheat inside a family's gallon and another denarius will fill the remainder of their container with three quarts of barley.

The third seal paints a grave picture for the poor, but it's not as distressing for the rich. The horseman concludes his instructions with the command, *"do not harm the oil and the wine."* This alludes to the luxury items that only the rich will be able to afford. In other words, in the process of rationing the food, do not harm the economic engine that drives the financial recovery, which sustains the existence of the global government.

Fourth Seal: The Pale Horsemen of the Apocalypse

> When He opened the fourth seal, I heard the voice of the fourth living creature saying, "Come and see." So I looked, and behold, a pale horse. And the name of him who sat on it was Death, and Hades followed with him. And power was given to them over a fourth of the earth, to kill with sword, with hunger, with death, and by the beasts of the earth. (Revelation 6:7-8)

As the seals progress in their chronological order, things go from bad to worse as the world welcomes in the Pale Horsemen of the Apocalypse. I say horsemen, rather than horseman, because unlike its three predecessors the Pale horse has two riders. This sinister tag team rides side saddle in their natural order, Death followed by Hades. Death deals with the material departure of a being from its body and Hades is concerned with the immaterial aspect of a person after death, which is their soul. Presently, when someone dies their soul is delivered to its destination, which is either Heaven if they're saved or Hades if they're not.

Whoever, or whatever their manifestations represent, this diabolical duo possesses power and authority over a quarter of the world's population to kill people via multiple means. Unlike the second horseman who only had a great sword in his sheath, Death and Hades have a lethal arsenal that enables them *to kill with sword, with hunger, with death, and by the beasts of the earth.*

The traditional teaching is that Death and Hades kill a fourth of mankind, but that's not necessarily what's being said here. Compare the differences in language between the fourth seal and the sixth trumpet in the book of Revelation.

> "By these three *plagues (of the sixth trumpet)* a third of mankind was killed—by the fire and the smoke and the brimstone which came out of their mouths." (Rev. 9:18 NKJV; emphasis added)

This above verse clearly states that *a third of mankind was killed* by the three plagues that followed the sounding of the sixth trumpet. However, Revelation 6:8 says that, "And *power* was given to them *over a fourth of the earth*, *to kill* with sword, with hunger, with death, and by the beasts of the earth."

It may mean that Death and Hades kill a fourth of the earth's population, but more than likely it implies that a quarter of the world's population are faithful followers of Death and Hades. These are devotees so committed to their cause that they are willing to kill their opposition. The fact that Hades takes a lead role in this massive operation infers that this involves a global religious crusade. This future scenario appears to be reminiscent of the historical inquisition periods when Roman Catholicism was martyring the so-called Protestant heretics centuries ago.

Who are Death and Hades?

Hades, which is translated as *Hell* in the King James Version, is the Greek equivalent for the Hebrew word *Sheol*. Hades is the abode of departed souls or spirits. Death and Hades appear together five times in the New Testament Scriptures. Below is a summary interpretation of their usages.

Death is likened to a lethal sting that kills its victim. If the deceased is an unsaved soul, the being goes to *Hades, who* in turn claims victory over that persons departed spirit, (1 Corinthians 15:55). In other words, Death detaches the soul from its body and then Hades imprisons it.

Christ, having His soul depart from His body after being stung by the death of His crucifixion, conquered Hades through the superior power of His resurrection. In His victory over Death and Hades, Christ now possesses the keys to their gates. This claim is made in Revelation 1:18, which says, "I *am* He who lives, and was dead, and behold, I am alive forevermore. Amen. And I have the keys of Hades and of Death."

As the gatekeeper, Christ determines who enters Hades and who doesn't. Upon death, a saved soul is locked out of Hades, but when an unsaved soul dies, it enters into Hades and the doors are sealed shut behind it.

As per Luke 16:19-31, Hades is an actual place and it is filled with unbearable torments. In order to avoid being locked into Hades, a person needs to accept Christ as their Savior, after which the gates of Hades can no longer prevail against it according to Matthew 16:18.

Revelation 1:18 is the only verse where Hades appears ahead of Death when they are paired together in scripture. When Death precedes Hades in scripture, it alludes to the death of the body, which is the first death. However, when Death follows Hades, it alludes to the second death pertaining to the eternal separation of the soul from God its maker. When Christ claims to have the *keys of Hades and* (then also) *of Death*, He is boldly declaring sovereign authority over the eternal destiny of each and every individual soul.

> "And do not fear those who kill the body, (Death), but cannot kill the soul, (Hades). But rather fear Him, (Jesus Christ), who is able to destroy both soul and body in hell." (Matthew 10:28; emphasis added)

Death and Hades are frightful, but a believer need not be fearful because they are unable to destroy both their soul and body in hell. These are words of comfort, especially to those that will be martyred by Death and Hades as the fourth horsemen of the apocalypse.

Lastly, Death and Hades make their final appearance during the White Throne judgment proceedings at the end of the millennial reign of Jesus Christ. After which, they and all the unsaved souls they had previously killed and incarcerated, are cast into the Lake of Fire.

> "Then I saw a great white throne and Him who sat on it, from whose face the earth and the heaven fled away. And there was found no place for them. And I saw the dead, small and great, standing before God, and books were opened. And another book was opened, which is the Book of Life. And the dead were judged according to their works, by the things which were written in the books. The sea gave up the dead who were in it, and Death and Hades delivered up the dead who were in them. And they were judged, each one according to his works. Then Death and Hades were cast into the lake of fire. This is the second death. And anyone not found written in the Book of Life was cast into the lake of fire." (Revelation 20:11-15)

Death and Hades will face the second death, but beforehand as the fourth horsemen, they exert power and authority over a large religious system. This massive institution comprised of at least a quarter of the earth's population, becomes the Harlot world religion of Revelation 17. This statement is qualified later in this thesis.

Is Islam the Fourth Horsemen of the Apocalypse?

Some relatively recent teachings have attempted to connect the fourth horsemen with Islam. They point out that the Greek word "chloros," which is used to identify the pale color of this horse, can also be translated as green. They make the connection with the flag of the prophet Mohammed, which was made of green silk, with this green horse.[29] They further suggest that Mohammed founded Islam in Mecca, Saudi Arabia, which also has a green flag.[30]

More green related topics are found in the Quran, which they believe adds further evidence that the fourth horsemen represent Islam.[31] Another correlation they make is that Islam is a religion of violence and has been responsible for many deaths, and one of the riders on the fourth horse is called "Death."

In my estimation, these arguments are weak and overridden by other prophetic factors, the primary one being previously mentioned, which is that Islam seems to be in a state of decline by the time the fourth horseman arrives on the scene. Also, the Islamic terrorist group called ISIS banners a black flag, but that does not make it the black horseman of the third seal. Similarly, the green flag of Saudi Arabia does not likely represent the pale horsemen of the fourth seal.

Is Islam the Harlot World Religion?

Joel Richardson teaches that Islam is the Harlot of Revelation 17 and Mecca is the central city of this world religion. In a personal face to face conversation that I had with him on October 27, 2016, I pointed out the following arguments against his new paradigm shift in thinking on this topic:

1.   After Psalm 83 and Ezekiel 38, Islam will be a religion in decline, which minimizes the potential for Islam to be the Harlot.

2.   Saudi Arabia becomes adversely affected by Middle East wars, which mitigate against Mecca becoming the central city of the Harlot. I provided the supporting prophetic verses below to Joel.

    a.   Jeremiah 49:8 - Saudi Arabia, who is identified by Dedan, is told to retreat prior to the calamity of Esau, which seems to allude to the concluding Arab-Israeli war of Psalm 83. Esau's descendants are referred to as the *"tents of Edom"* within the prophecy in Psalm 83:6. The Edomites have ethnical representations within some of the Palestinians today.

    b.   Ezekiel 25:13 – Which points out that Saudi Arabia, (*Dedan*), doesn't heed the warnings of Jer. 49:8 and thus suffers defeat in that war.

    c.   Psalm 83:6 – Saudi Arabia, under the banner of the *Ishmaelites,* are a member of the Arab confederacy of Psalm 83, which gets defeated. This war appears to occur before the Harlot becomes the world's dominant religion. Joel Richardson doesn't believe that Psalm 83 is an unfulfilled prophetic war. Below is a quote from him on this topic.

        "In conclusion, the Psalm 83 (war prophecy) *theory wrongly interprets the prophets, setting the Church up for confusion through unbiblical and false expectations. But the most*

THESIS

worrisome error of the Psalm 83 War theory is that it takes the righteous judgments of Jesus, and reallocates them to mere men."[32]

3. Ezekiel 38:13 – Saudi Arabia, (*Dedan*), is reduced to being a mere sideline protestor during the Gog of Magog invasion of Ezekiel 38. This is likely the weakened condition that the Saudis find themselves in after being defeated in Psalm 83.

4. Revelation 18:19-20 – which says that the "holy apostles" are avenged when Babylon is destroyed. I asked Joel, "If Babylon represents Islam with a central city of Mecca, then which two or more "holy apostles" were killed by Islam in the city of Mecca?" The answer is none! This is because Islam didn't exist until centuries after the apostles were martyred. However, two or more apostles were martyred in or nearby Rome. History suggests that they were Peter, Paul and possibly Andrew.

As this thesis progresses, I will further explain who I believe Death and Hades are and introduce the most important reason why I don't believe they represent Islam.

It is important to note that Death and Hades of Revelation 6:7-8 are probably one and the same with Death and Sheol in Isaiah 28:15, 18. This means that they are the probable perpetrators of the first leg of the "overflowing scourge." This scourge is what concerns Israel and causes them to become a signatory of the false covenant.

> "Because you (*Israel*) have said, "We have made a (*false*) covenant with death, And with Sheol we are in agreement. When the overflowing scourge passes through, It will not come to us, For we have made lies our refuge, And under falsehood we have hidden ourselves."" (Isaiah 28:15)

If there is a connection between Death and Sheol and Death and Hades, this means that the other party to the false covenant of Daniel 9:27 comes on the scene with the opening of the fourth seal. At that point, Israel, The Antichrist and Death and Sheol (Hades) are all together on the world stage. The Antichrist confirms the covenant between Israel and Death and Sheol. This implies that the false covenant could be confirmed and the Trib-period could begin when the fourth seal is opened. However, the details of the fifth seal suggest that won't be the case.

Who are Death and Hades Killing?

Now, it's time to examine who Death and Hades are killing. Understanding who they are martyring helps to answer the following important questions pertaining to them;

1.   Who or what do they represent?

2.   What is their mission on earth?

3.   Why are they killing people, especially believers?

4.   What is their role in the overflowing scourge?

Answering these questions should also help to uncover what is the true content of the false covenant and provide some insights as to when the treaty becomes finalized. Let's start by probing into what's taking place promptly after the fourth seal is opened, and some of those important details are provided within the fifth seal.

Fifth Seal: The Martyrs of the Apocalypse

> When He opened the fifth seal, I saw under the altar the souls of those who had been slain for the word of God and for the testimony which they held. And they cried with a loud voice, saying, "How long, O Lord, holy and true, until You judge and avenge our blood on those who dwell on the earth?" Then a white robe was given to each of them; and it was said to them that they should rest a little while longer, until both *the number of* their fellow servants and their brethren, who would be killed as they *were,* was completed. (Revelation 6:9-11)

Lo and behold, Death and Hades are killing believers for professing the word of God and living out their Christian testimony. True Christian believers may not be the only group they are killing, but they are at least one of them.

This means that Death and Hades must be perpetrating a spiritual message that runs contrary to the gospel of Jesus Christ. The fifth seal saints will hold fast, even to the point of death, to the biblical narrative, which is that Jesus Christ is the way, the truth and the life and the only means of salvation as per John 14:6.

This message of the fifth saints must be antithetical to the teachings of Death and Hades. As such, the quarter of the world's population that adheres to the religious view presented by Death and Hades, is called upon to martyr these Christian dissenters. The slaying of an untold number of Christians implies that the killing campaign of Death and Hades, is not religiously tolerant! Apparently, Death and Hades will not be propagating an ecumenical message, like "all roads lead to heaven."

This religious intolerance should terrify the Jews, who at the same time will be wanting to build the Third Jewish Temple and reinstate the Mosaic Law. When Death and Hades embark upon their unholy war against true believers, there will only be three powerful primary religions left in the world. They are the religions of the Harlot, Judaism, and biblical Christianity. Ultimately, there are four religions after the Rapture, but the fourth, which is the worship of the Antichrist, does not fully emerge until the Middle of the Trib-period. These four religions are explained in greater detail in the commentary section of the chapter called, "The EU Condemnation and Vatican Consecration of Russia."

Some noted Bible commentators believe that the Harlot will be a future apostate ecumenical world church that will embrace all religions except biblical Christianity. They believe this religiously tolerant church with its blending of all religious faiths will be in the war-torn country of Iraq, with a rebuilt Babylon as its central city. Unfortunately, the expositors don't usually explain which one of these religious faiths will arise and lead this ecumenical church. This teaching beckons the question, If Death and Hades represent a tolerant spiritual system, then why are they killing Christians?

The Two Killing Crusades that Martyr Christians After the Rapture

Unlike the indiscriminate deaths that will inevitably result from the war(s) of the second seal, there exist two religious systems that discriminately martyr true Christian believers after the Rapture. These two are the Harlot and the Antichrist.

Per Revelation 17:6, the Harlot is "drunk with the blood of the saints and with the blood of the martyrs of Jesus." Per Revelation 13:15-17 and 20:4, the Antichrist will kill believers for refusing to receive the "Mark of the Beast."

THESIS

Unless Death and Hades represents a third campaign of Christian martyrdom after the Rapture, which is not likely, then it must find association with either the Harlot or the Antichrist. It can't be related to the Antichrist for two reasons.

1.   The Antichrist is the White Horseman and Death and Hades are the Pale Horsemen of the Apocalypse. These two horses carry distinctly different riders who operate independent of each other. The Antichrist is given a crown and instructed to go out conquering and to conquer. Death and Hades are given authority over a quarter of the earth's population to kill believers.

2.   The Antichrist's killing crusade doesn't start until the middle of the Trib-period, but Death and Hades begin their targeted murders beforehand.

Therefore, based upon the minor premises above, the major premise is that Death and Hades seemingly finds association with the Harlot world religion. Or, more boldly and directly stated; DEATH AND HADES are associated with "MYSTERY, BABYLON THE GREAT, THE MOTHER OF HARLOTS AND OF THE ABOMINATIONS OF THE EARTH."

If this is the case then whoever THE MOTHER OF HARLOTS represents, could be the embodiment of the fourth horsemen of Death and Hades. One possible way to uncover the identity of Death and Hades, is to understand how the fifth seal saints become believers.

How Do the Fifth Seal Saints Get Saved?

How do the Fifth Seal Saints get saved? The "white robes" they are given in Rev. 6:11 symbolizes that they are indeed saved. These are committed saints, truly sold out to Christ, even to the point of dying for their faith? Providing they were alive when the Rapture happened, these people were left behind as unbelievers when the miraculous event took place. This means they received Christ as their Savior, after the Rapture.

These saints did not likely learn about Christ from the two witnesses in Revelation 11 or the angel with the everlasting gospel in Rev. 14:6, because the two witnesses and the angel appear during the Trib-period and these saints get saved beforehand. This statement will soon be qualified with an explanation about the timing of the Fifth Seal Saints.

Thus, these martyred saints likely learned about Christ through prior testimonies they had heard, Christian works that have been left behind, and / or by realizing that the Christians were Raptured. This prophetic truth about the Rapture will probably also be echoed by the 144,000 Jewish witnesses of Revelation 7, who will be ministering the gospel of Christ at the time. The 144,000 also get saved after the Rapture.

Here's how the process of conversion might go for the Fifth Seal Saint. After some very basic research, their analytical mind will quickly realize that those who vanished all had *one basic thing in common*; they all believed in Jesus Christ as the Messiah, *i.e.* they were believers. This fact will stick out for some like a sore thumb and be hard for them to deny.

Possessing that understanding, their analytical mind will then logically ask, "Did the Bible have anything to say about Christians vanishing instantly?" They will easily discover the answer is yes, and the event had been predicted about two-thousand years ago, by the Apostle Paul.

Their analytical mind will deliberate further and discover that the Bible also said, "Christ is the way the truth and the life and that God so loved the world that He sent Christ to die for their sins, so that they wouldn't perish but would have everlasting life." This realization will become a motivating factor in their ultimate decision to receive Christ as their Savior to obtain eternal life.

Moreover, after a little more basic study, their analytical mind will become aware that the same Bible predicted that a Harlot world religion and an Antichrist would emerge on the scene after the Rapture. This should cause their analytical mind to turn its attention to Rome and seriously question Roman Catholicism, which will still be mostly intact after the Rapture.

The sustained existence of Roman Catholicism after the Rapture is a prophecy contained in the letter to the Church of Thyatira, which is about to be explored and explained in this thesis. Revelation 2:22 foretells that Thyatira will be going into the Great Tribulation period, which is the second half of the seven year Trib-period.

The Catholics, represented by Thyatira prophetically, who are left behind will take issue with the Fifth Seal Saints when they question the unscriptural practices and beliefs of Roman Catholicism and its bold claims to be the one true Church. When confronted, some Catholics will likely say something like, *"We are the true church and the removal of many Protestants and Evangelicals brings clarity to this truth. The*

THESIS

disappearances of these individuals did not discredit Catholic claims, but to the contrary, proves our standing as the one true Church."

The analytical mind of the Fifth Seal Saint will likely respond with, "That doesn't make sense. It beckons the following questions, *"If the Catholic Church is the true Church, and the Bible predicted the unannounced and instantaneous removal of the true Church, then why:*

1. Is the Catholic Church still on earth?

2. Not only on earth, but why is the leadership still chiefly in place and the global infrastructure of Roman Catholicism mostly still intact?

3. Also, why did some Catholics disappear, but not all Catholics?

4. It seems more realistic to think that Roman Catholicism was a false religion. Can you convince me otherwise?"

Roman Catholicism will undoubtedly have answers for these and many other related questions, but the fact that the Fifth Seal Saints exist clearly evidences that not everyone will be convinced by their explanations.

Roman Catholicism believes that as the true Church, they are the rightful world religion. They believe that they are ordained to consecrate the world to Immaculate Heart of Mary, with the goal of creating a suitable earthy environment for the Second Coming of Christ. As such, they have no place in their theology for the Rapture. They will dismiss the event by explaining it away somehow.

The disappearances of millions of believers, coupled with the supernatural signs and lying wonders, which will be forwarded by Satan, should strongly reinforce their claims as the rightful one world religion. Believing this is their ordained calling, Catholic leaders will not likely feel the need, nor consider it wise, to be religiously tolerant. With the support of their Blessed Mother, they will carry the torch forward to be Christ's light of the world.

Those who deny Roman Catholicism the right to what it sincerely believes to be its calling will put theselves at odds with the Catholic Church. They will be marked as blasphemers and martyred as examples!

I realize that some of the readers are appalled by the scenario depicted in these preceding paragraphs, but these statements will be supported by exposing what's said in the Catholic Catechisms and explaining what the Holy Scriptures point out.

The Three Periods of Post Rapture Christian Martyrdom

Before I officially indict Roman Catholicism as the Harlot World Religion, it's important to discuss the three periods of Christian martyrdom that occurs after the Rapture. The Fifth Seal Saints are the first group, but they are not the only one. This section will also explain why I made the earlier statement that the Fifth Seal Saints get saved before the Trib-period beings.

The two Christian killing crusades, first of the Harlot and second by the Antichrist, take place over the three primary Post-Rapture time periods. They are;

1.   The Post-Rapture / Pre-Trib gap period,

2.   The first half of the Trib-period,

3.   The second half of the Trib-period, also referred to as the "Great Tribulation."

These time frames of martyrdom can be determined in part by interpreting Christ's response to the pleadings of the Fifth Seal Saints.

> "When He opened the fifth seal, I saw under the altar the souls of those who had been slain for the word of God and for the testimony which they held. And they cried with a loud voice, saying, "How long, O Lord, holy and true, until You judge and avenge our blood on those who dwell on the earth?" (Rev. 6:9-10)

Phase one of the killing spree perpetrated by Death and Hades is so deadly that these saints cry out with a loud voice for an answer as to how much longer it will continue. These saints have already been slain for the word of God and for their testimonies, but they are obviously concerned for their *"fellow servants"* who are still alive and experiencing this overflowing scourge.

The fact that they don't know how much longer stage one will continue, strongly suggests that they have been martyred during the Post-Rapture / Pre-Trib gap period. This period has no specific time attributed to it in the Scriptures.

The timing of the slaying of the Fifth Seal Saints can be logically deduced by realizing that if the seven-year Trib-period had already started, they would be able to calendar the days remaining until the

Second Coming of Christ. They don't know how much longer until Christ's return and that's why they ask Him this timing related question?

Other martyred saints, like the innumerable multitude mentioned in Revelation 7:9-17 who come out of the "great tribulation," don't ask this timing question. There is no need because they already know that the great tribulation, which they come out from, only spans the final three and one-half years of the Trib-period. They're not confused about their placement on the prophetic timeline.

However, the setting for the Fifth Seal Saints is different. The situation on earth is so dire, that their timing inquiry can hardly be classified as a naive question. It is doubtful that they ask this question out of prophetic ignorance. They likely realize that the Trib-period only lasts for seven years. I mean, these men and women were slain for the word of God. The fact that the Trib-period lasts for seven years is repeated numerous times in several different ways in the Scriptures. They must know that the Trib-period is coming, they just don't know "how long" until it starts.

By the way, if the Rapture happens soon, you probably know some of these men and women that will be asking this "how long" timing question of the Lord. Undoubtedly, you have important people in your lives that have not accepted Christ yet as their personal Lord and Savior. This puts them at risk of being left behind.

Perhaps you personally haven't made your decision to receive Christ as your Savior. If not, I encourage you to read the appendix entitled, "The Sinner's Salvation Prayer." This appendix will walk you through the process of getting saved. Don't put it off for even another chapter because at any given time you are only one heartbeat away from your eternal destiny.

Back to the question of, *"How long, O Lord, holy and true, until You judge and avenge our blood on those who dwell on the earth?"* Christ's response to their question is interesting. He sums up the metric of time by identifying their Christian condition. Christ says that He will return when the full number of believers who are martyred for their faith is complete. Christ identifies the three phases of Christian martyrdom for them.

> "Then a white robe was given to each of them; (*Group 1*) and it was said to them that they should rest a little while longer, until both the number of *"their fellow servants"* (*Group 2*) and *"their brethren,"* (*Group 3*) who would be killed as they were, was completed." (Rev. 6:11; emphasis added)

THESIS

The three phases of Christian martyrdom after the Rapture apparently, breakdown in the manner described below.

1. The Post-Rapture / Pre-Trib gap period: (*Group 1*) - This phase is when the *Fifth Seal Saints* are slain. It has previously been established in this thesis, that they are killed by Death and Hades. They are likely among those killed by the Harlot, who is "the woman" in Revelation 17:6, who is "drunk with the blood of the saints and with the blood of the martyrs of Jesus."

2. The first half of the Trib-period: (*Group 2*) - The second phase involves the "*fellow servants*" of the *Fifth Seal Saints*. They are killed during the first half of the Trib-period by the same executioner as the *Fifth Seal Saints*. The Harlot is drunk with their blood also. The fact that they are martyred by the same hands appropriately classifies them as *fellow servants* with the *Fifth Seal Saints*.

3. The second half of the Trib-period: (*Group 3*) - The final phase of martyrdom involves the "*brethren*" of the *fellow servants* who previously died in the second phase. By the time the *brethren* are martyred, the Harlot will have been desolated by the ten kings in Rev. 17:16. This means the *brethren* are killed by a different source. The *brethren* are beheaded by the Antichrist for refusing to worship him by taking his "Mark of the Beast." The fact that they die during the Trib-period adequately categorizes them with the *fellow servants*, who also died in the Trib-period, as *their brethren*.

Why is the Roman Catholic Church Cast into the Great Tribulation?

It's important to start this section by looking at an unfulfilled Bible prophecy that appears to find association with Roman Catholicism. The prediction is written in the letter to the Church of Thyatira. The prophetic link between Thyatira and Roman Catholicism is explained in the appendix entitled, "The Seven Letters to the Churches," and elsewhere in this book.

"Notwithstanding I have a few things against thee, (*Roman Catholicism*), because thou sufferest that woman Jezebel, (*The Blessed Mother*), which calleth herself a prophetess, to teach and to seduce my servants, (*Catholics*), to commit fornication, and to eat things sacrificed unto idols. And I gave her space to repent of her fornication; and she repented not. Behold, I will cast her, (*the Harlot world religion*), into a bed, and them that commit adultery (*idolatry*) with her into great tribulation, (*The second half of the Trib-period*), except they repent of their deeds. And I WILL KILL HER CHILDREN WITH DEATH; and all the churches shall know that I am he which searcheth the reins (*minds*) and hearts: and I will give unto every one of you according to your works. (Rev. 2:20-23, KJV; emphasis added)

Hold everything, before I complete the Scripture quote in the letter to Thyatira, let's hit rewind. Did God just say that He "WILL KILL HER CHILDREN WITH DEATH?" I apologize for pausing in the middle of these passages, but I'm sorry, these above verses seemingly state that God will kill children of one of the seven churches and that He will do it during the great tribulation, which seems to assign these killings during the second half of the seven year Trib-period.

A commentary by John Gill explains this verse to mean,

"And I will kill her children with death,.... Her popes, cardinals, priests, Jesuits, monks, friars, and all that join in the Romish apostasy, they shall be killed with death; there shall be an utter extirpation of them in God's own time;..."[33]

John Gill, (November 23, 1697-October 14, 1771) was an English Baptist, a biblical scholar and the first major writing Baptist theologian. He says that "*in God's own time,*" that He will kill with death "*all that join in the Romish apostasy,*" including the Catholic hierarchies. I explain shortly that God's own time appears to be during the great tribulation time-period.

This implies that, the institution of Roman Catholicism, as Thyatira, will still exist on the earth after the Rapture. That's interesting because it's counterpart, the Church of Philadelphia, seemingly ceases to exist after the Rapture. Per Revelation 3:10, Philadelphia is kept from experiencing the seven-year Tribulation period, but Thyatira experiences it in its entirety. If that's not terrible enough, not only do they experience the wrath of God taking place during the great tribulation, but they are going to be purposely afflicted by it!

These verses are addressing the children of Thyatira, which apparently alludes to the faithful followers of Roman Catholicism, rather than literal children. The Bible speaks of the "children of Israel" about 600 times and most of those references refer to the Jewish people in general, rather than singling out their kids.

Unless I'm misinterpreting this, the question is why? Why would God kill followers of Roman Catholicism with death? Considering that God is a just God, the answer becomes obvious. They are being killed because they have done something deserved of death. A likely reason that this Church merits being "cast into the sickbed of the great tribulation," and therein be killed, is because it must be guilty of killing God's people.

The Greek words used for kill, which is "apokteino," and death, which is "thanatos," can only be translated as to kill or slay someone to the point of their death. They are the same two words used in Rev. 6:8, which says that Death, "thanatos," and Hades have authority over a fourth of the earth to kill, "apokteino," the Fifth Seal Saints of Rev. 6:9-11.

This is not talking about Islam, which has a history of killing God's people, rather this is specifically alluding to the Church of Thyatira. The historic and prophetic connections that justifies this bizarre pronouncement are probably identified in the Catholic inquisitions of the past and in Revelation 17:6 of the future.

The Catholics have a bloody history of killing Christians, who they had identified as heretics. Presently, they are no longer committing these heinous atrocities, but do they deserve no punishment for their bloody past? God is merciful, so perhaps He gives them a pass, but Revelation 17:6 becomes the issue.

I interpret this verse elsewhere in the book, but it says the Harlot is drunk with the blood of the saints AND THE MARTYRS OF JESUS! My concern is that the Catholic inquisitions may repeat themselves again in the future!

I realize that it's hard to imagine that God would kill the precious Catholic Mother Theresa's of the world that are caring for the orphans in India, and I'm not saying that these nuns are going to volunteer to be on the front lines to slaughter the Fifth Seal Saints with AK 47's. However, if any Catholic gets left behind from the Rapture they are in jeopardy of being cast into the great tribulation and being killed!

During the Catholic Inquisitions, there were nuns who knew that the executions of the so-called heretics were occurring. They didn't necessarily do the slaying, but the fact that they remained faithful to their Catholic faith, rather than excommunicate themselves, made them guilty by association.

Generally, the Christians were sentenced by the Catholic authorities, but then turned over to the secular authorities for their executions. This process might repeat itself, Christian killings will not likely be done by the Catholic hierarchies, rather the martyrs of Jesus could be sentenced by some future Catholic inquisition court and then turned over to the civil authorities for their executions.

For more understanding into this prophecy it's important to pick up where I left off in the letter to Thyatira. The next verse contains some good, but also some dreadful news.

> But unto you I say, and unto the rest in Thyatira, as many as have not this doctrine, and which have not known the depths of Satan, as they speak; I will put upon you none other burden." (Revelation 2:20-24; KJV, emphasis added)

Let's hit rewind again, what are "the depths of Satan?" This can't be a good thing! How would you like to be a member of a Church that is steeped in Satanic doctrine? This is apparently what the letter to Thyatira says. Thyatira has allowed Satan to insert terrible false doctrines within Roman Catholicism. One of these erroneous teachings deals with a demonic feminine figure possessing similarities to Jezebel of the Old Testament. The only possible female candidate throughout the entire Church age that comes to mind is the Queen of Heaven, otherwise known as the Blessed Mother, the Virgin Mary, Our Lady of Fatima and many more titles. I compare the striking similarities between Jezebel and the apparition of Mary in the commentary of the chapter called, "Two Witnesses Prepare for the Tribulational Period."

So, the letter to Thyatira contains some dreadful claims that should severely concern Catholics today. The buzz words and phrases are, "Jezebel," "great tribulation," "kill her children with death" and "depths of Satan."

The Greek words for "great tribulation" are, "megas thlipsis." The first tandem use of these words together is in Matthew 24:21, and they identify the timing of prophetic events that happen during the second half of Daniel's 70th week.[34] This is one of the verses that some Bible teachers point to as a proof text for the great tribulation alluding to the latter three and one-half years of the Trib-period.

Concerning the great tribulation and its associated time frame, Dr. David Reagan of Lamb and Lion Ministries says this;

> "This view is based primarily on a statement Jesus made that is recorded in Matthew 24. According to this passage, Jesus referred to the last half of Daniel's 70th week of years as 'the great tribulation'" (Matthew 24:21).[35]

Megas thlipsis appears together a total of four times in the New Testament and three of them are associated with events that find fulfillment in the latter half of the Trib-period. These three are found in Matthew 24:21, Rev. 2:22 and Rev. 7:14. The one instance that does not is in Acts 7:11. This verse explains the great suffering associated with the historical famine that came over Egypt and Canaan at the time of Jacob. Most Bible versions translate Acts 7:11 as a great, affliction, suffering or trouble, rather than calling it the "great tribulation."

All four New Testament uses of megas thlipsis deal with specific time-periods. One was in the past, but the three others occur in the future within the second half of the Trib-period. Therefore, the great tribulation mentioned in Rev. 2:22 pertaining to the Church of Thyatira, should not simply be viewed as a period of great suffering that occurs during some undisclosed time-period.

I point out these four usages of megas thlipsis to emphasize that Thyatira apparently enters into the great tribulation period. It's important to compare the translations of Rev. 2:22 provided in the American Standard Version and the New King James Version.

> "Behold, I cast her, (*Thyatira*), into a bed, and them that commit adultery, (*idolatry*), with her into great tribulation, except they repent of her works." (ASV)

> "Indeed I will cast her, (*Thyatira*), into a sickbed, and those who commit adultery, (*idolatry*), with her into great tribulation, unless they repent of their deeds."

These two translations emphasize that Thyatira is cast into great tribulation, like a stowaway might get involuntarily cast off a ship into the sea. Moreover, what better place to punish an adulteress harlot than to confine her to a bed, which is her customary place of business. The NKJV calls it a sickbed, because the great tribulation period is the most sickening of time-periods.

Roman Catholicism became the religious institution that Satan found most suitable to introduce a female type of Jezebel into its theology. This erroneous teaching, which appears to be associated with Mariology, causes the Roman Catholic Church to be cast into the worst three and one-half years ever, which is the "great tribulation" period. Those Catholics who believe in this Jezebel deception, rather than repent of it, will likely be left behind. If they continue to subscribe to this form of idolatry they run the risk of being killed with death during the great tribulation.

How will these killings take place?

How Will God Kill the Children of Thyatira?

This section will explain how God plans on killing the children of Thyatira. There might be multiple means. One of them could understandably be by pouring out His wrath in the great tribulation period, but more than likely, He intends to use the ten prominent political leaders of the end times to fulfill this purpose.

> "And the ten horns which you saw on the beast, these will hate the harlot, make her desolate and naked, eat her flesh and burn her with fire. For GOD HAS PUT IT INTO THEIR HEARTS TO FULFILL HIS PURPOSE, to be of one mind, and to give their kingdom to the beast, until the words of God are fulfilled. (Rev. 17:16-17; emphasis added)

God apparently employs His proven method of the past, of using pagan Gentiles to accomplish His greater purposes. The Babylonians were used to discipline the Jews during their seventy years of Babylonian captivity. Then, He empowered the Persians to conquer the Babylonians so that the Jews could return from exile back into Israel. In the instance of the Harlot, He plans on killing her followers through the ten kings.

Will these ten kings only target the Pope, Cardinals, Bishops and Priests, and leave the kind-hearted nuns alone to feed and clothe the poor? Is that a realistic scenario? Or, will the armies executing the commands of their kings ravish and kill these helpless ladies, who happen to be mostly virgins? The verses above say that the Harlot is made desolate and naked, which should concern a Catholic nun dressed in her traditional habit garb at the time.

I apologize for painting a graphic portrayal, but these verses also say that the armies of the ten kings will eat her flesh, and burn her with fire. Burning with fire is reminiscent of the Catholic inquisitions. Many of the martyred Christians at that time were burned at the stake.

The Main Obsessions of the Blessed Mother

The next couple sections of this thesis explore what the devil has pre-planned for the Post-Rapture future of Roman Catholicism. What is the grander satanic plan that will unfold after the Rapture, when Satan is no longer restrained from performing supernatural signs and lying wonders, during the reign of the Harlot religion?

First, it is important to realize that the apparition of Mary is obsessed with at least five main issues. These must be matters of extreme importance to the Queen of Heaven! They all require her intercession and future intervention, which likely means that Satan's not done with the Virgin Mary. Satan's potential end game for the Marian apparitions is explained in the commentary of the chapter entitled, "The Queen of Heaven Appears Globally."

The Blessed Mother's main obsessions are;

1.   Becoming the Co-Redemptrix, Mediatrix and Advocate,

2.   Catholics praying the Rosary daily, (The Rosary was personally initiated by this demonic female character centuries ago during one of her apparition appearances).

3.   Creating World Peace through her,

4.   Consecrating Russia to her Immaculate Heart,

5.   The importance of the Eucharist in the salvation process.

Various visionary messages delivered from the apparition of Mary throughout time have often centered upon these topics above. One of my favorites is the apparitions quest to become the Co-Redemptrix, Mediatrix and Advocate. How convenient is it for Satan to position this imposter of the biblical Mary as a mediator between the Catholic and Christ? If the Devil wants to interfere with a personal relationship between Christ and a potential believer, one great way to accomplish this is to have a demonic intermediator. It has already been established in this thesis, that the apparition of Mary, as a type of Jezebel, is a creation from the "depths of Satan."

These five fixations of the Blessed Mother are addressed in various places within this book, so your thorough reading of the novel and commentary will acquaint you with the devilish deception linked to these topics.

Satan's Plan to Influence Mankind Through the Harlot

"In the beginning, there had been one will, the will of God, the Creator. After the rebellion of Lucifer there had been two wills, that of God and the rebel. *But now there are billions of wills*." (Donald Grey Barnhouse, from his book, *The Invisible War*). [36]

This Barnhouse quote illustrates one of the Devil's critical dilemmas, especially when he is no longer hindered by the restrainer of 2 Thessalonians 2:7-12. These 2 Thessalonian verses, which pertain to the end times, inform that Satan plans on employing supernatural signs and lying wonders to deceive people living on the earth. Satan's goal will be to influence the *billions of wills*, representing the mindsets of mankind, to believe in what the Bible refers to as "the Lie."

The Devil's predicament is that God created man as a free moral agent with the ability to exercise his own will and make his own choices. Presently, the Devil exerts a strong influence over the *billions of wills*, but he does not control them.

"We know that we are of God, and the whole world lies *under the sway (*not the control*) of* the wicked one." (1 John 5:19; emphasis added)

However, when the restraint is removed, it appears that Satan has a clever multi-faceted plan in place to gain greater control over the *billions of wills* within mankind. Signs and lying wonders working in tandem with the existing doctrines, dogmas and catechisms of Roman Catholicism should better align the free wills of man with Satan's diabolical plans, which are to put *billions of wills* into spiritual bondage.

The first phase of Satan's two phased plan to dominate the will of man, is the Harlot world religion of Revelation 17. In the second phase the Harlot will be replaced by the religious system of the Antichrist in Revelation 13. These are two differing satanic systems that are custom designed by the Devil to meet his needs for each time-period. The Harlot system prevails during the Post-Rapture / Pre-Trib gap period up to the midpoint of the Trib-period. The Antichrist reign is during the great tribulation period.

During the first phase of the Harlot, lawlessness will abound and misleading supernatural events will make the *billions of wills* who have been left behind susceptible to spiritual deception. Mysterious disappearances of millions of Christians, signs and lying wonders from Satan and generally chaotic world events will present people with uncertain futures. The *billions of unsaved souls* should be more religiously inclined then, than they are now. Mostly, people will probably stop denying or questioning the existence of god, rather they will be deciding which one to worship. Satan will employ supernatural deception to influence their decision in favor of the Harlot world religion.

Amidst this backdrop the Harlot enters in to soothe the sojourning souls seeking a more stable and predictable future. Nothing like a Blessed Mother, with her promises of world peace, to comfort the wearied *billions of wills* that are trying to survive in a war-torn world that is becoming increasingly lawless.

The paranormal will become the new normal and the supernatural will defy the natural and, as such, people's perceptions of reality should be dramatically altered. This becomes further complicated by the defeat of the Gog of Magog invaders in Ezekiel 38-39 via supernatural forces, which could find fulfillment around this time. Israel wins this Mideast war against a massive Russian coalition without hardly firing a shot according to the details in Ezekiel 38:18-39:6.

As temporal existence becomes more threatened, eternal security becomes of greater interest to the *billions of wills*. Salvation of the soul is what the Harlot will offer. So, how does Satan accomplish this through the Harlot world religion?

Salvation Comes Through the Roman Catholic Church

> "In order to be saved, I (*one*) must be baptized in the Catholic Church, belong to the One True Church established by Jesus, obey the Ten commandments, receive the Sacraments, pray, do good works and die with no mortal sin on my (*their*) soul."[37]

According to the teachings of Roman Catholicism, salvation can only be obtained through their religious institution via the means that they prescribe. This quote was taken from the book called, *A Catechism for Adults*, which was written by Willam J. Cogan. Father Cogan was a priest and author of the twentieth century, serving the diocese of Chicago. His book, which was published in 1951, received the coveted "Nihil Obstat" and "Imprimatur" around 1958.

"Nihil Obstat," in the Roman Catholic Church, is a certification by an official censor that a book is not objectionable on doctrinal or moral grounds. The "Imprimatur" is an official license by the Roman Catholic Church to print an ecclesiastical or religious book. Thus, the quote above and the ones below from Cogan's book represent the bonafide teachings of Roman Catholicism.

The quotations below are formatted in a question and answer format and are numbered to correspond identically with the related numbers in Cogan's book. Some of the unbiblical answers below illustrate how Roman Catholicism could easily be used by Satan to put people into spiritual bondage. By comparison, the biblically supported answers to these salvation related quotes are provided in the *Apocalypse Road* appendix entitled, "The Sinner's Salvation Prayer."

"Lesson 14

Q-23: Will I not be saved by accepting Jesus as my personal Saviour?

A-23:   No, I will not be saved merely by accepting Jesus as my personal Saviour or merely by believing in Him. (Cogan answers this question in the first person by using the word "I," which means neither he or anyone else can get saved by merely accepting Christ as their Saviour. It requires more than that).

Lesson 16

Q-3: Has the Catholic Church ever changed its teaching?

A-3:   No, in the 2000 years of its history, the Catholic Church has taught without change the same things taught by Jesus.

Q-4: Could the Catholic Church ever teach error?

A-4:   No, the Catholic Church could never teach error, because it is the only church which Jesus promised to protect from error.

Q-14:   Can the Pope make an error when teaching?

A-14:   No, the Pope cannot make an error when teaching religion as the head of the whole Catholic Church.

Q-15:   Do all Catholics have to obey the Pope?

A-15:   Yes, all Catholics all over the world have to obey the Pope because he has the authority of Jesus to rule the whole Church."

The answers above establish the fact that the Catholic Church dogmatically teaches that it is the one true church and that the Pope is infallible. Moreover, the teachings of the Catholic Church are never wrong and they have not changed over time. Most importantly a person can't be saved by simply accepting Jesus Christ as their Savior, they must also do the things dictated by the Catholic Church.

With those facts established the remainder of the answers to key questions about Catholic teachings from Cogan's book are summarized below.

Lesson 17, A-9: The Catholic Church can never be destroyed.

Lesson 10, A-3 to 6: There are two types of sins, mortal sins are big sins and venial sins are little sins. If someone dies with a mortal sin on their soul, they will be sent to hell forever. Mortal sins can be forgiven and they include;

1.   Refusing to accept all of God's teaching,

2.   Never praying,

3.   Telling serious lies,

4.   Not going to Mass on Sundays or Holy Days of Obligation,

5.   Getting very drunk,

6.   Killing an unborn baby in the womb,

7.   All sins of sex,

8.   Stealing something expensive.

Lesson 2, A-20: Since attending Mass is essential to avoid going to hell forever, a person must go to Mass every Sunday and on the six Holy Days of Obligation.

Lesson 15: A-17-22: Protestant churches were established by men who broke away from the Catholic Church. There are around 200 Protestant Churches, like Episcopalian, Presbyterian, Baptist, Methodist, Adventist, etc. All Protestant churches are false man-made churches. None of the men who established the Protestant churches had any authority whatsoever to start churches of their own. Everyone has an obligation to obey the Catholic Church because it alone has the authority of Jesus to rule and to teach. To disobey the Catholic Church knowingly is a sin, just as much as disobeying Jesus or His apostles.

Lesson 18: A-3 to 9: It is impossible for a soul to be saved outside of the Catholic Church! It is a serious matter to become a Catholic because, in so doing, a person commits themselves completely and forever under the authority of the Catholic Church. A committed Catholic must always believe everything that the Catholic Church teaches. It is a mortal sin to quit the Catholic Church because it amounts to the rejection of the authority of Jesus Christ.

Need I say more? These teachings compel people to become Catholics and faithfully attend Mass or else they run the genuine risk of going to Hell forever. These doctrinal themes are also included in the Baltimore Catechism, which was the Gold Standard of Catholic education from 1885 to the 1960s. It was commissioned by the Third Council of Bishops in Baltimore.

Below is a quote explaining the Baltimore Catechism from EWTN. com, which is a global, Catholic Television, Catholic Radio, and Catholic News Network.

"The Catechism with which we, (Catholics) are, perhaps, most familiar in pre-Vatican Council days, is known as the Baltimore Catechism. This catechism was collaborated on by the Bishops of the United States in the Third Plenary Council of Baltimore, which took place in 1884. It was put together and finally issued in 1885 by Cardinal Gibbons who, at the time, was the head of the American hierarchy. It took the American Bishops from 1829 to 1885 to put together the Baltimore Catechism, which in turn, derived from what was called the Roman Catechism or the Catechism of the Council of Trent. This document, similar to the Catechism of the Catholic Church which came out on June 22, 1994, was issued in 1565 by Pope Saint Pius V, and was to be the basis of various national catechisms and textbooks.... The new Catechism of the Catholic Church should be read and understood in the light of its (the Baltimore Catechism's) history, especially Catechesis Tradendae and the General Catechetical Directory."[38]

The quotes below from the Baltimore Catechism reinforce Cogan's claims and the unchanging teachings of all other Catechisms, past and present. At their core, these catechisms are designed to compel people to become Catholics.

Lesson Twenty-Ninth: On the Commandments of God.

#1125 - "It is not enough to belong to the Church in order to be saved, but we must also keep the Commandments of God and of the Church." [39]

Lesson Thirty-Fifth: On the First and Second Commandments of the Church.

#1325 – "The commandments of the Church are also commandments of God, because they are made by His authority, and we are bound under pain of sin to observe them." [40]

#1327 – "The chief commandments of the Church are six:

(1) To hear Mass on Sundays and (the six) holy days of obligation.[41]

(2) To fast and abstain on the days appointed.

(3) To confess at least once a year.

(4) To receive the Holy Eucharist during the Easter time.

(5) To contribute to the support of our pastors.

(6) Not to marry persons who are not Catholics, or who are related to us within the third degree of kindred, nor privately without witnesses, nor to solemnize marriage at forbidden times."[42]

#1329 – "It is a mortal sin not to hear Mass on a Sunday or a holyday of obligation, unless we are excused for a serious reason..."[43]

Some Catholics categorize sins in three categories, which are mortal, grave and venial. Mortal and venial sins were previously defined, but what are grave sins? Some ecclesiastical documents, like the Code of Canon Law and the Catechism of the Catholic Church, regularly use the phrase "grave sin" to mean "mortal sin," but are they really the same? What if a sin has been committed that has grave matter but lacks the knowledge and consent needed to make it mortal?

Fortunately, in 1984, Pope John Paul II answered this question once and for all and since, according to Cogan's claims, the Pope can never be wrong, the quote below is the final truth on this matter. The Pope wrote the following,

> "*During the synod assembly some fathers proposed a threefold distinction of sins, classifying them as venial, grave and mortal. This threefold distinction might illustrate the fact that there is a scale of seriousness among grave sins. But it still remains true that the essential and decisive distinction is between sin which destroys charity and sin which does not kill the supernatural life: There is no middle way between life and death.*"[44]

The article from which this quotation was taken goes on to conclude with this statement, "*Hence, in the* (Catholic) *church's doctrine and pastoral action, grave sin is in practice identified with mortal sin.*"

The point made by the Pope is that there is no distinction between mortal and grave sins. There is no middle ground! Mortal sin and grave sin are synonymous. Call the sin that kills supernatural life whatever you want, but if you commit a mortal sin as defined by Roman Catholicism, you go to Hell forever! Eight of these mortal sins, such as aborting a baby, telling serious lies, stealing something expensive and getting very drunk, were previously listed. Have any of you ever committed one of these mortal sins? Per Roman Catholicism, if you have, you are at risk of going to Hell!

At their core, these catechisms and Cogan claims identified in this thesis are designed to compel people to become Catholics. The explanations below make this conclusion relatively obvious.

1. Roman Catholicism is the One True Church. The Protestant churches are false. I point out in the commentary of the chapter called, "The Vatican Global Council Meeting," that the Second Vatican Council, (October 11, 1962 – December 8, 1965), made the Catholic Church more Protestant friendly, but did not substantially change the core doctrines of Roman Catholicism.

2. Salvation comes primarily through the Catholic Church, rather than merely receiving Jesus Christ as their personal Lord and Savior.

3. People can go to Hell forever if they don't receive forgiveness for their mortal sins in the manner prescribed by the Catholic Church.

4. In order to be saved a person must,

   a. Become a Catholic

   b. Faithfully partake of the Mass in the acceptable manner defined by the Catholic Church, which is;

      1. Take the Mass every Sunday, and on the days of obligation,

      2. Perform it inside the Catholic Church,

      3. Receive the Eucharistic elements by the Catholic Priest.

The plausible way that Satan can gain greater control over the *billions of wills* that have been left behind is to prop up the Catholic Church as the world's One True Church. He can accomplish this by using signs and lying wonders to deceive people, who are already vulnerable to spiritual deception because of the supernatural activities that are occurring in the world at that time.

If people who are left behind from the Rapture don't want to be banished to Hell forever, they need to seek forgiveness through the Catholic Church. The fear of eternal damnation will compel, and the satanic deception will encourage, many people to become Catholics. Even then, their eternity is only as secure as their commitment to the catechisms of the Catholic Church. They will need to take the Mass continually or run the risk of dying with a mortal sin attached to their soul.

This type of spiritual bondage can be easily manipulated by Satan, who has already infused demonic doctrine into Roman Catholicism as per the letter to the Church of Thyatira.

> "Now to you I say, and to the rest in Thyatira, as many as do not have this doctrine, who have not known the depths of Satan, as they say, I will put on you no other burden. (Rev. 2:24)

Stage two of Satan's plan of deception involves the Antichrist. Since this phase is executed primarily during the Trib-period, the commentary about this segment will be provided in the next book of this series, which deals with that seven-year period.

The False Covenant of Death in Agreement with Sheol

In addition to Daniel 9:27, Isaiah 28:15, 18 provides more details about the infamous false covenant. Whatever the true content of this false covenant contains, it is so problematic that it triggers the start of the seven year Trib-period.

Before interpreting portions of Isaiah 28 in this section, let me caveat that some commentaries believe that the prophecies contained in Isaiah's verses were fulfilled historically with the destruction of the Northern Kingdom of Israel by Assyria in 722 BC. and the Southern Kingdom of Judah by the Babylonians in 586 BC. A few problems with this view are in the following passages:

1. Isaiah 28:5, which addresses the faithful remnant of the Jews. The remnant of Israel is a theme that often finds association with the last days.

2. Isaiah 28:15-18, which informs of;

    a. The ratification and ultimate annulment of the false covenant of Daniel 9:27.

    b. The prior coming of Jesus Christ in typology as the *tried* and *precious cornerstone* of the Temple's *sure foundation*. These verses appear to state that the first coming of Christ had already happened in history. The coming of Christ happened over 500 years after the destruction of Judah, which nullifies the possibility that all of the prophecies of Isaiah 28 concluded in 586 BC.

3. Isaiah 28:21-22, which declares that the Lord will perform an awesome work. It is an unusual act that involves a *"destruction determined even upon the whole earth."* This judgment happens during the Trib-period when the Lord pours out His wrath on a Christ rejecting planet.

Considering the above qualifiers, this implies that some of the predictions in Isaiah 28 may remain unfulfilled. From that perspective, my interpretation of portions of Isaiah 28 is summarized below.

Isaiah 28:14 forewarns that the leadership of Israel at the time the false covenant is confirmed is a contemptuous group of scornful scoffers. They represent Israel in a condition of power after the wars of Psalm 83 and Ezekiel 38, but in unbelief that Jesus Christ is the Messiah.

Their response to their empowered national condition will not include recognizing Christ, but rather they plan to build their Third Temple and reinstate the Mosaic Law. They believe this is what needs to happen for the betterment of Israel. They will become a signatory to the false covenant to accomplish this. This thinking is pointed out in the verses below. These passages also include God's warning to them about this dangerous national mindset.

> "Therefore hear the word of the LORD, you scornful men, Who rule this people who *are* in Jerusalem, Because you have said, "We have made a covenant with death, And with Sheol we are in agreement. When the overflowing scourge passes through, It will not come to us, For we have made lies our refuge, And under falsehood we have hidden ourselves. Therefore thus says the Lord GOD: "Behold, I lay in Zion a stone, (*Jesus Christ*), for a foundation, A tried stone, (*Christ's first coming*), a precious cornerstone, a sure foundation; Whoever believes will not act, (*Concerning the false covenant*), hastily. Also I will make justice the measuring line, And righteousness the plummet; The hail will sweep away the refuge of lies, And the waters will overflow the hiding place." (Isaiah 28:14-17; emphasis added)

Isaiah 28:5-13 had previously explained that by the time the false covenant gets ratified, that the prophets, priests and rulers in Jerusalem were unschooled in the ways of God. The Word of God, which was measured out one precept at a time and was intended to be the guiding principle of their leadership, was not adequately understood by them. Isaiah 28:9 likened their spiritual maturity to that of a baby, *"just weaned from milk"* and *"just drawn from the breasts."*

Would anyone want a toddler to be the man of their house, let alone rule a thriving nation, especially in the critical last days? Heaven forbid!

Proverbs 25:2 says, *"It is the glory of God to conceal a matter, But the glory of kings is to search out a matter."* The scornful leadership of Israel at the time they sign the false covenant represents childish infants rather than glorious kings. They haven't thoroughly searched the Holy Scriptures to understand the totality of Gods prophetic word. They likely understand parts of the Old Testament (OT), but not in correlation with their related applications in the New Testament (NT).

Isaiah 28:10 is repeated in Isaiah 28:13 to emphasize that God's word is completed in both portions within the Bible. "Precept upon precept (OT), precept upon precept (NT), Line upon line (OT), line upon line (NT), Here a little (OT), there a little (NT)." According to 2 Timothy 3:16, which says that all Scripture is given by the inspiration of God, that means God's word is purposely distributed, a *little* in the Old Testament and *a little* in the New Testament.

Isaiah 28:15 says these deceived leaders are panicked by an overflowing scourge that is sweeping through the world. In order to avoid being overtaken by it, they hastily sign a treaty with the perpetrator of the scourge. God says this is a covenant of death that is originated from the pits of Hell, (Sheol in this instance). Concerning Isaiah 28:14-15, Dr. Arnold Fruchtenbaum explains,

> "In verse 14, God calls the ones making this covenant scoffers. Verse 15 gives the reason for this and provides God's viewpoint of the covenant itself. It is obvious that the leaders of Israel will enter into this covenant to obtain some measure of security and to escape the overflowing scourge. Hence they will believe that entering the covenant will free them from further military invasions. However, God declares that this is not a covenant of life, but a covenant of death. It is not a covenant of heaven, but a covenant of hell."[45]

Even worse, these scornful leaders of Israel realize that their underlying motive for covenanting is based upon deceit. Isaiah 28:15

exposes this when it says, *"For we have made lies our refuge, And under falsehood we have hidden ourselves."*

The motivation for covenanting is not only to avoid the scourge, but may also include the unrestricted ability to build the Third Jewish Temple. The Temple could be built before the false covenant gets confirmed, perhaps after Israel's victory over its Arab enemies in the Psalm 83 war. However, shortly I will provide the Scriptural clues that infer that the construction of the Jewish Temple may be one of Israel's stipulations contained within the false covenant.

The First Jewish Temple took Solomon twenty years to construct, (1 Kings 9:10). Legend has it that the Second Temple took forty-six years for the Jews to complete, (John 2:20). However, some suggest that the Third Temple could be built in one to two years. [46]

Presently, there are three prevailing points of view about when the Third Jewish Temple should be rebuilt.[47]

a. The Temple will miraculously float down from heaven and settle in its appropriate place.

b. The Messiah will come and facilitate the building of the Temple.

c. The Temple will be built and then the Messiah will come.

The odds are that the Temple will not be floating down from heaven any time soon. Moreover, the Messiah is Jesus Christ and He's not coming back just so the Jews can build their Third Temple. Thus, we can eliminate both of these scenarios. Therefore, the only viable alternative is that the Jews will seek to construct the Temple to hasten the coming of their Messiah, not accepting that He already came over 2000 years ago, in the person of Jesus Christ.

The correlation of the Temple and the coming of Messiah is the important point to the Jews. The coming of the Messiah eventually segues into the establishment of His Messianic Kingdom. The predictions and promises that are destined to find fulfillment during this messianic age epitomize the high point of unfulfilled Old Testament prophecies. The world essentially gets restored to a utopian condition during the Messianic Kingdom.

The probable thinking of the scornful rulers is driven by the belief that whatever it takes to hasten the coming of the Messiah must be done, and without further delay. If it means signing a covenant with a hellish party that's perpetrating a terrible scourge on the earth, then so be it. The means justify the ends because they can accomplish several things through this covenant;

1. Avoid the overflowing scourge,

2. Build the Third Temple,

3. Hasten the coming of the Messiah,

4. End the overflowing scourge, because the Messiah must make an end of it before establishing His benevolent kingdom on earth.

5. Enter into the glorious Messianic Kingdom age.

Isaiah says the covenant is based upon *lies* and *falsehood* and the Jews will believe they have found a *hiding place* by becoming a party to it. However, Isaiah says that like flood waters, the overflowing scourge will come upon them. He warns that their covenant will be short lived.

> "Your covenant with death will be annulled, And your agreement with Sheol will not stand; When the overflowing scourge passes through, Then you will be trampled down by it. As often as it goes out it will take you; For morning by morning it will pass over, And by day and by night; It will be a terror just to understand the report." (Isaiah 28:18-19)

What is the True Content of the False Covenant?

Isaiah 28:15 and 18 identify two deadly phases of the overflowing scourge, but before I explain what these phases seem to be, I will address what appears to be the true content of the false covenant. Isaiah 28 and Daniel 9 provide several of the contract particulars, but they don't clearly identify the actual content of the false covenant. What exactly is it that Israel and Death and Sheol agree to? Israel is trying to avoid a scourge, but how does Death and Sheol benefit from the deal?

Some Bible prophecy experts believe that the covenant has something to do with resolving the Arab-Israeli conflict. They suspect that the content spells out some acceptable arrangements for a Palestinian state that can harmoniously co-exist alongside a secure Jewish state.

THESIS

Below are the problems with this teaching;

1.   Nowhere in the covenant related scriptures does it say anything about an agreement between the Arabs and the Jews. Isaiah 28:15, 18 says nothing about the Arabs and neither does Daniel 9:27. However, Daniel 9:26-27 does say that the one who confirms the false covenant and ultimately makes an end of it comes from the revived Roman Empire.

2.   The Arab-Israeli conflict gets resolved militarily in Psalm 83 and other related verses, rather than diplomatically through a peace plan.

3.   Scriptural clues suggest that the covenant may have something to do with the construction of the Third Temple.

Identified below are some hints that suggest the false covenant has something to do with the construction of the Third Temple.

The first clues are contained in Isaiah 28:16-17. These two verses are sandwiched in between Isaiah 28:15 and 18, which are the verses referring to the false covenant. These passages use terms like a "tried stone," a "precious cornerstone," a "sure foundation," a "measuring line" and a "plummet." These are terms that can find association with constructing a Jewish Temple.

To build the Temple, you start with a *tried stone* that becomes the *precious cornerstone*. This *cornerstone* has a *sure foundation* built around it. The length and width dimensions of a building needs to be calculated with a *measuring line*, and the vertical accuracy of a structure is determined with a *plummet,* (plumb-line).

I interpret Isaiah 28:16-17 as a warning to the scornful rulers that drag Israel into being a signatory of this dreadful covenant. These leaders seem to think that they are going to build a Temple and hasten the coming of the Messiah, but Isaiah cautions them not to hastily enter this covenant, because the Messiah has already come as the, *tried stone, precious cornerstone* and *sure foundation.*'

A second clue is found in Daniel 9:27, which also is a proof text verse regarded with the false covenant.

> "Then he, (*the Antichrist*), shall confirm a covenant with many (*Israel and Death and Sheol*) for one week; (*of seven years*), But in the middle of the week, (*after three*

and one-half years) He shall bring an end to sacrifice and offering, (*taking place in the Temple*). And on the wing of abominations shall be one who makes desolate, Even until the consummation, which is determined, Is poured out on the desolate." (Daniel 9:27; emphasis added)

Jesus Christ foretells that this event predicted by Daniel happens in the holy place, which represents the Third Jewish Temple at the time.

"Therefore when you see the 'abomination of desolation,' spoken of by Daniel the prophet, standing in the holy place" (whoever reads, let him understand), "then let those who are in Judea flee to the mountains." (Matthew 24:15-16)

The intimations in these related verses above, are that by the middle of the Trib-period the Third Jewish Temple will exist. The Antichrist will make a bold statement by entering this Temple and stopping the priestly sacrifice and offering occurring therein. This is in fulfillment of Isaiah 28:18, which says the false covenant will be annulled. What better way to dissolve a covenant than to void out its terms? If the true content of the false covenant allowed the Jews to build their Temple and perform sacrifices and offerings inside of it, then the action taken by the Antichrist to go into the Temple and stop the sacrifice and offering terminates the contract.

A third interesting clue is in the book of Revelation. Several important details are provided in these passages below concerning the benefits to both parties of the covenant. These verses describe what happens in the immediate aftermath of the ratification of the false covenant.

"Then there was given me a measuring rod like a staff; and someone said, 'Get up and measure the temple of God and the altar, and those who worship in it. Leave out the court which is outside the temple and do not measure it, for it has been given to the nations; and they will tread under foot the holy city for forty-two months. And I will grant *authority* to my two witnesses, and they will prophesy for twelve hundred and sixty days, clothed in sackcloth.'" (Rev. 11:1-3, NASB)

The time frame of *"forty-two months"* is associated with one-half of the seven years of tribulation. The same increment of time is used in the ensuing verse but worded differently as, *"twelve hundred and sixty days."* It is commonly taught that both usages allude to the first half of the Trib-period.

Thus, the very first thing that appears to happen as part of the implementation of the covenant, is that the Temple gets measured for its construction. The apostle John is given a measuring rod and instructed to measure the temple of God, alluding to the Third Temple. If the covenant called for the construction of the Temple, then this would be one of the first order of events. Measure it so that it can be built.

Some of you might wonder if John is measuring an already existing Temple, but why would he be instructed to do that? That would be an arduous process with the measuring rod he is provided. It would make more sense to simply go to City Hall to get the measurement of an already existing Temple. A building of that magnitude certainly must have its blueprints approved by the city planning commission before it can be constructed. John could get the accurate measurements straight from the blueprints.

Moreover, the measuring process does not take place in the second half of the Trib-period because John, being a Jew and therefore representing the Jews at that future time, would be fleeing from the persecution of the Antichrist, rather than measuring the "temple of God and the altar." In fact, per Matthew 24:15-19, Jesus Christ instructed the Jews to flee from Judea when the Antichrist goes into the temple and commits the abomination of desolation. Jesus did not command the Jews to get a measuring rod to measure the temple of God.

Notwithstanding, the architectural instructions include some restrictions. In other words, the agreement contains some caveats about the building of the Temple that benefit the other covenanting party. The other party are Gentiles who must have some claims to the Temple's outer court and Jerusalem because they are given authority over the outer court, and access to trample through the holy city of Jerusalem.

The Greek word used for "Gentiles" in Rev. 11:2 is *"ethnos."* It used over 150 times in the New Testament and can be translated as Gentiles, nations, pagans or people.[48] The Greek word in that same verse used for "trample," is *"pateo,"* which can also be translated as "tread under foot."[49]

Thus, another possible way to translate this verse is, *the pagans will tread under foot, the holy city of Jerusalem*. They will need this access to make their way to the outer court of the Temple mount, which is given over to these pagan Gentiles. This is an important concession for these pagans. It implies that whoever they are, that they have valid claims to these sacred areas. Presently, the Old City of Jerusalem is divided into four quarters: Christian, Armenian, Jewish and Muslim. The Christian category includes Roman Catholicism.

When the covenant gets confirmed and the Gentiles get awarded access to Jerusalem and authority over the outer court, several Bible prophecies will have likely happened. Two important ones will be Psalm 83 and the Rapture, not necessarily in that order. After Psalm 83, the Muslims will probably lose substantial control over their quarter in the Old City and after the Rapture some Christian and Armenian sections will be vacated by the true believers that resided there. This leaves the Jews and probably a strong Vatican contingency.

It was pointed out earlier in this thesis that Roman Catholicism appears to remain mostly intact after the Rapture. It has also been pointed out that Roman Catholicism represents the Harlot World Religion. Therefore, the pagan Gentiles controlling the outer court and treading Jerusalem under foot are most likely the Catholics, who were not Raptured.

These three clues above seem to suggest that the true content of the false covenant has something to do with the building of the Third Jewish Temple. They also suggest that the covenanting parties are the Jews and the Catholics. But why? Why would the Jews cut a deal with the Catholics? Moreover, why would the Catholics deal with the Jews, especially if they have emerged as the dominant world religion of the Harlot?

The answer would likely be that at the time, Judaism and Roman Catholicism are at loggerheads with each other. The Jews will be following Judaism and they will not convert to Catholicism. They will be empowered from their Psalm 83 and Ezekiel 38 victories and on a quest to build their Temple, reinstate the Mosaic Law and hasten the coming of the Messiah. However, they will be troubled by the overflowing scourge that is being perpetrated by the Harlot world religion, which is probably why they come to the negotiating table. The Harlot is killing true Christian believers throughout the world at the time as per Revelation 17:6

On the flip side, the Vatican will be feeling somewhat invincible because Satan will be propping up Roman Catholicism after the Rapture via supernatural signs and lying wonders. The Vatican will also have the

THESIS

powerful allegiance of the Antichrist and his developing global political infrastructure.

With this global geo-political scenario, probably in place at that time, we can better understand the two phases of the overflowing scourge in Isaiah 28;15, 18.

The Two Deadly Phases of the Overflowing Scourge

THESIS

This is my two cents worth on explaining the two deadly phases of the overflowing scourge. If you haven't read the entire thesis, but have just skipped ahead to this part, then you will undoubtedly think I'm crazy after you read this section. So please, consider reading this entire thesis before you read my commentary below.

Phase One of the Overflowing Scourge – Isaiah 28:15

> "Because you have said, "We have made a covenant with death, And with Sheol we are in agreement. When the overflowing scourge passes through, It will not come to us, For we have made lies our refuge, And under falsehood we have hidden ourselves." (Isaiah 28:15)

The first phase of the scourge, *as I interpret it*, is when Israel signs the false covenant with the Harlot world religion so as not to be its next religious victim. The Harlot, represented by Roman Catholicism is drunk with the blood of the martyrs of Jesus because their biblical narrative is problematic for the advancement of the Harlot's choke hold on humanity.

The Harlot is not religiously tolerant, which sincerely troubles the Jews. They will not buy into her lies, because they are sold out on their own. They practice Judaism and its trappings contained in the sacrificial system of the Mosaic Law. They don't realize that true Christianity is the completion of Judaism. Jesus is the Messiah who already came, but they are in denial about this reality.

> "Therefore the, (Mosaic) law was our tutor *to bring us* to Christ, that we might be justified by faith. But after faith has come, we are no longer under a tutor." (Galatians 3:24-25; emphasis added)

The fact of the matter is that the law was fulfilled by Christ, (Matthew 5:17-18), which rendered it inoperative. Now people are saved by faith through the gift of God's grace, rather than by the works of the law, (Ephesians 2:8-9). Aren't you glad that's how God has now made salvation available to you?

By locking arms with the Harlot, the Jews believe that they can appease her temporarily. They believe that she will not attempt to be drunk with the blood of the martyrs of Jesus and, also the blood of the Jews. The Jews are willing to concede some sacred holy territory by giving the Harlot authority over the outer court and access to tread Jerusalem under foot, because they will be able to build their Temple and hasten the coming of their long-awaited Messiah.

The Jews reason that the means of signing this deceitful covenant justifies the ends of invoking the coming of the Messiah. In their estimation, once the Messiah comes He eliminates the pagan Harlot system. They believe that in the end, it's the Harlot and not them, who gets the short end of the stick in this seven-year covenant.

After the ratification of the covenant the Jews build their Temple and enjoy a temporary period of pseudo peace. They await the imminent coming of their Messiah to destroy the Harlot and usher in His Messianic Kingdom, which is the high point of all Old Testament prophecy.

Phase Two of the Overflowing Scourge – Isaiah 28:18

> "Your covenant with death will be annulled, And your agreement with Sheol will not stand; When the overflowing scourge passes through, Then you will be trampled down by it." (Isaiah 28:18)

However, something goes horribly wrong for the Jews and that's phase two of the overflowing scourge. This is a good place to lay out the likely chronological sequence of events that happen in the middle of the Trib-period. These prophecies set the stage for the second phase of the overflowing scourge.

1. Satan loses a war in heaven, which forces him and his fallen angels to depart from heaven and flee to the earth, (Rev. 12:7-9).

THESIS

2. Realizing his time is short, (Rev. 12:12), Satan commands his political point man on earth, the Antichrist, to exalt himself above all gods, (Daniel 11:36-37), and to ally with the False Prophet to usurp the religious system of the Antichrist over all others, (Rev. 13:11-17). Thus, the Antichrist needs to do several things, which are;

    a. Form an alliance with ten powerful political leaders, (ten kings), to desolate the Harlot religion, (Rev. 17:16), and replace it with his own religious system,

    b. Personally, go to Jerusalem and kill the Two Witnesses, (Rev. 11:7),

    c. Personally, enter the Third Jewish Temple and make an end of the Jewish sacrifices and offerings, which annuls the false covenant, (Matthew 24:15, Daniel 9:27 and 12:11),

    d. Begin a genocidal campaign of the Jews and in so doing end the religion of Judaism, (Zechariah 13:8),

    e. Force people to worship the Antichrist by taking the "Mark of the Beast," (Rev. 13:14),

    f. Martyr biblical Christians for not taking his beastly mark. (Rev. 13:15, Rev. 20:4).

It is phase two of the scourge that Jesus warned about in Matthew 24:15-22. He instructed the Jews to flee immediately to the mountains, alluding to Petra in Jordan. He issued this command because He wanted to protect the Jews from the final genocide attempt against them, which will be executed by the Antichrist. This was predicted in Zechariah 13:8 with imagery of the scenario provided in Isaiah 28:19-20. A faithful remnant of Jews will emerge in Petra Jordan, and Jesus ultimately comes for them there according to Isaiah 63:1-8.

Summary of the Two Phased Overflowing Scourge

The overflowing scourge has two phases and each phase is carried out by different sources. The perpetrator of phase one is the Harlot world religion and the executioner of phase two is the Antichrist. Both phases involve martyrdom of biblical Christians, but only phase two involves the killing of the Jews.

The irony for the Jews in Isaiah 28:15-18 is that they will trust the Antichrist to confirm the false covenant, but shortly thereafter he will betray their trust by annulling the covenant that he brokered. The warning from the prophet Isaiah in these verses might be restated as follows:

> "Behold you scornful rulers of Jerusalem that become signatories of the false covenant. You are making a grave mistake on behalf of Israel. This devilish deal will bring death upon your people. It has been designed by Satan out from the pits of Hell (Sheol). The political leader you believe will guarantee your national security, will betray you. He will first eliminate the other covenanting party of the Harlot world religion, and then he will commit genocide of the Jews. If you would have searched all the Scriptures thoroughly, you would have understood that Jesus Christ is the Messiah! You would not have acted in haste to sign this covenant with the hopes of hastening the coming of some other messiah. You would have known better!"

Congratulations, you have completed the reading of the Post-Rapture / Pre-Trib Thesis. I encourage you to read the Companion's Commentary next. The commentary will provide additional details to this thesis.

APOCALYPSE ROAD

Companion's Commentary

Introduction to The Companion's Commentary

Welcome to the commentary section of the book. As stated in the introduction, this segment provides "biblical believability" to the adventurous scenarios depicted in the novel. It's designed to enhance the fiction section, but has been conveniently positioned behind the novel for those who choose to read it independently. This dual format was selected to cater to both fiction and non-fiction audiences.

Maximum enjoyment and enrichment can be achieved by reading both the novel and the commentary together. This can be accomplished through either a chapter-by-chapter, or section-by-section, review of the book. Some might prefer to breeze through the novel before reading the supporting commentary. Others may seek to study the prophecies as they unfold one chapter at a time, by flipping back and forth between the novel and the corresponding commentary.

Throughout man's history a multitude of masterpiece manuscripts have been written. Many of them were based on true stories. Whereas those were inspired by people and events of the past, this story could easily become based upon the true accounts of someone in the future. This is entirely possible because, even though the characters are made up, their last days life struggles are realistic.

Certainly, we know from Revelation 19:10 that the testimony of Jesus Christ is the spirit of prophecy, and thus we confidently conclude that the Bible is based upon his story. However, as the powerful scenarios depicted inside *Apocalypse Road* unfold, they will undoubtedly serve to shape numerous additional autobiographies.

The question is, whose? Who will become the wiser for the reading? The world is about to undergo a significant period of unprecedented tribulation. Who will discern the times and heed the signs? Who among you will rise to the occasion and shine forth in the last days like a beacon of light in a dark world?

Some of the episodes explored in this commentary section deal with predicted events that the author believes could happen during the Post-Rapture / Pre-Tribulation gap period. Since the Rapture is an imminent event, this means they could happen before, during, or shortly after you read this book, but probably sometime within your generation.

The author is not making this statement because he claims to be a prophet, but because the world stage is set for the near-fulfillment of the primary prophecies described inside *Apocalypse Road*. That's right; the stage appears to be set up for dozens of prophecies to find near-fulfillment. This is a daunting possibility qualified by the fact that every weapon is fashioned, technology developed, empire-revived, and confederate-alliance-formed, enabling all of the end time's prophecies to be fulfilled.

Prophecies were issued through the ancient Hebrew prophets in both near and far formats. The near prophecies had to be fulfilled during the prophet's lifetime. Upon fulfillment of a near prophecy, the person earned the right to be identified as a true prophet, verses a false prophet. False prophets presented misleading information that often led to idol worship or loss of life. As such, they were punished by death.

The fulfillment of a near prophecy authenticated the prophet, and accredited all of his or her far prophecies. The logic was, if the prophecy occurred exactly as foretold during the person's lifetime, then all the prophet's future predictions could also be counted on to be fulfilled exactly.

Although the prophecies in the Companion's Commentary were far off prophecies when written centuries ago, they are rapidly approaching their near future fulfillment. Only those once far, but now near, prophecies that the author believes are soon forth-coming, are identified in this book and the first book of this series called, *Revelation Road*. Each "*Road*" series book picks up where the previous left off. Ultimately, the series intends to identify chronologically the prophecies scheduled to occur between now and the second coming of Jesus Christ.

Note: Only when a prophecy becomes history, can its exact details be known. Anticipating the coming of a prophecy by understanding its biblical description, and discerning its stage setting signs, is like looking through a glass; no matter how clear the glass, perfect vision is impossible. Describing a coming prophecy or ordering it chronologically, is an imperfect science. Therefore, the ordering of prophetic events outlined in *Apocalypse Road*, is the educated estimate of the author, and cannot be chronologically guaranteed!

COMMENTARY

Chapter 1
The Message Left Behind

Topics Covered

What is the Post-Rapture / Pre-Tribulation Gap Period?

How Long is the Post-Rapture / Pre-trib Gap Period?

Why the Gap Period Takes Time?

Identifying the Final Generation

The Post Rapture People Categories

Why Should a Believer Care About Those Left Behind?

The first chapter of this novel introduces a few of the important issues that will confront everyone who is left behind after the Rapture. The fact that they are left behind, means that they were unsaved at the time of the Rapture. These issues are:

1. There exists a gap of time that could be filled with perilous prophetic events between the Rapture and the Tribulation Period,

2. People are getting saved during this gap period,

3. Ezekiel 38 may be a gap period prophecy, rather than a Church Age prophecy,

What is the Post-Rapture / Pre-Tribulation Gap Period?

The Post-Rapture / Pre-Tribulation Thesis points out that one of the central purposes of this book is to explore and explain the mysterious gap period that exists between the Rapture of the Christian Church and the seven-year Tribulation-Period, (Trib-period). Many Bible prophecy experts today are recognizing that it's not the Rapture that starts the Trib-period. Rather, it begins with the confirmation of the covenant of Daniel 9:27 by the Antichrist, between Israel and some other party.

The other covenanting party is identified in Isaiah 28:15, 18 as "Death." Who or what "Death" represents in this estranged geo-political relationship, and what role "Death" plays in the end times, is explored in the "Post-Rapture / Pre-Tribulation Thesis." This important thesis provides the basis for the storyline scenarios of the novel, as well as, the conclusions drawn in the Companion's Commentary.

Everyone who is left behind will enter into this gap period. Therefore, it is critically important for them to know how long the time-gap is, and what happens within it.

How Long is the Post-Rapture / Pre-trib Gap Period?

This Post Rapture / Pre-Trib gap period is like the Church age in that neither was given a specified time frame of existence within the Scriptures. Although some prophetic periods of time are given prescribed time allotments, the time-span of the gap period is unspecified.

Some Bible prophecy teachers suggest that this time-gap could be as short as twenty-four hours. Their logic is generally based upon the thinking that once the Church is removed, the wrath of God quickly follows. Since the Church is not appointed to the wrath of God according to Scriptures like Romans 5:9, 1 Thessalonians 1:10 and 5:9 and elsewhere, they presume that the wrath of God could commence swiftly, without further restraint, after the Rapture occurs.

However, upon a closer examination it may not be as simple as saying, "Out with the good (grace) and in with the bad (wrath)." The gap period seems to include events that legitimately take time to manifest into action. Before exploring those events, it's important to recognize that if the gap period extends beyond a day, a week, or even a month, then it is safe to suggest that this period of time will contain some globally impacting events!

The Rapture itself will be a world changing episode and the biblically predicted scenarios that follow it, in the gap and on into the Trib-period, will also be earth shaking. The instantaneous disappearances of millions of people worldwide will likely deeply distress the masses left behind. Emotions of loneliness and despair will characterize those who have personally lost loved ones.

COMMENTARY

Unrestrained lawlessness will abound as people from various walks of life are raptured and permanently removed from their personal relationships and business positions. Uncontrollable civil disobedience will plague various parts of the world. All of this, along with the fulfillment of the prophecies identified within this book, which seemingly begin in the gap period, will make mankind vulnerable to supernatural deception and dictatorial leadership. 2 Thessalonians 2:1-10 foretells that Satan will use this scenario to deceive humanity through signs and lying wonders. Ultimately, the deception will provide the Harlot world religion and the Antichrist with the platforms they need to rule the world during their respective periods.

Why the Gap Period Takes Time?

If any or all of the prophecies identified in this book begin during the gap period, some time will elapse as they manifest sequentially. However, if none of the above events occur in the gap, there is another solid reason to believe that the gap lasts longer than a day, week or even a month. This alternative reason is predicated upon, a *MAJOR PREMISE*, which is supported by several *minor premises*. This topic was included in the thesis, but is expounded upon further below.

MAJOR PREMISE: The seven year Trib-period doesn't start until the Antichrist confirms the covenant of Daniel 9:27 between Israel and some other party.

> "Then he (*The Antichrist*) shall confirm a covenant with many for one week (*seven years*); But in the middle of the week He shall bring an end to sacrifice and offering. And on the wing of abominations shall be one who makes desolate, Even until the consummation, which is determined, Is poured out on the desolate." (Daniel 9:27; emphasis added)

Minor Premise #1: In order for the Daniel 9:27 covenant to be consummated; Israel, the Antichrist and the other party to the covenant must all exist.

Minor Premise #2: More than exist, the Antichrist must have also risen to a position of prominent political power. This world leader must achieve sufficient political prowess and power in order to earn the respect of both Israel and the other covenanting party. Otherwise, they would not allow him to confirm the covenant between them.

For instance, US Presidents Jimmy Carter and Bill Clinton confirmed separate agreements between Israel and Egypt in 1979, (Carter), and Israel and Jordan in 1994, (Clinton). In these scenarios, Israel, Egypt and Jordan trusted these political leaders to mediate between them. Likewise, Israel and the other covenanting party will trust the Antichrist as the intermediator between them.

Minor Premise #3: The overflowing scourge spoken of in Isaiah 28:15 must already be taking place within the world. According to Isaiah, Israel becomes a party to the covenant in order to avoid this overflowing scourge. The scourge can't be a figment of Israel's future fearful imagination, but it must have already become a legitimate active threat to the national interests of Israel.

The examples of Egypt and Jordan are cases in point. Both of these Arab nations had been in three major wars against Israel in 1948, 1967 and 1973. These two countries, along with Israel, all decided that it was in their collective national interests to make a peace-pact together. Likewise, Israel and "Death's" representation on earth at the time of the covenant's confirmation will mutually agree to make a seven-year agreement together.

> "Because you have said, "We have made a covenant with death, And with Sheol we are in agreement. When the overflowing scourge passes through, It will not come to us, For we have made lies our refuge, And under falsehood we have hidden ourselves."" (Isaiah 28:15)

These premises establish that Israel feels the need to make a covenant with some party that can prevent an overflowing scourge from adversely affecting the Jewish state. This implies that the other party is either the perpetrator of the overflowing scourge, or that they have the capability to protect Israel somehow from being victimized by the scourge. Israel would not make a pact with a party that was incapable of controlling this overflowing scourge.

The "Post-Rapture / Pre-Tribulation, (Pre-Trib for short), Thesis" explains who "Death" likely represents at the time of the confirmation of the Daniel 9:27 covenant. This commentary and the thesis will also implicate "Death's" earthy representative as the guilty perpetrator of the "overflowing scourge." Lastly, the thesis and remaining commentary will further explain why the gap period is likely much longer than a month. The gap period could actually last for a number of years.

Identifying the Final Generation

At the end of chapter one in the novel, Nathan says, "We need to come to grips with the fact, that this is the FINAL GENERATION." The Bible declares that there is a FINAL GENERATION. More prophetic information is devoted to them than any other generation that ever lived, including the generation that was alive at the first coming of Christ!

This invaluable information is God's gift to that generation. Apocalypse Road is written primarily for that FINAL GENERATION! Therefore, all the characters in the novel section of this book are members of the FINAL GENERATION.

There is a strong possibility that the FINAL GENERATION is alive today. If this is the case, then everyone that is alive today, and up until the time of the Rapture, is written about in some unfulfilled end time's Bible prophecy. This means that you, the reader can know your future!

If you are a believer and the Rapture has yet to occur, then you will be Raptured as long as you don't die beforehand. If you are an unbeliever at the time of the Rapture, then you fall into one of the Post-Rapture people groups. These populations are outlined below and further explained within various sections of the "Companions Commentary."

The Post Rapture People Categories

Saved – Jews and Gentiles

1. Jews

    a. *144,000 Witnesses*, (Revelation 7:1-8 and 14:1-5)

    b. *2 Witnesses*, (Revelation 11:1-12)

        CAVEAT: Please note that these two witnesses may not presently be on the earth, but might descend down to earth from heaven when the timing of their ministries commences.

    c. *Faithful Remnant*, (Zechariah 13:9)

2. Gentiles

    a. *5th Seal Saints*, (Revelation 6:9-11) These are people who appear to become believers in the Post Rapture-Pre-trib gap period. The 5th Seal Saints will be martyred for the word of God and their Christian testimonies. They are portrayed in prophecy as slain souls. If Nathan, Lisa or Jami were to die in the gap period, and you will have to read the entire novel to see if they do, then they become a 5th Seal Saint.

b. *Fellow Servants of the 5th Seal Saints*, (Revelation 6:11) These are people who appear to become believers during the first half of the Tribulation Period (Trib-period). They will also be martyred for the same spiritual reasons as the 5th Seal Saints.

c. *The Brethren of the Fellow Servants of the Fifth Seal Saints*, (Revelation 6:11, 7:9-17, 15:2 and 20:4) These are people who appear to become believers during the second half of the Trib-period, i.e. the "Great Tribulation." They will be martyred for refusing to worship the image of the Antichrist in Revelation 13:15.

d. *Sheep Gentiles*, (Matthew 25:31-40) These are Christians that survive through the Gap and the Tribulation Periods. They will likely include the faithful remnants from Egypt, (Isaiah 19:23-25) Assyria, (Isaiah 19:23-25) Jordan, (Jeremiah 48:47, 49:6) Iran, (Jeremiah 49:39) and elsewhere.

Unsaved- Jews and Gentiles

1. Jews

a. *Orthodox Jews*, (Isaiah 28:15, 18) These Jews will rebuild the third Jewish temple and reinstate the sacrificial system of the Mosaic Law. They will be among the two-thirds of the Jewish peoples that are killed by the Antichrist in Zechariah 13:8.

b. *Secular Jews,* this is a presumptive category for Jews that may not be classified as either the faithful remnant of saved Jews, or unsaved Orthodox Jews. Since they remain as unbelievers in Christ, their prophetic future is the same as the unbelieving Orthodox Jews.

COMMENTARY

2. Gentiles

   a. Harlot World Religion Worshippers (Revelation 2:20-23 and 6:7-8 and 17:6, 15)

   b. Antichrist worshippers, (Revelation 13:16-17, 16:2) These are those who receive the "mark of the Beast."

   c. Goat Gentiles, (Matthew 25:41-46) Unbelievers that survive the Trib-period. (Some of these may have or not have believed in either the Harlot or Antichrist systems).

Why Should a Believer Care About Those Left Behind?

When a Church age believer truly comprehends the tragic plights of the Post Rapture populations, they should be burdened with a sincere concern for their well-being. If this is the FINAL GENERATION, then these peoples are among us today. It could be a spouse, child, grandchild, friend, neighbor, co-worker, business associate, or someone else within the sphere of your influence. If they don't accept Christ as their Savior prior to the Rapture, they run the high risk of being killed for their faith, or being eternally damned for their lack of it.

Apocalypse Road is a FINAL WARNING to the FINAL GENERATION to get right with the Lord NOW, before it's too late!

COMMENTARY

Chapter 2
Rabbis Warn of the Future Russian Invasion

Topics Covered

Ezekiel 38: The Ezekiel 38 Battle Belongs to the Lord

Ezekiel 38: The Glory Belongs to the Lord

Is Ezekiel 38 a Church Age Prophecy?

Topics related to the Timing of Ezekiel 38

Israel Becomes Religious after Psalm 83 and Ezekiel 38

Ezekiel 38: The Ezekiel 38 Battle Belongs to the Lord

I n chapter two of the novel, Israeli Prime Minister Kaufman meets with Israel's Chief Rabbinate Council to inform them that a Russian led coalition is about to invade Israel from the north. To Kaufman's chagrin, the Rabbis attempt to still his fears by quoting several verses from the book of Ezekiel. They foresee Russia's aggression as just the beginning of a forthcoming massive Mideast invasion that was predicted thousands of years ago in Ezekiel 38 and 39.

The Rabbis instruct the Prime Minister to have the Israeli Defense Forces (IDF) stand down in this conflict because the ancient prophecy declares that this last days battle belongs exclusively to the Lord. According to the prophecy, neither IDF, American or any other forces are involved in the military defeat of these invaders. Through supernatural means only, these enemy troops are stopped dead in their tracks. Ezekiel 38:19-22 explains that a great earthquake in the land of Israel shakes up these invaders, which causes the attackers to panic and turn against one another. This is followed up with a barrage of flooding rain, great hailstones, fire, and brimstone.

In the aftermath, the world will have just cause to consider that the Jehovah of the Jews is the one true God over all the earth. Ezekiel says it this way,

> "So I will make My holy name known in the midst of My people Israel, and I will not let them profane My holy name anymore. Then the nations shall know that I am the Lord, the Holy One in Israel. Surely it is coming, and it shall be done," says the Lord God. "This is the day of which I have spoken." (Ezekiel 39:7-8)

Ezekiel declares that "*the nations shall know*," that the God of the Jews is the Lord of the universe. The Hebrew word that Ezekiel uses for the "Lord" is translated as Jehovah, which is the Jewish national name of God. In this prophecy, the Jews are identified as "*My people Israel*," which evidences that the Lord is not finished with the Jews.

A more in-depth analysis of Ezekiel 38-39 is provided within the Companion's Commentary of this book in the chapter entitled, "The Collapse of the Russian Coalition."

Unfortunately, many mainstream Christian denominations believe that God is done with the Jews. They subscribe to "Replacement Theology." Basically, this is the centuries old teaching that when the Jews rejected Jesus, God rejected the Jews. The adherents of this erroneous teaching believe that the church has become the benefactors of the plethora of unfulfilled promises and prophecies that were given to the Jews. According to Ezekiel 38-39 and Romans 9-11, this couldn't be further from the truth.

God has not chosen the Christian Church as the final means in the last days to let the nations know that He is the Lord, "*the Holy One in Israel*." Absolutely not! Instead, He has chosen His "*people Israel*" for that specific purpose. In fact, there's a strong possibility that the Church won't even be on the earth when the Lord makes His holy name known. Ezekiel 38 will possibly happen in the Post-Rapture / Pre-trib gap period.

Ezekiel 38: The Glory Belongs to the Lord

The fulfillment of Ezekiel 38 and 39 will clear up the massive confusion about what the centuries of Jewish Diaspora was all about. The verses below explain the truth of the matter from the Lord's perspective.

"I will set My glory (*in supernatural victory*) among the (*invading*) nations; all the (*world*) nations shall see My judgment which I have executed, and My hand which I have laid on them (*the Ezekiel 38 invaders*). So the house of Israel shall know that I *am* the Lord their God from that day forward. The Gentiles (*world nations*) shall know that the house of Israel went into captivity (*the diaspora*) for their iniquity; (*disobedience*) because they were unfaithful to Me, therefore I hid My face from them. I gave them (*to be chastened*) into the hand of their enemies, and they all fell by the sword. (*experienced centuries of persecution in the diaspora*) According to their uncleanness and according to their transgressions I have dealt with them, and hidden My face from them."' (Ezekiel 39:21-25; emphasis added)

Ezekiel explains that the Jews were intentionally evicted from the land of Israel because of their unfaithfulness to the Lord. They were adequately forewarned about this type of impending disciplinary action in the book of Leviticus. Leviticus 26:32-33 called for a desolation of the land and a dispersion from the land, whenever the people of Israel reached a level of irreversible apostasy.

Ezekiel warned that the worldwide Jewish dispersion was coming over six centuries before it happened.

"Can your heart endure, or can your hands remain strong, in the days when I shall deal with you? I, the Lord, have spoken, and will do *it*. I will scatter you (*Israel*) among the nations, disperse you throughout the countries, and remove your filthiness completely from you. You shall defile yourself in the sight of the nations; then you shall know that I *am* the Lord." (Ezekiel 22:14-16; emphasis added)

Subsequently, Ezekiel provided more supporting details into why the dispersion occurred and how the Gentile nations misperceived what the diaspora was about.

"Moreover the word of the LORD came to me, saying: "Son of man, when the house of Israel dwelt in their own land, they defiled it by their own ways and deeds; to Me their way was like the uncleanness of a woman in her customary impurity. Therefore I poured out My fury on them for the blood they had shed on the land, and for their idols *with which* they had defiled it. So I scattered them among the nations, and they were dispersed throughout the countries; I judged them according to their ways and their deeds. When they came to the nations, wherever they went, they profaned My holy name—when they said of them, 'These *are* the people of the LORD, *and* yet they have gone out of His land.' But I had concern for My holy name, which the house of Israel had profaned among the nations wherever they went." (Ezekiel 36:16-21)

These Scriptures inform that the Jews had upset the Lord, which provoked Him to chasten them. This chastening resulted in a national dispersion out of Israel into the nations of the world. This represents what occurred during the Jewish diaspora between 70-1948 A.D.

During the diaspora, the nations misperceived that the God of the Jews was an inept deity that was unable to protect and preserve His people inside their historic homeland. The Gentile countries misconstrued what was happening during the diaspora and the Jews did nothing collectively to correct their thinking. Furthermore, rather than learn their lessons and glorify the Lord, the Jews attempted to assimilate within the nations in a blatant disregard for God.

This behavior defamed God's holy name. The Jews were a chosen people that were set apart by God from the Gentiles. This is the point of Deuteronomy 7:6-8 and Ezekiel 20:32. Even though the Jews were being disciplined within the Gentile nations, they were to remain set apart for God.

"For you (Jews) *are* a holy people to the LORD your God; the LORD your God has chosen you to be a people for Himself, a special treasure above all the peoples on the face of the earth. The LORD did not set His love on you nor choose you because you were more in number than any other people, for you were the least of all peoples; but because the LORD loves you, and because He would keep the oath which He swore to your fathers, the LORD has brought you out with a mighty hand, and redeemed you from the house of bondage, from the hand of Pharaoh king of Egypt." (Deuteronomy 7:6-8)

"What you have in your mind shall never be, when you say, 'We (Jews) will be like the Gentiles, like the families in other countries, serving wood and stone.'" (Ezekiel 20:32; emphasis added)

Ezekiel 36:22-24, in conjunction with Ezekiel 39:7, explains how the Lord would remedy this problem. These verses inform that the Jews would return from the nations of the world back into Israel. This miraculous undertaking would disprove the mistaken international mindset that the God of the Jews was impotent or incompetent. Once the regathering was accomplished, then the Lord could uphold His holy name in the Ezekiel 38 and 39 prophecies.

Is Ezekiel 38 a Church Age Prophecy?

Many of today's top Bible prophecy teachers believe that Ezekiel 38 could happen at any time. In their haste to make Ezekiel 38 an imminent event, they overlook several important prophetic details, which have to be in place before this prophecy can occur. According to Ezekiel 38:7-13, Israel must be dwelling securely, in the midst of the land and without walls, bars or gates. Additionally, Israel's national coffers must be filled with sufficient wealth to entice Russia and its coalition to come after it. These are significant preconditions that have to be met prior to the fulfillment of Ezekiel 38-39.

Presently, Israel is not dwelling securely. Israel is one of the most fenced in and fortified nations in the world. The tiny country has walled itself in because it is surrounded by enemy Arab nations and radical terrorist organizations that mostly despise the Jews. Additionally, Iran wants to wipe Israel off of the map and seeks the nuclear means to accomplish this.

These dangerous, predominately Muslim, populations are at enmity with Israel and possess combined arsenals of hundreds of thousands of advanced missiles. This causes Israel to remain in a constant state of combat readiness. Therefore, at the time of this publication Israel is not dwelling in the nationally secure position that is predicted in Ezekiel 38.

Moreover, although Israel has discovered an abundance of oil and gas and is rapidly becoming an extremely prosperous nation, in my opinion, they do not yet possess the significant plunder and booty that the Russian coalition comes to capture.

Furthermore, Ezekiel 38 may not even be a Church Age prophecy. It could actually happen after the Rapture takes place. Several of my colleagues and myself suspect that this will prove to be the case. This

COMMENTARY

means that this prophecy could possibly be a Post-Rapture / Pre-Trib gap-period prophecy.

The Rapture is imminent, but Ezekiel 38 still requires that Israel dwell securely and possess great plunder and booty. If Ezekiel 38 is not a Church Age prophecy, then shouldn't Bible prophecy teachers put less emphasis on it, and place more emphasis on the other potential Church Age prophecies that seem to precede it? I call these the *Now Prophecies*, because they lack preconditions, which means they could happen at the present time. A few of them are;

- Disaster in Iran – (Jeremiah 49:34-39),

- Destruction of Damascus – (Isaiah 17, Jer. 49:23-27),

- Toppling of Jordan – (Jer. 49:1-6, Zephaniah 2:8-10, Ezekiel 25:14),

- Terrorization of Egypt – (Isaiah 19:1-18),

- Final Arab-Israeli War- (Psalm 83),

- Decline of America (Ezekiel 38:13), (*America is possibly identified as the young lions of Tarshish*)

- Expansion of Israel – (Obadiah 1:19-20, Jeremiah 49:2, Zephaniah 2:9, Isaiah 19:18),

- Vanishing of the Christians – (1 Corinthians 15:51-52, 1 Thessalonians

(These are among the prophecies, which are identified in my *Now Prophecies* book).

Topics related to the Timing of Ezekiel 38

Below are a few of my reasons for adopting the post-Rapture / Pre-Trib. gap view for the timing of Ezekiel 38.

1. *My people Israel* – God calls the Israelis "My people Israel" three times in Ezekiel 38 and 39. (Ezekiel 38:14, 16 and 39:7). This suggests that the Christian Church need not be present on the earth at the time of Ezekiel 38. This is all about Israel and the Israelis. This is one reason I believe the Rapture could occur before Ezekiel 38 finds fulfillment.

2. *Upholding His Holy name* – Ezekiel 39:7 informs that this is the singular prophetic event that the Lord chooses to uphold His holy name. The Russian confederacy wants to harm the *Chosen*

People, the Jews, and deprive them of their bounty in the *Promised Land*, of Israel. The *Chosen People* and the *Promised Land* are two integral components of the unconditional covenant that God made with Abraham in Genesis 15. The supernatural defeat of the Russian coalition is specifically designed to show the world that the Lord personally made good on His 4000-year-old promise to Abraham. The Abrahamic covenant extrapolates on to Isaac, and Jacob and their Jewish descendants today. The Christian Church is not the focus of Ezekiel 38.

The fulfillment of Ezekiel 38 in the Post-Rapture / Pre-trib gap accomplishes a couple important things. First, since the Christian Church would already be Raptured, it transfers the worlds focus back on the Chosen People and the Promised Land. The Rapture will signify that Christ keeps His promises to believers. The fulfillment of Ezekiel 38 proves that Jehovah keeps His covenants and promises with Israel.

Secondly, it gives the nations an advanced opportunity to know that the Holy One in Israel, is the one true God. After the Antichrist has risen to power in the Trib-period, the choice becomes more difficult for people because of the deceptive lie in 2 Thessalonians 2:8-12 that will be influencing people.

3. *Israel burns weapons for seven years* – in addition to the reasons above, I hold to the teaching that Ezekiel 39:9-10 presents yet another clue to the timing of Ezekiel 38 and 39.

> "Then those who dwell in the cities of Israel will go out and set on fire and burn the weapons, both the shields and bucklers, the bows and arrows, the javelins and spears; and they will make fires with them for seven years. They will not take wood from the field nor cut down any from the forests, because they will make fires with the weapons; and they will plunder those who plundered them, and pillage those who pillaged them," says the Lord GOD." (Ezekiel 39:9-10)

These Ezekiel verses say that Israel will make fires with the enemy's weapons. Israelis appear to utilize these weapons for energy consumption for a period of seven-years. This will be no problem during the first half of the tribulation because the Jews will be enjoying a temporary peace. This peace ends abruptly after three and one-half years when the

COMMENTARY

Antichrist begins a genocidal campaign against the Jews. This period of persecution happens in the second half of the Trib-period. During this period, many Jews will be fleeing from Israel, rather than burning weapons in Israel.

Therefore, some scholars, like Dr. Ron Rhodes and Dr. Arnold Fruchtenbaum, suggest that Ezekiel 38 and 39 should conclude no later than three and one-half years before the seven-years of tribulation even begins. This allows the Jews seven full years to burn the weapons before they begin fleeing for their lives. This could put the conclusion of Ezekiel 38 in the Post-Rapture / Pre-trib gap period.

Israel Becomes Religious after Psalm 83 and Ezekiel 38

In this novel chapter, the Rabbis gloated over their understanding of Bible prophecy. They explained that the destruction of Damascus was a direct fulfillment of Isaiah 17, and the annexation of Jordan a fulfillment of Jeremiah 49:1-6. (*These prophecies were fulfilled in the Revelation Road, Hope Beyond the Horizon storyline*).

The point is, that by the time the Now Prophecies above and Ezekiel 38 find fulfillment, the religious leadership of Israel will become increasingly esteemed and empowered by their people. At that future time, it will be undeniable that The God of the Jews has foretold the future accurately in the past and that He is the protector of Israel in the present and the future. This should elevate the Jewish religious leaders to a similar status that the Levite priests enjoyed in the past.

Even now, after having the won the Arab-Israeli wars of 1948, 1967 and 1973, against insurmountable odds, many Jews suspect that God is protecting Israel in fulfillment of His covenants, promises and prophecies. The more they realize that they are again the "Chosen People," they will turn their focus toward their God Jehovah. However, as a nation, the way they will do this is by reinstating the sacrificial system of the Mosaic Law.

Rather than embracing Jesus Christ as their Messiah, they will expand their borders, build their temple, raise up their Levite priests and once again sacrifice animals on the altar. This was how it was at the time of the first and second Jewish Temples. Returning to variations of those religious practices is what they plan to do. They are already preparing for their Third Jewish Temple to be constructed.

They will build this Temple with the goal of hastening the coming of the Messiah. Not realizing the futility of this thinking, because Jesus Christ is the Messiah, they will consider it politically and religiously expedient to enter into the covenant referenced in Isaiah 28:15, 18 and Daniel 9:27. This will be to the detriment of the nation because this is when the seven-year Trib-period begins, which concludes with the severe persecution of the Jews by the Antichrist. The probable true content of this disastrous false covenant is provided in the "Post-Rapture / Pre-Trib Thesis."

Below is a quote concerning the problematic nature of this covenant from the biblical scholar, Dr. Arnold Fruchtenbaum of Ariel Ministries. This quote identifies the two key passages, which evidence that the Trib-period commences when this tragic covenant is confirmed.

> "The Tribulation begins with Israel signing a seven-year covenant. Two key passages bear this out. The first passage is Daniel 9:24–27, the famous prophecy of the seventy weeks or seventy sevens of the prophet Daniel.... The second passage is Isaiah 28:14–22. In verse 14, God calls the ones making this covenant scoffers. He considers them mockers rather than serious leaders. Verse 15 gives the reason for this and provides God's viewpoint of the covenant itself. It is obvious that the leaders of Israel will enter into this covenant to obtain some measure of security and to escape the overflowing scourge. Hence they will believe that entering the covenant will free them from further military invasions. However, God declares that this is not a covenant of life, but a covenant of death. It is not a covenant of heaven, but a covenant of hell. Rather than gaining security, they will gain a strong measure of insecurity."[50]

COMMENTARY

Chapter 3
The European Union Consoles Israel

Topics Covered

The EU and the Revived Roman Empire

The Coming Greater, Safer and Wealthier Israel

Russia's evil plan against Israel in Ezekiel 38:10

The Decline of the USA and UK

The Biblical Indictment of America

T his novel chapter relates to several end times prophetic scenarios.

COMMENTARY

1. The EU and it's likely connection with the revived Roman Empire in Bible prophecy.

2. The greater, safer and wealthier Israel that Russia's coalition seeks to invade in Ezekiel 38-39.

3. Russia's evil plan against Israel in Ezekiel 38:10.

4. The decline of the USA and UK in the end times in Ezekiel 38:13.

5. The EU and the revived Roman Empire

The European Union is introduced in this early part of the novel. It is commonly taught among some of today's Bible prophecy teachers that the EU exists in fulfillment of the biblical prophecies that predicted the revival of the Roman Empire. Some related verses that deal with this subject directly are, Daniel 2:40-43, 7:23-25 and indirectly in Revelation 13:7-8.

According to Daniel, the Antichrist emerges out of this revived empire. It was the Roman Empire that conquered Jerusalem and destroyed the second Jewish Temple in 70 A.D.

> "And after the sixty-two weeks Messiah (*Jesus Christ*) shall be cut off (*crucified*), but not for Himself; (*but for the sins of mankind*) And the people (*the Romans*) of the prince (*Antichrist*) who is to come (*in the end times*) Shall destroy the city (*Jerusalem*) and the sanctuary (*second Jewish Temple*). The end (*this occurred in 70 A.D.*) of it *shall be* with a flood, (*military invasion*) And till the end of the war desolations are determined. (Daniel 9:26; emphasis added)

Europe stands to be one of the few regions that remains relatively intact as end times prophetic events begin to unfold. The Middle East becomes a war zone in Psalm 83 and other related prophecies. Many Arab countries will be decimated as a result. Russia, Turkey, Libya, Iran and other countries participating in Ezekiel 38 will be essentially conquered and incapacitated. America seems to have declined from its superpower status by then, which is pointed out at the end of this chapter's commentary. This will leave the revived Roman Empire as a strong candidate to pick up the pieces of a tattered and torn world.

The EU stands to play a vital role in uniting the global order of the end times. Ultimately, the world order divides into ten regions represented by the ten kings of Daniel 7:24 and Revelation 17:12 and the ten horns of Revelation 13:1 and 17:3-16.

The EU can be expected to endorse the world religion of the Harlot in Revelation 17. There is historical precedent and biblical predictions that support this conclusion.

Historically, when the Roman Empire began to collapse it became politically expedient for the Roman rulers to endorse Christianity as the official religion. When Constantine, the emperor of Rome, became a Christian it meant that the empire became Christian. By 313 AD, Constantine issued the Edict of Milan, which specifically guaranteed religious freedom to Christians throughout the Roman Empire.[51]

According to Revelation 17, the harlot world religion plays an important role in ruling over the masses. The world will be recovering from a plethora of overwhelming events. Many people will look to this world religion for guidance and direction. Revelation 17:3 says that the

Harlot and the Antichrist will be in cahoots with each other. This future political marriage between the Antichrist and the harlot world religion will somewhat rival what occurred when the Roman Empire fell.

The Harlot and the Antichrist are exposited upon further throughout various chapters of the Companion's commentary.

The Coming Greater, Safer and Wealthier Israel

According to several prophecies, Israel is predicted to someday expand its borders, improve its national security and increase its economic prosperity.

Ezekiel 38:8-13 depicts that in the "latter years" the Jewish state will be dwelling securely and in a very prosperous condition. Ezekiel 38:11 says that the Israelis will reside as *"a peaceful people, who dwell safely, all of them dwelling without walls, and having neither bars nor gates."* Observe that this verse acknowledges that *"all of them,"* alluding to the entire Israeli populous, abide as *"a peaceful people."*

Presently, this can't be said of anyone living in Israel. Most Israelis possess gas masks and know the locations of nearby bomb shelters. Additionally, there exists a security wall inside the country that was built to keep Palestinian terrorism out of Israel proper. This partition wall is over 400 miles long. Plus, there are security checkpoints throughout various parts of Israel.

Moreover, Hezbollah has over 100,000 missiles that could be launched into Israel at the rate of about 1500 per day. This headline on April 1, 2015, which was taken from "Breaking Israel News," points this out. *"IDF: Hezbollah Could Fire Up to 1,500 Rockets Per Day at Israel."*[52]

Many other reasons, like the looming risk to Israel of Iran possessing a nuclear weapon, the spillover of the Syrian revolution into Israel from its Northeast border and the daily threat of Hamas missiles landing inside of Israel, prohibit Israelis from dwelling safely. This means that something must happen before Ezekiel 38 commences, which turns Israel into a safer nation.

Some Bible teachers suggest that this secure Israel already exists today. They propose that the "dwelling securely" can be translated as residing confidently. The inference is that Israel presently dwells with the confidence that the IDF can defend the nation adequately. Some generalize it to mean that the Israelis dwell safely because God's protection is over them. However, Ezekiel explains ten chapters earlier exactly what "dwelling securely" means.

"And there shall no longer be a pricking brier or a painful thorn for the house of Israel from among all *who are* around them, who despise them. Then they shall know that I *am* the Lord God." 'Thus says the Lord God: "When I have gathered the house of Israel from the peoples among whom they are scattered, and am hallowed in them in the sight of the Gentiles, then they will dwell in their own land which I gave to My servant Jacob. And they will dwell safely there, build houses, and plant vineyards; yes, they will dwell securely, when I execute judgments on all those around them who despise them. Then they shall know that I *am* the Lord their God."'"

The only way that Israel will achieve the peace that Ezekiel 28:24-26 and 38:8-13 describes is to eliminate the dangers posed to it by Iran and its Arab neighbors. These Arabs are identified in Psalm 83 by their ancient names. The map below calls them the "*Inner Circle of Psalm 83*" because they share common borders with Israel. It's highly unlikely that Ezekiel 38 will happen until the Inner Circle of Arab nations and terrorist populations are eradicated.

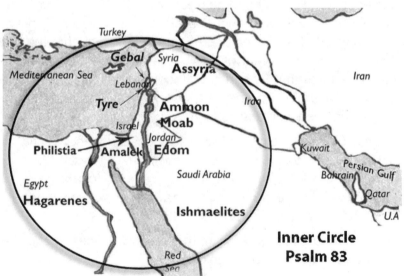

The map superimposes the ancient names of the Psalm 83 populations upon their modern day equivalents.

The biblical remedy for removing this problem is to curse those that curse Israel. This is God's foreign policy toward the Gentiles as per Genesis 12:3. On the flip side, this policy is also designed to benefit those who bless Israel. If Iran and the Inner Circle of Arabs were blessing Israel, the Israelis would currently be dwelling securely as a peaceful people. There would be no further need to maintain walls, bars or gates.

The international prescription to remedy the Arab-Israeli conflict is to have Israel contract in size by relinquishing land to the Palestinians. Conversely, the Bible predicts that the opposite will happen. Israel will expand according to Obadiah 1:19-20, Jeremiah 49:2, Zephaniah 2:8-9, Isaiah 19:18 and elsewhere.

What biblically permits Israel to expand its borders into these Arab territories is found in Genesis 15:18, which measures the Promised Land as existing between the Nile River in Egypt and the Euphrates River in Iraq and Syria. When the IDF, who exists in fulfillment of Bible prophecies, defeats the Inner Circle of Psalm 83 in a concluding Arab-Israeli war, Israel will be free to capture more of the Promised Land.

There is historical precedent for this in both history and modernity. Historically, Joshua conquered and captured lands around 3300 years ago. King David and King Solomon did the same about 3000 years ago. In modern times, the IDF did the same thing in June of 1967. In all of these incidences, the Jewish state became greater, safer and ultimately it facilitated their ability to become wealthier.

Ezekiel 38:13 says that when Russia and its allies of Turkey, Iran, Libya and several other nations come to invade Israel, that the country will possess booty and great plunder. This depicts Israel as a wealthy nation. The point is that when Israel becomes safer and greater, it will also become wealthier. The nation's economy seems to be so strong that the Russian coalition covets Israel's prosperity.

> "Sheba, Dedan, the merchants of Tarshish, and all their young lions will say to you, 'Have you (*Russia*) come (*to invade Israel*) to take plunder? Have you gathered your army to take booty, to carry away silver and gold, to take away livestock and goods, to take great plunder?" (Ezekiel 38:13; emphasis added)

Another telling passage of Scripture along the lines of the coming wealthier Israel is described in Ezekiel 36.

> "Therefore thus says the Lord God: "I have raised My hand in an oath that surely the (*Inner Circle of Psalm 83*) nations that *are* around you shall bear their own shame. But you, O mountains of Israel, you shall shoot forth your branches and yield your fruit to My people Israel, for they are about

to come (*out from the Diaspora*). For indeed I *am* for you, and I will turn to you, and you (*the land of Israel*) shall be tilled and sown. I will multiply men upon you, all the house of Israel, all of it; and the cities shall be inhabited and the ruins rebuilt. I will multiply upon you man and beast; and they shall increase and bear young; I will make you inhabited as in former times, and do better *for you* than at your beginnings. Then you shall know that I *am* the Lord. (Ezekiel 36:7-11; emphasis added)

Ezekiel informs that when the Inner Circle of nations are cursed, that Israel will be blessed. These verses also point to the coming of the wealthier Israel of Ezekiel 38:13.

Russia's evil plan against Israel in Ezekiel 38:10

Thus says the Lord God: "On that day it shall come to pass *that* thoughts will arise in your (Russian leader's) mind, and you will make an evil plan (Ezekiel 38:10; emphasis added)

Israel's greater, safer and wealthier condition is short lived because the Russian leader at that time will devise an evil plan against Israel. In the novel he is portrayed as Vladimir Zirosky. His covetous plan consists of forming a predominately Muslim coalition of nations to invade Israel for its booty and great plunder. The general consensus of who the nations are that enlist with Russia are displayed in the "Outer Ring of Ezekiel 38" map.

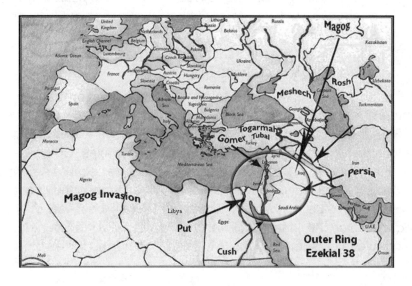

This Outer Ring map superimposes the ancient names in Ezekiel 38:1-5 upon their modern day equivalents. It's important to note that none of them are in the Inner Circle of Psalm 83. Furthermore, not one of them share common borders with Israel. Also, not any of the Outer Ring of nations has ever been an overt enemy of the nation of Israel, which can't be said about the Inner Circle of Psalm 83.

The Russian alliance seems to begin their aggression against Israel by blockading all the important waterways needed to export its commerce into world markets. We can conclude from the mention of merchants in Ezekiel 38:13, that a prosperous Israel is involved in international commerce at the time.

The map above shows how this alliance could be selected with this potential boycott strategy as part of Russia's evil plan. Turkey and Libya can blockade the Mediterranean Sea. Ethiopia can prevent passage through the Red Sea. Iran can shut down the Strait of Hormuz in the Persian Gulf. I develop this scenario in more detail in the *Revelation Road* book. Ultimately, the evil plan manifests into an invasion of Israel to capture Israel's booty and great plunder.

The Decline of the USA and UK

The quote below is taken from this chapter of the novel.

> *"Western armies, especially the USA and UK, are still in a state of disarray, from the massive unexplained disappearances. But Russia's coalition, comprised mainly of Muslim countries, experienced very few disappearances, leaving their armies virtually intact. Moreover, the Muslim populations residing inside Europe are mostly supportive of the Russian coalition, and are crowding our streets in large numbers in protests against Israel."*

The context of this scene takes into consideration that both the Rapture and Psalm 83 have previously occurred. Only believing Christians get Raptured, which means that the Muslim forces within the Russian coalition will still remain within their respective armies. Conversely, the US military will be adversely affected by the Rapture because a significant number of Christians will have permanently abandoned their posts.

European Muslims will be upset with Israel because of the IDF conquest over the Inner Circle of the Psalm 83 Arab countries. It is reasonable to presume that these Muslims will be supportive of Russia's coalition plans to invade Israel. They will seek retaliation upon Israel. If the EU condemns Russia in support of Israel, it is likely that European Muslims will line up in the streets of Europe in protests.

Ezekiel 38:13, quoted earlier in this commentary, appears to identify the USA and UK in Bible prophecy. I devote an entire chapter to this subject in the *Now Prophecies* book. The chapter is entitled, *"Is America in Ezekiel 38?"* I conclude that the UK is the *"merchants of Tarshish"* and the USA is identified as *"their young lions."*

These countries appear to be sideline spectators in this massive Mideast Gog of Magog invasion. They don't appear to lift a finger to defend Israel in this battle, rather they simply protest Russia's evil intentions. It's easy to understand why the UK wouldn't want to confront this Russian coalition, but the USA still possesses the world's most powerful military.

Why doesn't America come to the side of Israel, its greatest Middle East ally, in this matter? Is it because the USA is no longer the world's greatest superpower at that time? I believe the answer is yes. In my estimation, something drastic happens to dethrone the USA from its superpower status. It could be the Rapture, which would certainly cripple the nation to a large extent. However, it could be a menu of disastrous events that serve to downgrade America as a superpower.

Many of today's top Bible prophecy teachers are sounding the alarm that America is presently experiencing the early stages of divine judgment. I conclude this section of commentary by biblically indicting the USA. This country has straight armed God out of this nation and the indictment below explains how.

The Biblical Indictment of America

World history confirms what the Bible boldly declares: The establishment and future of a city, territory, nation or empire, is determined by the Lord. Concerning the creation of a nation, we are told in Acts 17:26,

> "And He (God) has made from one blood every nation
> of men to dwell on all the face of the earth, and has
> determined their preappointed times and the boundaries
> of their dwellings."

The prophet Jeremiah explains how the future of a nation is determined.

COMMENTARY

"The instant I speak concerning a nation and concerning a kingdom, to pluck up, to pull down, and to destroy it, if that nation against whom I have spoken turns from its evil, I will relent of the disaster that I thought to bring upon it." (Jer. 18:7-8)

"And the instant I speak concerning a nation and concerning a kingdom, to build and to plant it, if it does evil in My sight so that it does not obey My voice, then I will relent concerning the good with which I said I would benefit it." (Jer. 18:9-10)

This section of commentary takes a look at the epic tales of two infamous cities, Nineveh and Jerusalem. These comparisons are made to determine which one of these locations best characterizes America's current spiritual condition. If such a historical comparison can be applied now, then the relevant question is: Should Americans find hope in Jeremiah 18:7-8, with the story of Nineveh at the time of Jonah, or feel despair in the story of Jeremiah 18:9-10, which describes Jerusalem at the time of the Babylonian conquest? To determine the answer, I propose the examination of two principles that I call *"The Nineveh Principle"* and *"The Jerusalem Principle"*.[53]

The Nineveh Principle

"I think in many ways America is like Nineveh. The wickedness of Nineveh was so great that God effectively said it was recognized up in heaven – 'the sin of Nineveh has come before me' – and I believe America is at such a state." (Senior Calvary Chapel Pastor and Evangelist Greg Laurie.)[54]

The Nineveh Principle has its origin in the 8th century BC before Jeremiah 18:7-10 was written. It is rooted in 2 Chronicles 7:14;

"If My people who are called by My name will humble themselves, and pray and seek My face, and turn from their wicked ways, then I will hear from heaven, and will forgive their sin and heal their land."

Although these verses primarily dealt with the Lord's response to King Solomon's petition for the protection of the nation of Israel around 957 BC, they apparently also laid the groundwork for the Lord's treatment toward other nations. The Assyrian city of Nineveh at the time of Jonah about 760 BC evidences this.[55] Nineveh, the capital city of the Assyrian empire, was ultimately destroyed around 612 BC; however, the empire had become exceedingly evil long before it came to its end.

At the height of its wickedness, the Lord sent Jonah, a prophet, to warn of Nineveh's fast approaching destruction.

> "And Jonah began to enter the city on the first day's walk.
> Then he cried out and said, "Yet forty days, and Nineveh
> shall be overthrown!"" (Jonah 3:4)

Jonah's warning was well received by the king and the people of Nineveh. They took it upon themselves to turn from their evil ways and Nineveh received a stay of execution.

> "Then God saw their works, that they turned from their evil
> way; and God relented from the disaster that He had said
> He would bring upon them, and He did not do it." (Jonah
> 3:10)

Although it can be argued that the Assyrians at the time were not classified as "My people," the fact that they repented and turned from their evil ways changed their spiritual standing with the Lord.

With the historical precedents of 2 Chronicles 7:14 and Jonah 3:10 already in place, Jeremiah 18:7-8 reinforces this Nineveh Principle: if an evil people repent and turn from their wicked ways, the Lord will relent from bringing disaster upon them.

The Jerusalem Principle

In sharp contrast to the Nineveh Principle, is the Jerusalem Principle. The Jerusalem Principle applies when a nation reaches a point of no return and the Lord determines that its destruction will not be postponed. This happened to the city of Jerusalem and the Southern Kingdom of Judah about 2700 years ago during the time of the Hebrew prophet Jeremiah. Three times Jeremiah was told to stop praying for the people of Judah.

> "Therefore do not pray for this people, nor lift up a cry or
> prayer for them, nor make intercession to Me; for I will
> not hear you. Do you not see what they do in the cities of
> Judah and in the streets of Jerusalem?" (Jer. 7:16)

COMMENTARY

> "So do not pray for this people, or lift up a cry or prayer for them; for I will not hear them in the time that they cry out to Me because of their trouble." (Jer. 11:14)

> "Then the LORD said to me, "Do not pray for this people, for their good. When they fast, I will not hear their cry; and when they offer burnt offering and grain offering, I will not accept them. But I will consume them by the sword, by the famine, and by the pestilence."" (Jer. 14:11-12)

After Jeremiah received his instructions to quit praying for the people of Judah, he forewarned them of their impending judgment. The people were captured and transported into Babylonian captivity where they remained for seventy years. Their homeland sat desolate during that period.[56]

In His foreknowledge the Lord knew that Judah would not have a Nineveh or 2 Chronicles 7:14 moment. Jeremiah's intercessory prayers on behalf of Judah would have no effect on the Lord's decision and he was told to cease praying for the people. The Lord explained why:

> "Therefore you (Jeremiah) shall speak all these words to them, (in Judah) but they will not obey you. You shall also call to them, but they will not answer you." (Jer. 7:27)

In essence, Jeremiah was informed that the people of Judah would not respond to his warnings in the similar way that the people of Nineveh did to Jonah's forewarnings. As per the provision of forgiveness given in Jeremiah 18:7-8, if Judah would have repented, like Nineveh did, then the Lord would certainly have relented from judgment. However, due to their evildoings and disobedience the Lord implemented the provision of judgment in Jeremiah 18:9-10, which was ultimately executed through the Babylonian conquest.

The people of Judah forsook their God Jehovah and became idolatrous. Jeremiah 19:4-9 provides the indictment of, and verdict for, Judah. These verses paint a graphic picture of despair and they are summarized below.

The Indictment of Judah (Jeremiah 19:4-5)

- The people forsook the Lord and alienated Him from Judah.
- They worshipped false gods instead.

- They sacrificed the innocent blood of their children to the false god Baal.

- Child sacrifice appalled the Lord.

The Verdict of Judah (Jeremiah 19:6-9)

- A judgment in the form of a slaughter would come as sequenced below.

- The counselors of Judah would provide foolish counsel.

- The people of Judah would be killed by the swords of their enemies.

- Their corpses would be eaten by the vultures and carnivorous animals.

- The land would be desolated and contaminated with plagues.

- The survivors would become cannibals in order to survive.

- They would even eat their own sons and daughters due to their despair.

It is important to note that the Lord told Adam and Eve in Genesis 1:22, 28 and Noah and his three sons in Genesis 9:1, 7 to be fruitful and multiply upon the earth. The goal was to populate the earth with godly offspring. Contrary to the Lord's command, the people of Judah were murdering and ultimately reduced to eating their children!

The Jerusalem Principle depicts what has historically happened when judgment and destruction occurs to an evil people who forsake the Lord.

America's Indictment

"We have taken God out of the public debate…I want to put Him back in." Evangelist Franklin Graham.[57]

(Tombstone image quotes Daniel 5:24-28 – MENE, MENE, TEKEL, UPHARSIN. God has numbered your kingdom, and finished it; You have been weighed in the balances, and found wanting; Your kingdom has been divided). (June 26, 2015 is when the Supreme Court approved same sex marriages).

UNITED STATES OF AMERICA
BORN: JULY 4TH 1776
DIED: JUNE 26 2015

MENE, MENE, TEKEL
UPHARSIN

America has crossed every forbidden biblical boundary and in so doing has forsaken God. Throughout history nations and empires have been judged and destroyed for transgressing these biblically defined moral and spiritual boundaries! Boundaries such as:

- SEXUAL PERVERSION, like that of Sodom and Gomorrah at the time of Abraham around 2000 BC.

- IDOL WORSHIP, which in its worst conditions led to child sacrifice, which resulted in the destruction of the Northern Kingdom of Israel in 722 BC and the Southern Kingdom of Judah in 586 BC.

- WICKEDNESS AND MORAL DECADENCE, which caused the ultimate destruction of the Assyrian empire about 612 BC by the Babylonians and Medes.

- ANTI-SEMITISM, which led to the destruction of the Egyptian army at the time of Moses about 3500 BC. The treatment of Israel by a nation is reciprocated upon that nation according to Genesis 12:3. This policy pertains to Abraham, Isaac, Jacob and their descendants, the Jews today. Blessings are in store for those who treat Israel favorably, but troubles are guaranteed to them that curse Israel.

In every instance the destructions caused unbearable sufferings and hardships to everyone, including believers in God and unbelievers that did not heed the prophetic warnings given in advance by the Hebrew prophets.

America's In the Danger Zone

Over the past fifty years, America has transgressed over all of these dangerous boundaries. This is attested to by the Supreme Court decisions listed below.

- *1962 – Engel v. Vitale*: the removal of Prayer in public schools by the Supreme Court.

- *1963 – Abington School District v. Schempp*: the removal of Bible reading in public schools by the Supreme Court.

- *1973 – Roe v. Wade*: legalized abortions by the Supreme Court. Since then, America has performed over 58 million abortions. Presently about 1 million abortions occur every year in America. This law means that about 1 million children annually will not be able to grow up, populate the earth and potentially become Godly offspring.

- *1980 – Stone v. Graham*: in this case the Supreme Court ruled that a Kentucky statute requiring the posting of a copy of the Ten Commandments on the wall of each public classroom in the state was unconstitutional. The Court ruled that because they were being placed in public classrooms they were in violation of the First Amendment.

- *2003 – Lawrence v. Texas*: This was the landmark decision by the United States Supreme Court that struck down the sodomy law in Texas, which by extension, invalidated sodomy laws in 13 other states.

- *2013 – United States v. Windsor*: the case that the Supreme Court struck down the Defense of Marriage Act (DOMA). DOMA stated that one man should be married to one woman. DOMA was biblically supported according to Genesis 2:24, which says; "Therefore a man shall leave his father and mother and be joined to his wife, and they shall become one flesh." Marriage is the ordained relationship through which a man and woman can become fruitful and multiply the earth with godly children.

- *2015 – Obergefell v. Hodges*: the Supreme Court case that ruled in favor of Same Sex Marriages, which is unbiblical according to Romans 1:27 and elsewhere. Same sex couples are unable to procreate naturally. Therefore, it is humanly impossible for them to be fruitful and populate the earth with godly kids.

- *2015* – The present White House Administration has turned its back on Israel. As an example, Obama believes the Iran JCPOA nuclear deal is good, but Israeli Prime Minister Netanyahu believes it's the worst deal imaginable. A recent poll conducted by the "Panels Politics in Tel Aviv" confirmed the concerns that Israelis have about U.S. President Barrack Obama. The poll overwhelmingly rated him as the worst president for Israel in the last 30 years.

The Lord has provided ample warnings to Americans that the country is headed for destruction. These forewarnings have come in the forms of remedial judgments, prophetic voices, and ultimately by giving them the ungodly leaders they deserve. For instance, U.S. President Barack

Hussein Obama is the most pro-abortion, pro-homosexual, and anti-Israel president in America's history!

America's Verdict

Which of these two cities does America most resemble today, forgiven Nineveh or judged Jerusalem? Most would agree that once upon a time the Lord planted, built up and blessed this nation. This would connect the USA with Jeremiah 18:9, which says, "And the instant I speak concerning a nation and concerning a kingdom, to build and to plant it."

It appears safe to also suggest that from the Supreme Court decisions provided above, that America has, as Franklin Graham stated, "Taken God out of the public debate." Thus, if the Lord's voice is not even in the public debate, then how can we be obeying the Lord's say-so in the important matters of this country? If we are not obeying the Lord's commands, then we are doing evil in His sight. This would connect the USA with Jeremiah 18:10a, which states, "if it (a nation) does evil in My sight so that it does not obey My voice, then..."

> *Then what?* "Then I will relent concerning the good with which I said I would benefit it?" (Jer. 18:10b) Let's substitute America for Jerusalem and Judah in Jeremiah 7:16 to see if the shoe fits.

> "Therefore do not pray for this people, nor lift up a cry or prayer for them, nor make intercession to Me; for I will not hear you. Do you not see what they do in the cities of Judah and in the streets of Jerusalem?" (Jer. 7:16)

> *This verse is paraphrased below for potential American application.*

> "Therefore do not pray for Americans, nor lift up a cry or prayer for them, nor make intercession to Me; for I will not hear you. Do you not see the forbidden biblical boundaries their Supreme Court has crossed over in the city of Washington D.C., the sale of aborted baby body parts by Planned Parenthood of the Pacific Southwest, and the LGBT Gay Pride Parades in the streets of San Francisco and San Diego?"

COMMENTARY

Will America Have a Nineveh or Jerusalem Experience?

Is it possible that the historical example of Nineveh could be repeated in America? If indeed America is headed for a disaster, could America receive a similar pardon from the Lord? The answer is yes, but the Lord does not issue "get out of jail free" cards as in the game of Monopoly. Americans and their leaders must sincerely emulate the actions of Nineveh in order for the Lord to relent from destroying the nation.

I'm not saying that Americans should stop praying for their country, nor am I suggesting that Americans will become so desperate that they will someday eat their sons and daughters. In fact, Ezekiel says that was a one-time episode for Judah that wouldn't be repeated.

> "And I will do among you (*Jerusalem)* what I have never done, and the like of which I will never do again, because of all your abominations. Therefore fathers shall eat their sons in your midst, and sons shall eat their fathers; and I will execute judgments among you, and all of you who remain I will scatter to all the winds." (Ezekiel 5:9-10; emphasis added)

What I am asking Americans to consider is, does America have a national repentance forthcoming in the near future? If the answer is yes, then America will most resemble forgiven Nineveh and Jeremiah 18:7-8. If the answer is no, then...*Then what?* Then, at the very least, the Lord will no longer bless this nation and America's greatness will never return! Only God, who knows the end from the beginning, knows America's final verdict!

> "Remember the former things of old, For I am God, and there is no other; I am God, and there is none like Me, Declaring the end from the beginning, And from ancient times things that are not yet done, Saying, 'My counsel shall stand, And I will do all My pleasure.'" (Isaiah 46:9-10)

COMMENTARY

Chapter 4

The EU Condemnation and Vatican Consecration of Russia

Topic Covered

The Four Final Religions of the Last Days

This novel chapter introduces the global Church and State relationship that is predicted to manifest after the Rapture. Revelation 17: foretells of this.

> "So he (*an angel*) carried me (*John the apostle*) away in the Spirit into the wilderness. And I saw a woman (*The Harlot*) sitting on a scarlet beast (*The Antichrist*) *which was* full of names of blasphemy, having seven heads and ten horns. (Revelation 17:3; emphasis added)

> John marvels at the revelation he receives and Revelation 17:7 says, "But the angel said to me, "Why did you marvel? I will tell you the mystery of the woman (*Harlot*) and of the beast (*Antichrist*) that carries her, which has the seven heads and the ten horns."

John sees the future union between the harlot world religion and the Antichrist. These verses picture the Harlot sitting on the Antichrist and him carrying her to the heights of her power. Notice that these verses portray the Antichrist supporting the ambitions of the Harlot. When this unholy church and state matrimony takes place, the masses will embrace it. This merger accomplishes several important things.

1.   The Harlot will serve as the religious opiate the masses will crave after the Rapture occurs.

When millions of believers vanish in an instant without warning, the world is involuntarily ushered into an age where the paranormal becomes the new normal. Secular explanations from scientific circles will likely not sufficiently placate the concerns of the masses who are left behind. The harlot system must satiate their spiritual appetites for answers.

This means that the harlot religion must already be in place prior to the Rapture in order for it to rapidly rise to the supernatural occasion. It can't be a sluggish afterthought that evolves over time out of world chaos. Global order has to be reinstated swiftly for Satan to forward his campaign of deception identified in 2 Thessalonians 2:8-12.

Since the timing of the Rapture is the Lord's best kept secret, Satan has undoubtedly already put this system in place. It is safe to assume that the Harlot is already prepped to fill the spiritual void that results after the Rapture.

2.   Supernatural signs and wonders, and the political endorsement by world leaders of the Harlot, will give this world religious system its credibility and prestige in the eyes of the masses.

According to the apostle John, the Harlot is wealthy, violent and embraced worldwide. Although this religion has a global grasp, Revelation 17:18 informs that its main headquarters are centralized in a "great city." A clue to which great city is found in Revelation 17:9, which says that the city sits upon seven mountains, or seven hills in some translations.

> Revelation 17:4 explains that the Harlot is arrayed in purple and scarlet, and adorned with gold and precious stones and pearls. This verse along with Revelation 18:3, which says the merchants of the earth have become rich through the harlot's abundance, evidences that this is a wealthy religion.
>
> Revelation 17:6 warns of the violent nature of the Harlot; "I saw the woman, drunk with the blood of the saints and with the blood of the martyrs of Jesus. And when I saw her, I marveled with great amazement."
>
> Revelation 17:15 addresses the harlot's global influence; "Then he said to me, "The waters which you saw, where the harlot sits, are peoples, multitudes, nations, and tongues."

COMMENTARY

The point of all the above is that after the Rapture, it's the Harlot that Satan puts forth first to deceive those left behind. The initial role of the Antichrist is to support the Harlot. After the Rapture, Satan has a one-two punch planned for man. Eventually, the Harlot over extends her usefulness and the Antichrist has her desolated.

> "And the ten horns which you saw on the beast, these will hate the harlot, make her desolate and naked, eat her flesh and burn her with fire. For God has put it into their hearts to fulfill His purpose, to be of one mind, and to give their kingdom to the beast, until the words of God are fulfilled." (Revelation 17:16-17)

The dominion of the Harlot is during the Post-Rapture / Pre-trib gap period and it extends throughout the first three and one-half years of the Trib-period. Then, at the midpoint of the Trib-period, Revelation 17:16-17 finds fulfillment and then the Antichrist activities that are described in Revelation 13 begin.

The Four Final Religions after the Rapture

Presently, there are more gods to worship than there are days on the calendar and among the plethora of choices is the NO god option of agnosticism. However, without warning, that's all about to suddenly change! A time is coming when people will no longer ask if there is a god, instead they will be deciding between at least four choices. Ultimately, as the world's time clock ticks off its final three and one-half years, the options narrow down to just two.

The religious turning point kicks off with the Rapture.[58] After Christ snatches up His bride, the church, into heaven everything on earth swings into high spiritual mode. According to the Bible, signs and wonders become commonplace in the last days.[59] It becomes a period of time when paranormal events become normal and only supernatural explanations make any sense.

True Christianity

Christianity continues to flourish after the Rapture. Multitudes receive Christ as their Savior through Christian works, such as books and movies that were left behind, the preaching of the 144,000 Hebrew witnesses (Rev. 7:1-8), the two witnesses (Rev. 11:1-13) and the angel that proclaims the gospel in (Rev. 14:6-7)

COMMENTARY

However, this period of time is characterized by Christian martyrdom (Rev. 6:9-11, 7:9-17). Christ alludes to this time as the "patience of the Saints" period (Rev. 13:10, 14:12-13). Choosing Christ then will be unpopular for two primary reasons. First, it will likely turn into a death sentence. Second, the satanic deception described in 2 Thessalonians 2:9-10 will be so persuasive that it will allure many to believe in the religions of the Harlot (Rev. 17) and ultimately the Antichrist (Rev. 13).

False Religion Part One (The Harlot of Revelation 17)

After the Rapture many will be on the lookout for a charismatic world leader to emerge on the scene. Christianese buzz words like the "Apocalypse," "Antichrist," "Mark of the Beast" and the number "666" will cause many a sleepless night. However, the Antichrist and his Mark of the Beast system won't be the first false religion to take center-stage after the Rapture.

The first religious jeopardy for humanity is "MYSTERY, BABYLON THE GREAT, THE MOTHER OF HARLOTS AND OF THE ABOMINATIONS OF THE EARTH."[60] As previously stated, the Antichrist initially plays second fiddle to this globally recognized religious system. He allows the Harlot to strum her song of strong deception until his appointed time in the sun arrives.

Ultimately, the Harlot becomes problematic to the grander schemes of the Antichrist and he has her system desolated by the ten kings of Revelation 17:16. The devastation of the harlot religion paves the way for the Antichrist to implement his global scheme, which comes replete with a religion, economic system and world government. This Antichrist system becomes one of the final two religions, alongside true Christianity, competing for the souls of men.

The identity of the Harlot has been the subject of some prophetic controversy. Many, like me, believe it is spearheaded by Roman Catholicism and is based out of Rome. Others believe it is an ecumenical system that tolerates all religions, which could be headquartered in Babylon (Iraq), New York City, Jerusalem or Mecca. These are the five primary location choices among most Bible scholars.

This counterfeit religion is vehemently opposed to the true Christianity taking place simultaneously. Revelation 17:6 seems to suggest that this system will shed the blood of God's saints in the future. The book of Revelation says that at least three types of religious persecutions occur after the Rapture. The first sure pathway to a Christian death is the refusal

COMMENTARY

of worshipping the image of the Antichrist (Rev. 13:15). However, this offer is not made available to mankind until after the Harlot is desolated. Therefore, the alternative murderous system is that of the Harlot's! Lastly, the third form of targeted killings occurs when the Antichrist attempts the genocide of the Jews in Zechariah 13:8.

Some teach that Islam is the Harlot; however, this thinking fails to recognize that the Islam of today is not likely the same as that of the time of existence of the first false religion. For reasons pointed out in my *Psalm 83, The Missing Prophecy Revealed* book, Islam is degraded by devastating defeats in the predominately Muslim wars of Psalm 83 and Ezekiel 38. If my prophetic conclusions are correct, Islam's best days are behind it, but Roman Catholicism is headed for an upswing.

Judaism

Speaking of religious upswings, one of the last days religions that will continue to flourish will be Judaism. It should become much more dominant within Israel in the last days. The Jews will be emboldened by their victories in the wars of Psalm 83 and Ezekiel 38. Psalm 83 brings the Arab-Israeli conflict to its conclusion. The Israeli Defense Forces defeat the Arab confederacy identified in the prophecy.[61] Their God Jehovah destroys the Russian led coalition of Ezekiel 38:1-6 through supernatural means.[62]

In the aftermath of Israel's victories, the Israelis appear to embrace the religious practices prescribed in their Levitical Law. They will want to rebuild their temple and reinstate their former worship practices therein. This temple is identified prophetically in Matthew 24:15, Revelation 11:1-2 and elsewhere.

Another prophecy that supports the rise of Judaism in Israel is found in Ezekiel 39:12-16. These verses describe an Israeli campaign to *cleanse the land* after the defeat of the Ezekiel invaders. Decontaminating the land was a requirement of the Mosaic Law. Concerning this practice, Dr. Ron Rhodes writes in his book *Northern Storm Rising*:

> "From the perspective of the Jews, the dead must be buried because exposed corpses are a source of ritual contamination to the land (Numbers 19:11-22; Deuteronomy 21:1-9). The land must therefore be completely cleansed and purged of all defilement. Neither the enemies nor their belongings (their weapons) can be left to pollute the land!"[63]

Although Judaism will exist after the Rapture, it will not survive much beyond the midpoint of the seven-year Tribulation period. The Antichrist will attempt to kill all the Jews and the byproduct of that holocaustic event should be the rapid decline of Judaism. Concurrently, the faithful remnant of Zechariah 13:9 that survive the genocidal campaign will abandon Judaism and embrace true Christianity. The prophet Hosea informs us that during the Jewish persecution that the surviving Jews will recognize Jesus as their Messiah.

> I will return again to My place, (Christ ascended to His heavenly home after resurrecting). Till they, (The Jews), acknowledge their offense, (Generational rejection of Jesus as the Messiah). Then they, (A Jewish remnant), will seek My face; In their affliction, (The Trib-period), they will earnestly seek Me." (Hosea 5:15)[64]

False Religion Part Two (The Antichrist of Revelation 13)

When the Antichrist rises to power, he will attempt to end every other religion and pedestal his own. The apostle Paul calls him the "*Son of Perdition*" and informs us in 2 Thessalonians 2:4 that he is the one, "*who opposes and exalts himself above all that is called God or that is worshiped, so that he sits as God in the* (Third Jewish) *temple of God, showing himself that he is God.*"[65]

It is safe to presume that the spiritual system introduced by the Antichrist, which is propelled into position supernaturally by Satan through powerful deceptive wonders and lying signs, will be unlike anything before. [66] It may incorporate some old pagan religious beliefs and practices, but it will likely include new concepts as well. Some suggest it could be a new age spiritual movement that could include things like;

- Proof that mankind is not alone in this universe,

- Alien beings created mankind and influenced ancient religions, (*These would likely be fallen angels, masquerading around as benevolent alien beings*),

- How a person can become a god,

- And, how to achieve super human psychic abilities.

Whatever deceptive trappings come wrapped up in this final scheme, they will be effective in bringing many people to a belief in the Antichrist as the god above all gods.

Once the Antichrist system is put in place, Judaism and the religious system of the Harlot are in serious trouble! The harlot religion gets taken out first in Revelation 17:16. Once she is removed, the Jews and Judaism come under a severe attack. Zechariah 13:8 predicts that it will be a genocidal attack of the Jews that will make the holocaust of World War II pale in comparison.

The good news is that Zechariah 13:9 explains that one-third of the Jews survive. These Jews become a "faithful remnant" who all believe in Jesus Christ. They are identified in Romans 11:26 and elsewhere.

> And so all Israel (*represented by the faithful remnant*) will be saved, (*as believers in Christ*) as it is written: "The Deliverer (*the Messiah*) will come out of Zion, And He (*Jesus Christ*) will turn away ungodliness from Jacob; (*Israel*) For this *is* My covenant with them, When I take away their sins." (Romans 11:26; emphasis added)

GOD WINS!!!

Jesus Christ wins! That's the great news! That's the end of the previously foretold story. God prevails, and that's why all believers in true Christianity can rejoice before and after the Rapture. We, who believe in the Bible as the inerrant Word from God, know the end from the beginning. It's all been given to us in the Holy Scriptures.[67]

Jesus returns on a white horse, (Revelation 19:11), and rescues the faithful Jewish remnant single handedly according to Isaiah 63:1-8. Subsequently, He establishes His kingdom on the earth for 1,000 years (Revelation 20:4).

Jesus Christ will be the last man standing after all the other religions fall by the wayside. About 2,000 years ago He came to earth, died for mankind's sins, conquered death, and because of His supernatural resurrection, He is alive and well right now. Believe it or not, He is returning soon. Are you ready?

> "And behold, I (Jesus) am coming quickly, and My reward *is* with Me, to give to every one according to his work. I am the Alpha and the Omega, *the* Beginning and *the* End, the First and the Last." (Rev. 22:12-13)

For more information about the topics covered in this chapter, I highly recommend the reading of the script of, "*The Coming Global Transformation: An End Times Audio Presentation*," *by Jim Tetlow, Brad Myers and Bill Salus.* The audio and written versions of this timely end times work are available at the links included within this endnote.[68]

Chapter 5
144,000 Jewish Evangelists

Topics Covered

People Get Saved After the Rapture

Is Receiving Christ a Now or Never Proposition Before the Rapture?

COMMENTARY

This chapter introduces the 144,000 witnesses in Revelation 7:1-8. In the storyline they are evangelists who are familiar with Bible prophecy. Two of these 144,000 lead Lisa's brother's family to the Lord. Now the novel includes nine characters that have been saved after the Rapture during the Post-Rapture / Pre-Trib gap period. They include, Nathan, Lisa, Jami, Tovia, Amber, Bella, Jaxon and two of the 144,000 witnesses.

The 144,000 witnesses are from the 12 Tribes of Israel. Revelation 7:4 says, *"And I heard the number of those who were sealed. One hundred and forty-four thousand of all the tribes of the children of Israel were sealed."*

This verse clearly identifies that they are descendants from *"all the tribes of the children of Israel."* They appear to play a large part in the salvation of the multitudes listed in Revelation 7:9-17. In the verses below, the apostle John says that after the 144,000 are sealed for Godly service, that an innumerable multitude gets saved.

> "After these things I looked, and behold, a great multitude which no one could number, of all nations, tribes, peoples, and tongues, standing before the throne and before the Lamb, clothed with white robes, with palm branches

in their hands, and crying out with a loud voice, saying, "Salvation *belongs* to our God who sits on the throne, and to the Lamb!" (Revelation 7:9-10; emphasis added)

The topic of the 144,000 witnesses surfaces again in future chapters of this novel. As such, more will be written about who they are, and what role they play after the Rapture, in the commentary of those upcoming chapters.

People Get Saved After the Rapture

The good news is that many people get saved after the Rapture. The 144,000 witnesses and the great multitude spoken of in Revelation 7:9 are among them. The bad news is that becoming a believer after the Rapture will lead to a life of severe persecution and probable martyrdom! Christian persecution will be a worldwide phenomenon, making it virtually impossible for believers to hide and survive. Revelation 6:15 declares that even world rulers, great men, rich men and commanders will hide in caves to avoid the dangers occurring across the globe.

Apocalypse Road addresses some of the devastating prophetic events that occur during the Post-Rapture / Pre-trib period, but the seven-year Trib-period that follows will be the worst seven-years on earth since the flood of Noah. If you or a loved one are not saved prior to the Rapture, then you need to accept Christ as your Savior now, during this "Age of Grace!"

Salvation is achievable then in the same way it is gotten now, and that's through receiving Jesus Christ as your Savior. The appendix entitled, "The Sinners Salvation Prayer," explains what salvation is and how it can be attained right now!

There is an important question to address in this regard. Can people who hear about the gospel before the Rapture get saved after the Rapture occurs? Every true believer existing before the Rapture gets Raptured. If someone alive before the Rapture gets left behind that means they were an unbeliever before the spectacular event happened.

If they had never heard the gospel beforehand, then that explains why they never became believers and why they were left behind. However, what if someone left behind did hear the gospel before the Rapture, but did not receive Christ at the time? Can that person have a second chance to get saved?

Surprisingly, some Bible prophecy teachers say NO! They teach that there is no second chance after the Rapture for them to receive Christ and get saved. I disagree with this teaching for the various reasons below.

Is Receiving Christ a Now or Never Proposition Before the Rapture?

Topics covered below

The No Second Chance Argument

Salvation is part of God's loving plan for mankind

The Rapture is an amazing evangelistic event

Multitudes of people get saved after the Rapture

It only takes one exception to nullify the entire now or never view

The text of 2 Thess. 2 does not clearly support the no second chance view

There is a gap between the Rapture and the Point of No Return

The timing and context of 2 Thess. 2 does not support this view…

In chapter one of the novel, Nathan, Lisa and Jamie are left behind individuals who became believers after the Rapture. Each of them had heard the gospel of Christ before the Rapture, but found themselves left behind because they didn't accept it at the time. After their loved ones vanished in the Rapture, they all received Christ and became true believers. In their cases the Rapture became sufficient proof that Jesus Christ was the true Savior!

A frequently asked question of Bible prophecy experts is, "Do people who get left behind from the Rapture still have a second chance to get saved afterwards?" This question specifically applies to individuals who have heard the *good news* about Jesus Christ before He comes to

Rapture His Bride, the Church, up to heaven. They, like Nathan, Lisa and Jamie, need a second chance after the Rapture because they did not become believers beforehand when they had initially heard the gospel.

Believers who ask this question are mostly concerned that people they cherish, whom they know have heard the gospel, may not accept Christ before the Rapture. The thought that these loved ones are disqualified from receiving a second opportunity at salvation deeply disturbs them.

On a personal note, my decision to receive Christ as my Lord and Savior was a process. It took me some time to research the matter. The process took several months, after which I settled the matter and took my altar call at Calvary Chapel, Big Bear Lake, CA in 1990. Fortunately, I had a second chance. In fact, I heard the gospel numerous times before making my decision, which means I was given a third, fourth and fifth chance. If the Rapture would have occurred during my months of indecision, and if there's no second shot, I guess I wouldn't be saved.

The remainder of this chapter will present and refute the no second chance theory. Before I present both sides to the second chance scenario, let me direct your attention to the appendix entitled "The Tribulation Saints." This appendix was authored by my dear friend, Brother Al Gist. I was so impressed with Al's teaching on this topic, that I asked him to provide me with his message about this matter. I recommend that you consider this appendix as part of the required reading of this chapter.

The No Second Chance Argument

The teaching that no second chance is given to a select group after the Rapture is based primarily upon what I believe are questionable interpretations of 2 Thessalonians 2:1-12. There are two precepts to understand inside these verses in order to come up with the no second chance conclusion.

First, the advocates of this teaching believe that the Rapture is alluded to somewhere in either or all of the verses below.

- 2 Thess. 2:1 – Concerning the coming of Jesus and the gathering of believers to Him. The gathering together of believers with Christ is the essential theme of the Rapture.

- 2 Thess. 2:3 – Some believe the *"apostasy,"* which in some translations is interpreted as the *"departure,"* *"departing away"* or *"falling away"* spoken about in this verse represents the Rapture.

- 2 Thess. 2:6-7 – Some interpret the *"restrainer"* in these verses to be the Holy Spirit. Since the Holy Spirit dwells within each believer, when they are Raptured, the restraint is removed.

Second, the select group that is being shunned from salvation is identified in 2 Thess. 2:10-11. This crowd is eternally condemned *"because they did not receive the love of the truth that they might be saved."* As such, they are damned because they *"did not believe the truth."*

This implies that this faction has heard the truth, which according to John 14:6 is the good news gospel of Jesus Christ, but they did not love or believe it enough to receive it.

> Jesus said to him, "I am the way, the truth, and the life. No one comes to the Father except through Me. (John 14:6)

Linking the two parts together the thinking goes as follows; Since the Rapture has occurred prior to the condemnation of those who do not receive Christ, those who heard the gospel beforehand are damned for not becoming believers. In short, to become a member of this unenviable assembly one only needs to hear, but not receive, the good news gospel of Jesus Christ before the Rapture.

I like how Bible prophecy teacher Brother John Haller sums this thinking up.

> "If there is no second chance, the sure fire way to send someone you love to hell is to ineffectively share the gospel with them before the Rapture."

The Bible says this concerning the gospel,

> "How then shall they call on Him (*Jesus Christ*) in whom they have not believed? And how shall they believe in Him of whom they have not heard? And how shall they hear (*the gospel of Christ*) without a preacher? (Romans 10:14, emphasis added)

Haller points out the irony of this no second chance teaching. On the one hand, in order to receive Christ someone needs to hear the gospel, but on the other hand, once they hear the gospel they run the risk of going to hell if they vacillate in making their decision for Christ. This intensifies the issue for both the preacher and hearer of the gospel.

Not every Christian is a world class evangelist like Billy Graham, and even he can't force someone to receive Christ. So, if someone adheres

COMMENTARY

to the no second chance thinking, these questions should concern someone about to preach the gospel.

1.   Can I preach it effectively enough to bring about an immediate decision for Christ?

2.   Am I really even qualified to take the risk to tell someone about Jesus?

3.   What if I blow it?

4.   What if the timing isn't right for them to be receptive to the gospel message?

5.   If they don't accept Christ, should I inform them that they made the biggest mistake of their life because now they are going to hell without a second chance after the Rapture?

6.   What if they don't even know what the Rapture is?

7.   Is it imperative that I explain what the Rapture is along with the gospel?

8.   Am I even qualified to explain what the Rapture is all about?

Imagine that you preach the gospel to someone and they don't decide to receive Christ in that moment. Then without notice, as the person is departing, the Rapture occurs. You go to heaven, but thanks to your sincere efforts they are forced to hell. This isn't how it works, and I give several reasons why below.

The Reasons Supporting a Second Chance at Salvation After the Rapture

There are several reasons that I believe strongly support the possibility that people do get a second chance at salvation after the Rapture. They are;

•   Salvation is part of God's loving plan for mankind,

•   The Rapture is an amazing evangelistic event,

•   Multitudes of people get saved after the Rapture,

•   It only takes one exception to nullify the entire *now or never* view,

•   The text of 2 Thess. 2 does not clearly support the no second chance view,

•   There is a gap between the Rapture and the Point of No Return,

•   The timing and context of 2 Thess. 2 does not support this view.

Salvation is part of God's loving plan for mankind

John 3:16 tells us that God loves everyone and wishes that no one would be denied the gift of salvation. He sent His only begotten Son, Jesus Christ to the cross for this purpose. Depriving anyone of the opportunity of being saved goes against the heart of God. God is love (1 John 4:8). He is merciful, gracious and slow to anger (Psalm 103:8). The Lord delights in people (Proverbs 8:31). God is the heavenly Father (Matthew 6:8). Jesus encouraged the apostle Peter to extend forgiveness a minimum of 490 times (Matthew 18:20-21). God's goodness is what leads men to repentance (Romans 2:4).

It seems illogical to think that God, possessing the attributes above, would single out a select group and deprive them of a second chance at salvation.

Although there is a forthcoming event that justifiably blocks out a select group from salvation, it's not the Rapture. It's the global implementation of the mark of the Beast in Revelation 13. Those who receive this mark, make a conscious choice to worship the Antichrist, and in so doing, separate themselves from eternal salvation through Christ Jesus.

The Rapture is an amazing evangelistic event

Christ catching up His believers into heaven in fulfillment of Bible prophecies evidences that He is the Savior. The Rapture represents Christ making good on His promises to give His true followers eternal life. People left behind, who have heard about the Rapture before it happens, will have the opportunity to recognize this.

As such, the Rapture has the potential to be an amazing witnessing tool. Why would the loving God of the Bible, not seize the inherent evangelistic opportunity provided by this supernatural event? Apparently, the Lord does capitalize on the Rapture to this positive end, because multitudes get saved after the event.

Multitudes of people get saved after the Rapture

The fact that multitudes are getting saved after the Rapture supports the thesis that *Salvation is part of God's loving plan for mankind*. A few examples of those Jews and Gentiles being saved after the Rapture were previously identified in the *"Post Rapture Peoples Categories."* It is probable that many of these Jews and Gentiles will have been alive when the Rapture took place and will have heard, but not accepted, the gospel of Christ prior to the event. In fact, the Rapture could be a primary reason many of them become Christians.

The text of 2 Thess. 2 does not clearly support the no second chance view

Many biblical predictions are very specific. For instance;

- Isaiah 17:1 informs that the city of Damascus is going to be reduced to rubble and cease from being a city. This is a prophecy that many of us believe remains unfulfilled and could occur in the near future.

- Jeremiah 25:11 accurately predicted seventy years of desolation for the land of Israel.

- Isaiah 45:1 foretold that King Cyrus of Persia would subdue nations, which occurred during the reign of the Persian Empire.

These examples provide clear and concise prophetic information. They are to be interpreted literally. This is not the case with the 2 Thess. 2 verses. Nowhere do these verses clearly state that those condemned in 2 Thess. 2:12 were privy to having heard the gospel prior to the Rapture.

Since the deprivation of a select group's salvation is such a severe punishment and goes against the character of God's nature, it seems like more prophetic specificity should have been provided within the pertinent text. Because the text fails to undeniably support the no second chance interpretation, some of those who teach it humbly admit that they can't be dogmatic about their view.

The no second chance view would be more believable if somewhere in 2 Thess. 2 it said something like.

> "Now, brethren, concerning the coming of our Lord Jesus Christ and our gathering together to Him, we beseech you who hear our good report before His coming, that you believe upon Him, because there is no salvation available for you afterward." (2 Thess. 2 nowhere)

It only takes one exception to nullify the entire now or never view

It's impossible to know precisely how many of those left behind from the Rapture will have heard the gospel beforehand. Obviously, if they are left behind, they did not seize the opportunity to receive Christ when it was first presented to them. It would be safe to suggest that they could number in the hundreds of thousands, if not the millions.

It only takes one conversion from this bunch to nullify the entire no second shot at salvation view. One person, having heard the gospel before the Rapture, dropping to their knees sometime after the event to receive Christ as their Lord and Savior wipes out the whole now or never interpretation.

Take for instance, a single member of the 144,000 witnesses in Revelation 7. These are servants of the living God. Certainly they must be saved souls. Most of the no second chancers would agree that these are individuals that have been left behind. If just one of them has heard the gospel before the Rapture, the no second chance teaching is nullified in the exact moment of their salvation. Thus, according to the now or never theology, none of the 144,000 witnesses can have ever heard the gospel before the Rapture.

I find this thought preposterous! How could these 144,000 be as effective in preaching the gospel as they will be unless they knew something about the gospel beforehand? They appear to be partially responsible for the multitudes being saved during the great tribulation period. (Revelation 7:9-17)

I believe members of the 144,000 could include, for instance, a certified Israeli tour guide. Some of these guides know more about the New Testament than many of the Christians on their tour. If they witnessed the Rapture and the sudden decline of Christian tourism as a direct result, then they could easily realize that Christ is the Messiah.

There is a gap between the Rapture and the Point of No Return

Another foreseeable problem with the now or never theology is the gap that exists between the Rapture and the implementation of the strong delusion referenced in 2 Thess. 2:11. This verse calls this delusion "the lie." According to the no second chance argument, it is "the lie" that prohibits people from obtaining salvation.

For the sake of this section the lie will also be referred to as the "POINT OF NO RETURN," because once someone accepts the lie, they officially reject Christ and there is no turning back. The only line of no return referenced elsewhere in the Scripture is when someone receives the "MARK OF THE BEAST." (Revelation 13:11-18 and 14:9-11)

2 Thessalonian 2:5-12 points out that the implementation of the *"strong delusion"* that comes upon mankind involves a process. It does not appear to occur simultaneously with the timing of the Rapture. Why that's a problem for the now or never thinking will be discussed at the end of this section.

The process of perpetrating *the lie* involves Satan. The devil is allowed to utilize all of his power, signs, lying wonders and unrighteous deception to delude mankind.[69] The verses below inform that it is belief in this *lie* that condemns those alive after the Rapture to damnation.

> And for this reason God will send them strong delusion,
> that they should believe *the lie*, that they all may be
> condemned who did not believe the truth but had pleasure
> in unrighteousness. (2 Thess. 2:11-12; emphasis added)

This gap between the rapture and full implementation of *the lie* becomes problematic for the no second chance argument because it implies that at the instant the rapture occurs, those left behind that had previously heard the gospel, are doomed to damnation by some other factor than *the lie*.

The *major premise* is that *the lie* is what condemns all the unbelievers after the rapture, whether or not they had heard the gospel. The *minor premise* is that no human living in the world after the Rapture can be properly condemned to damnation until *the lie* is put in place as the point of no return. If one buys into *the lie* by accepting the *mark of the beast*, they cross this point of no return.

> (*The exception would be those who die as an unbeliever
> between the rapture and the implementation of the lie.
> According to the Bible, belief in Christ is the prerequisite
> of salvation, regardless of the timing of one's death.)*[70]

Herein lays the problem for the now or never proposition. *The lie*, which is probably embodied by the mark of the beast, is not put into place until a minimum of three and one-half years after the Rapture. It is commonly taught that implementation of the mark takes place in the middle of the seven year Trib-period.

The establishment of the lie will probably take longer, because there is a gap of unspecified time between the Rapture and the commencement of the seven years of tribulation. The seven-year time clock starts with the confirmation of the false covenant referenced in Daniel 9:27.

Sequentially, the Rapture occurs and then sometime afterward the false covenant is confirmed. Then three and one-half years later the mark of the beast is instigated.

Simply stated, all people can be saved up to the point of no return. This means that between the Rapture and the midpoint of the Trib-period, everyone on the planet has the ability to receive Christ, even if they had heard the gospel before the Rapture! Unless the Lord supernaturally puts blinders on those needing a second chance, they have at least three and one-half years to become believers.

Nowhere in Scripture does it allude to some zombie like group with no hope for salvation that exists in a condition of limbo until they can get in line to receive the mark of the beast.

The timing and context of 2 Thess. 2 does not support this view.

Another important argument against the now or never view is that the timing and context of 2 Thess. 2 addresses events that climax in the Trib-period, rather than prior to the Rapture.

Respected Bible teacher, Dr. Arnold Fruchtenbaum explains the timing and context as follows;

> "These (2 Thess. 2) verses have often been interpreted as teaching that if one hears the gospel before the Rapture and rejects it, he will not have an opportunity to be saved after the Rapture. But this is not the teaching of this passage. The point of no return is the acceptance of the "big lie" of the Antichrist's self-proclaimed deity and the submission to the worship of him by means of taking the mark of the beast. It is only then that the point of no return is actually reached. The option of taking the mark of the beast only begins in the middle of the tribulation. Even the context of this passage shows that it speaks of events that occur in the middle of the tribulation. The worshippers of the Antichrist do so because they are deceived by the Antichrist's power of miracles. They are deceived because they received not the love of the truth. The rejection of the gospel was not what they may have heard before the Rapture but rather the preaching of the 144,000 Jews and the Two Witnesses."[71]

COMMENTARY

Bestselling Christian author, Dr. Tim Lahaye, of the *Left Behind* book series echoes this same sentiment in the quote below;

> "*First*, 2nd Thessalonians 2 does not say anything about an individual hearing, understanding and then rejecting the Gospel. It does make a universal statement about those who do not love the truth. Thus, all unbelievers are referred to in the same way as one group. There is no basis in this passage for identifying a subclass of unbelievers, such as those who have heard the Gospel, understood it, and rejected it... *Second*, the context of the entire passage relates to what will happen in the forthcoming Trib-period ...The 2nd Thessalonians 2 passage is talking about the response of unbelievers during the Tribulation. If the passage were referring to an unbelieving response prior to the Tribulation, with a result that such a decision would impact one's destiny during the Tribulation, then the passage would have probably been worded differently in order to convey such a message.[72]

The arguments provided in this article should give the reader hope that there is always a second chance to receive salvation unless a person accepts *the lie*, which is evidenced by taking the *Mark of the Beast*. Remember, if you receive Christ, Who is the truth, you will never believe in *the lie* that is soon forthcoming!

COMMENTARY

Chapter 6

Hooked in the Jaws - Russia Covets Israeli Contracts with the West

Topics Covered

The Role of the USA and UK in Ezekiel 38

I n this chapter of the novel, Russia and Iran prepare to lead the Gog of Magog coalition into the battle of Ezekiel 38. The president of Russia is not concerned about meeting with resistance from the USA or the UK. He says,

> "*Their* (the USA and UK) *armies are weakened and disoriented due to the disappearances. They are no match for our coalition forces and weapons. Our troops have not vanished into thin air like many of theirs. They will protest our invasion from the sidelines, but they won't draw us into a multi-front war.*"

The theory behind this quote is three-fold.

1.   The Rapture is the supernatural event whereby Christ comes to catch up into the clouds everyone on earth that has personally received Him as their Savior. This is their blessed hope according to Titus 2:3, which says that believers are, "*looking for the blessed hope and glorious appearing of our great God and Savior Jesus Christ.*"

Anyone who has not received Him will be left behind. Excluding most of Russia, the Gog of Magog coalition is mostly comprised of Muslim nations. Muslims worship Allah and not Jesus Christ, which means that every Muslim will be left behind. Thus, Russia's confederacy will remain mostly intact. This coalition will present an existential threat to Israel and an intimidating military force to the international community.

2.   Predominately Christian countries stand to suffer severely when a presumably large portion of its countrymen and women permanently vanish from the earth. A pew research report in 2014 estimated about 70% of Americans identified themselves as Christians.[73] This doesn't mean that all of them have accepted Jesus Christ as their Savior, but if even half of that percentage is removed, that equals about one-hundred million people. The sudden disappearance of that many people will negatively impact the nation. As of 2016, an estimated 64 million people live in the UK. Percentage estimates of Christians in the UK are slightly lower than in America, but imagine if about twenty million UK citizens also vanished. This scenario would have a crippling effect on that country as well.

3.   The disappearances of so many people in these two countries, which support the world's #1 (USA) and #6 (UK) ranked armies will undoubtedly marginalize their potential roles in Ezekiel 38.[74]

The Roles of the USA and UK in Ezekiel 38

This commentary was taken from a chapter in my timely new book entitled, "*The NOW Prophecies.*" It unpacks Ezekiel 38:13 to unmask the mysterious modern day identities of ancient Tarshish and their young lions, or "villages" in some translations. Additionally, it examines their specific roles within the prophecy. If Tarshish is the UK and the young lions are partially represented by the USA, then the ramifications for the future of America are staggering!

Ezekiel 38 and 39 involves at least fourteen participants in the prophecy. They are;

1.   *The Victor:* God.

2.   *The (intended) Victim:* Israel.

3.   *The 9 Invaders:* Rosh, Magog, Meshech, Tubal, Persia, Ethiopia, Libya, Gomer, and Togarmah. (Refer to the Ezekiel 38 map image in the chapter called, "The European Union Consoles Israel," to find out the modern-day equivalents).

4.   *The 4 Protestors:* Sheba, Dedan, the merchants of Tarshish and their Young Lions.

The prophecy informs that in the latter years the invaders will attack Israel to capture plunder and booty. They covet Israel's economic prosperity and conspire militarily to confiscate this livelihood as part of their spoils of war. As the victor, the Lord prevents this from occurring by utilizing supernatural means to defeat these invaders. More details of Ezekiel 38-39 are provided in the commentary of the chapter called, "The Collapse of the Russian Coalition."

Meanwhile, as the epic event unfolds, the protestors complain about the evil intentions of the invaders. Their protests are lodged in the questions in Ezekiel 38:13 quoted below. Ultimately, after the invaders are conquered, Israel graduates from being the intended victim and instead becomes the resultant benefactor.

> "Sheba, Dedan, the merchants of Tarshish, and all their young lions will say to you, 'Have you come to take plunder? Have you gathered your army to take booty, to carry away silver and gold, to take away livestock and goods, to take great plunder?" (Ezekiel 38:13)

The modern day equivalents of these protestors today are commonly understood and taught to be;

1. *Sheba*: Yemen.

2. *Dedan*: Saudi Arabia and perhaps parts of the Gulf Cooperative Council (GCC) Arab Gulf States.

3. *Tarshish*: Either the UK or Spain.

4. *Young Lions*: Either the colonies that came from the UK, namely North America, or the offshoots of Spain, mainly the Latin American countries.

Ezekiel 38:13 imparts several important clues to the reader. One of them is that the merchants (of Tarshish) are concerned about the motives of the invaders. They are not referred to as soldiers, politicians, athletes, entertainers, etc., but as merchants. The Hebrew word used by Ezekiel is clearly talking about commerce. Being labeled as merchants in Ezekiel 38:13 insinuates that at least some of the protestors have commercial interests at stake within Israel at the time of the Magog invasion. This is not a new phenomenon. According to Ezekiel 27:12, Tarshish has been conducting foreign trade in the Middle East for centuries.

These merchants appear distraught over the possibilities of the invaders seizing Israel's national assets. This raises the questions, "If

COMMENTARY

they are concerned about protecting their foreign trade relations within Israel, why do they not appear to be fighting alongside the Jewish state in this conflict? Why don't they coalesce militarily to oppose the Magog coalition?"

In 1990, George H. Bush had no problem assembling an alliance of nations against Saddam Hussein's Iraq in Operation Desert Storm. That American led coalition was comprised of several Arab states, including Saudi Arabia, who is represented as Dedan in Ezekiel 38:13. However, in the Ezekiel invasion, a Desert Storm scenario does not seem to be repeated.

This might mean that passive political leadership is in place, but more likely implies that the protestors lack military prowess at the time. Maybe, these abstaining countries are concerned that their forces won't match up against the invading armies. This is the possible conclusion that I favor.

Who was Tarshish?

According to the Table of Nations in Genesis 10, Tarshish was Noah's great grandson through his son Japheth, who fathered Javan, who in turn fathered Tarshish.

> And the sons of Javan: Elishah, and Tarshish, Kittim, and Dodanim. Of these were the isles of the nations divided in their lands, every one after his tongue, after their families, in their nations. (Genesis 10:4-5, ASV)

Where was Tarshish?

The two most favored locations for Tarshish among historians, archaeologists and Bible teachers are Spain or Britain. My research leads me to conclude that Britain is the location of "Tarshish" and the North American countries most resemble their "young lions."

Tarshish settled in the isles or in some translations the coastlands. In addition to the verse above, the theme of Tarshish in connection with the isles shows up in Psalm 72:10, and Isaiah 23:6, 60:9, 66:19. A careful reading of these verses uncovers a clear connection between Tarshish and a geographical location associated with isles or coastlands. One example is below.

> The kings of Tarshish and of the isles shall render tribute: The kings of Sheba and Seba shall offer gifts. (Psalm 72:10)

The isles alluded to could be the British Isles, which are a group of oversized islands off the northwestern coast of continental Europe that consist of the islands of Great Britain, Ireland and over six thousand smaller isles.[75]

Many of the maps that display the location of ancient Tarshish locate it around or beyond the Strait of Gibraltar. The Strait of Gibraltar is the westernmost part of the Mediterranean Sea before it merges with the Atlantic Ocean. It is the water barrier that separates Southern Spain from Northern Morocco. It is far to the west of Israel, which is also a point made in Psalm 48:7. The Psalm says, *"As when* You break the ships of Tarshish With an east wind."* This implies that the ships are coming to the Middle East from the west, rather than the east.

Bible prophecy expert Dr. Mark Hitchcock points out a possible connection between Tarshish and Britain in his book entitled, *"The Late Great United States."* Hitchcock states;

> *"Some archeologists believe that Tarshish was the ancient name of Britain. "Tarshish" can also mean "beyond Gibraltar" depending on your translation. Tarshish and her villages or young lions — in other words Britain which then settled Canada and the United States and Australia."*[76]

COMMENTARY

Dr. J. R. Church, the founder of Prophecy in the News, says the following about Tarshish in his book called, *"The Guardians of the Grail."*

> *"An inscription discovered in 1780, on a cliff above Mt. Hope Bay in Bristol, Rhode Island, contained an engraving that read "Voyagers from Tarshish this stone proclaims." … Believed to be inscribed around 533 B.C….Harvard University has found five locations within the United States where the merchants of Tarshish had colonies."*[77]

Another respected Bible prophecy expert that advocates this same connection is Dr. David Hocking, of Hope for Today Ministries. We shared a speaking platform together on July 3, 2011. During that event, Dr. Hocking provided several sound biblical, historical and archaeological reasons that support America as the Young Lions of Tarshish. Dr. Hocking's conclusion that he gave at the event is quoted below. [78]

> "If you ask me today if the USA is in Bible prophecy, I would have to say on the basis of historical documentation and on the basis of the British museum and all of its records around Glastonbury that it begins with Great Britain (Tarshish), and undoubtedly as a seed-bearing people it refers to the USA as the "Young Lions.""

What was Tarshish famous for?

Tarshish's claim to historical fame was primarily two-fold. *First,* they were known for their vast wealth and abundant mineral and metal resources. We glean this from historical accounts as well as several Scriptures. One example is found in Ezekiel 27:12, which says, "Tarshish *was* your (Tyre) merchant because of your many luxury goods. They gave you silver, iron, tin, and lead for your goods."

This verse, written around 587 BC, acknowledged that "tin" was among the primary metals that came from Tarshish. Cornwall, a county on England's rugged southwestern tip, was the only major source of tin in Europe for the past 2,500 years. In the 19th century there were approximately 400 mines in Cornwall employing 18,000 people. It is also true that the mountains of Wales, just north of Cornwall have been a source of all the minerals and metals listed above in Ezekiel 27:12.[79]

Second, Tarshish gained renown for their extremely sturdy ships. These seaworthy vessels would take extended voyages to transport their exports and imports across the Atlantic Ocean and the Mediterranean

Sea. These ships of Tarshish are alluded to at least nine times in the Bible.

> The ships of Tarshish were carriers of your (Tyre's) merchandise. You were filled and very glorious in the midst of the seas.. (Ezekiel 27:25; emphasis added)

What About Tarshish Today?

Ezekiel 38:8, 16 notifies that this is a prophecy that finds fulfillment in the last days. Ezekiel 38:13 places Tarshish in the epic event. Since these appear to be the last days, then it's safe to say that ancient Tarshish has a modern day equivalent. This logical deduction applies geographically in the world, and geo-politically in the Middle East. Furthermore, Tarshish and their young lions have a relationship with Israel in this prophecy. This beckons the questions, what nation or nations have played instrumental roles in modernity in the Mideast? What countries have been interacting with Israel the most since its rebirth in 1948?

This seemingly rules out Spain as Tarshish and the Latin American countries as the young lions. The Spanish Empire was a dominant world influence in between the late 15th century until the early 19th century. During that time, Spain shared the global power struggle with the Ottoman Empire, which controlled the Middle East between 1517-1917. Today both empires have faded from their former glories and neither has much influence in the geo-political affairs of the Middle East in general and Israel specifically.

Around the end of the 18th century, the second rise of the British Empire began. At its height it was considered the largest empire in history. No other nation in history created as many colonies (young lions).[80] The empire grew so rapidly that it became characterized by the phrase, *"the empire on which the sun never set."* By 1922, the British Empire held sway over about 458 million people, one-fifth of the world's population. Moreover, the empire covered more than 13,000,000 square miles, almost a quarter of the Earth's total land area.[81]

The Ottoman Empire's control over the Middle East ended with its defeat in World War I. Subsequently, Britain and France took sovereignty over the territory. When Israel was rebirthed in 1948, it was Britain, rather than Spain, that controlled the subject territory, which at the time was called Palestine.

COMMENTARY

Presently, America, not Latin America, is playing a young lion's role in the Mideast. In 1979, the USA was instrumental in brokering a peace deal between Israel and Egypt with President Jimmy Carter, and again in 1994 with Israel and Jordan by President Bill Clinton. It seems as though today, Britain, as Tarshish, is now playing a subservient role behind the young lions of America in important geo-political issues of interest to Israel. On the other hand, Spain and the Latin American countries are not involved much at all in Mideast matters.

Conclusion

I am convinced that the majority of biblical, historical, archaeological, geographical and geo-political arguments for the identity of Tarshish and their young lions favor Britain and America. My conclusions are also based upon a thorough examination of several respectable commentaries that clumsily attempted to connect Tarshish to Spain. In my estimation, the arguments I uncovered in favor of Spain were easily refutable.

If Britain and the USA are mentioned as mere protestors in Ezekiel 38:13, then this should trouble Americans. Why does the greatest superpower that ever existed seem to abstain from fighting alongside Israel at this critical point in its future? We have historically been Israel's greatest ally!

The USA, in the past, has consistently voted pro-Israel in the United Nations, even when it was unpopular to do so. We provide Israel with state of the art weaponry and other forms of foreign aid. As of June 15, 2015, Israel is the largest cumulative recipient of U.S. foreign assistance since World War II. To date, the United States has provided Israel over $124 billion in bilateral assistance.

Why does the USA seem content to remain on the sidelines when Russia and its hordes invade Israel? Is it because America declines from superpower status between now and Ezekiel 38? Britain already has! In only seventy years, between 1920 and 1990, in the midst of Israel's rebirthing process, Britain collapsed as a world superpower. Now the sun always sets on the British Empire. Today the UK only spans 94,058 square miles and has a population of only about 64 million.

It's easy to see why Britain, as Tarshish in the prophecy, would tremble at the thought of fighting against the Magog coalition. But what about the USA? Is America following in Britain's same failed footsteps? Will America turn its back on God and Israel, like Britain did when it failed to enact the Balfour Declaration, which was drafted in 1917? Britain's failure to provide territory for a Jewish State at the time contributed to the extermination of approximately 6 million Jews in World War II!

Will America's decades long push to divide the land of Israel into two states have the same consequences? Is this type of anti-biblical geo-political behavior one of the reasons that America is portrayed as cowardly young lions in Ezekiel 38:13? Joel 3:2 says that one of the reasons God judges the nations is for dividing his land. In modernity, America is at the forefront of attempting to divide God's land.

Chapter 7
Jews Flee Israel as the Russian Invasion Begins

Topics Covered

The Gog of Magog Invasion from the Israeli Perspective

Does the ISRAEL of EZEKIEL 38 EXIST NOW?

What are the conditions in Israel before the Gog of Magog invasion?

The Mysterious Message Concealed in the Names of the 144,000 Witnesses

Are the 144,000 Witnesses Virgins?

COMMENTARY

This chapter of the novel concludes with Simeon and Gershom explaining how the 144,000 Witnesses of Revelation 7 were supernaturally sealed for godly service. They also describe how their prior careers required them to be biblically literate. Thus, when the time came for the 144,000 Witnesses to emerge in fulfillment of Bible prophecy, they were already prepped for their callings. At the conclusion of this chapter's commentary, I will provide more intriguing information about this elite group of 144,000 Jews. The commentary will point out that the ordering of their tribal names contains a hidden message and whether they are truly virgins as per Revelation 14:4.

The Gog of Magog Invasion from the Israeli Perspective

By the time the Ezekiel 38 prophecy finally arrives, several other biblical prophecies should have already found fulfillment. These prophecies are identified in my "Now Prophecies" book. So, just prior to the beginning of Ezekiel 38, Israel will likely be responding to, and the world recovering from, the following plethora of prophetic events, (listed below in no specific chronological order);

1. Jeremiah 49:34-39, the Elam prophecy about the disaster in Iran,

2. Isaiah 17 & Jeremiah 49:23-27, the destruction of Damascus,

3. Jeremiah 49:1-6 and Zephaniah 2:8-9, the toppling of Jordan,

4. Isaiah 19:1-18, the terrorization of Egypt,

5. Psalm 83, the concluding Arab-Israeli war,

6. The groundbreaking for the third Jewish temple,

7. Obadiah 1:19-20, Jeremiah 49:2 and Zephaniah 2:9, the expansion of Israel,

8. Ezekiel 37:10, 25:14, Obadiah 1:18, the rise of the exceedingly great Israeli army,

9. Ezekiel 38:11, the safer Israel that dwells without partition walls and security fences,

10. Ezekiel 38:13, the wealthier Israel in receipt of great plunder and booty,

11. 1 Corinthians 15:51-53 and 1 Thessalonians 4:15-18, the Rapture of the Church,

12. Ezekiel 38:13, the decline of the UK and USA, (Tarshish and their young lions),

This commentary section of this book will present the events described in Ezekiel 38-39 form the Israeli perspective. Listed below are the three categories that will be explained.

1. What are the conditions in Israel before the Gog of Magog invasion? (Ezekiel 38:1-13).

2. What are the conditions in Israel during the Ezekiel 38 invasion? (Ezekiel 38:14-39:8).

3. What are the conditions in Israel in the aftermath of Ezekiel 38? (Ezekiel 39:9-21).

The emphasis of this chapter's commentary will address the first point and the chapter called, "The Collapse of the Russian Coalition," will address points two and three.

Does the Israel of Ezekiel 38 Exist Now?

Most contemporary commentaries on Ezekiel 38 approach the prophecy as if it could happen as Israel exists in its present state. However, that is not the perspective presented in this book.

Currently, Israel is slightly over 8,000 square miles, which is about the size of New Jersey. It is surrounded by Arab states and terrorist populations that don't recognize Israel's right to exist as the Jewish State. If you believe that Ezekiel 38 finds fulfillment while Israel exists in its current geo-political condition, then how would you answer the following questions?

1. Why does Russia (Magog) need such a big coalition to invade today's tiny little Israel? (The list of invaders includes Russia, Turkey, Iran, Tunisia, Libya, Ethiopia, Sudan, Somalia, Morocco and others). The first five listed above, not including the other invaders, have populations that currently total over 300 million. When you compare this to Israel's estimated Jewish population of about 6 million, it seems a bit like overkill. Additionally, the Russian army is ranked #2, the Turkish army is ranked #10 and Iranian army is ranked #23 among world armies. In comparison, Israel is presently ranked #11.82

2. Why doesn't Ezekiel include the Arab states that share common borders with Israel among the Gog of Magog invaders? After all, these Arabs are the notorious enemies of Israel in the past and still today, but none of the invaders in Ezekiel 38 have ever been historic enemies of Israel. (Excluding perhaps Persia at the time of Esther around 486-468 BC).

3. Is Israel dwelling securely without walls, bars or gates as per Ezekiel 38:11? Israel has approximately a 400-mile-long wall that runs through much of Israel. In fact, it can be argued that Israel is the most fenced in and fortified country in the world.

4. Does Israel possess the enormous amount of booty and plunder that the Magog invaders desire as per Ezekiel 38:12-13? Israel has recently discovered large amounts of natural gas, but Russia has no shortage of natural gas. It is doubtful that Israel's current economic wealth, although substantial, is significant enough presently for the Russian coalition to come to capture.

These are just a few questions, which upon a scrutineer's examination, seems to suggest that the Gog of Magog invaders won't coalesce to invade today's Israel. However, if some of the NOW prophecies precede Ezekiel 38, then these same four questions could be answered in this manner;

1. *Why does Russia (Magog) need such a big coalition to invade today's tiny little Israel?*

    Russia needs to formulate a big coalition to invade Israel because;

    a. The Israeli Defense Forces (IDF) have become an exceedingly great army in fulfillment of Ezekiel 37:10, 25:14.

    b. The IDF accomplished this by decisively defeating the Arabs in Psalm 83, destroying Damascus in Isaiah 17 and toppling Jordan in Jeremiah 49:2.

    c. Furthermore, the tiny Jewish state of 2015 has become a significantly larger Israel. This resulted from annexing the formerly occupied Arab lands identified in Obadiah 1:19-20, Zephaniah 2:9, and Jeremiah 49:2.

2. *Why doesn't Ezekiel include the Arab states that share common borders with Israel among the Gog of Magog invaders?*

    The most likely answer to this question is, the Arab states are already defeated by the IDF in fulfillment of the Psalm 83 war. Ezekiel 28:24-26 calls these nations a prickling briar and a painful thorn to Israel. Ezekiel says these Arab states that share common borders with Israel despise the Jewish state and prevent it from dwelling securely. These Ezekiel verses clearly state that judgments will be executed upon them, and that afterward Israel dwells in the security described in Ezekiel 38:8-11. Jeremiah 12:14-17 identifies these surrounding Arabs as Israel's "evil neighbors." Ultimately these Muslim nations will be "utterly plucked up and destroyed."

3. *Is Israel dwelling securely without walls, bars or gates as per Ezekiel 38:11?*

    a. After the fulfillment of Psalm 83 and the related peripheral prophecies, Israel is dwelling securely. This is because the IDF has defeated their neighboring enemies. As a result, they have militarily, rather than politically, achieved the national security that they had desperately longed for since becoming a nation in 1948.

COMMENTARY

b.   Another possible reason is that they have torn down the partition wall and removed all security checkpoints within the country, after the defeat of their enemies in Psalms 83. With the conquest over these enemies, the need for partition walls and security checkpoints becomes mostly eliminated.

4.   *Does Israel possess the enormous amount of booty and plunder that the Magog invaders desire as per Ezekiel 38:12-13?*
Once the Now Prophecies are fulfilled the answer is yes. These prophecies enable Israel to become safer and larger as answered in the three prior questions. Israel will also be able to elevate its national economy up to the level depicted in Ezekiel 38:8-13. The potential for this increased prosperity is explored below.

What are the conditions in Israel before the Gog of Magog invasion?

Ezekiel 38:1-13 are the telling verses that describe what Israel looks like geopolitically prior to the Gog of Magog invasion. Presuming some or all of the NOW Prophecies have occurred; then Israel will be reshaping itself in response to the twelve scenarios presented at the beginning of this chapter. The Jewish state should be understandably *larger, safer* and *wealthier*.

These three conditions should be conducive to an influx of more Jewish Aliyah, (Jewish migration into Israel). Jews have been making Aliyah into Israel continuously for over a century and this process will likely increase once Israel is freed from the torment of Arab terror. Terrorism should slow down substantially after Israel defeats its Arab foes in Psalm 83.

Some Jews living outside of Israel today are contemplating making Aliyah to avoid present or perceived future persecution in their present countries of residence. This includes some of the 5.4 million Jews presently living in America. Concerning many Jews residing abroad, is the reality that currently worldwide Jew-Hatred is at a modern-day all-time high. A September 8, 2016 Breitbart headline reads,

> "Israeli UN Envoy: Jew-Hatred At 'Highest Level of Our Lifetimes'"

These are the opening quotes from the article, *"Over 1/3 of European Jews are afraid to wear a yarmulke or Star of David in public," "More than half of French Jews have considered emigrating because they don't feel safe living as Jews in France. Today we hear things about Jews and the Jewish people that we thought belonged to the pages of history. ... Anti-Semitism is returning to everyday life without shame."*

However, when Israel is *larger* and *safer*, Jews can make Aliyah, not only to escape mounting international Anti-Semitism, but also to participate in the expansion of Israel into a *wealthier* nation. The skills and wealth they bring with them could become a contributing factor that leads to the type of prosperous condition described in Ezekiel 38:12-13. These verses portray Israel as possessing a very robust economy.

More land, Jews, economic wealth, military strength and international influence should characterize Israel just before the Gog of Magog invasion. This burgeoning Israel should be bursting at the seams, which will be conducive to improved and expanded foreign relations with other countries. However, this won't be the case for most surviving Muslim nations, like Iran, Turkey, Libya etc. These countries will probably not be pleased with Israel after the fulfillment of several NOW prophecies, like Psalm 83, (Arab-Israeli war), Isaiah 17, (destruction of Damascus), and Jeremiah 49:1-6, (toppling of Jordan).

Leading up to Ezekiel 38, the focus of the participating Muslims nations will largely be to extract revenge from Israel. The IDF will have decisively conquered their "evil Arab neighbors." The Arab casualties of that war, prisoners of that war and displaced Muslim refugees, will aggravate these Ezekiel 38 Muslim nations.

Additionally, Israel should also be capturing war spoils, which could include increased territory. These spoils of war could be part of the plunder and booty described in Ezekiel 38:12-13. Israel has a pattern of territorial expansion after winning wars. Joshua did this about 3300 years ago. David and Solomon also did this about 3000 years ago. Israel did this in 1967 after the infamous "Six-Day" war.

Israel feels justified in seizing neighboring lands for two primary reasons. *First*, it is part of the land God gave to Abraham in Genesis 15:18. *Second*, because it increases the defensibility of their borders.

The Muslim nations will also be upset with Israel if, after defeating the Arabs of Psalm 83, they break ground on the construction of their third Jewish temple. According to Bible prophecy, Israel will rebuild their temple sometime before the middle of the seven-year tribulation period. Today, the Temple Institute in Jerusalem declares that its ultimate goal is,

COMMENTARY

"To see Israel rebuild the Holy Temple on Mount Moriah in Jerusalem, in accord with the Biblical commandments."[83]

Although the surviving Muslim nations should be upset with Israel, and some Western nations supportive of the improved Israel, Russia will be jealous of the thriving Jewish state. A cruel Russian leader surfaces on the scene. In light of Russia's apparent bid to re-emerge as a superpower, some speculate that this ruthless ruler could be Russian President Vladimir Putin. Whoever he is, we are informed in Ezekiel 38:10 that he devises an "evil plan" against Israel.

The formulation of the evil bent Magog coalition will ruffle more than Israel's feathers. The protestors of Yemen, Saudi Arabia, the UK and USA, who are all identified in Ezekiel 38:13, will become extremely tense at the time.

All eyes throughout the world will undoubtedly be focused upon the mainstream news channels to see what Russia's evil intentions are. As the Magog coalition takes shape and begins to assemble to the north of Israel, according to Ezekiel 38:6, 15 and 39:2, the onlookers will watch their televisions with bated breath. *"What in the world is Russia up to*?" They will wonder.

Just when the hordes of Ezekiel 38 invaders are marching upon the soil of Israel, with all their weapons of warfare locked and loaded, something catches them completely off guard! Television viewers around the world become shocked to see that a massive earthquake rocks the area! The sequences of supernatural catastrophes that follow are explained in Ezekiel 38:14-39:8. What happens next is explained in the commentary of the chapter called, "The Collapse of the Russian Coalition."

The 144,000 Witnesses

This chapter reveals the hidden message concealed in the ordering of the tribal names of the 144,000 witnesses of Revelation 7:1-8. It also explores the marital status of the 144,000. The common teaching is that the 144,000 witnesses are virgins, but that may not be the best interpretation.

The Mysterious Message Concealed in the Names of the 144,000 Witnesses

Oddly, the listings of the names are out of chronological order, which suggests that there is a spiritual reason for this. The Bible doesn't make forgetful mistakes when it comes to important genealogical sequences.

Therefore, it appears the reason is because a mysterious message about the ministry of the 144,000 is cleverly concealed in the way their names are arranged.

Revelation 7:1-8 identifies twelve tribes who show up on the scene after the Rapture. They appear to arrive on the world stage in correlation with the timing of the opening of the seal judgments Revelation 6. These are clearly Jews called to the service of God. They come on the scene at a very interesting time and represent Israel in a preferred national condition. They are identified genealogically from their ancestral Hebrew tribes, and the ordering of the usage of their tribal names, though puzzling, may contain a ministerial meaning.

The Bible calls these 144,000 Jews "the servants of our God" in Revelation 7:3. They receive their ministry after the Church is raptured. Per some Bible prophecy teachers, the simple interpretation of Revelation 2 and 3 represents the Church on Earth, and Revelation 4 and 5 represents the Church, raptured and residing in heaven. Revelation 7 starts with the Greek words "*meta tauta*," interpreted in English as "*after these things*." After the summation of events of the Church age on Earth and the rapture of the Church, the events of Revelation 7 occur.

This adds credence to the fact that, if the "fullness of the Gentiles" is regarded with the completion of the Church during the Church Age, then the fullness of the Gentiles has been completed and it is time for the historic, "Chosen People," also referred to in the Bible as, "My people Israel" to again take front-and-center stage as God's people.

> "For I do not desire, brethren, that you should be ignorant of this mystery, lest you should be wise in your own opinion, that blindness in part has happened to Israel until the fullness of the Gentiles has come in." (Romans 11:25)

This verse informs that Israel was partially blinded to the gospel truth during the Church Age. However, it is commonly taught that after the Rapture, this blindness is removed.

For the most part, all Jewish tribal genealogical records were destroyed in AD 70, yet a Revelation 7:5–8 prophetic event still to occur distinctly identifies the emergence of twelve thousand members from each of their twelve ancestral tribes.[84] This is not a random selection; rather, God orchestrated it and ordained it by the angel having the "seal of the living God."

COMMENTARY

It is not an accident that there are not 11,999 from one tribe and 12,001 from another. There are exactly 12,000 from each tribe sealed for service. From these specifics, we can assume God is administering His earthly program once again through His chosen Jewish people. This safely suggests that these Jews are not "My people the Church," which by this time will have likely been raptured. Rather, they represent a significant component within "My people Israel." In my *"Psalm 83: The Missing Prophecy Revealed, How Israel Becomes The Next Mideast Superpower,"* I devote an entire chapter to the topic of "My people Israel."

These 144,000 servants minister after the Church age, and should therefore be very familiar with the gospel and the mystery of fellowship quoted in Ephesians, which says;

> "How that by revelation He made known to me (The apostle Paul) the mystery (as I have briefly written already, by which, when you read, you may understand my knowledge in the mystery of Christ), which in other ages was not made known to the sons of men, as it has now been revealed by the Spirit to His holy apostles and prophets: that the Gentiles should be fellow heirs, of the same body, and partakers of His promise in Christ through the gospel." (Ephesians 3:3-6; emphasis added)

Thus, the 144,000 Hebrew witnesses would know—and therefore teach—that salvation now comes through faith in Christ and not the Mosaic Law. They also teach that it is God's will that Gentiles should be partakers along with the Jews through the gospel.

With this understanding, we can interpret the possible ministerial message within the ordering of the names of the twelve tribes in Revelation 7:5–8.

> of the tribe of *Judah* twelve thousand *were* sealed;
> of the tribe of *Reuben* twelve thousand *were* sealed;
> of the tribe of *Gad* twelve thousand *were* sealed;
> of the tribe of *Asher* twelve thousand *were* sealed;
> of the tribe of *Naphtali* twelve thousand *were* sealed;
> of the tribe of *Manasseh* twelve thousand *were* sealed;
> of the tribe of *Simeon* twelve thousand *were* sealed;
> of the tribe of *Levi* twelve thousand *were* sealed;
> of the tribe of *Issachar* twelve thousand *were* sealed;

of the tribe of *Zebulun* twelve thousand *were* sealed;
of the tribe of *Joseph* twelve thousand *were* sealed;
of the tribe of *Benjamin* twelve thousand *were* sealed.
(Rev. 7:5–8, NKJV; emphasis added)

The names of the twelve tribes are listed in this non-chronological order, perhaps to describe the ministerial purposes of the 144,000 Hebrew Christian witnesses of Revelation 7:5–8. Normally, the Bible lists descendants in the chronological order of their birth. However, the apostle John lists these tribes out of order, apparently giving us insight into the ministry of these witnesses.

The tribe of Judah is listed first in Revelation 7:5, however, in birth order, Judah was the fourth son. Similarly, the Bible lists the other tribes out of order in Revelation 7:5–8. An astute student of the Word watches for these abnormalities within the scriptures and, as such, is always encouraged to dig deeper to discover what the Holy Spirit intends for him or her to understand relative to the text.

The Meanings of the Names:

Judah (Praise God), *Reuben* (behold a son), *Gad* (good fortune), *Asher* (happiness), *Naphtali* (my wrestling), *Manasseh* (God has caused me to forget), *Simeon* (hearing), *Levi* (joining or adhesion), *Issachar* (God hath given me my hire, or man for hire), *Zebulun* (elevated or elevated dwelling), *Joseph* (adding or increaser), *Benjamin* (son of the right hand).

The Message of the Names:

Praise God! Behold, a son of good fortune and happiness. My wrestling God has caused me to forget. Hearing of our joining, God hath given me my hire and elevated dwelling increased by the son of the right hand.

Inherent in these oddly ordered names, appears to be the ministerial message of the 144,000 witnesses. Their "Mission Statement" should read as follows:

"Praise God for the gospel of Christ. Behold, His Son of good fortune and happiness. My struggle with sin and the Mosaic Law, God has caused me to forget. Hearing of the mystery of our grafting in with the Gentiles,[85] God has reinstated me into an elevated position of ministry once again, and is increasing those being saved through Christ, the Son of the right hand."

Are the 144,000 Witnesses Virgins?

> These are the ones who were not defiled with women, for they are virgins. These are the ones who follow the Lamb wherever He goes. These were redeemed from *among* men, being firstfruits to God and to the Lamb. And in their mouth was found no deceit, for they are without fault before the throne of God. (Rev. 14:4–5, NKJV; emphasis added)

These 144,000 servants become "firstfruits to God and to the Lamb," (Jesus Christ), [86] suggesting that after the rapture the subsequent dispensation has the 144,000 as its firstfruits. This further suggests that at that time God will again administer His sovereign program through "My people Israel." These 144,000 servants likely represent the first crop of harvested souls after the Rapture of the Church. They are the first of many saved souls which were foretold to follow the sudden disappearance of the Christian Church. These saved souls are identified in Revelation 7:9-17, and elsewhere. Below is a definition of "Firstfruits."

> The choice examples of a crop harvested first and dedicated to God. In accordance with Mosaic law, individual Israelites brought to the house of the LORD "the first (that is, 'the best') of the firstfruits of thy land." (Ex. 23:19; 34:26)[87]

Per Revelation 14:4 we can easily understand that the 144,000 witnesses are "*firstfruits*" who "*follow the Lamb*," who is Jesus Christ. Also, they are saved and thus forgiven of their sins, which classifies them as being "*without fault*," and having no "*deceit*" in their mouths. However, are they true "*virgins*?" Maybe, but there is another possibility.

This topic came up in the novel in the chapter entitled, "*Jews Flee Israel as the Russian Invasion Begins*." In that part of the story Simeon, one of the 144,000 witnesses, explains why the common view that they are virgins, may not be the best and only interpretation. It would be helpful to compare his comments to what is said about this topic in this chapter. Some of the pertinent excerpts from Simeon's comments from the storyline are restated below.

Amber had her Bible open to Revelation chapter 14, where she read aloud: "*The hundred and forty-four-thousand who were redeemed from*

the earth. These are the ones who were not defiled with women, for they are virgins."

Jami blushed, and her mother winked at her. Looking up from the Bible, Amber inquired, "Does this mean that neither of you have been married before, or does it mean that you won't get married from this point forward?"

Young Jami, who was finding it hard to keep her eyes off handsome Simeon, found this question of particular interest, and she leaned in to hear Simeon's response.

Since this question was based on the New Testament, Simeon responded, "That's an excellent question and being an eligible bachelor, one of particular interest to me. Certainly, on the surface it suggests that we are all virgins and in that condition, we can devote 100% of our attention toward serving the Lord. I have looked closely at the original Greek language of the biblical text and I have compared it to the teachings of Paul about married life in 1 Corinthians 7. ... In 1 Corinthians 7:6-9, Paul makes an interesting comment after having laid down the groundwork for a successful marriage. He says, *'But I say this as a concession, not as a commandment. For I wish that all men were even as I myself. But each one has his own gift from God, one in this manner and another in that. But I say to the unmarried and to the widows: It is good for them if they remain even as I am; but if they cannot exercise self-control, let them marry. For it is better to marry than to burn with passion.'* I understand that to mean that Paul was unmarried and preferred to carry out his ministry in that capacity."

"What are you saying, that you are never getting married?" Jami blurted out. Then, having embarrassed herself, she sunk back into her seat.

Simeon smiled and wisely dodging her question, he went on: "Amber, you only read part of Revelation 14:4, about the *defiled by woman* and us being *virgins*, would you kindly read the rest of the verse?"

Revisiting the verse, Amber read, *"These are the ones who follow the Lamb wherever He goes. These were redeemed from among men, being firstfruits to God and to the Lamb."*

Now, let me explain the problems I have with simply saying we are virgins. First, the verse implies that women are defiling and that's why we remain as virgins. It's as if we don't want to become contaminated by a woman. That's utter nonsense! God didn't create Eve to defile Adam. In fact, a good woman can serve a vital role in a man's ministry.

In my estimation, the apostle Paul didn't remain single out of a fear that he would become corrupted by a woman. He calculated that he could better devote his undivided attention to his calling in an unmarried capacity..."

Pausing momentarily, he asked, "Does that make sense so far?"

Jami responded giddishly, "Yes, especially the part about *a good woman can serve a vital role in a man's ministry*."

Chuckling for a moment, Simeon continued: "I had Amber read the rest of the verse because it emphasizing that we are the ones who follow the '*Lamb wherever He goes*.' This is in stark contrast to, we are the ones who follow the Harlot, wherever she goes. This may be difficult to explain until you learn about the coming global religion, which is represented in Revelation 17 and elsewhere as a harlot. It appears that these verses may teach that the 144,000 witnesses remain chaste solely to the Lord, and are not stained, soiled, or defiled by the coming false world religion represented by the Harlot. One of the distinguishing characteristics of our 144,000 witnesses will definitely be that we will not be defiled by the harlot religion. Or another way of explaining it would be that we are considered virgins because we won't partake of the pagan idolatries that come out of the harlot global religion."

Below are some commentaries that support the notion that the marital status is not the central issue of Revelation 14:4.

Believers's Bible Commentary - William MacDonald

> "They are described as virgins, those who have not defiled themselves with women. They had kept themselves free from this terrible idolatry and immorality of this period and followed the Lamb in unquestionable obedience and devotion."[88]

Jamieson-Fausset-Brown Bible Commentary

> "Virgins—in contrast to the apostate Church, Babylon (Rev. 14:8), spiritually "a harlot" (Rev. 17:1-5; Isa 1:21; contrast 2 Cor. 11:2; Ephesians 5:25-27). Their not being defiled with women means they were not led astray from Christian faithfulness by the tempters who jointly constitute the spiritual "harlot.""[89]

John Gill's Exposition of the Bible

"These are they which were not defiled with women,.... With the whore of Rome, and her harlots, she is the mother of; while the kings and inhabitants of the earth were drunk with the wine of their fornication, or committed idolatry with them, which is spiritual fornication, and is here meant by being defiled with them, these were free from such pollutions, or idolatrous practices: for they are virgins; for their beauty and comeliness in Christ, chastity, sincerity of their love, uncorruptness in doctrine and worship, and for the uprightness of conversation."[90]

Matthew Poole's Commentary

"These are they which were not defiled with women; for they are virgins; that is, that would not comply with antichristian idolatry and superstition; for idolatry is all along in holy writ compared to whoredom and fornication."[91]

Chapter 8
The Antichrist and the Coming Global Religion

D ue to the vast amount and complex nature of the prophetic topics introduced in this novel chapter, the accompanying commentary is provided in the "Post-Rapture / Pre-Trib Thesis" of *Apocalypse Road*. This thesis, which is inserted at the end of the Companion's Commentary, is devoted to the thorough explanation of the events that occur within this vastly unexplored gap period of time. This exposition also explains the events that segue from the gap period on into the Trib-period.

The overall intent of the thesis is to present the reader with an overview of several end time's Bible prophecies in general, but more specifically, to provide a detailed glimpse of the author's gap period hypothesis. The novel storyline reflects the conclusions taken from the end time's model that is postulated in this thesis.

The decision to consolidate several chapters of Companion's Commentary into this single thesis, was based upon the awareness that the gap hypothesis must be presented in its entirety, rather than be chopped up into individual commentary sections.

Chapter 9
The Collapse of the Russian Coalition

Topics Covered

What are the conditions in Israel during the Ezekiel 38 invasion?

What are the conditions in Israel in the aftermath of Ezekiel 38?

This chapter looks at prophecies described in Ezekiel 38 and 39 through the lens of Israel's perspective. The first topic of the three below was previously covered in the commentary of the chapter entitled, "Jews Flee Israel as the Russian Invasion Begins." This chapter exposits upon the second and third topics.

1. What are the conditions in Israel before the Gog of Magog invasion? (Ezekiel 38:1-13).
   (Topics covered in this chapter are below).

2. What are the conditions in Israel during the Ezekiel 38 invasion? (Ezekiel 38:14-39:8).

3. What are the conditions in Israel in the aftermath of Ezekiel 38? (Ezekiel 39:9-21).

What are the conditions in Israel during the Ezekiel 38 invasion?

The previous few paragraphs along with those about to follow in this section are admittedly somewhat speculative. However, author liberties are being taken in order to paint a biblically based portrait of how the

Ezekiel 38 invasion might unfold. You are encouraged to have your Bibles open to the pertinent passages to confirm that my interpretations are not too far-fetched.

Ezekiel 38:19-20 says there will be a *"great earthquake in the land of Israel."* The magnitude of the quake will cause all men upon the face of the whole earth to *"shake."* Affected *mountains* will crumble and *walls* will fall. When was the last time you saw mountains, (plural), topple as the result of an earthquake? Also, wonder who might be killed when the affected mountains are thrown down.

Imagine watching this spectacular scene that interrupts the advance of the Magog invaders on your TV set. What is about to follow is all supernatural. Neither the IDF, nor the American military plays any role in what happens next.

Ezekiel 38:21 declares that *"Every man's sword will be against his brother."* This is alluding to the Magog invaders. Apparently, the powerful repercussions from the seismic event causes panic among the troops, who then begin attacking one another. This is not an example of "friendly fire." This is an illustration of what happened in Israel's history when Gideon's 300 man army fought against the Midianites. Judges 7:22 says, *"the LORD set every man's sword against his companion throughout the whole camp."*

Ezekiel 38:22 informs, *"I will rain down on him, on his troops, and on the many peoples who are with him, flooding rain, great hailstones, fire, and brimstone."* As if the earthquake, which will topple mountains, crumble walls and result in the killing of one another wasn't enough, matters go from terrible to horrendous for the invaders. Flooding rains accompanied by stone size hailstones pummel the invaders. Fire and brimstone finish them off. By the time all the supernatural events above concludes,

1. The Magog invaders are destroyed,

2. The television watchers around the world are in shock,

3. And, Israel is counting their blessings and praising Jehovah the God of Abraham, Isaac and Jacob.

Ezekiel 39:1-6 provides more graphic details about what happens to the invaders and then Ezekiel 39:7-8 sheds light on the purpose of the experience. These verses have been quoted before in this book, but bear repeating again here.

> "So I will make My holy name known in the midst of My people Israel, and I will not *let them* profane My holy

name anymore. Then the nations shall know that *I am* the LORD, the Holy One in Israel. Surely it is coming, and it shall be done," says the Lord GOD. "This *is* the day of which I have spoken." (Ezekiel 39:7-8)

It will be hard for anyone that watched or experienced this event first hand to walk away with any other conclusion than what is said in these two verses.

What are the conditions in Israel in the aftermath of Ezekiel 38?

Ezekiel 39:9-21 explains what happens in Israel in the aftermath of God's supernatural victory over the Magog invaders.

Israel uses the enemy's weapons

Ezekiel 39:9-10 clues us in to the types of weaponry the invaders possess. The weapons must be of the sort that Israel will be able to convert into fuel. Ezekiel says that *"they will make fire with them for seven years."* The picture is of energy provision for the entire nation, rather than a few isolated households. Verse 9 says, *"those who dwell in the cities,"* utilize this converted weapons-grade fuel.

The widespread use and lengthy seven year span suggests that the weapons must be far more sophisticated than wooden bows and arrows, which would undoubtedly only last a short while. I mention this because some expositors today limit the weapons to wooden ones. I doubt nuclear non-proliferation will reduce Russian arsenals to wood between now and then.

These missiles and rockets that are being converted to fuel in Ezekiel 39:9-10 probably include the ABCs of weaponry—atomic, biological, and chemical. We can presume this because these types of weapons already exist inside the arsenals of Russia and some of their cohorts. Additionally, the dead soldiers appear to require Hazmat (Hazardous Materials) teams to assist with their burial according to Ezekiel 39:14-16. The fascinating fact is that whatever the weapons configuration, Israel will possess the technological know-how to convert them into national energy. Today, whether it is cell phones or irrigation techniques, Israel is on the cutting-edge of technological advances.

The Magog invaders intended to use these weapons to dispossess Israel of its booty, which would include its energy resources, but the opposite occurs. Israel converts the enemy weaponry into additional energy sources for themselves, instead of having their energy sources stolen.

Israel buries the Magog invaders

Ezekiel 39:11-16 describes the location of the mass burial grounds of the destroyed armies of Gog. A valley east of what is probably the Dead Sea is renamed the Valley of Hamon Gog, which means the "hordes or multitudes" of Gog, in Hebrew. Why I believe it refers to a valley in modern-day Jordan is explained in the chapter called, "Israel Cleanses the Holy Land."

We also find in Ezekiel 39:11-16 that the Israelis will be burying the dead in order to cleanse the land. This could imply two things. *One*, that the hordes of Gog's dead soldiers are contaminated, which would require a professional quarantined burial. This contamination could come from either the fallout from their atomic, biological and / or chemical weapons, or the deteriorating corpses strewn across the battlefield. *Two*, the Jews are adhering to their ancient Levitical Law according to Numbers 19:11-22 and Deuteronomy 21:1-9. These verses set forth specifications about the appropriate handling of dead bodies lying on the land of Israel.

Ezekiel 39:17-20 is an invitation "to every sort of bird and to every beast of the field" to partake of the sacrificial meal of the "flesh" and "blood" of the invaders. This passage is not for the faint of heart. I remember hearing prophecy expert Joel Rosenberg teach this topic at a Calvary Chapel Chino Hills prophecy conference, and he brought tears streaming down from my eyes.

Ezekiel 39:21-29 concludes the chapter with a recap of some Jewish history and a promise to the faithful remnant of Israel that the Lord will pour out His spirit upon them in the end. The Holy Spirit will be bestowed to the faithful remnant when they recognize Christ as their Messiah. This is one of the rewards for believing in Jesus Christ. (John 14:16-17, 26, 15:26, 16:7).

Summary

Ezekiel 38 and 39 provides the most important, well explained, and easy to understand prophecies in the Bible. This is because these chapters foretell of the coming marquis event, whereby the Lord upholds His holy name before the watchful eyes of humankind. The event is so epic that the Lord achieves the undivided attention of mankind. Israelis continuing to inhabit their homeland of Israel, after the prophetic wars of

Psalm 83 and Ezekiel 38, will provide humanity with ample evidence to recognize that the God of the Bible is the one true God!

The timing of Ezekiel 38 is critical. It occurs in the end times when the Promised Land of Israel hosts the Chosen People (Israelis). The Rapture of the church could occur before, during or after the event. My personal view is that the Ezekiel 38 is a post-Rapture, but Pre-Tribulation (Pre-Trib) event. I non-dogmatically believe that Ezekiel 38 finds fulfillment prior to the implementation of the Antichrist's "Mark of the Beast" campaign in Revelation 13:11-18.

Lastly, this novel chapter ends with Nathan shocked to read how some Catholics were accrediting Our Lady of Fatima with stopping the Ezekiel invasion. This concluding portion was included in the storyline to inform you that the Catholics may attribute the supernatural defeat of the Gog of Magog invasion to the Blessed Mother, rather than the God of the Bible, especially if Russia has already been consecrated to the Immaculate Heart of Mary prior to the fulfillment of the event. The appendix entitled, "The Marian Apparitions Connection with Ezekiel 38," explains how this could be what happens.

COMMENTARY

Chapter 10
Letter to the Saints Left Behind

The commentary for this chapter is integrated within the "Post-Rapture / Pre-Tribulation Gap Thesis" of *Apocalypse Road*. The Fifth Seal Saints are part of the seven seals in the book of Revelation. These seals are explained in the Thesis...

Fifth Seal: The Cry of the Martyrs

"When He opened the fifth seal, I saw under the altar the souls of those who had been slain for the word of God and for the testimony which they held. And they cried with a loud voice, saying, "How long, O Lord, holy and true, until You judge and avenge our blood on those who dwell on the earth?" Then a white robe was given to each of them; and it was said to them that they should rest a little while longer, until both *the number of* their fellow servants and their brethren, who would be killed as they *were,* was completed." (Revelation 6:9-11)

Chapter 11
The Queen of Heaven Appears Globally

Topics Covered

Is the Catholic "Virgin Mary" the Mary of the Bible?

What is the End Game of the Marian Apparitions?

Will there be more apparitions of Mary to come?

Will Future Apparitions of Mary Create the World Religion of Revelation 17?

The Marian Apparitions Connection with Ezekiel 38

In the storyline, the apparition of Mary speaks directly, rather than transmitting her message through a visionary. Although this is uncommon, it is not unprecedented. On at least one past occasion the apparition has spoken directly. This was alleged to have occurred in the Philippines in 1986. Below is a quote from an article dealing with this apparition message.

> "Then a Lady of enormous splendor appeared to them..." the Cardinal told in a review. "She was beautiful, and Her eyes were shining. And that beautiful woman spoke out to the soldiers using the words: 'Stop, my dearest soldiers! Don't go any further! Do not harm my children'. Having heard this the soldiers abandoned everything, left the tanks and joined the people" – said Cardinal Sin." [92]

This chapter delves into the five important topics below. Topics #1-4 will be covered in this chapter's commentary, but topic #5, which deals with the Eucharist, will be addressed in the commentary of the chapter entitled, *"The Harlot Rides the Beast to Peace and Prosperity."*

1.　Who is the Catholic "Virgin Mary," "Blessed Mother," "Queen of Heaven," "Our Lady," etc.? Is she the true mother of Jesus, i.e., the Mary of the Bible?

2.　Do the multitude of Marian apparitions play a grand purpose in the coming Satanic deception of 2 Thessalonians 2:9-11?

3.　Could a series of strategically located apparitions of Mary occur after the Rapture? Is this how the harlot world religion of Revelation 17 might come together?

4.　Why did the "Blessed Mother" issue a prediction at the 1917 Fatima apparition about Russia?

5.　What is the important role of the Eucharist in Roman Catholicism?

Is the Catholic "Virgin Mary" the Mary of the Bible?

Catholics believe that their "Virgin Mary" is the actual Mary in the Bible. They believe that the Vatican approved apparitions over the past centuries were actual visitations from the mother of Jesus. One of those supernatural appearances spawned the infamous Catholic Rosary.

The Rosary is a form of devotion in which the "Hail Mary" prayer is recited. The Hail Mary, *Ave Maria* in Latin, is a Roman Catholic prayer to the Virgin Mary that consists of salutations and a plea for her intercession. Catholics worldwide recite this prayer daily. The prayer consists of 42 words that are recited an astonishing 53 times during the course of praying a standard Rosary. The quote below briefly explains the history of the Rosary.

> "It was only in the year 1214, however, that the Church received the Rosary in its present form and according to the method we use today. It was given to the Church by St. Dominic, who had received it from the Blessed Virgin as a means of converting the Albigensians and other sinners...
> At this point our Lady appeared to him, accompanied by three angels, and she said, "Dear Dominic, do you know which weapon the Blessed Trinity wants to use to reform the world?" "Oh, my Lady," answered Saint Dominic, "you know far better than I do, because next to your Son

Jesus Christ you have always been the chief instrument
of our salvation."[93]

There are fifteen promises rewarded to those who recite the Rosary
and a few of them are listed below. These pledges are not specifically
spelled out within the words of the Rosary itself, but were assurances
made directly by the apparition herself. The promises identified below
and the history quoted above were gathered from the holyrosary.org
website.[94] Some of these claims from the Blessed Mother are things
that only God can do. After reading them one might justifiably wonder, is
there anything that the apparition of Mary can't do?

•   I (The Blessed Mother) promise my special protection and the
     greatest graces to all those who shall recite the Rosary.

•   The soul which recommends itself to me by the recitation of the
     Rosary, shall not perish.

•   Whoever shall recite the Rosary devoutly, applying himself to the
     consideration of its Sacred Mysteries shall never be conquered
     by misfortune. God will not chastise Him in His justice... he (one
     who recites the Rosary) shall remain in the grace of God, and
     become worthy of eternal life.

•   You shall obtain all you ask of me by the recitation of the Rosary.

Many Catholics believe that she never died, rather she was assumed
into heaven because she possesses an Immaculate (unstained, sinless)
Heart. As such, they believe that she is alive and actively interceding
between Christ and the Catholic Faithful. When they pray to Mary, it is
not in honor of whom she once was, but in accordance with whom they
presently believe she is. I write about the fatal fallacies of this thinking in
the *Revelation Road* book appendix entitled, "The Fallible Assumption
of Mary."[95]

The Bible clearly debunks this teaching by acknowledging in Mary's
own words, that she was simply Christ's maidservant who was in need of
a Savior. This means that she died about 2000 years ago in accordance
with the wages of sin.

> And Mary said: "My soul magnifies the Lord, And
> my spirit has rejoiced in God my Savior. For He has
> regarded the lowly state of His maidservant; For
> behold, henceforth all generations will call me blessed.
> For He who is mighty has done great things for me,

And holy *is* His name. And His mercy *is* on those who fear Him From generation to generation. (Luke 1:46-50)

Therefore, being a sinner, Mary died. "For the wages of sin *is* death, but the gift of God *is* eternal life in Christ Jesus our Lord. (Romans 6:23)

Thus, the Catholic "Queen of Heaven," although a real supernatural phenomenon, is nothing more than an imposter masquerading as the Mary of the Bible. She is cleverly deceiving the Catholic Faithful and people from other religious backgrounds and yet, millions continue to buy her statues and pilgrimage to her apparition sites around the world.

In fact, at www.catholicjourneys.com a few thousand dollars will get you a ticket to the 100-year anniversary of the Fatima apparition. (1917-2017). Or, this website will also sell you tickets to other famous apparition locations like Guadalupe, Mexico, Medjugorje, Bosnia Herzegovina, Lourdes, France and several other popular Catholic related tourist destinations.

The cult of Mary is good business for many in the Catholic Church, but it also provides a method for the deceived clergy to manipulate the spiritual mindset of the Catholic masses. Many Catholics are so captivated by this false prophetess that they believe she should be elevated to the status of Co-Redemptrix, which associates her with having a potential role in the redemption of man. Another name currently being associated with this Catholic heroine is, "The Co-Redemptrix, Mediatrix and Advocate."

Many visionaries have uttered direct messages from the "Blessed Mother," which acknowledge her personal claim to be called the Co-Redemptrix.

Below are quotes to this effect.

> "In her message of March 18th in Medjugorje, Bosnia-Hercegovina, the apparition, calling herself Queen of Peace, tells visionary Mirjana Dragicevic-Soldo *"Dear children! I am coming among you because I desire to be your mother - your intercessor. I desire to be the bond between you and the Heavenly Father - your mediatrix. I desire to take you by the hand and to walk with you in the battle against the impure spirit."*

COMMENTARY

In the 1950's in a series of apparitions in Amsterdam, Holland, an apparition, calling herself Lady of All Nations, tells visionary Ida Peerdeman that she demanded of the Church to declare her *"Co-redemptrix, mediatrix and advocate"*.[96]

What is the End Game of the Marian Apparitions?

Before spelling out the likely Satanic end game of the Marian apparitions, it's important to comprehend the relatively complex official Catholic position on the topic of the biblical end times. In order to accomplish this, a researcher is required to understand the Catholic stance on Replacement Theology, Amillennialism and the pertinent teachings on the last day's topics provided in their Catechism.

Basically, the Catholics believe in the end times, but not exactly in the same context as some of their Evangelical Christian counterparts. For instance, the Catholics are not expecting Christ to come for His Bride the Church in the Pre-Tribulation Rapture![97]

Replacement Theology

It is important to understand how Replacement Theology plays a part in the Catholics understanding of the end times. The Catholics believe that they have replaced Israel, the "Chosen People" of the Old Testament. They believe that the promises and prophecies that were made to and through Israel, those which were intended to find fulfillment between the start of the Church age and the end of the Messianic kingdom, for the most part, have been transferred to the Catholic Church. Remember that the Catholic Church considers itself to be the "True Church." Thus, they now esteem themselves as God's people. They believe that like the Jews were the "Chosen People of the Promise," that they have become the "Chosen People of the Fulfillment."[98]

The general justification for this thinking is, that when the Jews rejected Jesus as their Messiah, God rejected the Jews as His Chosen People of the Fulfillment. This thinking gained momentum during the Jewish Diaspora between 70 A.D. and 1948 A.D. As each year passed, the replacement theologians deduced that because the Jews remain under relatively constant persecution and without a homeland in which to return, that God must have rejected them.

Amillennialism

Part of the Catholic confusion about the end times is caused by their infusion of "Amillennialism" into their theology. Amillennialism involves the rejection of the belief that Jesus will have a literal, thousand-year-long, physical reign on the earth. This rejection contrasts with premillennial interpretations of chapter 20 of the Book of Revelation. Pre-Millennialism teaches that Christ will return to establish His Messianic Kingdom on earth prior to the Millennial period identified in Revelation 20:4.

The quote below, which was taken directly from a Catholic forum website, adequately summarizes the Catholic Amillennial perspective.

> "*Amillennialism is the belief that the prophesied* (Messianic) *kingdom of Jesus and the Old Testament is being fulfilled now in the Church. It comes from the belief that Israel's promises are to be fulfilled in the Church.* (Replacement Theology). *Amillennialism is in opposition to premillennialism, which believes that Jesus will come back to reign for a literal 1000-year kingdom on the earth.*"[99]

For reasons further explained below, the Catholics do not believe that Jesus is returning before this kingdom age in order to reign throughout this period. The high point of Old Testament prophecy was this Messianic kingdom age. Some of the most comforting prophecies were clearly designed to find fulfillment during this special age. Isaiah provides a partial description of this period below.

> "The wolf also shall dwell with the lamb, The leopard shall lie down with the young goat, The calf and the young lion and the fatling together; And a little child shall lead them. The cow and the bear shall graze; Their young ones shall lie down together; And the lion shall eat straw like the ox. The nursing child shall play by the cobra's hole, And the weaned child shall put his hand in the viper's den. They shall not hurt nor destroy in all My holy mountain, For the earth shall be full of the knowledge of the Lord As the waters cover the sea. (Isaiah 11:6-9)

The apostle John reveals in Revelation 20:2-7 that the Messianic kingdom will last for one-thousand years, which is a millennium. Interestingly, mankind has recently entered into the third millennium of the Church Age. Because the Catholics believe that they are destined to fulfill the promises and prophecies instead of Israel, including those during the Messianic period, this means that the next nine plus centuries should prove to be critically important to Catholics.

From the Roman Catholic perspective, the Church can't be removed from the earth in the Rapture. This is an utter impossibility because of the pivotal position they believe the Church fulfills during the kingdom age. When Isaiah 11:9 says, "For the earth shall be full of the knowledge of the Lord as the waters cover the sea," the Catholics believe that, in large part, this is accomplished through them.

Stimulating their thinking in this regard is their allegorical, rather than literal, interpretation of some Bible prophecies and their unshakable belief that the Eucharist represents the actual presence of Jesus Christ on earth. They believe that Christ's literal body and blood mystically inhabit the bread and wine elements of this sacrament. This process is called "Transubstantiation."

Because of Amillennialism, in conjunction with Replacement Theology, the Catholics are not anxiously awaiting the imminent return of Christ in the Pre-Trib Rapture, rather they are eagerly hoping for a reappearing of the Queen of Heaven in one or more future apparitions. They trust that this central feminine figure of their faith will fulfill in the near future, the apparition promises she has made in the not so distant past. These prophecies were issued primarily through visionary messages at Fatima and elsewhere.

Thus far, the assortment of supernatural Marian apparitions and visionary messages have helped convince many Catholics that they belong to the "One True Religion." Possessing this authoritarian mindset, the Catholic clergy believes that Roman Catholicism exclusively represents the ordained embodiment of Christ upon the earth. The Catholic hierarchies sincerely believe that Christ has appointed them to spread Roman Catholicism throughout the world in this third millennium of Christendom.

The Catholic leaders are hoping that their Blessed Mother will support their cause to promote Catholicism by ushering in an era of worldwide peace. As this momentous feat is underway, they anticipate that the Virgin Mary will complete the consecration of the world to her Immaculate Heart.

At the beginning of this new third millennium of Christendom, Pope John Paul II set the stage for these two critical things, world peace and consecration, to happen. On October 8, 2000, the Holy Father, with the collegial union of all the Bishops of the Church, consecrated the world to the Immaculate Heart of Mary.[100] The process of consecrating the world to the Immaculate Heart of Mary, essentially involves the conversion of the masses to Christ through Roman Catholicism.

World peace is the novel concept that most beauty pageant contestants wish for, but in the new millennium the Catholics are planning to award the Miss Universe crown to their "Queen of Heaven." With her supernatural power and continued spiritual guidance, the Catholics hope to fulfill their obligations as the replacement for Israel.

When Christ returns in fulfillment of a Pre-trib Rapture, the Catholics will be proven wrong on all of the above!

Will there be more apparitions of Mary to come?

There are a few things to consider when answering this question.

1. *The Queen of Heaven has unfinished business on earth.* Some of the direct messages from the Blessed Mother, which have been uttered through her selected visionaries, declare that she will play a vital role in the future. As previously mentioned, the Queen of Heaven promises to usher in a period of global peace and to fulfill the consecration of the world to her Immaculate Heart.[101]

2. *The Bible predicts a double religious jeopardy for mankind after the Rapture.*

    a. First, the Harlot of Revelation 17, will form a global religion. After she has overextended her usefulness the Antichrist will have the ten kings desolate her as per Revelation 17:16.

    b. Second, after the Harlot Queen is dethroned, the False Prophet and the Antichrist of Revelation 13 will rise up and replace her. At this point the Antichrist seeks the world to worship him instead of the desolated harlot.

3. *Supernatural deception is predicted to occur after the Rapture in 2 Thessalonians 2:1-12.* In my opinion, this implies that first Satan will deceive mankind through supernatural means by the Harlot. This favors the probability that more supernatural sightings of Mary are forthcoming. This would be in alignment with what the Blessed Mother has also prophesied. This false prophetess has promised

to consecrate the world to her Immaculate Heart. The presumption to make is that the Catholic "Virgin Mary" will be returning to make good on her promises.

4. *The Bible predicts that a female typology within the church gets left behind and ends up in Trib-period.* In the letter to the Church of Thyatira we are informed of the following.

> "Notwithstanding I have a few things against thee, (*Roman Catholicism*), because thou sufferest that woman Jezebel, (*The Queen of Heaven*), which calleth herself a prophetess, to teach and to seduce my servants, (*Catholic Clergy*), to commit fornication, and to eat things sacrificed unto idols. And I gave her space to repent of her fornication; and she repented not. Behold, I will cast her, (*Harlot world religion*), into a bed, and them that commit adultery with her, (*Marian worshippers*), into great tribulation, (*The second half of the Trib-period*), except they repent of their deeds. And I will kill her children with death; and all the churches shall know that I am he which searcheth the reins and hearts: and I will give unto every one of you according to your works. But unto you I say, and unto the rest in Thyatira, as many as have not this doctrine, and which have not known the depths of Satan, as they speak; I will put upon you none other burden." (Revelation 2:20-24; KJV, emphasis added)

I took liberties by inserting my suggested interpretations in the (*italicized parentheses*) in the verses above. In the appendix entitled, "The Seven Letters to the Churches," I provide additional connections between Roman Catholicism and the letter to the Church of Thyatira. The reference to a female type of Jezebel within the church that gets cast in the tribulation period has Post-Rapture prophetic implications. The great tribulation is commonly taught to be the second half of the seven-year tribulation period.

In my estimation, the best candidate for a female figure that has typified Jezebel the prophetess of the Old Testament, which has been dominant within the church age, is the Catholics "Blessed Mother." The striking similarities between these two female figures are provided in the commentary of the chapter called, "Two Witnesses Prepare for the Tribulational Period."

If these Revelation 2 verses connect Jezebel in typology with the Blessed Mother, then it's the Roman Catholic Church that gets cast into the "sickbed" of the "great tribulation." This implies that, unlike the first half of the Trib-period when Catholicism is in its heyday, the second half of the Trib-period casts Catholicism into a diametrically different role, "a sickbed of great tribulation." A harlot confined to a sickbed finds herself unemployed. She is unable to conduct any further fornication. In other words, the harlot world religion of Revelation 17 will be finished and unable to further spread its false teachings.

These are just four considerations supporting the probability that the Marian apparitions have an end game in sight. It is preposterous to think that Satan has no diabolical future plans in the end times for this supernatural being. Furthermore, it is doubtful that the Rapture will cause the collapse of Catholicism and the complete cessation of the apparitions. Unless all the Catholics get Raptured, it is probable that the Blessed Mother will reappear to comfort any of her faithful Catholic followers that have been left behind. Won't her supposed sacred heart have a soft spot for them?

In fact, the perfect time for the Queen of Heaven to reappear is swiftly on the heels of the Rapture. She will have some serious explaining to do. The Rapture represents the removal of the Church from the earth, yet if many Catholics and their leaders are left behind, then something went horribly wrong for all of them. The Queen of Heaven, being no stranger to the supernatural realm, would be the perfect source to answer their questions and dispel their concerns about what happened and what will happen in the future.

Her timely reappearing would provide the reassurance these Catholics need. Also, it could provide the perfect platform to usher in the era of world peace that she has promised.

Will Future Apparitions of Mary Facilitate the World Religion of Revelation 17?

It is commonly taught that Revelation 17 describes a coming world religion. It is depicted as a harlot in this prophecy. If this harlot world religion is embodied by Roman Catholicism, which I and some of my colleagues believe, then future supernatural apparitions of Mary could be the catalyst to its emergence. What better way to deceive a world that will be traumatized after the miraculous disappearance of millions of Christians, than to have some supernatural sightings of the Blessed Mother in strategic world locations.

Below are a couple of quotations along these lines. These quotes illustrate what is commonly accepted in some Catholic circles, that more apparitions of Mary are forthcoming.

The first one is from the Marian apparition expert Thomas W. Petrisko.

> *"After the warnings will come the great miracles. Some of these miracles are to be wondrous signs to the world that God exists and that Jesus Christ is Lord. Others will confirm the Virgin Mary's apparitions throughout the world."*[102]

The second quote comes from a visionary message written about by Isabel Bettwy.

> *"At the end of all the apparitions in the world, I* (the Marian apparition) *will leave a great sign in this place and in all those where I have been."*[103]

Author liberties were taken in this novel chapter by speculating that multiple apparition sightings occur at differing locations. However, it would only take one powerful supernatural Mary sighting to garnish the world's undivided attention. One or more timely Post-Rapture apparition(s), along with a reassuring message, could comfort and reconfirm the faith of any Catholics that were left behind.

Remember, Catholics do not believe in a literal Pre-trib Rapture of the Church. It's safe to suggest that left behind Catholics will be susceptible to alternative explanations, especially if they come from their Blessed Mother. All the apparition message has to say, is "That was not the removal of the true Church, rather it was the *yada, yada, yada, blah, blah, blah*…, or whatever the deceptive explanation might be.

The apparition message might even render a biblical quote like,

> *"Soon the wicked will disappear. Though you look for them, they will be gone. The lowly will possess the land and will live in peace and prosperity.* (Psalm 37:10, NLT)

> *"The righteous will never be removed, But the wicked will not inhabit the earth."* (Proverbs 10:30)

> *"The Son of Man will send out His angels, and they will gather out of His kingdom all things that offend, and those who practice lawlessness…So it will be at the end of the age. The angels will come forth, separate the wicked from among the just."* (Matthew 13:41, 49)

Imagine if the Pope, some Cardinals, Bishops, Priests and other members of the Catholic clergy get left behind. It is doubtful that any of them will want to hear that Christ left them behind. Most, if not all of them, would prefer to teach that the righteous remained, whereas the wicked were removed from the earth. Moreover, her timely Post-Rapture reappearing would reconfirm their already established beliefs that;

1. Their Queen of Heaven is playing an active lead role within the world,

2. Roman Catholicism is the embodiment of Christ on earth, the "One True Church,"

3. Christ is still present in the Eucharist,

4. There is no Pre-trib Rapture,

5. The Reformation is over,

6. Global peace is finally forthcoming along with the completion of world consecration to the Immaculate Heart of Mary. This would include Russia as per the Fatima predictions.

The unification of a world religion after the Rapture will require supernatural support. Something spectacular will likely have to occur in order to capture mankind's attention, gain its spiritual trust and persuade it to worship within the harlot system. If Roman Catholicism stays mostly intact and some of its key leaders remain in their places after the Rapture, then this well-established worldwide religious institution could easily be embraced by humanity at large, and the Antichrist, as he begins his nascent rise to political power.

According to Revelation 17:2, this religious system is *"with whom the kings of the earth committed fornication, and the inhabitants of the earth were made drunk with the wine of her fornication."* These idioms express a church and state relationship, through which the masses not only embrace, but become intoxicated by its teachings. Additionally, Revelation 17:15 confirms that the harlot system has a worldwide reach. It says that she presides over *"peoples, multitudes, nations, and tongues."*

Revelation 17:9 and 18 point out that the religious headquarters of the Harlot is in a *"great city"* that sits on seven hills. At the time these verses were inscribed, Rome was referred to as the city that was built upon seven hills. Below is a quote about this from the Encyclopedia Britannica.

"Seven Hills of Rome, group of hills on or about which the ancient city of Rome was built. The original city of Romulus was built upon Palatine Hill (Latin: Mons Palatinus). The other hills are the Capitoline, Quirinal, Viminal, Esquiline, Caelian, and Aventine (known respectively in Latin as the Mons Capitolinus, Mons Quirinalis, Mons Viminalis, Mons Esquilinus, Mons Caelius, and Mons Aventinus)."[104]

Revelation 17:16, predicts that this system will eventually be desolated by ten kings in order for the Antichrist to introduce his beastly religious system in Revelation 13. This desolation seemingly eliminates the possibility that the harlot system is comprised of an ungoverned interfaith based conglomeration of multiple world religions. Some Bible prophecy experts teach that the Harlot is just that, some sort of a loosely assembled ecumenical cooperative that's religiously tolerant.

There are several problems with this thinking.

1.   *How do you desolate all world religions?* How do you eliminate all the snake charmers, witches of Wicca, and New Age mystics, not to mention the far more difficult task of decimating the major world religions of Hinduism, Buddhism and Islam?

Since they are not believers, all of these religious pagans will be left behind. Also, how will all their temples, shrines and mosques become enjoined under one religious canopy? What single primary city has to be desolated among these religions to make an end of this type of a harlot system? Would it be Muslim Mecca, Saudi Arabia, Hindu Mathura, India or Buddhist Beijing, China? Whichever city, it has to be situated on seven hills and hold the reigns over the harlot system.

If Roman Catholicism turns out to be the harlot system, then Rome becomes the target city. If the desolation occurs at Vatican City, then the entire Roman Catholic system becomes disconnected from its head. Additionally, sizeable amounts of the institutions wealth can be easily captured by the Antichrist and the ten kings. This may be a motivator in the minds of some of these ten political leaders.

It's important to note that Mary is the most venerated woman in Catholicism and she is highly regarded within Islam. Additionally, the Hindus worship multiple female goddesses like Lakshmi (goddess of wealth and prosperity), Saraswati (goddess of knowledge and learning) and Parvati (who is the wife of Shiva - the destroyer). The Muslims and

COMMENTARY

Hindus would probably be mesmerized if Marian apparitions followed on the heels of the Rapture.

Moreover, Islam will probably be on a severe downward spiral at the same time because the prophetic wars of Psalm 83 and Ezekiel 38 will have happened, or be about to happen. These involve predominately Muslim populations that will be decimated. Should this be the geopolitical scenario at the time the harlot system comes on the scene, then it's doubtful that the Muslim city of Mecca is the city that will be desolated.

2.   A second problem with interfaith view of the Harlot is, how do you convince passive religions to kill true believers in Christ? Revelation 17:6 says, "I saw the woman, drunk with the blood of the saints and with the blood of the martyrs of Jesus. And when I saw her, I marveled with great amazement."

The apostle uses clear and strong language that depicts a religious system with blood stained hands. It's hard to imagine that a passive Buddhist will embark upon a manhunt to martyr a follower of Jesus. Additionally, whomever the Harlot represents, it must have a history of killing God's saints. The woman is drunk with the blood of two differing groups of believers, the past *saints* and the future *martyrs of Jesus*.

Many religions have no history of killing God's saints. However, the Catholic inquisitions in the 12th and 15th centuries do favor Roman Catholicism as a potential candidate. The Catholics have in the past, stained their hands with the blood of the saints. Interestingly, the prophetess Jezebel, who was previously mentioned in a possible connection with Roman Catholicism, was guilty in 1 Kings 18:5, 13 of killing God's saints in the Old Testament.

Some of you might be thinking that currently the Catholics have turned a new, more religiously tolerant, page from their bloody past. I agree, but when the world is in utter chaos and those who become believers after the Rapture likely speak out against Roman Catholicism, the geo-political environment will be drastically different and much more dangerous. As they did in the past, the Catholics will likely call anyone who denies the actual presence of Christ in the Eucharist a blasphemer. This might be among the reasons that the Harlot is martyring people who become believers in Christ after the Rapture.

For example, J. C. Ryle, writing about the history of the Eucharist from another perspective, explains what happened when people refused to accept the Roman Catholic belief in the Real Presence of Christ within the Eucharist:

COMMENTARY

"The point I refer to is the special reason why our reformers were burned. Great indeed would be our mistake if we supposed that they suffered in the vague charge of refusing submission to the Pope, or desiring to maintain the independence of the Church of England. Nothing of the kind! The principal reason why they were burned was because they refused one of the peculiar doctrines of the Romish church. On that doctrine, in almost every case, hinged their life or death. If they admitted it, they might live, if they refused it, they must die. The doctrine in question was the real presence of the body and blood of Christ in the consecrated elements of bread and wine in the Lord's Supper."[105]

Revelation 17:6 expresses the utter amazement the apostle John experienced when he glimpsed into the future and witnessed the killings committed by the harlot religion. He says, "*I saw the woman, drunk with the blood of the saints and with the blood of the martyrs of Jesus. And when I saw her, I marveled with great amazement.*"

This same apostle John was the one whom Jesus delegated to take care of His mother Mary at the time of the crucifixion. He personally knew the real Mary, the blessed virgin through whose womb the Savior of all men was birthed.

"Now there stood by the cross of Jesus His mother, and His mother's sister, Mary the *wife* of Clopas, and Mary Magdalene. When Jesus therefore saw His mother, and the disciple (the apostle John) whom He loved standing by, He said to His mother, "Woman, behold your son!" Then He said to the disciple, "Behold your mother!" And from that hour that disciple (John) took her to his own *home.*" (John 19:25-27; emphasis added)

Imagine if the Harlot that John is describing in Revelation 17:6 has a connection with Roman Catholicism and the Marian apparitions. The thoughts that would be running through his mind and causing him to marvel with great amazement would presumably be,

"*Unbelievable, Satan has deceived the Church into believing that the most blessed virgin of the Bible has been turned into the bloodiest whore of all whores, the mother of harlots. I was with Mary when she passed on to be in heaven with her son. I wept over her grave. Yet, Satan has deceived people into thinking that she didn't die, but rather was assumed into heaven. Mary should be venerated as the mother of the Savior, but Satan has tarnished her legacy by turning her into a type of Jezebel that kills those who are true followers of the Savior."*

The Marian Apparitions Connection with Ezekiel 38

It's puzzling to wonder why some of the apparition messages have addressed Russia. This was the case with the Fatima apparitions in 1917, which occurred at the same time that Russia was fighting in World War I. Britain, France, Italy and America were allies with Russia, but for some reason, the apparition singled out Russia, as an important country in the future.

Below is a fascinating discourse between the child visionary Lucy of Fatima and the apparition. This is concerning the third apparition message at Fatima and it includes references to Russia.

On July 13, 1917, Lucy asked (the apparition): *"What do you want from me?"*

The apparition answered: *"Continue to recite the Rosary every day to our Lady of the Rosary to obtain peace in the world and the end of the war, (World War I), because only She, (the apparition), will be able to aid you."*

Lucy said " *I want to ask you to tell us who you are, and to make a miracle for the crowd to believe that you appear."*

She answered: *"In October (1917), I will tell you who I am, that which I want, and I will do a miracle that all can see and believe. Sacrifice yourselves for sinners, and say often this prayer, especially during any sacrifice: "O my Jesus, I offer this for love of Thee, for the conversion of poor sinners, and in reparation for all the sins committed against the Immaculate Heart of Mary... To save future souls God wishes to establish in the world the devotion to My Immaculate Heart. If people do what I tell you, many souls will be saved."*

Then She, (the apparition), continued: *"If my requests are granted, Russia will be converted and there will be peace. If not, she (Russia) will scatter her errors throughout the world, provoking wars and persecution of the Church. The good will be martyred, the Holy Father will have much to suffer, and various nations will be destroyed...But in the end, my Immaculate Heart will triumph. The Holy Father will consecrate Russia to me, Russia will be converted, and a certain period of peace will be granted to the world".* "

Why is the apparition so concerned about Russia? Over the past century, the actions of and visionary messages from, the Marian apparitions have focused upon several main things, including this bizarre infatuation with Russia. The list of topics that presently seem to be of utmost concern to the apparition are, her;

1. Desiring to be co-equal to Christ as the Co-Redemptrix, Mediatrix and Advocate,

2. Wishing to be an intercessor for sinners in her role as the Co-Redemptrix,

3. Pleading for people to believe that she has an Immaculate Heart,

4. Requesting that people don't sin against her,

5. Longing for the world, including Russia, to be consecrated to her,

6. Appealing for people to focus on the actual presence of Christ in the Eucharist,

7. Ability to perform supernatural wonders,

8. Aspiring to be recognized as a supernatural source to aid in ending world wars and ushering in global peace,

9. Concerns about the future of Russia.

At the time of this writing, there are 193 recognized countries in the United Nations, but for some reason the "Our Lady of Fatima" seems to be mostly fixated upon Russia, rather than the others. Why is this? Is the apparition aware of Russia's lead role in Ezekiel 38? Is that why the Blessed Virgin Mary warned at Fatima that Russia, *"will scatter her errors throughout the world, provoking wars and persecution of the Church?"*

I believe there exists a possible prophetic connection between Ezekiel 38 and the Queen of Heaven's obsession with Russia. For more information about this potential correlation, read the appendix entitled, "The Marian Apparitions Connection with Ezekiel 38."

COMMENTARY

Chapter 12
The Harlot Rides the Beast
to Peace and Prosperity

Topics Covered

The Supremacy of the Eucharist from the Catholic Perspective

The prior chapter of commentary discussed the potential non-ecumenical nature of the coming Harlot world religion of Revelation 17. This chapter of the novel emphasizes the strong probability that Roman Catholicism becomes the canopy that covers the one world religion. Some reputable globally established institution has to organize and govern such a vast global network. Now the storyline describes how this enormous end times entity could become cohesively united.

For a non-Catholic religion to participate in this worldwide organization they will likely be required to pledge their allegiance to the will of the Queen of Heaven, the dogmas of the Catholic Church, and the supremacy of the Eucharist.

The Supremacy of the Eucharist from the Catholic Perspective

It is important to understand what the Eucharist is and the central role it plays within Roman Catholicism. The Eucharist is the ceremony commemorating the Last Supper, in which the bread and wine elements are consecrated and consumed. Evangelicals generally call it communion and when they partake of these elements, they do it symbolically in remembrance of Christ's crucifixion. However, the Catholics elevate the Eucharist to an entirely higher mystical level of significance.

The Catholic interpretation of the Eucharist is deeply ingrained in the "Paschal Mystery." Paschal is the English adjectival form of the Greek word pascha, which is derived from the Hebrew word pesah (or pesach), which means "passover."

The Paschal Mystery is a core doctrine of the Catholic Church, one of the essential beliefs of all Catholics. Though all doctrines are important, it can also be said that some doctrines define the very heart of the Catholic Faith. The Paschal Mystery is one of those doctrines, making it similar to the doctrines of the Incarnation of Christ and the Holy Trinity of the Father, Son and Holy Spirit.

This is the definition of the Paschal Mystery in the glossary of the Catechism of the Catholic Church:

> "Christ's work of redemption accomplished principally by his Passion, *which involved his arrest, trial and crucifixion*, and his death, Resurrection, and glorious Ascension... The paschal mystery is celebrated and made present in the liturgy of the Church, and its *saving effects* are communicated through the sacraments, especially the Eucharist, which *renews the paschal sacrifice of Christ* as the sacrifice offered by the Church."[106]

The operative words in this prior paragraph are, "*its saving effects*" and "*especially the Eucharist, which renews the paschal sacrifice of Christ*." Before identifying the inherent problem with the usage of this language, it's important to understand what was the "*sacrifice of Christ*."

The sacrificial death of Christ upon the cross accomplished, once and for all, the final forgiveness for mankind's sins. When He was confirmed that His sacrifice was fully completed He said, "*It is finished*." As such, this unprecedented event does not need to be continuously *renewed* in some mystical Paschal mystery in order to accomplish its *saving effects*.

> After this, Jesus, knowing that all things were now accomplished, that the Scripture might be fulfilled, said, "I thirst!" Now a vessel full of sour wine was sitting there; and they filled a sponge with sour wine, put *it* on hyssop, and put *it* to His mouth. So when Jesus had received the sour wine, He said, "It is finished!" And bowing His head, He gave up His spirit. (John 19:28-30)

These above verses confirm that Christ accomplished the ultimate mission of His first coming. His appointed assignment, which cost Him His life, is spelled out in the Scriptures paraphrased below.

COMMENTARY

- Christ was put to death once for our sins, (1 Peter 3:18).

- Christ was delivered up to the cross because of our offenses, and was raised from the dead for our justification, (Romans 4:25).

- Christ was crucified, buried and resurrected in fulfillment of the Scriptures, (1 Corinthians 15:3-4).

When Christ presented Himself in the elements of the bread and wine at the Passover meal He said,

> When the hour had come, He sat down, and the twelve apostles with Him. Then He said to them, "With *fervent* desire I have desired to eat this Passover with you before I suffer; for I say to you, *I will no longer eat of it* until it is *fulfilled in the kingdom of God*." Then He took the cup, and gave thanks, and said, "Take this and divide *it* among yourselves; for I say to you, *I will not drink of the fruit of the vine until the kingdom of God comes*." And He took bread, gave thanks and broke *it,* and gave *it* to them, saying, "This is My body which is given for you; *do this in remembrance* of Me." *Likewise* He also *took* the cup after supper, saying, "This cup *is* the new covenant in My blood, which is shed for you. (Luke 22:14-20; emphasis added)

Christ's instructions were to eat the bread (His body) and, *"likewise"* for the similar reason, drink the wine (His blood). The intent of ingesting both of these elements was to memorialize His sacrifice for sin. Moreover, He said that this would be His last Passover meal until it was fulfilled in the kingdom of God. He also declared that He would not drink the wine again until the kingdom of God comes. The kingdom of God ultimately gets established when Christ returns in His Second Coming.

At the infamous Last Supper celebration of the Hebrew Feast of Passover, Christ was acknowledging Himself as the required Passover Lamb of God. John the Baptist had attributed this title to him beforehand.

> *"The next day John saw Jesus coming toward him, and said, "Behold! The Lamb of God who takes away the sin of the world!"* (John 1:29)

Exodus 12 introduces the Passover and provides the description of the significance of the Passover lamb within the feast. The lamb had to be unblemished, sacrificed, cooked in a specific way and completely consumed by the entire household from which it came. The blood of the lamb was to be put on the two doorposts and on the lintel of the houses where it was eaten. The bloodstained doorposts served as a sign to the Lord to pass over that marked property when He passed through Egypt in judgment.

When Christ said this is My body and blood in the Last Supper on the Passover, He was distributing the bread and wine to symbolize the essential elements of the Passover lamb, which was its *flesh* and *blood*. The intended application of ingesting the bread and wine in remembrance of Christ's sacrifice, is to acknowledge that the reason judgment passes over believers, is because they are covered by Christ's dead *flesh* and shed *blood*. In other words, the Paschal (Passover) sacrifice of Christ protects believers from judgment by sealing them for salvation. If Christ was not sacrificed as the Passover Lamb of God, then divine judgment would not pass over anyone.

> "But He *was* wounded for our transgressions, *He*
> *was* bruised for our iniquities; The chastisement for our
> peace *was* upon Him, And by His stripes we are healed.
> All we like sheep have gone astray; We have turned, every
> one, to his own way; And the Lord has laid on Him the
> iniquity of us all He was oppressed and He was afflicted,
> Yet He opened not His mouth; He was led as a lamb to
> the slaughter, And as a sheep before its shearers is silent,
> So He opened not His mouth." (Isaiah 53:5-7)

The Paschal sacrifice of Christ is a fact in world history, rather than an ongoing Catholic mystery. The Paschal mystery as taught in Roman Catholicism, is that Christ continues to be an active participant in the Passover event. When the ordained priest beckons Christ to be present in the bread and wine, Christ is expected to honor his request.

This is what Catechism 1410 says about the Eucharist,

> "*It is Christ himself, the eternal high priest of the New*
> *Covenant who, acting through the ministry of the priests,*
> *offers the Eucharistic sacrifice. And it is the same Christ,*
> *really present under the species of bread and wine, who*
> *is the offering of the Eucharistic sacrifice.*"

Romans 8:34, Ephesians 1:20 and Colossians 3:1 all point out that Christ is presently dwelling in heaven where He is seated on the right hand of God. This means that at the invitation of thousands of Catholic priests worldwide on Sundays that Christ has to voluntarily vacate His post from the right hand of God and exist in the Eucharist. This also means that Christ has to be present in the wine that He promised never to drink again until He returns to set up the kingdom of God. It seems a bit bold for any man to ask Christ to inhabit a chalice that is symbolically filled with the very wine that He promised not to drink. Yet week after week for centuries, the Catholics have continuously petitioned Christ to present Himself in the Eucharist.

Speaking of the wine, here is a quote of interest taken from the ETWN Global Catholic Network that correlates with Christ's ability to be present in the elements of the Eucharist.

> "As Jesus was capable of changing water into wine, he is equally capable of making the bread and wine his body and blood for the life of the world."[107]

The body of evidence presented in the commentary of this and the last chapter strongly supports the probability that Roman Catholicism is primed to be the harlot world religion of Revelation 17. The menu of mystical characteristics shrouded in this religion must have been cleverly designed by Satan to fulfill a grand deceptive purpose in the end times.

The rise of the harlot world religion will come during a time period that is plagued with unrestrained lawlessness and characterized by the common occurrences of supernatural events. Spiritual soul searching within humanity will make it vulnerable to the mystique behind the Paschal mystery and the reoccurrence of one or more Marian apparitions.

The *Marian apparitions, Paschal Mystery* and their inseparable association to the *Eucharist* will be explored further in the chapter entitled, "Millions Witness Eucharistic Miracles from Rome." That section of commentary, in addition to the "Post-Rapture / Pre-Trib Thesis," will explain how the supernatural aspects of these three central subjects within Roman Catholicism can be used by Satan go gain greater control over the will of man in the last days.

COMMENTARY

Chapter 13
Israel Cleanses the Holy Land

Topics Covered

Is the Valley of Hamon Gog in Jordan?

Did Jesus Instruct Jews to Flee from The Antichrist into Jordan?

Is the Valley of Hamon Gog in Jordan?

Prior commentary explained that Israel would be burying the Ezekiel 38 invaders for seven months and burning their weapons for seven years. This chapter will attempt to locate their future burial grounds. Ezekiel provides the following details.

> "It will come to pass in that day *that* I will give Gog a burial place there in Israel, the valley of those who pass by east of the sea; and it will obstruct travelers, because there they will bury Gog and all his multitude. Therefore they will call *it* the Valley of Hamon Gog. For seven months the house of Israel will be burying them, in order to cleanse the land. Indeed all the people of the land will be burying, and they will gain renown for it on the day that I am glorified," says the Lord God. "They will set apart men regularly employed, with the help of a search party, to pass through the land and bury those bodies remaining on the ground, in order to cleanse it. At the end of seven months they will make a search. The search party will pass through the land; and *when anyone* sees a

man's bone, he shall set up a marker by it, till the buriers have buried it in the Valley of Hamon Gog. *The* name of *the* city *will* also *be* Hamonah. Thus they shall cleanse the land."' (Ezekiel 39:11-16)

These verses identify a place that has never been known by this name. However, someday it will be put on the map. This mass gravesite will be called Hamon Gog, which means the *multitude* or *hordes* of *Gog*. The Israelis will manage to gather the enemy weapons and dispose of the slain invaders in such a professional manner that they gain national renown.

The burial grounds will be located in a valley east of some sea, which will be strategically selected for some of the following reasons;

1. So as not to adversely affect tourism, commerce and other societal transportation needs, since Ezekiel says that this enormous cemetery *will obstruct travel*.

2. To provide effective environmental control, since the bodies appear to be contaminated and the affected lands need to be cleansed.

3. To provide logistical support to assemble all the strewn corpses expeditiously and orderly into one quarantined area.

There are four possible seas that Ezekiel could be referring to above. They are, the Red Sea, Dead Sea, Mediterranean Sea or the Sea of Galilee. I believe the future location of the Valley of Hamon Gog is east of the Dead Sea. I provide my detailed reasons for this in my book called, *Psalm 83: Missing Prophecy Revealed, How Israel Becomes the Next Mideast Superpower*.

Presently, the most suitable valley to become Hamon Gog is east of the Dead Sea in the country of Jordan. This implies that between now and the fulfillment of Ezekiel 38, Israel needs to annex a significant part of Jordan. Several unfulfilled prophecies predict that this will happen.

"Therefore behold, the days are coming," says the Lord, "That I will cause to be heard an alarm of war In Rabbah of the Ammonites; It shall be a desolate mound, And her villages shall be burned with fire. Then Israel shall take possession of his inheritance," says the Lord." (Jeremiah 49:2)

"I have heard the reproach of Moab, And the insults of the people of Ammon, With which they have reproached My people, And made arrogant threats against their borders. Therefore, as I live," Says the Lord of hosts, the God of Israel, "Surely Moab shall be like Sodom, And the people of Ammon like Gomorrah— Overrun with weeds and saltpits, And a perpetual desolation. The residue of My people shall plunder them, And the remnant of My people shall possess them." (Zephaniah 2:8-9)

In these verses above, Ammon represents Northern Jordan, and Moab is located in Central Jordan. Jeremiah and Zephaniah prophesy that Israel wins a war and captures territory that presently exists in Jordan. Both Ammon and Moab are listed in the unfulfilled war predicted in Psalm 83. The process of prophetic events should be as follows:

1. Israel wins the Psalm 83 war.

2. Israel captures and annexes a sizeable portion, if not all, of Jordan.

3. Ezekiel 38 finds fulfillment.

4. Israel creates the city of Hamonah in the Valley of Hamon Gog, which at that time will exist "*in Israel*." Ezekiel 39:11 declared that Hamonah will be "*in Israel*." Presently, this future territory is in Jordan, but at the conclusion of Psalm 83, it should be rezoned "*in Israel*."

5. Israelis will bury the dead for seven months in the Valley of Hamon Gog.

Did Jesus Instruct Jews to Flee from The Antichrist into Jordan?

This section below happens during the Trib-period after the events described in *Apocalypse Road* occur. So, technically it belongs in the next book in this series, which deals with that future time period. However, because it addresses the topic of Israel taking possession of Jordan, I have included it here to further reinforce the probability that Israel will annex Jordan as a result of the Psalm 83 war. This annexation should take place prior to the fulfillment of Ezekiel 38, which is then followed by the Trib-period.

In Matthew 24, Christ instructs Israelis to flee hastily to the mountains when they witness the "abomination of desolation" spoken of by the prophet Daniel (Daniel 9:27, 12:11).

> "Therefore when you see the 'abomination of desolation,' spoken of by Daniel the prophet, standing in the holy place" (whoever reads, let him understand), "then let those who are in Judea flee to the mountains. Let him who is on the housetop not go down to take anything out of his house. And let him who is in the field not go back to get his clothes. But woe to those who are pregnant and to those who are nursing babies in those days! And pray that your flight may not be in winter or on the Sabbath. For then there will be great tribulation, such as has not been since the beginning of the world until this time, no, nor ever shall be. (Matthew 24:15-20)

Jesus, born as a Jew, provided these instructions in order to warn and protect a future generation of His kinship from the perilous predictions in Zechariah 13:8-9. These prophecies inform that the Antichrist will someday attempt a final genocide of the Jews. Zechariah 13:8 says that two-thirds of the Jews will be killed in the land. The timing of this closely correlates with the "abomination of desolation," which was referenced in the Matthew 24 verses above. It is the Antichrist that commits this abomination in the "holy place," which alludes to the coming third Jewish temple. We glean from connecting passages in Isaiah 63 and elsewhere that the specific mountains Christ instructs the Jews to flee to are located in ancient Edom, which is in modern-day southern Jordan.

> Who *is* this who comes from Edom, With dyed garments from Bozrah, This *One who is* glorious in His apparel, Traveling in the greatness of His strength? — "I who speak in righteousness, mighty to save." Why *is* Your apparel red, And Your garments like one who treads in the winepress? "I have trodden the winepress alone, And from the peoples no one *was* with Me. For I have trodden them in My anger, And trampled them in My fury; Their blood is sprinkled upon My garments, And I have stained all My robes. For the day of vengeance *is* in My heart, And the year of My redeemed has come. (Isaiah 63:1-4)

These Isaiah verses address how the Messiah, (Jesus Christ), comes to single-handedly rescue the faithful Jewish remnant. In Matthew 24, Jesus told them to flee to this area and in Isaiah 63, He promises to save them there.

This remnant of Israelis emerges out of the Antichrist's final genocidal attempt of the Jews. This horrific holocaust episode takes place during the final three-and-one-half years on the earth's timeline, in a period commonly called the "great tribulation." Zechariah says this remnant will consist of one-third of the Jews who ultimately become believers and say, "The Lord is my God." (Zechariah 13:9). Thus, they are often referred to as the "faithful remnant of Israel." They are the saved Israel, described in Romans 11:26-27.

> "And so all Israel will be saved, as it is written: "The Deliverer will come out of Zion, And He will turn away ungodliness from Jacob; For this is My covenant with them, When I take away their sins."" (NKJV)

According to Hosea 5:15, this Jewish remnant recognizes Christ as their Messiah during their great tribulation. Subsequently, they plead for Him to return and rescue them from the onslaught of the Antichrist. The precise words that they will utter in their pleadings for Christ to return are; *"Blessed is He who comes in the name of the Lord!"*

> "For I say to you, (the Jews) you shall see Me (Jesus Christ) no more till you say, 'Blessed is He who comes in the name of the Lord!'" (Matthew 23:39; emphasis added)

Isaiah 63 above tells us that the Messiah first touches down at their location in Edom. The verses go on to declare that Christ's garments are subsequently stained with the blood of the Antichrist and his Armageddon armies. Ultimately, Christ wins the war and then makes His victory ascent up to the Mount of Olives, as per Zechariah 14:3-4.

Ancient Bozrah of Edom is located in modern day Petra in Jordan. Presently, this area is a tourist destination under Jordanian sovereignty. It's about a six-hour drive from. Jerusalem. The natural mountain cliffs and manmade caves and waterways, which were carved out mostly by the Nabateans in ancient times, make this territory an excellent place of refuge.

Christ's instructions for the remnant to *"flee to the mountains"* of ancient Edom seems like excellent strategic advice because of its protective geographical conditions and its relatively close proximity to Jerusalem. It's excellent advice as long as Petra, Jordan, comes under Israeli sovereignty prior to the "abomination of desolation."

If Israel controls Petra, then the Jewish remnant can flee there. However, if Jordan still controls the territory at that time, then these Jews would not likely be provided unrestricted passage to Petra, Jordan.

COMMENTARY

Presently, if a remnant of Israelis numbering in the hundreds of thousands, perhaps millions, attempt to cross the Israeli borders for refuge in the Jordanian mountains, the Jordanian government would undoubtedly protest. Under current pre-Psalm 83 conditions the historical account inscribed in Numbers 20, would likely repeat itself.

> Then Edom said to him, "You [Moses and the Hebrews at the time of their exodus out of [Egypt] shall not pass through my land, lest I come out against you with the sword." So the children of Israel said to him, "We will go by the Highway, and if I or my livestock drink any of your water, then I will pay for it; let me only pass through on foot, nothing more." Then he said, "You shall not pass through." So Edom came out against them with many men and with a strong hand. Thus Edom refused to give Israel passage through his territory; so Israel turned away from him. (Numbers 20:18-21)

However, in a post-Psalm 83 Middle East, Israel can annex defeated Jordan in fulfillment of Jeremiah 49:2 and Zephaniah 2:8-9. This would enable two critical things to happen.

1.   The Valley of Hamon God could be created east of the Dead Sea.

2.   The faithful Jewish remnant could flee to Petra, Jordan.

Chapter 14
Doomsday Conference Erupts
Into Deadly Chaos

Topics Covered

Who is the Woman Drunk with the Blood of the Saints?

Why Did the Apostle John Marvel at the Harlot?

What is the Blood of the Saints?

As the title of this chapter alludes to, when the days of doom arrive after the Rapture, they will be characterized by deadly chaos. The book of Revelation is filled with threatening predictions, including a lot of death and destruction. It is the time frame when God finally pours out His wrath upon a Christ rejecting world. Therefore, it is illogical to expect that this process is going to be pleasant.

This is why this book encourages the reader to make a decision for Christ now during the age of grace, before the Rapture. Regardless, the reader is reminded continually throughout this manuscript that they always have a second chance to get saved, as long as they receive Christ as their Savior as per Romans 10:8-11, and unequivocally reject the Antichrist's mark in Revelation 13:16-17.

The "Second Chance" topic has already been covered extensively in the commentary of the chapter entitled, "144,000 Jewish Evangelists."

In this novel chapter, deadly violence erupts. This chaos is orchestrated by the Vatican. This scene will undoubtedly disturb some of the readers, but I remind them that the Catholic Church has a history of violence especially toward those who oppose its teaching and authority. In addition, Revelation 17:6 says that the harlot world religion has a past history, as well as a forthcoming future, filled with violence.

I saw the woman, drunk with the blood of the saints (*in the past from our current time perspective*) and with the blood of the martyrs of Jesus (*in the future*) And when I saw her, I marveled with great amazement. (Revelation 17:6; emphasis added)

Who is the Woman Drunk with the Blood of the Saints?

Below are some quotes from respected sources concerning the violent nature of the coming Harlot world religion.

"Those who do come to Christ will be subject to her persecution, and the woman is described as "drunk with the blood of the saints" (Rev. 17:6). The apostate church has been (past tense) *unsparing in its persecution of those who have a true faith in Christ. Those who come to Christ in the end time will have the double problem of avoiding martyrdom at the hands of the political rulers and at the hands of the apostate church."* (John Walvoord).[108]

John Walvoord, the former president of Dallas Theological Seminary from 1952 to 1986, connects the Harlot with the apostate church. He says, that as per Revelation 17:6, true believers have faced *"unsparing"* persecution from the apostate church in the past and that this process gets repeated in the future. Tim LaHaye's quote below also emphasizes the future persecution and potential martyrdom of believers at the hands of the Harlot of Revelation 17.

"In Revelation 13 we saw that the beast and the false prophet come on the scene in the midst of the Tribulation Period, seeking to make men worship anti-Christ. The complete tyranny of the Tribulation Period is seen in the fact that during the first three and one-half years the ecumenical church of Revelation 17 is so powerful she dominates anti-Christ and kills all believers who refuse to participate with her. During the second half of the Tribulation Period it will be antichrist and the false prophet who kill those that refuse to worship his image and receive his mark."[109]

Tim LaHaye acknowledges that during the first three and one-half years of the Trib-period, that Harlot holds a superior role to the Antichrist. Revelation 17:3 pictures the Harlot sitting on the Antichrist and Rev.

17:7 says that the Antichrist carries her during this process. LaHaye also states that the Harlot *"kills all believers."* The next quotes connect Roman Catholicism with the harlot religion.

> *"The meaning here* (Revelation 17:6) *is, that the persecuting power referred to had shed the blood of the saints; and that, in its fury, it had, as it were, drunk the blood of the slain, and had become, by drinking that blood, intoxicated and infuriated. No one need say how applicable this has been to the papacy* (Roman Catholicism) *... Let the blood shed in the valleys of Piedmont; the blood shed in the Low Countries by the Duke of Alva; the blood shed on Bartholomew's day; and the blood shed in the Inquisition, testify."* [110] (American Theologian Albert Barnes - December 1, 1798 – December 24, 1870)

> *"When the true church is caught up* [raptured]*... the Roman Catholic "church" will see a great revival. For a time she has been stripped of the temporal power she once had, but it will be restored to her... And she was drunken with the blood of the Saints and with the blood of the martyrs of Jesus, so that John wondered with a great wonder. Such were her cruel, wicked, Satanic deeds in the past... It could never be true of the literal Babylon. Nor does it mean, as Romish expositors of this book claim, pagan Rome, for if it meant the persecutions under the Roman Emperors, John would not have wondered with a great wonder. And the last page of her* (Roman Catholicism) *cruel, horrible, persecutions is not yet written. When she comes to power again, she will do the same thing."* (Arno C. Gaebelein) [111]

Why Did the Apostle John Marvel at the Harlot?

> *"And when I saw her, I* (the apostle John) *marveled with great amazement."* (Rev. 17:6b)

The distinction made above by Arno C. Gaebelein is between *pagan* Rome and *papal* Rome. Pagan Rome alludes to the political Roman Empire during John's time and papal Rome refers to the religious realm that followed a few centuries later.

COMMENTARY

"Pagan Rome ended and Papal Rome began with the CROSS!! Imperial Rome became PAPAL Rome on October 28, 312 A.D., when Constantine exchanged the eagle for the cross: And not only so, but he (Constantine) also caused the sign of the salutary trophy to be impressed on the very shields of his soldiers; and commanded that his embattled forces should be preceded in their march, not by golden eagles, as heretofore, but only by the standard of the cross. (Eusebius, Life of Constantine, p. 545)."[112]

Arno Gaebelein makes the point that John "*would not have wondered with a great wonder*" from merely witnessing "*the persecutions under the Roman emperors,* (pagan Rome)." These persecutions were commonplace during John's time. Gaebelein also explains that for the same reason "*it could never be true of the literal Babylon.*"

Some teachers believe the Harlot of Revelation 17 alludes to pagan Rome and there are others who believe that it refers to the literal city of Babylon, Iraq. Gaebelein clearly believed that it was papal Rome, i.e., Roman Catholicism.

The argument could be raised against Gaebelein's statements by saying that John marveled with amazement mostly because he saw the Harlot drunk with the martyrs of Jesus in the future. However, contextually it was both distinctly different periods of persecution, the blood of the saints and the martyrs of Jesus, that shocked John. From John's perspective both periods were yet future because papal Rome did not come on the scene until after he died. From our present vantage point, we can suggest that the blood of the Saints period has already transpired during the period of the Catholic inquisitions. Now, the period awaiting final fulfillment is the "martyrs of Jesus."

What John apparently witnessed was two future periods of Christian persecution that would be perpetrated by the same apostate religious system. The system was destined to have a papal affiliation with pagan Rome, and this is probably partially why he gave it the code name of,

"MYSTERY, BABYLON THE GREAT, THE MOTHER OF HARLOTS AND OF THE ABOMINATIONS OF THE EARTH." (Revelation 17:5b)

During John's time, Christians would sometimes allude to Rome as Babylon. This was primarily done to avoid political harassment and religious persecution for being Christians. This practice appears in New

Testament Scripture. This quote below is from the apostle Peter, who was thought to be in Rome when he issued this greeting.

> "She who is in Babylon, (Rome) elect together with you, greets you; and so does Mark my son." (1 Peter 5:13; emphasis added)

Another example of Christians concealing their faith to avoid Roman persecution was the Christian fish symbol ⊂✕.

> "Greeks, Romans, and many other pagans used the fish symbol before Christians. Hence the fish, unlike, say, the cross, attracted little suspicion, making it a perfect secret symbol for persecuted believers. When threatened by Romans in the first centuries after Christ, Christians used the fish mark meeting places and tombs, or to distinguish friends from foes. According to one ancient story, when a Christian met a stranger in the road, the Christian sometimes drew one arc of the simple fish outline in the dirt. If the stranger drew the other arc, both believers knew they were in good company. Current bumper-sticker and business-card uses of the fish hearken back to this practice."[113]

What is the Blood of the Saints?

History demonstrates that the Harlot has already become drunk with the blood of the saints. All that awaits her final inebriation is to become intoxicated with the future blood of the martyrs of Jesus. Will history repeat itself with the return of the Catholic inquisitions after the Rapture?

Sadly, the Roman Catholic Church was responsible for the death of numerous Christians who held to their true, biblical convictions. Most notable are those who were put to death for refusing to worship the Eucharist. Below are several historical accounts whereby papal Rome was intoxicated from the blood of the saints.

Historical accounts from Foxes Book of Martyrs.

> "At his trial, [Andrew] Hewet was accused of not believing that the consecrated host was the actual body of Christ. Asked what he truly believed, Hewet replied, "As John Frith believes." "Do you believe it is really the body of

Christ, born of the Virgin Mary?" his accusers insisted. "No!" The Catholic bishops smiled at Hewet and the Bishop of London said, "Frith is a heretic, already sentenced to burn. Unless you revoke your opinion, you will burn with him." Hewet said that he would do as Frith did. On July 4, 1533, Andrew Hewet was burned with John Frith."[114]

"Kerby and Clarke were captured in Ipswich in 1546 and brought before Lord Wentworth and other commissioners for their examination. At that time, they were asked if they believed in transubstantiation. Admitting they did not, both stated their belief that Christ had instituted the Last Supper as a remembrance of His death for the remissions of sins, but there was no actual flesh or blood involved in the sacrament. Kerby was sentenced to burn in Ipswich the next day; Clarke the following Monday in Bury."[115]

These are just a couple historical examples among many others, which strongly suggest that Roman Catholicism has already fulfilled part one of Revelation 17:6. Papal Rome has already become *drunk with the blood of the saints*.

It is interesting that one of the primary reasons that believers were martyred by the Catholic Church is because they refused to acknowledge the actual presence of Christ in the Eucharist. Catholics still consider this a grave offense and they take it very seriously as the "Post-Rapture / Pre-trib Thesis" points out.

When Roman Catholicism is called upon in the future to serve the revived Roman Empire, as it did in the past, as the official Church of the former Roman Empire, they can be expected to hold fast to their historic doctrines, especially transubstantiation. More Marian apparitions and Eucharistic miracles, which many Catholic leaders still await, will likely be coming in the future as part of the satanic deception in 2 Thessalonians 2. If these supernatural phenomena continue to occur, they will further fuel this religion's quest for greater global control.

In the novel, the event program read as follows:

Topics

1.   The Confirmation of the False Covenant Causes Tribulation.

2.   Are the Apparitions Divine or Demonic?

3.   Israel is the Woman of Revelation 12, Not the Queen of Heaven!

4.   The Four Horsemen of the Apocalypse.

5.   Does God Give Second Chances After the Rapture?

6.   True Christians; Prepare to Be Martyred.

Topics number 2, 5 and 6 have been covered thus far in previous portions of the Companion's Commentary. Numbers 1 and 4 will be covered in the "Post-Rapture / Pre-Trib Thesis" commentary.

COMMENTARY

Chapter 15
Jews Return Home as Rumors of Nuclear Wars Abound

Topics Covered

Jews Continue to Return to Israel

Brief Storyline Overview

T his chapter of the novel covers several powerful prophetic topics. The story alludes to rumors of global nuclear wars and other global tensions that facilitate the return of world Jewry back to Israel. Additionally, it depicts how these world schisms lead to the unholy matrimony between the Revived Roman Empire and the harlot world religion. All of these events are predicted to occur in the end times.

Jews Continue to Return to Israel

COMMENTARY

The Arab aim to destroy the Jews and banish the name of Israel, which was predicted in the ancient biblical prophecy of Psalm 83, and is presently playing out in the Middle East, is destined to fail.

> They (The Arabs) have said, "Come, and let us cut them (the Jews) off from being a nation, That the name of Israel may be remembered no more." (Psalm 83:4; emphasis added)

Far from being destroyed and remembered no more, the Jews and Israel are here to stay. In fact, there are Bible prophecies that remain unfulfilled that predict more Jews are coming to Israel in the future. The influx of Jews returning to Israel will likely surge as global tensions threaten Jews living abroad. Anti-Semitism should intensify concurrently, precipitating more Jewish Aliyah. Lastly, improved political, military and socio-economic conditions in the Jewish state, especially after the Psalm 83 and Ezekiel 38 wars, will also motivate more Jewish migration to Israel.

The return of Jews into Israel is happening now in fulfillment of several prophecies and it is going to continue on into the early inception of the messianic kingdom. Several prophecies being fulfilled now by Jewish Aliyah are found in Isaiah 11:11-12, Jeremiah 23:7 and Ezekiel 20:34, 36:11, 24. Other Jewish Aliyah prophecies to be fulfilled between now and the millennium are located in Isaiah 49:22, 60:9, and Ezekiel 39:25-29.

Brief Overview of the Storyline

The preponderance of this chapter's commentary will be included in the "Post-Rapture / Pre-trib Thesis." The unholy union between the Revived Roman Empire and the harlot world religion is a central theme of the thesis. Also, the potential for global nuclear wars will be discussed in relationship to the "Seal Judgments" of Revelation 6 in the thesis.

Now it's time to take a brief review of the setting thus far established in the first two books of this apocalyptic "Road" series.

1. The Church is in heaven, having already been Raptured. This happened at the conclusion of book one, *Revelation Road, Hope Beyond the Horizon*.

2. Israel is gaining territory and world renown for having won the biblical wars of Psalm 83 in *Revelation Road* and Ezekiel 38 in *Apocalypse Road*. They are also making plans to build the Third Jewish Temple and reinstate their ancient Mosaic Law and its entire sacrificial system,

3. Islam is steadily crumbling due to the crushing blows of these two predominately Muslim wars,

4. The Antichrist has come on the world scene in *Apocalypse Road* and is rising to power in the character of EU President Hans Vandenberg,

5. Supernatural phenomenon associated with the Queen of Heaven and the Eucharist are occurring that are influencing people toward Roman Catholicism as the "True Church."

6. The Catholic Church is emerging as the harlot world religion of Revelation 17,

COMMENTARY

7.   The EU is becoming like the Revived Roman Empire and forming an unholy Church and State union between itself and Roman Catholicism.

8.   Other world countries are preparing to war against each other.

9.   People are getting saved and becoming persecuted by the harlot world religion.

All of the above are powerful world events that were predicted to occur in the last days. Ultimately, these events usher in the final seven-years of tribulation. However, these enumerated events are occurring in this storyline prior to the tribulation, in correlation with the first five seal judgments of Revelation 6:1-11. The thesis will explain how this controversial claim can be made.

The theory presented in this book is that the first five seal judgments begin after the Rapture but before the Trib-period. Although these judgments commence during this period, they mostly carry over and conclude at various stages within the Trib-period.

Chapter 16
The Vatican Global Council Meeting

Topics Covered

The Problems with Vatican Council Meetings

The Importance of the Zeitoun Marian Apparition

The Future Pope Receives Unprecedented Power

This chapter describes a future Vatican global council meeting that is used to unite world religions under the canopy of Roman Catholicism. At various times in the past, the Vatican has hosted important councils at critical points in its history. Two notable meetings were "The Council of Trent" and "The Second Vatican Council" (Vatican II).

The most serious time in Roman Catholic history, if it is the Harlot, is forthcoming after the Rapture when the religion rises to unprecedented global prominence as MYSTERY, BABYLON THE GREAT, THE MOTHER OF HARLOTS AND OF THE ABOMINATIONS OF THE EARTH (Rev. 17:5). As such, it is highly probable that another major Vatican council meeting, perhaps like the one described in this chapter of the novel, will occur after the Rapture.

The Problems with Vatican Council Meetings

Vatican council meetings can be very problematic because in the past they have produced heretical doctrine. A couple of past examples are below in "The Council of Trent" and "The Second Vatican Council." It is important to note that the Catechism of the Catholic Church spells out the infallibility of an ecumenical council, which means that the outcome of a Vatican council meeting becomes official Catholic doctrine.

COMMENTARY

"The Roman Pontiff, head of the college of bishops, enjoys this infallibility in virtue of his office (as the Pope), when, as supreme pastor and teacher of the faithful - who confirms his brethren in the Faith - he proclaims by a definitive act a doctrine pertaining to Faith or morals.... The infallibility promised to the Church is also present in the body of bishops when, together with Peter's successor, they exercise the supreme Magisterium," *above all in an ecumenical council*.[116]

The Council of Trent

The Council of Trent was held in Trento (Trent) and Bologna, northern Italy. It was one of the Roman Catholic Church's most important ecumenical councils. It was prompted by the Protestant Reformation and it has been described as the embodiment of the Counter-Reformation.[117] This meeting was primarily conducted to clarify and solidify Catholic doctrine in order to justify the persecutions of the so called "heretics" during the inquisition periods.

Several important things came out of The Council of Trent which convened twenty-five times between 1545-1563.[118] As a result of the Council of Trent, the Catholic Church:

- Condemned and refuted the *beliefs of Protestants*, like Martin Luther and John Calvin.

- Condemned as heresy the Protestant teaching of *justification by faith* alone apart from anything else, including good works.

- Rejected the Protestants view that the additional books found in the *Apocrypha* were not part of the approved biblical canon.

- Rejected the Protestants teaching against the doctrine of "*Transubstantiation*," which claims that the actual presence of Christ is experienced during the partaking of the Eucharist.

- Damned those who said that *indulgences* were useless or that the Church does not have the power to grant them. At the time, the selling of indulgences was a common practice of the Catholic Church. In Catholic theology, an indulgence is a remission of temporal punishment due to sin, the guilt of which has been forgiven.

- Affirmed the doctrine of "*Purgatory*." Purgatory means to make clean or purify. In accordance with Catholic teaching, it is a place or condition of temporal punishment for those who, departing this life in God's grace, are, not entirely free from venial faults, or have not fully paid the satisfaction due to their transgressions. (Venial sins are considered lesser sins in contrast to "Grave" sins, which can cause a person to go to Hell).

These Catholic doctrines above are all unbiblical. Salvation is justified by faith alone, apart from works, according to Ephesians 2:8-9 and Romans 10:8-11. The additional books of the Apocrypha are not part of the widely accepted translations used by most Protestant and Evangelical Churches. Transubstantiation, whereby the actual presence of Christ manifests in the Eucharist is a papal fallacy. This topic was already addressed in the Companion's Commentary of the chapter called, "The Harlot Rides the Beast to Peace and Prosperity."

The selling of indulgences for money and the place of afterlife limbo called Purgatory are nowhere to be found in the Bible. These are Catholic contrivances that were created to guilt trip the faithful into buying favor for their sins. It was a way for the Catholic Church to generate revenues. Conversely, what is found in the Bible is; *And as it is appointed for men to die once, but after this the judgment.*" (Hebrews 9:27). When someone dies they either get rewarded at the "Bema Seat" in 2 Corinthians 5:10 as a believer, or condemned as an unbeliever at the "White Throne" in Revelation 20:11-15. Nobody manipulates either process by bribing God with some prepaid indulgences purchased from the Catholic Church!

The Second Vatican Council

The Second Vatican Council occurred in four sessions between 1962-1965 during the tenures of Pope John XXIII (1958-1963) and Pope Paul VI (1963-1978). Vatican II was the first ecumenical council to settle doctrinal issues in over a century. The meeting addressed church practices in light of cultural changes that occurred after World Wars I and World Wars II. Between 2,000 and 2,500 bishops and thousands of observers, auditors, sisters, laymen and laywomen participated. These observers included many religious leaders from non-Catholic faiths.

As a result of Vatican II, sixteen documents in total were released that made Roman Catholicism appear more Protestant friendly and ecumenically embraceable. These official papers laid a foundation for Catholics to pray with other Christian denominations, encourage friendship with other non-Christian faiths, and open the door for languages besides Latin to be used during Mass. Vatican II modified the position of the Catholic Church in relationship to non-Christian religions. It affirmed that people of all religions form one community and that the Catholic Church respects the spiritual, moral and cultural values of Hinduism, Buddhism and Islam.

This was an innovative attempt to reform a religion that was becoming antiquated in modernity, without substantially compromising the importance of its sacraments, main dogmas and doctrines, and its claim to be the "True Church." For instance, Vatican II never changed the erroneous teaching that salvation cannot be obtained apart from the Catholic Church. This dangerous doctrinal teaching is further exposited upon in the "Post-Rapture / Pre-Trib Thesis."

To the dismay of many Traditionalist Catholics, this progressive trend of conforming the Catholic Church to be more ecumenically and culturally inclined is continuing. Traditionalist Catholics are those who believe that there should be a restoration of many of the customs, traditions and authoritative teachings of the Church before Vatican II. Some of these tradionalists known as "Sedevacantists," hold that the post-Vatican II popes have forfeited their position through their acceptance of heretical teachings connected with the Second Vatican Council and consequently there is at present no known true pope.[119]

A serious concern to the traditionalists is that the moral and spiritual authority entrusted to the Catholic Church and its pontiff, the Pope, is being threatened. Ideally, as the "True Church," with the Vicar of Christ as its helm, Roman Catholicism should be the uncontested arbiter of morality and spirituality. However, since Vatican II this perception of religious prestige has been gradually eroding. Moreover, cultural and social issues dealing with things like marriage, abortion and homosexuality continue to challenge the overall influence of the Catholic Church.

A few problems with Vatican II are that all religions don't form one respectable community and the Church is not supposed to buckle under ecumenical pressures, nor conform to the cultural issues of the world. Jesus said in John 14:6, "*I am the way, the truth, and the life. No one comes to the* (Heavenly) *Father except through Me.*" This means, according to Jesus Christ, that Christianity is respectable, but all other religions should be disrespected because they don't lead to the Heavenly Father.

In John 17:3, Jesus narrowed the focus even further when He said, "*And this is eternal life, that they may know You,* (Heavenly Father), *the only true God, and Jesus Christ whom You have sent."* In essence, eternal life is only obtained by going through Jesus Christ in order to form a righteous and acceptable relationship with the Heavenly Father. The other world religions will not deliver a soul in the right condition to the same destination.

Christ's resurrection from the grave serves as His certificate of accuracy and authenticity for everything that He taught before and after He died upon the cross. No other spiritual teacher ever resurrected to authenticate the accuracy of their teachings before they died.

Concerning the directional course that the Christian Church is to take, the Bible teaches something entirely different than ecumenism and cultural conformity.

> "I beseech you therefore, brethren, by the mercies of God, that you present your bodies a living sacrifice, holy, acceptable to God, which is your reasonable service. *And do not be conformed to this world, but be transformed by the renewing of your mind*, that you may prove what is that good and acceptable and perfect will of God." (Romans 12:1-2; emphasis added)

The Importance of the Zeitoun Marian Apparition

Another important aspect of the novel deals with the apparition of Mary in Zeitoun, Egypt between 1968-1970. Millions witnessed this supernatural event, including Egyptian President Gamal Abdel Nasser. The quote below briefly summarizes what took place.

> "For more than a year, starting on the eve of Tuesday, April 2, 1968, the Blessed Holy Virgin Saint Mary, Mother of God, appeared in different forms over the domes of the Coptic Orthodox Church named after Her at Zeitoun, Cairo, Egypt. The late Rev. Father Constantine Moussa was the church priest at the time of these apparitions. The apparitions lasted from only a few minutes up to several hours and were sometimes accompanied by luminous heavenly bodies shaped like doves and moving at high speeds. The apparitions were seen by millions of Egyptians and foreigners. Among the witnesses were Orthodox, Catholics, Protestants, Moslems, Jews and non-religious people from all walks of life. The sick

COMMENTARY

were cured and blind persons received their sight, but most importantly large numbers of unbelievers were converted"[120]

Healings and miracles occurring at an apparition site is not unique to what happened at Zeitoun. In their well- researched book entitled, *"Queen of All, The Marian apparition's plan to unite all religions under the Roman Catholic Church,"* Jim Tetlow, Roger Oakland and Brad Myers state the following,

"Numerous healings and miracles have been reported at apparition sites around the globe. In addition, the apparition of the Blessed Virgin Mary has repeatedly announced that her most significant signs and wonders are yet future! She admits that she has not yet revealed her full glory to the world. She predicts heavenly signs and wonders that the whole world will soon witness."[121]

The Zeitoun apparition occurred within the past century, which supports the possibility the more apparitions will follow in the future. In fact, the quote below from a visionary message predicts that Mary will appear again so that everyone can see her.

"I wish to also tell you that before my apparitions end completely, I shall be seen by every denomination and religion throughout this world. I will be seen among all people, not for just a moment, but everyone will have a chance to see me. As I appeared in Zeitoun, I shall appear again so everyone may see me. Pray and help my plans to be realized, not just here, but throughout the world."[122]

The Future Pope Receives Unprecedented Power

The trend in Roman Catholicism to be more culturally inclined and ecumenically minded will probably continue after the Rapture. This is predictable because when the world is recovering from the supernatural disappearances of millions of believers, epic biblical Mideast wars and other end times catastrophic globally impacting events, the Pope will need to become everything to everyone.

Being elevated into the role of becoming the world's foremost religious authority through supernatural deception will burden the leader of the harlot religion with enormous responsibility, but it will also bestow upon him unprecedented power. The lesson learned from Vatican II is that Roman Catholicism can rebrand its religious image, without having to significantly sacrifice the sacraments, dogmas and doctrinal substance. The future Pope, like his post-Vatican II predecessors, will be able to exercise some cultural conformity without compromising the core essentials of Catholic doctrine. Salvation and sanctification through the manners prescribed in Roman Catholicism can never drastically change, or it would mean the end of the religious institution.

In the post-Rapture world, humankind will likely still look to the Pope for spiritual guidance and for Roman Catholicism to be its moral compass. Human dependency in these areas should increase, especially when the paranormal becomes the new normal. Social, cultural and moral issues are still going to need addressing, and they will become intensified by the supernatural phenomena and unrestrained devilish deception occurring during that time period.

The international political establishment will probably be propping the Pope up while it attempts to restore some semblance of order in the world. Non-Catholic religious leaders will also be more susceptible to the influences of the Vatican, if supernatural phenomena associated with the Roman Catholic Church are taking place. The overall climate should be conducive for the final Pope to become the most powerful pontiff in the history of Roman Catholicism.

COMMENTARY

Chapter 17
Millions Witness Eucharistic Miracles from Rome

Topics Covered

Past Eucharistic Miracles Encourage That More Will Follow

The Blessed Mother's Obsession with Russia and World Peace

COMMENTARY

T his chapter of the novel describes a Eucharistic miracle that begins with a consecrated wafer turning into human blood and flesh. The plasma spurts to the ceiling out of the Pope's chalice and then turns from red blood into white light. Then an image of a man estimated to be in his early thirties, representing the Eucharistic Jesus, appears and delivers a powerful message to the assembly through a visionary. The entire scene lays out like something you would only expect to see in a Hollywood movie. However, this futuristic depiction may not be too far-fetched when you consider that past Eucharistic miracles have involved somewhat similar occurrences.

Past Eucharistic Miracles Encourage That More Will Follow

Eucharistic miracles have occurred throughout much of the history of Roman Catholicism. A Google search under the key words, "Eucharistic Miracles," can achieve well over one-hundred thousand results. Most Eucharistic miracles involve incidences in which the Host has transformed into actual human flesh and blood. Catholics are taught that the consecrated Host is the body, blood, soul, and divinity of Jesus Christ, under the appearances of the sacred bread. A few examples of Eucharistic miracles are provided below.

Eucharistic Miracle of Ferrara, Italy in 1171 A.D.

In the Eucharistic miracle of Ferrara, Italy, blood gushed upward from the consecrated Host and stained the ceiling above. Also, the wafer transformed into flesh. The account of this incident is summarized below.

"This Eucharistic miracle took place in Ferrara, in the Basilica of Saint Mary in Vado, on Easter Sunday, March 28, 1171. While celebrating Easter Mass, Father Pietro da Verona, the prior of the basilica, reached the moment of breaking the consecrated Host. At this point he saw that blood gushed from the Host, staining the ceiling of the crypt above the altar with droplets. In 1595, the crypt was enclosed within a small shrine and is still visible today in the monumental Basilica of Santa Maria in Vado."

"Not only did the witnesses see the blood, they also saw that the Host had turned into Flesh. The local Bishop of Ferrara and Archbishop Gherardo of Revenna came and saw the blood and the Host turned to Flesh and declared that this was the Body and Blood of Jesus Christ. Pope Eugenio IV and Pope Benedict XIV recognized the miracle, and Pope Pius IX visited the miracle in 1857 and noted that the drops of Blood were similar to those of the miracle of Orvieto and Bolsena." [123]

Eucharistic Miracle of Bordeaux, France in 1822 A.D.

In this miraculous account described below, an image of a man about thirty years old, thought to be Jesus, appeared in front of the entire parish. Someone testified that this Eucharistic Christ audibly spoke at the time.

"In the Eucharistic miracle of Bordeaux, Jesus appeared in the Host exposed for public adoration for more than 20 minutes, giving a blessing. Even today it is possible to visit the chapel of the miracle and venerate the precious relic of the Monstrance of the apparition, which is kept in Martillac, France, in the church of the contemplative community "La Solitude". In addition, someone testified to have heard Jesus saying: *I Am He Who Is*". [124]

COMMENTARY

345

Michael Freze says in his book called, "*Voices, Visions and Apparitions,*" that, "The entire parish in Bordeaux, France saw the image of Jesus appear. The image appeared as an attractive man about the age of thirty, moving his hands and smiling to all the people who were present."[125]

This is not the only example of someone hearing the voice of the Eucharistic Jesus during the miracle. Joan Carroll Cruz, who authored 15 Catholic books before she died in 2012, at the age of 81, says the following in her book entitled, "*Eucharistic Miracles and Eucharistic Phenomena in the Lives of the Saints.*"

> "Many saints have had the privilege of hearing the voice of Jesus speaking from consecrated Hosts…Not only did our Savior favor some of His saints with a vision of Himself as an Infant, but for others the consecrated Host took the form of Our Lord as a grown man.[126]

The National Catholic Register, which refers to itself as, "America's most complete Catholic news source," put forth an article about this supernatural speaking phenomenon. The piece dated, August 5, 2013, was entitled, "Truth or Hoax? Alleged Eucharistic Miracle Under Investigation in Mexico."[127] The article subtitle reads, "The parish priest said a 'voice' spoke to him before the miracle, and the Archdiocese of Guadalajara is investigating." Below are some quotes from this article.

> "According to Father Jose Dolores Castellanos Gudino, pastor of Mary Mother of the Church, he saw a flash of light and heard a voice while kneeling in prayer July 24 before the Blessed Sacrament." … "Ring the bells so that everyone comes," Father Gudino alleged the voice had told him. "*I will pour blessings upon those present, and the entire day. Take your small tabernacle for private adoration to the parish altar, and put the large monstrance next to the small tabernacle. Don't open the tabernacle until three in the afternoon, not before… I will perform a miracle in the Eucharist,*" the voice allegedly continued. "*The miracle that will take place will be called, 'Miracle of the Eucharist in the incarnation of love together with our Mother and Lady.' Copy the image that I will give you now and show it to others.*"

Eucharistic Miracle of Regensburg, Germany in 1255 A.D.

Some Eucharistic miracles have occurred when a Catholic priest was doubting that transubstantiation truly occurred during his delivery of the Mass. A priest's doubt is usually dispelled when a Eucharistic miracle occurs. An example of this comes from one of the more famous miracles, which occurred in Regensburg, Germany.

> "A priest was celebrating the Holy Mass in the little chapel, when he was struck by doubt regarding the Real Presence of Jesus in the Eucharist. He delayed, therefore, in elevating the chalice and suddenly heard a light noise come from the altar. From the wooden crucifix above the altar, the Lord slowly extended his arms to the priest, took the chalice from his hands and exhibited the Blessed Sacrament for the adoration of the faithful. The priest, repentant, fell to his knees and begged forgiveness for having doubted. The Lord returned the chalice to him as a sign of pardon. The miraculous crucifix is still preserved to this day in the nearby town of Regensburg, and many of the faithful go to the place every year in pilgrimage."[128]

Eucharistic Miracle of Lanciano, Italy in 750 A.D.

This fourth and last miracle provided in this chapter, demonstrates that some Eucharistic miracles have been scientifically proven to be credible.

> "An inscription in marble from the 17th century describes this Eucharistic miracle which occurred at Lanciano in 750 (A.D.) at the Church of St. Francis. "A monastic priest doubted whether the Body of Our Lord was truly present in the consecrated Host. He celebrated Mass and when he said the words of consecration, he saw the host turn into Flesh and the wine turn into Blood. Everything was visible to those in attendance. The Flesh is still intact and the Blood is divided into five unequal parts which together have the exact same weight as each one does separately... In 1970, the Archbishop of Lanciano, with Rome's approval, requested Dr. Edward Linoli, director of the hospital in Arezzo, to perform a thorough scientific

examination on the relics of the miracle which had occurred twelve centuries earlier. On March 4, 1971, the professor presented a detailed report of the various studies carried out."[129] Below are the findings:

1. The "miraculous Flesh" is authentic flesh.
2. The "miraculous Blood" is truly blood.
3. The flesh and the blood are human, and the blood type is AB – the same blood type as that of the man of the Shroud and the type most characteristic of Middle Eastern populations.
4. The proteins contained in the blood have the normal distribution, in the identical percentage for normal fresh blood.
5. No histological dissection has revealed any trace of salt infiltrations or preservative substances used in antiquity for embalming.

The Blessed Mother's Obsession with Russia and World Peace

Also in this novel chapter, the Pope makes the bold claim that the Blessed Mother supernaturally intervened in order to terminate the Russian invasion of Israel. The Queen of Heaven has become obsessed with Russia and world peace. The inseparable connection between the apparition called, "Our Lady of Fatima" and the nation of Russia is explored in the appendix entitled, "The Marian Apparitions Connection with Ezekiel 38." Below are a few related quotes concerning the association with Marian apparitions, Russia and world peace. These quotations taken from an article entitled, "Why World Peace Depends On It." This article was posted on the Fatima Network Website. [130]

> "One of the main themes of the Fatima Message is the establishment of peace throughout the world. At Fatima, the Mother of God presented to the world the conditions necessary for peace. They are the widespread practice of the devotion of the First Saturdays of Reparation to the Immaculate Heart of Mary, and the Consecration of Russia to the Immaculate Heart by the Pope together with all of the Catholic bishops. Our Lady told the three

shepherd children at Fatima, "If My requests are heeded, Russia will be converted and there will be peace."

Notice in this next quote how this imposter, posing as the mother of our Savior, has convinced the author and many Catholics that she has a sinless Immaculate Heart, and that she is the only source for providing a lasting world peace in the future.

> "At Fatima Our Lady, referring to Herself under the title Our Lady of the Rosary, said, "Only She can help you." No government or institution has been successful at bringing any kind of lasting peace to our war-torn world. That is because God has determined that peace will come through one source only: the hands of the Blessed Virgin Mary. And only by our obeying the simple yet profound requests She made at Fatima will She bestow upon mankind true peace...Sister Lucy asked Our Lord why He would not convert Russia without the Pope making the Consecration. He answered that He wanted the whole Church to recognize it as the Triumph of the Immaculate Heart of Mary; then, as a result of the triumph, His Church will subsequently place public homage to the Immaculate Heart beside the public homage to His Sacred Heart."[131]

The quote below is a distorted attempt to twist scripture to support false apparition claims. The prophecies of Isaiah and Micah below have nothing to do with "Our Lady," but will be fulfilled by the Messiah when He reigns in Jerusalem in His Messianic Kingdom during the millennium. As you read this quote, be reminded that the Catholics are "Amillennialists," which means they don't believe that Christ will come to the earth before the millennium to reign in a literal fulfillment of Revelation 20:4.

> "The peace Our Lady promised is the peace that Isaias (Isaiah) prophesied in Sacred Scripture: "The house of the Lord shall be exalted above the hills, and all nations shall flow unto it. And many people shall go, and say: Come and let us go up to the mountain of the Lord, and to the house of the God of Jacob, and he will teach us His ways, and we will walk in His paths. For the law shall come forth from Sion, (Zion) and the word of the Lord from Jerusalem they shall turn their swords into plowshares, and their spears

into sickles. Nation shall not lift up sword against nation, neither shall they be exercised any more to war" (Is. 2:2-4; cf. Mic. 4:1-3). This was prophesied over 2,500 years ago, and will be brought to fruition when the Immaculate Heart triumphs and reigns...The peace of Our Lady, as indicated by Isaias above, also includes the conversion of the world to Catholicism. This is the clear meaning of the first part of the passage, which states that nations will flock to the house of the Lord. It has been infallibly defined three times that there is no salvation outside the Catholic Church. Therefore, it follows that God wants all men to be Catholic."[132]

For more information on how Eucharistic Miracles and apparitions of Mary could play out in the end times scenario, I highly recommend the reading of the two books listed below. Both books are available at Amazon and the links are provided in this endnote.[133]

1. *Messages from Heaven; A Biblical Examination Of The Queen Of Heaven's Messages In The End Times*, by Jim Tetlow.

2. *Another Jesus: The Eucharist Christ and the New Evangelization*, by Roger Oakland and Jim Tetlow.

Chapter 18
Two Witnesses Prepare for the Tribulational Period

Topics Covered

Who Are The Two Witnesses of Revelation 11?

The Two Witnesses Are The Lord's Rebuttal To The False Covenant

This chapter of the novel introduces the Two Witnesses of Revelation 11 and the seven-year covenant of Daniel 9:27. The covenant is exposited upon in the "Post-Rapture / Pre-Trib Thesis," but the identities and ministries of the Two Witnesses will be explored briefly in this chapter's commentary.

It is commonly taught that the Two Witnesses are active during the first half of the Trib-Period. As such, they will be explored in greater detail in the final book of this trilogy, which deals with that specific time-period. The verse below establishes their three and one-half years of ministry. (1260 days ÷ 360 days = 3.5 years).

> 'And I will give power to my two witnesses, and they will prophesy one thousand two hundred and sixty days, clothed in sackcloth." (Rev. 11:3)

Their arrival is documented toward the end of this novel section to conclude this book and prepare for the final book. This dynamic end times duo will probably surface on the scene at the end of the Post-Rapture / Pre-Trib gap period to establish themselves for their important roles in the first half of the Trib Period.

Who Are The Two Witnesses?

It is possible, from the clues provided in Revelation 11:3-13, to make an educated guess as to who the Two Witnesses are. Some believe that they are Moses and Elijah. Others suggest they are Elijah and Enoch. Some have posited that they could be none of the above, but might be two entirely new faces.

I don't favor the "new faces" possibility for the following two reasons.

First, Revelation 11:4 says, *"These are the two olive trees and the two lampstands standing before the God of the earth."* This seems to correlate directly with a vision described in Zechariah 4 of the Old Testament. The same two olive trees show up three times in Zechariah's verses, (Zechariah 4:3,11-12). Referring to the identity of the two olive trees, Zechariah 4:14 says, "So he said, *"These are* the two anointed ones, who stand beside the Lord of the whole earth." If these are the two anointed ones, then it is highly doubtful that they are new faces on the earth in the end times, who serve the Lord for only three and one-half years.

Second, the overwhelming clues presented below, which solidly support Moses and Elijah as the prime two candidates, mitigates against the idea that the Two Witnesses are new faces.

Listed below are a few reasons why I favor Moses and Elijah as the Two Witnesses.

1. Moses and Elijah appeared together on the mount of transfiguration. (Matthew 17:3-4). If they appeared together in a significant event of the past, they will likely appear together in the future as well.

2. Moses and Elijah possessed in the past the similar supernatural powers that the Two Witnesses possess in the future. The verses below describe these powers.

> "These are the two olive trees and the two lampstands standing before the God of the earth. And if anyone wants to harm them, *fire* proceeds from their mouth and devours their enemies. And if anyone wants to harm them, he must be killed in this manner. These have power to shut heaven, so that *no rain* falls in the days of their prophecy; and they have power over *waters to turn them to blood*, and to *strike the earth with all plagues*, as often as they desire." (Revelation 11:4-6; emphasis added)

Elijah's former powers concerning *rain* are documented in 1 Kings 17:1, 1 Kings 18:1, 45, James 5:17-18. Elijah also called down *fire* from heaven in 1 Kings 18:38, and 2 Kings 1:10. Moses turned the *waters to blood* in Exodus 7:20-21. Concerning Moses and his ability to strike the earth will all plagues, he struck Egypt with ten plagues, which led to the Exodus of the Hebrews out of Egyptian bondage. The plagues were;[134]

- *First Plague*: Water turned to blood, (Exodus 7:20-21),

- *Second Plague*: Frog infestation throughout Egypt, (Exodus 8:2-4),

- *Third Plague*: Gnats or lice infestation throughout Egypt, (Exodus 8:16-17),

- *Fourth Plague*: Swarms of flies on the people and in their houses, (Exodus 18:21),

- *Fifth Plague*: Livestock diseased, (Exodus 9:3),

- *Sixth Plague*: Boil infections upon the Egyptians, (Exodus 9:8-11),

- *Seventh Plague*: Hailstones rain down upon Egypt, (Exodus 9:18),

- *Eighth Plague*: Locusts cover the face of the earth, (Exodus 10:4-5),

- *Ninth Plague*: Thick blanket of darkness over Egypt, (Exodus 10:21-22),

- *Tenth Plague*: Deaths of the firstborn in Egypt, (Exodus 11:4-5).

It's worthy to note, that some of these plagues seem to be repeated in some variation within some of the trumpet judgments in Revelation 8-9. The first trumpet involves hail and fire mingled with blood (Rev. 8:7). The second trumpet predicts that one-third of the seas will turn into blood (Rev. 8:8). The fourth trumpet says that one-third of the sun, moon and stars become darkened (Rev. 8:12). The fifth trumpet involves a plague of locusts (Rev. 9:3). However, this locust plague is not caused by Moses, but rather it appears to be outsourced by Satan.

It is possible that the trumpet judgments are occurring within the same time-period that the Two Witnesses are ministering on the earth. They may not have anything to do with these worldwide plagues, but something they do severely angers most of mankind as per the verses below. People around the world rejoice, rather than grieve, when these Two Witnesses are killed by the Antichrist in Jerusalem. This suggests that even though they are stationed in Jerusalem, their ministries and powers have a global impact.

COMMENTARY

When they finish their testimony, the beast (Antichrist) that ascends out of the bottomless pit will make war against them, overcome them, and kill them. And their dead bodies *will lie* in the street of the great city which spiritually is called Sodom and Egypt, where also our Lord was crucified. Then *those* from the peoples, tribes, tongues, and nations will see their dead bodies three-and-a-half days, and not allow their dead bodies to be put into graves. And those who dwell on the earth will rejoice over them, make merry, and send gifts to one another, because these two prophets tormented those who dwell on the earth. (Rev. 11:7-10)

More reasons why I favor Moses and Elijah as the Two Witnesses continues below.

3. Elijah was caught up in a whirlwind to heaven and never experienced death, (2 Kings 2:11-12). Enoch was also caught up to heaven, which is partially why some believe that he could be one of the Two Witnesses, (Genesis 5:24, Hebrews 11:5).

4. The Old Testament prophet Malachi predicts the return of Elijah.

> "Behold, I will send you Elijah the prophet Before the coming of the great and dreadful day of the Lord. And he will turn The hearts of the fathers to the children, And the hearts of the children to their fathers, Lest I come and strike the earth with a curse." (Malachi 4:5-6)

> Some scholars suggest that John the Baptist may have been the fulfillment of this Malachi prophecy according to the communication exchange between Jesus and His disciples in Matthew 17:10-13. However, below is a quote from Dr. Henry M. Morris negating this possibility.

> "Some assume that this prophecy was fulfilled in John the Baptist, but John the Baptist himself denied it. *"And they asked him, What then? Art thou Elias (Elijah)? And he saith, I am not"* (John 1:21). John did indeed come *"in the spirit and power of Elias"* (Luke 1:17), but he was not Elias, and his coming did not fulfill Malachi's prophecy. Jesus Himself confirmed this. *"Elias truly shall first come, and restore all things"* (Matthew 17:11)[135]

COMMENTARY

Although John did come before the *"great and dreadful day of the Lord,"* the prophetic implication is just prior to this period, rather than over two thousand years beforehand when John existed. Also, John did not *"turn the hearts of the fathers to the children, and the hearts of the children to their fathers."*

5.   Moses represents the Law and Elijah the prophets. When the Two Witnesses are on the earth, the Jews are wanting to reinstate the Mosaic Law and its animal sacrificial system. Moses and Elijah would be prime candidates to rebuke this effort. Both know that Jesus Christ is the Messiah. This was evidenced clearly to them at the mount of Transfiguration when the Lord said, *"This is My beloved Son, in whom I am well pleased. Hear Him!"* (Matthew 17:5). Jesus Christ fulfilled the Law, (Matthew 5:17), and in so doing, He rendered it inoperative. Galatians 3:24 clarifies the purpose of the law. It reads, "Therefore the law was our tutor *to bring us* to Christ, that we might be justified by faith."

6.   There was a dispute between Satan and Michael the archangel over the body of Moses. This could imply that Satan is concerned about Moses returning to the earth again as one of the Two Witnesses, (Jude 1:9).

The Two Witnesses Are The Lord's Rebuttal To The False Covenant

The Two Witnesses serve on the scene immediately after the false covenant of Daniel 9:27 is confirmed by the Antichrist between Israel and some other party. The "Post-Rapture / Pre-Tribulation Thesis" identifies the other probable party as the harlot world religion. The timing of the Two Witnesses is strategic. They appear to be the Lord's rebuttal to the dangerous covenant between Israel and the Harlot. The true content on the false covenant must be problematic because its starts the seven-year Tribulation clock ticking.

These two covenanting agencies not only represent the probable two main parties of the false covenant, but also represent the two dominant cities of the world at the time, Rome and Jerusalem. John alludes to Rome as Mystery, Babylon the Great. Babylon, referenced 258 times, and Jerusalem, mentioned 778 times, are the two most mentioned cities within the entire Bible.[136] Thus, the location of the Two Witnesses in Jerusalem, is also highly tactical on the Lord's part.

COMMENTARY

Moses will be able to stand before the Jewish Temple and explain to the Jews that Jesus was the Messiah and that their reinstated animal sacrifices and the Third Temple are not going to atone for their national sins, nor usher in the coming of the Messiah. He will proclaim to them that they must receive Christ as their Messiah, and a remnant of Jews will as per Zechariah 13:9.

Elijah will be able to point out the errors of the Harlot of Roman Catholicism. The Jezebel mentioned in the letter to the Church of Thyatira in Revelation 2:20. The Harlot is killing true believers in Revelation 17:6, just like Jezebel was killing true believers during his time in 1 Kings 18:4.

In the appendix entitled, "The Seven Letters to the Churches," a prophetic connection is made between the Church of Thyatira and Roman Catholicism. As the verses below demonstrate, Thyatira is the church that introduces a demonic feminine character. In fact, it is the only church in the seven letters to do so! The only possible female personage this could represent within the church age is the Catholic version of the Queen of Heaven.

> "Nevertheless, I have a few things against you, because you allow that woman Jezebel, (*Virgin Mary*), who calls herself a prophetess, (*Marian apparitions often issue prophecies*), to teach and seduce My servants to commit sexual immorality, (*idolatry*), and eat things sacrificed to idols, (*Transubstantiation in the Eucharist*). And I gave her time to repent of her sexual immorality, and she did not repent, (*Mariology is burgeoning, rather than repenting*). Indeed, I will cast her into a sickbed, and those who commit adultery with her into great tribulation, (*The final three and one-half years of the Trib-Period*), unless they repent of their deeds. I will kill her children with death, and all the churches shall know that I am He who searches the minds and hearts. And I will give to each one of you according to your works." (Rev. 2:20-23; emphasis added)

When Satan read these Thyatira verses about 2000 years ago in correlation with 2 Thessalonians 2:5-12, they probably prompted him to conceive his plan of deception partially through Thyatira, because he realized that this aspect of Christianity would survive the Rapture and be cast into the final days of the Trib-Period. Hence when Pagan Rome morphed into Papal Rome during the Church Age, the devil put his plan of deceit into action. 2 Thessalonians 2 foretold of the time when Satan would be freed from further restraint to deceive mankind.

Thyatira provided the perfect Christian platform to hatch his harlot religious scheme, rather than, in comparison, to the Church of Philadelphia. The letter to the Church of Philadelphia promised that church would be prevented from even entering the Trib-period. Choosing Philadelphia to use Christianity as a platform for deception would have been a poor decision.

> "Because you (*Philadelphia*) have kept My command to persevere, I also will keep you from the hour of trial (*Trib-Period*) which shall come upon the whole world, to test those who dwell on the earth." (Rev. 3:10; emphasis added)

Notice the spiritual dichotomy in Satan's scheme. The devil used Bible prophecy to prepare for his campaign of deception. The tip off was that Thyatira would be a good choice, but Philadelphia would be a bad choice. On the flip side, the Lord knowing the future realized that Satan would infiltrate Roman Catholicism and so He reported this in advance within the letter to Thyatira. The letter further states that this Jezebel campaign becomes a church doctrine from the depths of Satan, (Rev. 2:24). The apostle John apparently identified Jezebel of the past, as the representation for the Catholic Virgin Mary of the future because of some of the parallels below.[137]

Jezebel's Traits	End Time Harlot's Traits
A queen - 1 Kings 16:29-31	A queen - Revelation 18:7
Encourages idolatry - 1 Kings 21:25-26	Encourages idolatry – Rev. 2:20; 17:4
Described as a harlot -2 Kings 9:22	Described as a harlot – Rev. 17:1, 5; 19:2
She uses witchcraft - 2 Kings 9:22	Uses witchcraft - Isaiah 47:9, 12; Rev.18:23
Seductress; Outward beauty - 2 Kings 9:30	Seductress; Outward beauty - Rev. 17:4
Sheds the saints blood - 2 Kings 9:7	Sheds the saints blood - Rev. 17:6; 19:2
Massacres God's prophets - 1 Kings 18:4	Massacres God's prophets – Rev. 18:24
She is destroyed - 2 Kings 9:33-37	She is destroyed - Rev. 17:16; 18:8

A further thematic connection between Jezebel and the Catholic Virgin Mary is goddess worship. Believe it or not, the Queen of Heaven of Roman Catholicism is very much like a goddess to the millions of people who visit her shrines worldwide. They come from all faiths and religions. Here is just one example taken from a news article entitled, *"Twist of globalisation: All faiths come together."* Below is a quote from this article.

> "In an unexpected twist of globalisation, Hindus, Buddhists, Muslims and other pilgrims regularly worship at famous Roman Catholic shrines to the Virgin Mary such as Lourdes in France and Fatima in Portugal. They drink the holy water, light votive candles and pray fervently to the Madonna for help with life's hardships. Many venerate her like one of their own goddesses, a view that would be a heresy if a Catholic theologian tried to defend it."[138]

> Below is a separate quote along these same lines.

> "Mary was declared to be the "Mother of God" by the Christian church in the 7th century at Ephesus, Turkey. Ephesus was the home of a magnificent temple to the Goddess, Artemis Diana, one of whose sacred titles was "Queen of Heaven". Mary is a more recent and much loved incarnation of the Great Goddess of the ancient Middle-eastern cultures. Mary shares many standard Goddess attributes and symbols."[139]

The worship of the goddess Asherah during the time of Elijah was widespread in ancient Israel. In addition to being a personal devotee of Asherah, Jezebel employed 400 prophets that were entirely devoted to this demonic goddess.

> "So go gather all of Israel to meet me on Mount Carmel. Bring along 450 prophets of Baal and 400 prophets of the Asherah who are funded at Jezebel's expense. (2 Kings 18:19, ISV)

> Who was Asherah? Below are a couple quotes that answer this question.

> "Asherah was a fertility goddess, the mother of Baal. The Asherah existed in both the Southern and Northern Kingdoms of Israel. Jezebel of Tyre apparently installed Asherah worship in the north when she married King Ahab."[140]

"The Book of Jeremiah, written circa 628 BC, possibly refers to Asherah when it uses the title "Queen of Heaven", stating: "pray thou not for this people...the children gather wood, and the fathers kindle the fire, and the women knead their dough, to make cakes to the Queen of Heaven, and to pour out drink offerings to other gods, that they may provoke me to anger. (Jeremiah 7:18, 44:17–19, 25)"[141]

Elijah sounding the alarm about a false Roman Catholic goddess in the end times would be reminiscent of when he sounded the alarm in former times of Jezebel's pagan goddess Asherah.

Moses and Elijah are the two individuals most qualified to expose the flaws in the false covenant and the problems plaguing the primary covenanting parties. In addition to this, the Two Witnesses will be prophesying.

"And I will give *power* to my two witnesses, and they will prophesy one thousand two hundred and sixty days, clothed in sackcloth." (Revelation 11:3)

Perhaps they will be the ones to reveal what the "seven thunders" are in Revelation 10. The apostle John was told to, *"Seal up the things which the seven thunders uttered, and do not write them."* (Revelation 10:4)

Since the Two Witnesses are prophesying to the final generation during the short seven-year Trib-period, they are probably discerning and disseminating already foretold prophecies, more so than issuing new ones.

COMMENTARY

Chapter 19
The Encounter between Satan and his Seed

Topics Covered

Introduction to the Antichrist...

Introduction to the Antichrist

Satan introduces himself to his "seed" of Genesis 3:15 in this chapter. Commonly referred to as the Antichrist, this end times persuasive personality arrives on the world scene as the first horseman of the Apocalypse.

> Now I saw when the Lamb opened one of the seals; and I heard one of the four living creatures saying with a voice like thunder, "Come and see." And I looked, and behold, a white horse. He who sat on it had a bow; and a crown was given to him, and he went out conquering and to conquer. (Revelation 6:1-2)

The Antichrist rises to political prominence, military power and religious dominance through a process of two stages. The two stages are apparent in these verses by the usage of the words "*conquering and to conquer.*" They are both the same Greek word *nikaoô,* which in addition to conquering and conquer, can be translated to *prevail, overcome, overpower* or be victorious.[142]

The Antichrist will *prevail* politically, *overcome* militarily and *overpower* religiously. He will become victorious in these three important arenas. He is wearing a stefanos crown, which is a wreath or crown of victory. It is the type of crown that was awarded to a victor in the ancient athletic games, like the Greek Olympics.[143] Thus, he is victorious when he goes forth *conquering and to conquer.*

He prevails politically in Daniel 9:26-27 as the future prince, (political leader), that is called upon to confirm the all-important false covenant between Israel and another party. Modern day comparisons of a political leader possessing similar respect would be US Presidents Jimmy Carter and Bill Clinton, who were called upon to confirm covenants between Israel and Egypt, (Carter), and Israel and Jordan, (Clinton).

As a powerful political leader, he achieves military power. Once he achieves both political and military power, he uses them to springboard into religious dominance. This is understood in the sequence of verses below.

1. Revelation 17:3, 7 – The Antichrist, as the beast, is pictured in an unholy church and state relationship with the harlot world religion. He appears to be somewhat subservient to the Harlot, in that *she "sits" on him* in verse 3, and *he "carries" her* to her religious heights in verse 7.

2. Daniel 9:27 – As stated above, this verse evidences that the Antichrist becomes the esteemed political leader who Israel and some other party, probably the Harlot, trust to confirm a seven-year covenant between them.

3. Revelation 17:12, 16 – These verses state that the Antichrist will join forces with ten kings, who then desolate the harlot world religious system.

4. 2 Thessalonians 2 and Daniel 11 – These chapters explain that the Antichrist will go into the third Jewish Temple and exalt himself above every god, so that he shows himself as god. This happens after the harlot world religion is eliminated.

5. Daniel 7:24-25 – These verses describe that three of the ten kings, who were aligned with the Antichrist when the harlot world religion was desolated, decide to come against the Antichrist shortly thereafter. They appear to rebel against his claims to be god. As such, the Antichrist subdues them.

6. Daniel 11:40-41 – These verses explain how two of the three kings, the king of the South and the king of the North, are subdued by being defeated in a war with the Antichrist.

COMMENTARY

7.   Revelation 13 – This chapter says that the Antichrist is afflicted
      with a mortal head wound. Thus, he appears to die. However,
      he then appears to resurrect from the dead, at which point, the
      world at large begins to worship him. The mortal wound might
      result from a war between one of the three subdued kings.

The two stages in which the Antichrist rises to power, "*conquering
and to conquer*," occur after the Rapture of the Church. In *Revelation
Road*, I explain how the Church is pictured dwelling on earth in Revelation
2-3 and Raptured up into heaven in Revelation 4-5. It is from the vantage
point of being in heaven that the Christian Church experiences Christ
receiving the scroll in Revelation 5:7-8, and opening it in Revelation 6:1
to reveal the seven-seal judgments.

The first stage, which is predominately dealing with his political and
military empowerment, occurs after the Rapture on up to the middle of
the Trib-period. The second stage, which involves all three-fold aspects
of his ascent, occurs in the second half of the Trib-period. His religious
mission commences around the middle of the Trib-period after the Harlot
is removed and he subsequently enters the Jewish Temple. By that time,
Satan will have fully convinced the Antichrist that he is god and is worthy
of worldwide worship.

The predominant and traditional teaching of the origin of the
Antichrist is that he will come out of the Revived Roman Empire. This
is what I, along with Dr. David Reagan, Dr. Arnold Fruchtenbaum,
Dr. Ron Rhodes, Dr. Mark Hitchcock and a host of others believe.
However, some, like Joel Richardson and Walid Shoebat, believe that
the Antichrist will be a Muslim. A few others, like Terry James and LA
Marzulli, entertain the possibility that he might be a Nephilim. Whatever
his origin, he must come out for the Revived Roman Empire according
to Daniel.

> "And after the sixty-two weeks Messiah (*Christ*) shall be
> cut off, (*Crucified*) but not for Himself; (*But, for the sins of
> mankind*) And the people (*Romans*) of the prince (*Antichrist*)
> who is to come Shall destroy the city (*Jerusalem*) and
> the sanctuary, (*Second Jewish Temple*). The end of it (*70
> A.D.*) *shall be* with a flood, (*Military invasion*) And till the
> end of the war desolations are determined. (Daniel 9:26;
> *emphasis added*)

Since the Antichrist plays a more prominent role throughout the Trib-period, more information about his identity and his role will be provided in the final book of this series. Meanwhile, I highly recommend a book about the Antichrist by Dr. David Reagan entitled, *"The Man of Lawlessness: The Antichrist in the Tribulation."*[144]

I hope that you have enjoyed reading Apocalypse Road and I invite you to stay tuned for the final book of this series, which deals with the events that take place during the seven-year Tribulational period.

COMMENTARY

APOCALYPSE ROAD

Appendices

Appendix 1

The Sinners Salvation Prayer

> *"In an acceptable time I have heard you, And in the day of salvation I have helped you."* Behold, now *is* the accepted time; behold, now *is* the day of salvation. (2 Corinthians 6:2)

The most important decision one can make in their entire lifetime is to receive Christ as their personal Lord and Savior. It is the sinner's passport to paradise! It's an all-inclusive package that provides a forgiven and changed life on earth now and a guaranteed future admission into heaven afterward.

Without God's forgiveness, the sinner cannot enter into heaven because earthly sin is not allowed to exist there. Otherwise, it would not be rightfully called "heaven." Jesus was sent into the world to provide a remedy for man's sin problem. The Bible teaches that we are all sinners and that the wages, (what we deserve), of sin is death, (spiritual separation from God forever). But God so loved us that He wanted to make a way so anyone could be forgiven and thus be allowed to enter heaven. God doesn't want anyone to perish, and has been patient with us so that we can turn from sin and find forgiveness, (by faith), in His son, Jesus.

> "For God so loved the world that He gave His only begotten Son, [*Jesus Christ*] that whoever believes in Him should not perish but have everlasting life. (John 3:16, NKJV)

> And this is eternal life, that they may know You, the only true God, and Jesus Christ [*Begotten Son of God*] whom You have sent." (John 17:1-3, NKJV)

These passages point out that people are perishing to the great displeasure of God, who loves them immeasurably. He wishes that none would perish, but that everyone would inhabit eternity with Him and His only begotten Son, Jesus Christ. Quintessential to eternal life is the knowledge of these two concepts.

Sin Separates Us from the Love of God

The apostle John reminds us in 1 John 4:8, 16 that God is love, but man lives in a condition of sin, which separates him from God's love. Romans 8:5-8 explains how sin manifests into carnal behavior that creates enmity between God and man.

> "So then, those who are in the flesh cannot please God." (Romans 8:8, NKJV)

The book of Romans instructs that sin entered into the world through Adam, and spread throughout all mankind thereafter. Additionally, Romans informs that sin is the root cause of death, but through Jesus Christ eternal life can be obtained.

> "Therefore, just as through one man [Adam] sin entered the world, and death through sin, and thus death spread to all men, because all [men] sinned." (Romans 5:12; emphasis added)

> "All we like sheep have gone astray; We [mankind] have turned, every one, to his own way; And the LORD has laid on Him [Jesus Christ] the iniquity of us all." (Isaiah 53:6; emphasis added)

> "For the wages of sin is death, but the gift of God is eternal life in Christ Jesus our Lord." (Romans 6:23, NKJV)

If this makes sense to you, and you:

1. Have humbled yourself to recognize that you are a sinner, living under the curse of sin, which has separated from your Creator.

2. Believe that Jesus Christ took your punishment for sin so that you could be pardoned, as the only way to be saved

3. Want to repent and start letting God make changes in your life to be in a right relationship with God,

4. And, want to do it right now,

Then you have come to the right place spiritually. It is the place where millions before you, and many of your contemporaries alongside you, have arrived.

Fortunately, you have only one final step to take to complete your eternal journey. This is because salvation is a gift of God. Christ paid the full price for all sin, past, present, and future, when He sacrificed His life in Jerusalem about 2000 years ago. Your pardon for sin is available to you through faith in the finished work of Jesus Christ, which was completed upon His bloodstained cross. His blood was shed on our behalves. He paid sins wages of death on our account.

You must now take the final leap of faith to obtain your eternal salvation. It is your faith in Christ that is important to God.

> "But without faith *it is* impossible to please [*God*] *Him*, for he who comes to God must believe that He is, and *that* He is a rewarder of those who diligently seek Him." (Hebrews 11:6, NKJV; emphasis added)

> "In this you [*believer*] greatly rejoice, though now for a little while, if need be, you have been grieved by various trials, that *the genuineness of your faith, being much more precious than gold that perishes*, though it is tested by fire, may be found to praise, honor, and glory at the revelation of Jesus Christ, whom having not seen you love. Though now you do not see *Him,* yet believing, you rejoice with joy inexpressible and full of glory, receiving the end of your faith—the salvation of *your* souls." (1 Peter 1:6-9, NKJV)

Before the necessary step to salvation gets introduced it is important to realize and appreciate that salvation is a gift provided to us through God's grace. We didn't earn our salvation, but we must receive it. If you are one who has worked hard to earn everything you have achieved in life then you are to be commended. However, apart from living a sinless life, which is humanly impossible, there is nothing you as a sinner could have done to meet the righteous requirement to cohabitate in eternity with God. In the final analysis, when we see our Heavenly Father in His full glory, we will all be overwhelmingly grateful that Christ's sacrificial death bridged the chasm between our unrighteousness, and God's uncompromised holiness.

> "But God, who is rich in mercy, because of His great love with which He loved us, even when we were dead in [*sin*] trespasses, made us alive together with Christ (*by grace you have been saved*), and raised *us* up together, and made *us* sit together in the heavenly *places* in Christ Jesus, that in the ages to come He might show the exceeding riches of His grace in *His* kindness toward us in Christ Jesus. *For by grace you have been saved*

through faith, and that not of yourselves; *it is the gift of God,* not of works, lest anyone should boast." (Ephesians 2:4-9; emphasis added)

The Good News Gospel Truth

The term gospel is derived from the Old English *"god-spell,"* which has the common meaning *"good news,"* or *"glad tidings."* In a nutshell, the gospel is the good news message of Jesus Christ. Jesus came because God so loved the world that He sent His Son to pay the penalty for our sins. That's part of the good news, but equally important is the "Resurrection."

This is the entire good news gospel;

> "For I delivered to you first of all that which I also received: that Christ died for our sins according to the Scriptures, and that He was buried, and that He rose again the third day according to the Scriptures." (1 Corinthians 15:3-4; NKJV)

Christ resurrected which means He's alive and able to perform all of His abundant promises to believers. The Bible tells us that He is presently in heaven seated at the right hand side of God the Father waiting until His enemies become His footstool. Furthermore, from that position Christ also intercedes on the behalf of Christians. This intercession is an added spiritual benefit to you for becoming a believer.

> "But this Man, [*Jesus Christ became a Man, to die a Man's death*] after He had offered one sacrifice for sins forever, sat down at the right hand of God, from that time waiting till His enemies are made His footstool. For by one offering He has perfected forever those who are being sanctified." (Hebrews 10:12-14; emphasis added)

> "Who *is* he who condemns? *It is* Christ who died, and furthermore is also risen, who is even at the right hand of God, who also makes intercession for us." (Romans 8:34)

The resurrection of Christ overwhelmingly serves as His certificate of authenticity to all His teachings. He traveled through the door of death, and resurrected to validate His promises and professions. This can't be said of the claims of Buddha (Buddhism), Mohammed (Islam), Krishna (Hinduism), or any of the other host of deceased, human, non-resurrected, false teachers. All the erroneous teachings they deposited on the living side of death's door were invalidated when they died and lacked the power to conquer death itself, as Jesus has done.

One of Christ's most important claims is;

> "Jesus said to him, "I am the way, the truth, and the life. No one comes to the [*heavenly*] Father except through Me."" (John 14:6; emphasis added)

This is a critical claim considering eternal life can only be obtained by knowing the heavenly Father, and Christ, whom He [the Father] sent, according to John 17, listed earlier in this chapter. Most importantly, the resurrection proves that death has an Achilles heel. It means that its grip can be loosed from us, but only by Christ who holds the power over death.

> *"O Death, where is your sting? O Hades, where is your victory?"* The sting of death *is* sin, and the strength of sin *is* the law. But thanks *be* to God, who gives us the victory [*over Death and Hades*] through our Lord Jesus Christ." (1 Corinthian 15:55-57; emphasis added)

How to be Saved – You Must Be Born Again

> "Jesus answered and said to [*Nicodemus*] him, "Most assuredly, I say to you, unless one is born again, he cannot see the kingdom of God."" (John 3:3; emphasis added)

Jesus told Nicodemus, a religious leader of his day, that entrance into the kingdom of god required being born again. This is a physical impossibility, but a spiritual necessity, and why faith plays a critical role in your salvation. You can't physically witness your new birth; it is a spiritual accomplishment beyond your control that happens upon receiving Christ as your Lord and Savior. God takes full responsibility for your metamorphosis into a new creation at that point.

> "Therefore, if anyone *is* in Christ, *he is* a new creation; old things have passed away; behold, all things have become new." (2 Corinthians 5:17, NKJV)

You must trust God to perform on His promise to escort you through the doors of death into eternity, and to process you into the likeness of

Christ. This is the ultimate meaning of being born again, and alongside Christ, is a responsibility undertaken by the third member of the Trinity, the Holy Spirit. Christ holds the power over Death and Hades, but the Holy Spirit is your *"Helper"* that participates in your spiritual processing.

> "I *am* He [*Jesus Christ*] who lives, and was dead, and behold, I am alive forevermore. [*Resurrected*] Amen. And I have the keys of Hades and of Death." (Revelation 1:18; emphasis added)

> "If you love [*Christ*] Me, keep My commandments. And I will pray the Father, and He will give you another Helper [*Holy Spirit*], that He may abide with you forever— the Spirit of truth, whom the world cannot receive, because it neither sees Him nor knows Him; but you know Him, for He dwells with you and will be in you." (John 14:15-17; emphasis added)

> "These things I have spoken to you while being present with you. But the Helper, the Holy Spirit, whom the Father will send in My name, He will teach you all things, and bring to your remembrance all things that I said to you." (John 14:25-26, NKJV)

In order for you to successfully crossover from death to eternal life, *at the appointed time*, God has to work his unique miracle. Christ's resurrection demonstrated that He possesses the power to provide you with everlasting life. Death was not eliminated in the resurrection, it was conquered.

This is why the full gospel involves both God's love and power. His love for us would be of little benefit if it ended with our deaths. His love and power are equally important for our eternal assurance.

Therefore, we are informed in Romans 10, the following:

> "But what does it say? *"The word is near you, in your mouth and in your heart"* (that is, the word of faith which we preach): that if you confess with your mouth the Lord Jesus and believe in your heart that God has raised Him from the dead, you will be saved. For with the heart one believes unto righteousness, and with the mouth confession is made unto salvation. For the Scripture says, *"Whoever believes on Him will not be put to shame."* For

there is no distinction between Jew and Greek, for the same Lord over all is rich to all who call upon Him. For *"whoever calls on the name of the Lord shall be saved.""* (Romans 10:8-13, NKJV)

These Romans passages sum it up for all who seek to be saved through Christ. We must confess that Jesus Christ is Lord, and believe in our hearts that God raised Him from the dead.

The Sinner's Prayer for Salvation

Knowing that confession of Christ as Lord, coupled with a sincere faith that God raised Him from the dead are salvation requirements, the next step is customarily to recite a sinner's prayer in order to officiate one's salvation.

Definition of the Sinner's Prayer

"A sinner's prayer is an evangelical term referring to any prayer of humble repentance spoken or read by individuals who feel convicted of the presence of sin in their life and desire to form or renew a personal relationship with God through his son Jesus Christ. It is not intended as liturgical like a creed or a confiteor. It is intended to be an act of initial conversion to Christianity, and also may be prayed as an act of recommitment for those who are already believers in the faith. The prayer can take on different forms. There is no formula of specific words considered essential, although it usually contains an admission of sin and a petition asking that the Divine (Jesus) enter into the person's life."[145]

Example of the Sinner's Prayer

Below is a sample Sinner's Prayer taken from the Salvation Prayer website. If you are ready to repent from your sins, and to receive Jesus Christ as your personal Lord and Savior, read this prayer will all sincerity of heart to God.

Dear God in heaven, I come to you in the name of Jesus. I acknowledge to You that I am a sinner, and I am sorry for my sins and the life that I have lived; I need your forgiveness.

I believe that your only begotten Son Jesus Christ shed His precious blood on the cross at Calvary and died for my sins, and I am now willing to turn from my sin.

You said in Your Holy Word, Romans 10:9 that if we confess the Lord as our God and believe in our hearts that God raised Jesus from the dead, we shall be saved.

Right now I confess Jesus as the Lord of my soul. With my heart, I believe that God raised Jesus from the dead. This very moment I receive Jesus Christ as my own personal Savior and according to His Word, right now I am saved.

Thank you Jesus for your unlimited grace which has saved me from my sins. I thank you Jesus that your grace never leads to license for sin, but rather it always leads to repentance. Therefore Lord Jesus transform my life so that I may bring glory and honor to you alone and not to myself.

Thank you Jesus for dying for me and giving me eternal life. Amen.[146]

Congratulations and welcome into the household of God!

Below are the congratulatory words and recommendations also taken from the Salvation Prayer website. If you just prayed the Sinner's Prayer please be sure to read this section for further guidance.

"If you just said this prayer and you meant it with all your heart, we believe that you just got saved and are born again. You may ask, "Now that I am saved, what's next?" First of all you need to get into a bible-based church, and study God's Word. Once you have found a church home, you will want to become water-baptized. By accepting Christ you are baptized in the spirit, but it is through water-baptism that you show your obedience to the Lord. Water baptism is a symbol of your salvation from the dead. You were dead but now you live, for the Lord Jesus Christ has redeemed you for a price! The price was His death on the cross. May God Bless You!"[147]

Remember, being born again is a spiritual phenomenon. You may have felt an emotional response to your commitment to Christ, but don't be concerned if fireworks didn't spark, bands didn't march, sirens didn't sound, or trumpets didn't blast in the background at the time. There will be plenty of ticker-tape for us in heaven, which is where our rewards will be revealed. If you believed and meant what you said, you can be assured God, Who sent His Son to be crucified on our behalf, heard your every word. Even the angels in heaven are rejoicing.

> *"Likewise, I say to you, there is joy in the presence of the angels of God over one sinner who repents."* (Luke 15:10; emphasis added)

Welcome to the family and love the Lord with every aspect of your being*!*

> *"And you shall love the Lord your God with all your heart, with all your soul, with all your mind, and with all your strength. 'This is the first commandment.'"* (Mark 12:30)

Appendix 2

The Tribulation Saints

> This appendix was written by expert Bible prophecy teacher and respected evangelist, Al Gist. He is the founder of Maranatha Evangelistic Ministries. His website is: http://www.maranathaevangelisticministries.com/

I have often been asked this question: "Will those who reject the Lord's offer of salvation *before* the Rapture have a chance to be saved *after* the Rapture, or during the Tribulation?" My first response is to ask, "What motivates you to ask such a question?" It seems to me that anyone who would ask this is a person who is either trying to put off their own salvation until after the Rapture, or is concerned about some lost person whom they hope will have a change of heart after all the Christians disappear from this earth (in the Rapture) and will *then* begin to seek a relationship with God.

It's kind of a "quasi-faith" approach. It's the thinking that once a person *sees* the Rapture, *then* he will believe that the Bible is true and will seek salvation from the Lord. But the Bible says that *"faith is the substance of things hoped for, the evidence of things not seen."* (Heb. 11:1) Hence, I would submit to you that anyone who takes the approach of "Let me see it first and then I'll believe it" has not really believed by faith, but has made *sight* a prerequisite, which is not real faith at all!

Also, anyone who is thinking along the lines of belief after sight obviously does not realize just how bad The Tribulation is going to be. Jesus said that it would be a time of *great* tribulation... a time of suffering that will supersede all times in the history of mankind for its pain! (Matt. 24:21) Think of that!

There have been some horribly dark times in history when men have been demonically cruel to their fellow humans... times when men devoted themselves to inventing new ways to inflict pain and take the lives of people by the millions (The Inquisition, the Holocaust, etc.). But *no time* in all of history will compare to the dreadfulness of The Tribulation. It will be Hell on earth! It will be a time unparalleled in history for its pain, heartache and suffering. It will be a time so bad that Jesus said *"except those days should be shortened, there should no flesh be saved:"* (Matt.

24:22). [148]Most of those who *are* saved during the Tribulation will be persecuted unto death.

On the other hand, *today* (before the Rapture and following tribulation), we have the wonderful gift of salvation of our Lord that can be received through simple faith. Today, we can with child-like faith, believe in what Jesus did for us on the cross and accept His free gift of salvation. It is a salvation from death, Hell, and The Tribulation that is to soon come to this world!

Who in their right mind would want to pass up being saved *today* by faith, preferring instead of being saved *then* in a time of severe persecution and martyrdom? Whether a person is asking this question for himself or for someone else, the exhortation is the same... *Be saved today! Don't wait! Don't plan on being saved just moments before you die or after the Rapture!* Chances are that if you won't receive Christ today in this wonderful age of grace, you won't receive Him then in a time of intense persecution.

But, let's suppose for a moment that some lost friend (we'll call him "Lost Larry") has not actually made plans to wait until later to be saved, but has just been caught up in the things of this world and has not considered eternity. He's heard the Gospel, but has chosen to go the way of the world instead. Then, the Rapture occurs. Is it possible for him to have a change of heart and then give his life to Christ during The Tribulation?

Some Bible scholars who say it would be impossible for "Lost Larry" to be saved during the Tribulation, (we'll call them the "Larry-is-doomed" bunch), point to 2 Thessalonians 2 for their proof text. It says that *"God shall send... strong delusion"* (2 Thess. 2:11) to those who *"received not the love of the truth"* (2 Thess. 2:10) *"that they all might be damned..."* (2 Thess. 2:12). In other words, if Lost Larry rejected Christ before the Tribulation, then he will be so deceived by the *"power and signs and lying wonders"* (2 Thess. 2:9) of the Antichrist that he will have no desire for God and will ultimately be damned to Hell for an eternity without God. And, they emphasize the word "all" to show that this applies to *everyone* who has rejected Christ prior to the Rapture.

Let's take a close look at these verses. But first, we need to make one point clear... *There will be many people saved after the rapture,* (even the "Larry-is-doomed" people acknowledge that). Revelation 6:9 and 7:14 are a few scriptural examples. The "Larry-is-doomed" theologians would say the "numberless multitude" had never heard the Gospel before the Tribulation, so they're not like Lost Larry.

Paul told the Thessalonians that the *"mystery of iniquity"* (i.e., the mystery that pushes men toward sinfulness) was already at work (2 Thess. 2:7), but that it was being restrained ("let" in the KJV) until the One who restrains that wickedness (the Holy Spirit) is taken out of the way. During the Tribulation, the Holy Spirit's ministry of restraining evil will be removed.

The Holy Spirit will not be removed from the earth, just His particular ministry of restraining evil will be. Then, the Antichrist will be revealed (2 Thess. 2:8), the one who through the power of Satan will work power and signs and wonders (2 Thess. 2:9). Now, the next verse is a key. It says, *"And with all deceivableness of unrighteousness in them that perish;"*

In other words, the Antichrist will deceive through unrighteousness *those that perish* with his power, and signs, and wonders. The lost (those that perish) of the Tribulation era will be deceived by the Antichrist *"because they received not the love of the truth, that they might be saved."* (2 Thess. 2:10).

Here's where those who say Lost Larry can't be saved during the Tribulation base their theology. They say that this is a clear reference to people like Lost Larry who refused the Gospel message *("received not the love of the truth")* before the Rapture. 2 Thess. 2:11-12 goes on to say, *"And for this cause God shall send them strong delusion, that they should believe a lie: That they all might be damned who believed not the truth, but had pleasure in unrighteousness."*

Here's my question: What makes them think that the reference that says they *"received not the love of the truth"* is speaking of a time *before* the Rapture? Could it not just be saying that those people of the Tribulation period will be presented the Gospel, and those that reject it will then be deceived by the power, signs, and lying wonders of the Antichrist? And, that God will send those that reject Him strong delusion so that they will believe the lies of the Antichrist and as such, they will be damned because they did not believe the truth, but had pleasure in the unrighteousness of Antichrist?

The difficulty is in determining the antecedent of the pronoun "they" in 2 Thess. 2:12 where it says *"that they all might be damned"*. Who is the *"they"* it is referring to? Tracing it backwards, "they" are identified in 2 Thess. 2:11, as *"they should believe a lie"*. And, the "they" of verse

11 refers back to the "them" in the same verse where it says *"God shall send them a lie".*

This is the same "they" in verse 2 Thess. 2:10 that says, *"they received not the love of the truth, that they might be saved."* It is the same "they" who will be deceived by the Satanic powers of the Antichrist during the Tribulation and will ultimately perish (suffer eternal damnation).

All of these descriptive phrases point back to *"them that perish"* in verse 10, which is a reference to those who are deceived by the Antichrist *during* the Tribulation. I see nothing here that specifically points to the fact that these people *were, or were not,* presented the Gospel *before* the Tribulation, and nothing that says they rejected Christ *before* the Rapture and Tribulation.

In fact, we know that the *"...Gospel of the Kingdom shall be preached in all of the world for a witness unto all nations: and then shall the end come."* (Matt. 24:14), which will probably find ultimate fulfillment *during* the Tribulation through the work of the 144,000 servants of God (Rev. 7:2-8), the two witnesses of God (Rev. 11:3-14), and the special preaching angel of God (Rev. 14:6-7).

Most people living on earth after the Rapture will reject these preachings of the Gospel (as they do today) and will perish without Christ. They will believe the Lie and reject the Truth. As far as I can see, the passage in 2 Thess. 2 is a reference to them.

Finally, let's observe one last critical rule of Biblical Interpretation. Let's look at this passage *in context.* Paul begins chapter two by reassuring the Thessalonians that the day of the Lord had not yet come. It's possible that they felt that they were being so persecuted, that they thought the Tribulation had already begun.

Paul says in 2 Thess. 2:3 that day would not come until (1) *"there come a falling away first"* (i.e., a time of great apostasy) and (2) *"that man of sin be revealed, the son of perdition"* (the Antichrist). From there, he goes on to talk about the Antichrist in 2 Thess. 2:4-9, pausing momentarily to remind them, *"Remember ye not, that, when I was yet with you, I told you these things?"* (2 Thess. 2:5). He proceeds from there to talk about those many people who will be deceived by the Antichrist (2 Thess. 2:10-12).

Thus, one might safely conclude that it has nothing at all to do with those who heard the Gospel *before* the Rapture. It is all about the Antichrist and his deceit during the Tribulation. I have no doubt that those who reject God during that awful time will be swept up by the lies and deception of the Antichrist. Their ultimate end will be to perish eternally. However, just as there always has been a remnant of faithful believers, there will be a small minority that will recognize the Antichrist's deception. They will read the Bible and understand the final outcome of all those who show loyalty to Antichrist and his kingdom by taking his mark, and they will resist him.

In my heart, I have to believe that some of those will be people who, like Lost Larry, heard about Jesus, His salvation, the Rapture and the Tribulation in our time, but were too bound by the things of this world to give themselves to Christ. After the Rapture, knowing what is before them, and feeling the loneliness of being left behind without Christian support and fellowship, and feeling the conviction of the Holy Spirit for not having already received the Lord, they will cry out to God, and our God, Who possesses a multitude of mercies, will receive them into His waiting arms in that midnight hour.

But friend, do not try to wait until that last moment to be saved. Do it today and be sure!

Appendix 3

The Seven Letters to the Churches

The seven letters to the seven churches in Revelation 2 and 3 have multiple applications. First, they were instructional for the seven actual churches existing at the time. Second, similarities of these types of churches could be found throughout the church age. Third, they were intended to chronologically order the seven stages of church development throughout its earthly existence in a prophetic application.

Fortunately, we have the opportune advantage of looking back upon church history, which enables us to determine each church period. Below is an outline of the chronological development of the Christian church in accordance with the blueprints of the seven letters in Revelation. This outline reveals that we are living in the final days of church development, the "days of Laodicea."

Ephesus (Revelation 2:1-7; AD 40-150) The first stage of Christianity was primarily an apostolic period. Christians operated in compliance with Matthew 28:18-20. It was a time of reconciliation wherein the disciples successfully preached the good news gospel of Jesus Christ outwardly from Jerusalem into the surrounding Gentile populations of the world. This was Christianity in its infancy, and as a religion it was rapidly spreading throughout the broader Middle East region and into the greater Roman Empire.

Smyrna (Revelation 2:8-11; AD 100-312) This segment of church history was characterized by a period of persecution. Rome was conducting wide-scale Christian executions in an attempt to prevent the growth and spread of the religion. Martyrdom was the unfortunate predicament forced upon the church by the Roman Empire (Pagan Rome) during the Smyrna era. However, to Rome's chagrin, the persecutions actually bolstered the growth of Christianity. Christians dying for their faith caught the attention of multitudes that in turn fixated their focus upon Christ as their Savior.

Pergamos (Revelation 2:12-17; AD 300-600) The period of Pergamos, meaning "mixed marriage" in Greek, is associated with the paganization of the church. As the Roman Empire began its decline, it embraced Christianity as its state religion. This served two primary purposes. First, it began to fill deepening political rifts developing in the deteriorating Roman government; and secondly, it facilitated the survival of faltering pagan religious practices by cleverly integrating and incubating them into Christianity. Also, the martyrdom period of Smyrna that experienced Christianity flourishing became problematic for Rome. Each martyr's death brought new and renewed strength among fellow Christians. Thus, Rome adopted the attitude, "If you can't beat them [kill all the Christians], join them."

As time passed this Roman attitude eventually led many Christians to reciprocate and romanticize Romanism, and to believe that *"When in Rome, do as the Romans do."* During the Pergamos period, Christianity essentially was asked to compromise itself — and in so doing, create an end to the persecutions occurring during the Smyrna stage. By marrying up with Roman paganism, Christianity was insured its survival. Shortly thereafter, ancient Roman religious practices began to permeate and adulterate the church. Christian traditions, such as Christmas trees and Yule logs, can likely be traced to this Pergamos period of church history.

Thyatira (Revelation 2:18-29; AD 600-Tribulation) This church is commonly thought to represent the Roman Catholic Church, (Papal Rome), which evolved out of the Pergamos period. Thyatira tends to be a works-based, rather than a faith-based church. In so doing it emphasizes the religious rather than relational importance between God and humanity. Revelation 2:22 declares that an apostate element within Thyatira will exist in the end times and be cast into the "sickbed" of the great tribulation period.

> *"Nevertheless I have a few things against you,* (Roman Catholicism) *because you allow that woman* (The Queen of Heaven) Jezebel, *who calls herself a prophetess, to teach and seduce My servants to commit sexual immorality and eat things sacrificed to idols. And I gave her time to repent of her sexual immorality, and she did not repent. Indeed I will cast her into a sickbed, and those who commit adultery with her into great tribulation, unless they repent of their deeds. I will kill her children with death, and all the churches shall know that I am He who searches the minds and hearts. And I will give to each one of you according to your works."* (Revelation 2:20-23, emphasis added)

The comparisons between Jezebel and the Blessed Mother of Roman Catholicism are made in the chapter called, "Two Witnesses Prepare for the Tribulational Period."

Sardis (Revelation 3:1-6; AD 1500-Tribulation) This period is best described as the Protestant Reformation; however, it lacked true transformation. Salvation through faith rather than works was here reintroduced within Christianity; however, the Reformation continued to be more about religion than about a personal relationship with God.

Philadelphia (Revelation 3:7-13; AD 1800-Rapture) Philadelphia means "*brotherly love*." Powerful, worldwide missionary movements beginning in the mid-1600s characterize the period of Philadelphia. In accordance with Matthew 28:18-20, this church answered the call to the "Ministry of Reconciliation." The Philadelphian period concludes with the rapture as per Revelation 3:10, which says that this church will be kept from "*the hour of trial which shall come upon the whole world*," alluding to the Trib-period.

Laodicea (Revelation 3:14-22; AD 1900-Tribulation) Laodicea means "*people's rights*." Inherent in its name is the inference that this is a church predominately ruled by the people rather than the Lord. This church began in the twentieth century and will continue into the seven-year tribulation period. Laodicea believes that it is a prosperous church having need of nothing; conversely, Christ considers it "*wretched, miserable, poor, blind, and naked,*" (Rev. 3:17). IN Rev. 3:18, Christ encourages this church to abandon its apostate practices and purchase gold from Him that is refined through the fire. By the reference to gold refined through fire, Christ implies that Laodicea is an impure and undisciplined church in need of repentance.

Laodicea treats Christ more like an ordinary stranger, rather than an extraordinary Savior. They position Him mostly outside the church, which causes Him to say,

> "Behold, I stand at the door and knock. If anyone hears
> My voice and opens the door, I will come in to him and
> dine with him, and he with Me." (Rev. 3:20)

Most Bible prophecy teachers believe that these are the days of Laodicea.

Appendix 4

The Marian Apparitions Connection with Ezekiel 38

In 1917, after three years of nations raging against nations in World War 1, the apparition of Mary came to Fatima, Portugal to deliver a message. "Our Lady of Fatima," as she has ever since been called, spoke of heaven, hell and the sins of man which were being penalized by war. Many Catholics believe that in her message she provided the means to the end of World War 1 through her divine intervention. World War 1 ended about a year later on November 18, 1918.

> *"Continue to recite the Rosary every day to our Lady of the Rosary to obtain peace in the world and the end of the war, (World War I), because only She, (Our Lady of Fatima), will be able to aid you."*

During that same sequence of messages, the apparition spoke about the nation of Russia.

> *"I (the apparition) shall come to ask for the consecration of Russia. ... If my requests are heeded, Russia will be converted, and there will be peace; if not, she will spread her errors throughout the world, causing wars and persecutions of the Church. The good will be martyred; the Holy Father will have much to suffer; various nations will be annihilated. In the end, my Immaculate Heart will triumph. The Holy Father will consecrate Russia to me, and she shall be converted, and a period of peace will be granted to the world."[149]*

Twelve years later on June 13, 1929, Our Lady of Fatima made a follow up request to visionary Sister Lucy, who at the time was living at Tuy, Spain. This communication provided specific instructions about the manner in which Russia was to be consecrated.

> *"The moment has come in which God asks the Holy Father to make, and to order that in union with him and at the same time, all the bishops of the world make the consecration of Russia to My Immaculate Heart."*

"Consecration" is the act of separating something away from its current condition for a sacred use. In this case Russia is to be consecrated. After receiving this message from the apparition, Sister Lucy eventually delivered these instructions below to the Pope.

1. Russia must be specifically mentioned as the object of consecration.

2. The Pope must join with the world bishops in a public ceremony for the consecration.

The consecration of Russia to the Immaculate Heart of Mary alludes to the abandonment of atheism, paganism, heresy or schism and the acceptance of the Catholic Faith and the Church established by Christ.[150]

There is a relatively rigorous debate within Catholic circles as to whether or not Russia has been officially consecrated. The general consensus is no not yet. Then the question arises as to why it hasn't happened yet? The answer to this question gets complicated due to the staggered timing of the messages and the generally confusing and secretive nature of the predictions concerning Russia. In the end analysis, it appears as though Our Lady at Fatima may have had an ulterior motive looming behind her foretellings of Russia's future.

CAVEAT: All of the above is a supernatural reality. Most of what is below is spiritual speculation. However, it is provided because it finds potential relevance to the harlot world religion, which is a topic of this book.

These Fatima messages singled out Russia as the only nation to ever be called out for consecration to the Immaculate Heart of Mary. This sole inclusion of Russia is interesting considering at the time, the British Empire was referred to as the *"Empire on which the sun never sets."* Why didn't the apparition give at least an honorable mention to the UK, USA, France or Italy, who were all Russia's allies in World War 1?

Is it possible that Our Lady of Fatima, who is not really the "Virgin Mary" of the Bible like the Catholics teach, was concerned about Russia's future lead role in the Ezekiel 38 prophecy? This ancient prophecy predicts that Russia will be a dominant world warring power in the end times.

Although there is some dispute about the identity of some of the nations in this prophecy, most Bible experts believe that Russia is the lead nation in the Gog of Magog coalition of Ezekiel 38:1-6. It's safe to suggest that the supernatural entity calling herself Our Lady of Fatima,

APPENDICES

385

knows exactly whether or not Russia is identified in these verses. This intelligent being that is masquerading as the apparition of Mary has probably existed before there ever was a land of Magog.

Why would Our Lady of Fatima be concerned about Russia, and why in the same sequence of messages is this Mary imposter seemingly taking credit for ending World War 1? The answer may be hidden in identifying who Our Lady of Fatima really is, and in understanding two of the marquee end times prophecies.

First, the apparition claims to be the benevolent biblical character Mary, the mother of Jesus. It has already been revealed in the commentary of the chapter entitled, "The Queen of Heaven Appears Globally," that is not her true identity. Rather than being the biblical Mary, she or it must be diabolical. Whoever, or whatever, Our Lady of Fatima represents, her boss is the Devil. Thus, it's Satan who's concerned about the prophecy of Ezekiel 38. But why?

One of the two marquee prophecies concerning Satan must be Ezekiel 38, but why is the Devil so concerned about this prediction? The answer is understandably found in Ezekiel 39:7, which points out the overall purpose of the prophecy is the glorification of the Holy name of God.

> "So I will make My holy name known in the midst of My people Israel, and I will not *let them* profane My holy name anymore. Then the nations shall know that *I am* the Lord, the Holy One in Israel." (Ezekiel 39:7)

This is the prophecy, which according to Ezekiel 38:8, 16 occurs in the "latter days," that God uses to inform the world that He is the only God, *i.e.*, the one true God of the Bible. The Lord accomplishes this by supernaturally defeating the Russian led coalition in the manner described in Ezekiel 38:18-39:6. These verses are interpreted in the commentary of the chapter called, "The Collapse of the Russian Coalition."

This supernatural divine defeat appears to be accomplished at a time when Satan is attempting to perpetrate a campaign of strong deception in another latter days marquee prophecy found in 2 Thessalonians. Below is the second prediction that must be of particular interest to Satan.

> "The coming of the lawless one (*Antichrist*) is according to the working of Satan, with all power, signs, and lying wonders, and with all unrighteous deception (*including*

APPENDICES

APOCALYPSE ROAD

possible future Marian apparitions) among those who perish, (*left behind after the Rapture*) because they did not receive (*Jesus Christ*) the love of the truth, that they might be saved. And for this reason God will send them strong delusion, that they should believe the lie, that they all may be condemned who did not believe the truth but had pleasure in unrighteousness. (2 Thessalonian 2:9-12; emphasis added)

Since these are the latter days and neither of these marquee prophecies have happened as of yet, then should they happen about the same time, that complicates matters for Satan's spread of "the lie" alluded to above. Satan will be attempting to deceive mankind into thinking that the God of the Bible is not the one true God, but the fulfillment of Ezekiel 38 will prove otherwise.

Therefore, Satan has likely communicated the Fatima messages of 1917 in order to confuse the Lord's obvious future message to the masses that the supernatural defeat of the Russian coalition was orchestrated entirely by the God of the Bible. Instead, since Our Lady of Fatima took credit for ending World War 1, then certainly she is qualified to end Russia's ability to "*spread her errors throughout the world, causing wars,*" like Ezekiel 38, which she forewarned about at Fatima over a century prior.

Below is a quote from the article entitled, "*Pope Benedict XV Demands World Peace,*" (May 5, 1917), that documents the historical time-period involving the Lady of Fatima and World War I.

"In 1917 the First World War was raging, without showing any sure sign of concluding peacefully. By this time the Holy Father, Pope Benedict XV, who had been in the diplomatic service of the Vatican, had exhausted all of the natural means in his power to bring about peace, but to no avail. Realizing the limited power of even Papal diplomacy, the tired and frail Pope turned to the Blessed Mother of God, through Whom all graces are dispensed. He urgently requested all Christians to beg the Virgin Mary to obtain peace in the world, and to solemnly entrust the task to Her alone. The Pope wrote of his plea for peace in a letter dated May 5, 1917... The Blessed Mother responded quickly to this agonizing plea of the Pope

386

APPENDICES

and the Christian people. Only eight days later, at Fatima, the Virgin Mary came in response to the cries raised to Her from a warring world. She came to demonstrate Her maternal care for us, and that, as Mediatrix of all Graces, She alone can show us the way to peace."[151]

This quote points out that the Lady of Fatima appeared at the precise time when the Pope and Catholics around the world were desperately petitioning the Blessed Mother to intervene and bring peace during World War I. Does it seem reasonable to believe that a similar thing could take place during the war of Gog of Magog in the future? Might some Catholics tragically give the glory to the Lady of Fatima for the supernatural defeat of the Magog invaders of Ezekiel 38? The following quote about the future from John Paul II, who was very devoted to "Our Lady of Fatima," adds further credence to this possibility.

"In his book, *Crossing the Threshold of Hope*, the Pope made a prophetic statement that the Church's future victories will come through Mary, stating:... On this universal level, if victory comes it will be brought by Mary. Christ will conquer through her, because He wants the Church's victories now and in the future to be linked to her."[152]

Another episode in history worth mentioning along these lines took place on October 7, 1571, at the Battle of Lepanto. Below are quotes about this epic event, whereby the Blessed Mother intervened to defeat the Muslim Turkish Navy.

"No discussion of the history of the Rosary would be complete without a description of the epic and historic Battle of Lepanto. While engaged in a protracted war with the Muslim Turks over the control of Eastern Europe and in particular the Mediterranean, Pope Pius V organized a fleet of ships to engage the Muslim Turkish navy. Pope Pius V implored all the faithful to fervently pray the Rosary and ask our Blessed Mother to intercede on behalf of the Christians. Despite being hopelessly outnumbered in quantity of ships and fighting men, the Muslim Turks were defeated at the Battle of Lepanto on October 7, 1571...Pope Pius V declared this day to be the Feast of the Holy Rosary and asked all to give thanks to "Our Lady of Victory" for her timely intercession in answer to the faithful's praying of the Rosary."[153]

Catholic historian, Professor Plinio Corrêa de Oliveira, adds the following description of what took place at the Battle of Lepanto.

"Descriptions of the Battle of Lepanto based on the Catholic chronicles of the time do not mention an important fact found in the Muslim sources. The latter report that at a certain moment during the battle when the Catholic forces were being defeated, the Turkish fleet saw a majestic and terrible Lady in the sky. She was looking at them with such a menacing gaze that they could not bear it, lost their courage, and fled."[154]

For almost 2000 years, Satan foreknew that a time would come when he would be unrestrained to perpetrate strong delusion in the world. That time appears to be drawing near. However, for almost 2600 years, he has also known that the Lord predicted to destroy the Magog invaders supernaturally. In order to mitigate against the Lord getting due credit for stopping the Magog coalition, Satan may think that he has found a possible way, through Our *lying* Lady of Fatima, to usurp God's prophetic word.

If Our Lady of Fatima appears again, just once, with supernatural signs and wonders before, during or in the immediate aftermath of the divine defeat of Russia, then it's highly likely that some Catholics worldwide will believe that she intervened again in another major war. She could get the credit, rather than the God of the Bible.

But, what about the UK and the USA? Why didn't Our Lady of Fatima allude to them? After all, at the time of the Fatima messages the UK was the world's dominant empire and now America is. Perhaps, it's because Satan realized that in the Ezekiel 38 prophecy, they are no longer pictured in superpower statuses.

The UK and the USA appear to be identified in Ezekiel 38:13 as protestors of the Russian invasion of Israel. Ezekiel 38 portrays Russia as *powerful*, but the UK and USA as *powerless*. To learn more about the decline of America and the role Brexit plays in the end times read the following article **Are the UK and USA in Ezekiel 38?**, which is available at this web link: http://www.prophecydepotministries.net/2016/how-brexit-supports-the-uk-and-usa-in-ezekiel-38/

Appendix 5

The Apocalypse Road Timeline

The appendix provides a timeline for the unfulfilled biblical predictions of the last days. It is formatted to correspond closely with the books in this end time's trilogy, which are, *Revelation Road, Apocalypse Road* and *Tribulation Road*.[155] These three books are identified and bracketed in their appropriate time slots directly beneath the timeline.

NOW, NEXT and LAST Prophecies

There are three categories of coming biblical prophecies. They are the;

1.   *NOW Prophecies*, which are covered in *Revelation Road*.

2.   *NEXT Prophecies*, which are covered in *Apocalypse Road*.

3.   *LAST Prophecies*, which will be covered in *Tribulation Road*.

The *NOW Prophecies* are the unfulfilled ancient biblical predictions that appear to be imminent, which means they could happen NOW! These ancient foretellings have either minor or no remaining preconditions inhibiting them from happening at the present time. These predictions are identified and explained in detail within my book entitled, "*The Now Prophecies*."

The *NEXT Prophecies* are those that follow the fulfillment of the NOW Prophecies. In essence, the NOW's provide the necessary nexus of events that pave the path for the execution of the NEXT Prophecies. Although the NEXT Prophecies are rapidly racing toward fulfillment, they require the completion of the NOW's in order for their stage to become appropriately set.

The *LAST Prophecies* still have significant preconditions preventing them from finding fulfillment. They will find fulfillment relatively soon, but the LAST's have to wait in line behind the NOW's and NEXT's for their turn on the prophetic timeline.

The image below includes the numbers between #1 through #8 that identify the probable timing of the unfulfilled prophecies listed beneath the timeline. These numbers are sequenced in the three primary periods of the last days, which are;

1. *The Church age*, which ends with the Rapture.

2. *The Post-Rapture / Pre-Tribulation Gap Period*, which begins one second after the Rapture and concludes when the seven-year Tribulation period, (Trib-period), starts.

3. *The Seven-Year Tribulation Period,* which concludes with the Second Coming of Christ.

CAVEAT: In no way, does this timeline appendix attempt to set a date, time or any preconditions for the fulfillment of the Rapture prophecy. I believe that the Rapture is an imminent event that could happen at any time between now and the start of the seven-year Trib-period. It is a sign-less event, which means that the prophecy has no preconditions!

Apocalypse Road Timeline

The prophecies below are listed in the chronological order that the I believe they could happen. However, these events might find fulfillment differently than they are sequenced. Moreover, these predictions only represent some of, rather than all of, the prophecies of the end times. Each prediction begins with its time slot between numbers #1 through #8.

#1-Time Slot: The Church Age - *(Revelation Road)*

The **#1-time slot** concludes with the Rapture. Thus, all of these prophecies in the #1-time slot automatically shift to the **#2**-time slot of the Post-Rapture / Pre-Tribulation Gap Period, if they have not found fulfillment prior to the Rapture.

#1-Disaster in Iran – (Jeremiah 49:34-39),

#1-Destruction of Damascus – (Isaiah 17, Jer. 49:23-27),

#1- Final Arab-Israeli War- (Psalm 83),

#1-Toppling of Jordan – (Jer. 49:1-6, Zephaniah 2:8-10, Ezekiel 25:14),

#1-Terrorization of Egypt – (Isaiah 19:1-18),

#1- Expansion of Israel – (Obadiah 1:19-20, Jer. 49:2, Zephaniah 2:9, Isaiah 19:18),

#1-Vanishing of the Christians – (1 Corinthians 15:51-52, 1 Thessalonians 4:15-18).

#2-Time Slot: The Post-Rapture / Pre-Tribulation Gap Period - (*Apocalypse Road*)

Some of the **#2-time slot** begin in the #2 slot, but conclude in a subsequent time slot.

#2- Ezekiel 38; the Gog of Magog war, (Ezekiel 39-39),

#2- Supernatural signs and lying wonders from Satan, (2 Thess. 2:9),

#2- The 144,000 Jewish Witnesses emerge, (Rev. 7:1-8),

#2- First Seal: The White Horseman; the Antichrist, (Rev. 6:1-2),

#2- Second Seal: The Red Horseman; wars, (Rev. 6:3-4),

#2- Third Seal: The Black Horseman; famines, (Rev. 6:5-6),

#2- Fourth Seal: The Pale Horsemen; Death and Hades, (Rev. 6:7-8),

#2- Fifth Seal: The martyrdom of Christians, (Rev. 6:9-11),

#2- The Harlot World Religion emerges, (Rev. 17).

#3-6 Time Slots: The Seven-Year Tribulation Period - (*Tribulation Road*)

The Tribulation Period begins when the false covenant of Daniel 9:27 gets confirmed. This period is also referred to in the Bible as Daniel's Seventieth Week.

#3- The opening of the 6th and 7th Seal judgments, (Rev. 6:12-17 and Rev. 8:1),

#3- The sounding of the seven Trumpet judgments, (Rev. 8-9),

#3- The ministry of the 2 Witnesses, (Rev. 11:1-12),

#3- The building of the 3rd Jewish Temple, (Rev. 11:1-2),

#4- War in heaven and casting out of Satan and the fallen angels from heaven, (Rev. 12:7-9),

#4- The desolation of the Harlot World Religion, (Rev. 17:16),

#4- The killing and resurrection of the 2 Witnesses, (Rev. 11:1-12),

#4- The Abomination of Desolation, (Matthew 24:15),

#4- The campaign of Jewish genocide by the Antichrist begins, (Zechariah 13:8),

#4- The Mark of the Beast campaign by the False Prophet and the Antichrist, (Rev. 13:14-18),

#5- The pouring out of God's wrath in the seven Bowl judgments, (Rev. 16),

#5- The Armageddon campaign, (Joel 3:2, Rev. 16:6),

#5- The Remnant of Israel receives Christ as their Messiah, (Hosea 5:15, Matt. 23:39),

#6- The Second Coming of Christ, (Isaiah 63:1-6 and Matt. 24:30),

#6- The destruction of the Antichrist and his armies, (Daniel 11:45, 2 Thess. 2:8).

#7-8 Time Slots: The 75-day interval period and the Millennium

#7- Christ's victory ascent to the Mount of Olives, (Zechariah 14:4),

#7- The Sheep and Goat gentile judgments, (Matt. 25:31-46),

#8- The 1000-year millennial reign of Christ, (Rev. 20:4).

Endnotes

1   Characters not found inside Apocalypse Road are found in Revelation Road, Hope Beyond the Horizon, which is Book One of this series.

2   The "Message of Fatima" is available on the Internet as of 9/4/16 at this website: http://www.vatican.va/roman_curia/congregations/cfaith/documents/rc_con_cfaith_doc_20000626_message-fatima_en.html

3   Tanakh is the name used in Judaism for the canon of the Hebrew Bible. It includes the – The Torah ("Teaching", also known as the Five Books of Moses), Nevi'im ("Prophets") and Ketuyim ("Writings"). The Jewish Tanakh is the equivalent of the Christian Hebrew Old Testament

4   Jahannam is the word for Hell in Islam

5   Joel 2:28 and Acts 2:17 informs that in the last days that old men will dream dreams and young men will see visions.

6   1 Peter 1:7-9

7   Revelation 7:9 informs that all nations, tribes, peoples, and tongues are benefited by the ministry of the 144,000 witnesses.

8   Pogroms are defined as "The organized killing of many helpless people usually because of their race or religion by the Merriam Webster dictionary at this website: http://www.merriam-webster.com/dictionary/pogrom.

9   Information about the Griffon Vultures obtained over the Internet on 1/3/12 at this website: http://en.wikipedia.org/wiki/Griffon_Vulture Information about carnivores animals of Israel was obtained on the Internet on 1/3/12 at this website: http://www.listofcountriesoftheworld.com/is-animals.html

10   Information about carnivores animals of Israel was obtained on the Internet on 1/3/12 at this website: http://www.listofcountriesoftheworld.com/is-animals.html

11   Based upon Surah 3:40 in the Koran, which says: *And remember the angel's words to Mary. He said: "Allah has chosen you. He has made you pure and exalted you above all women. Diary, be obedient to your Lord; bow down and worship with the worshippers."*

12   The message of the third secret at Fatima is on this website: http://www.vatican.va/roman_curia/congregations/cfaith/documents/rc_con_cfaith_doc_20000626_message-fatima_en.html

13   Quote taken from Revelation Road page 224, and is duly footnoted to have been gathered from Dr. Ron Rhodes book, Northern Storm Rising.

14   S.O.S. is sometimes translated as "save our souls" or "save our ship."

15   Africanized Bees - The Africanized Bee is a descendant from 26 Tanzanian queen bees accidentally released from a lab in Brazil. The Biologist working with the bees was trying to develop a strain better adapted to tropical and subtropical conditions. Instead of more productive bees, he ended up with a strain of extremely defensive bees. The released queens gave rise to what is commonly called the Africanized Bee. They have since spread throughout the Americas. One sting from an Africanized bee is no worse than a sting from the common honey bee. It hurts but is rarely fatal. Unfortunately, the Africanized bees attack in swarms. Their victims may be stung thousands of times. That many stings can and does kill. Information gathered on 7/28/12 from this Internet site - http://www.squidoo.com/dangerous-bugs#module17098722

16   For more information on Mary of Agreda visit these two websites: https://en.wikipedia.org/wiki/Mary_of_Jesus_of_Ágreda / http://www.traditionalcatholicpublishing.com/n-city.html

17   Mary of Agreda quote is taken from the book by Thomas W. Petrisko called, "Call of the Ages," Santa Barbara, CA, Queenship Publishing, 1995, p. 449.

18   Quote from the book, "For the Soul of the Family," by Thomas W. Petrisko, Santa Barbara, California, Queenship Publishing, 1996, page 92.

19   The quotes of the Nostra Aetate were taken from the Internet on August 15, 2012 at this link http://www.vatican.va/archive/hist_councils/ii_vatican_council/documents/vat-ii_decl_19651028_nostra-aetate_en.html

20   St. Thomas Aquinas quote taken from the Internet on 10/20/16 from this website: http://www.catholictradition.org/Mary/mary18a.htm

21   St. Peter Chyrsologus quote taken from Internet on 10/20/16 from this website: http://www.catholictradition.org/Mary/mary18a.htm. As the Dr. of Homilies - http://www.dailycatholic.org/dec4doc.htm

22   Pope Gregory XVI quote from (Encyclical, Summo Jugiter), was taken on 10/20/16 from this website: http://catholicism.org/eens-popes.html

23   St. Bonaventure quotes taken on 10/20/16 from these websites: http://www.catholictradition.org/Mary/mary18a.htm, http://www.catholicgallery.org/quotes/quotes-about-mary-2/

24 The sign of peace is a ritual that is normally performed at a Catholic Mass. Read more about it at this website under the subtitle, "CDWDS Circular Letter on the Ritual Expression of the Gift of Peace at Mass." The website is: http://www.usccb. org/about/divine-worship/newsletter/upload/newsletter-2014-07-and-08.pdf

25 The Intinction is the administration of the sacrament of Communion by dipping bread in wine and giving both together to the communicant

26 Portions of this section, beginning with the word, "Many," was quoted from the book Message in Heaven by Jim Tetlow on pages 238-239. The quotes originated from, John Leary, *Prepare for the Great Tribulation and the Era of Peace,* Volume 7, Santa Barbara, CA. Queens Publishing, 1997, pp 8,57,58. Message from "Jesus" to John Leary.

27 Fruchtenbaum quote came from this website: http://lastdayscalendar.tripod.com/ twenty_four_elders.htmThe website quoted from his book called, The Footsteps of the Messiah, p.114

28 Definition of mystery is taken from the New American Standard Exhaustive Concordance.

29 The flag of Mohammed is described at this website: http://kenraggio.com/KRP-N-GreenHorse.html

30 The flag association between Saudi Arabia and the fourth horseman is made at this website: http://kenraggio.com/KRPN-GreenHorse.html

31 This website also associates Islam with Death and Hades of the fourth seal: http:// www.hope-of-israel.org.nz/GreenMustang6.html

32 Joel Richardson quote taken from this website: http://www.joelstrumpet. com/?p=5731

33 John Gill quote taken from the internet on 12/15/16 from this website: http://bible-hub.com/commentaries/gill/revelation/2.htm

34 Daniel's 70th week is located in Daniel 9:27. This 70th week is also commonly referred to as the Tribulation Period.

35 Dr. David Reagan quote was taken on 12/14/16 from this website: http://christin-prophecy.org/articles/the-great-tribulation/

36 Barnhouse quote taken from this website on page 88 of the PDF. http://timothy-tanministries.yolasite.com/resources/eBook/The%20Invisible%20War%20-%20 Donald%20Grey%20Barnhouse%20iPad.pdf

37   Quote taken from the book called, "*A Catechism for Adults*," page 43.

38   EWTN quote taken from this internet site on 12/15/16: http://www.ewtn.com/library/CATECHSM/NCOFCC.HTM

39   Baltimore Catechisms: Page 256 from this website: https://www.pcpbooks.net/docs/baltimore_catechism.pdf

40   Baltimore Catechisms: Page 290 from this website: https://www.pcpbooks.net/docs/baltimore_catechism.pdf

41   Six days of holy obligation are on Page 292 / #1333 of this website: https://www.pcpbooks.net/docs/baltimore_catechism.pdf

42   Baltimore Catechisms: Page 291 from this website: https://www.pcpbooks.net/docs/baltimore_catechism.pdf

43   Baltimore Catechisms: Page 291 from this website: https://www.pcpbooks.net/docs/baltimore_catechism.pdf

44   Pope John Paul II quote came from this website: http://jimmyakin.com/2010/05/grave-sin-mortal-sin.html

45   Dr. Fruchtenbaum quote taken on 12/7/16 from this website: http://chafer.nextmeta.com/files/v6n1_3.pdf

46   The timing determined to build the third temple is at this website: http://www.ldolphin.org/gano.html

47   The three prevailing views about the timing of the Third Temple are identified at this website: https://www.breakingisraelnews.com/48944/age-old-biblical-debate-searches-to-answer-which-comes-first-messiah-or-the-temple-jewish-world/#4krHl3HdfclpOBWl.97

48   Ethnos translations taken from the New American Standard Hebrew and Greek Dictionaries under G1484.

49   Pateo translation taken from Strong's Hebrew and Greek Dictionaries under G3961.

50   Dr. Fruchtenbaum quote was taken on 9/2/16 from this website: http://chafer.nextmeta.com/files/v6n1_3.pdf

51   Information about the Edict of Milan was taken on 9/3/16 from this website: http://quatr.us/religion/christians/constantine.htm

52 Headline taken on 9/2/16 from this website link: http://www.breakingisrael-news.com/34946/hezbollah-1500-rockets-israel-day-middle-east/#HsM-vUWEyoEas4Q1T.99

53 The Nineveh and Jerusalem Principles are newly designed concepts for this article and are not to be confused with other previously used concepts with the same name found on the Internet.

54 Greg Laurie quote taken from this Internet site: Read more at http://www.wnd.com/2013/08/94-year-old-billy-grahams-warning-for-america/#WMF23Ojl-wHL8rXlb.99

55 The date that Jonah went to Nineveh is located on this website: http://biblehub.com/timeline/jonah/1.htm

56 Jeremiah 25:11-12, 29:10

57 Franklin Graham quote taken from this Internet site: http://www.christianpost.com/news/franklin-graham-god-political-debate-put-him-back-in-decision-amer-ica-159090/

58 The Rapture is described in 1 Thessalonians 4:15-18, 1 Corinthians 15:51-52 and elsewhere. It is the event whereby Jesus Christ catches His bride, the Church, up to heaven.

59 2 Thess. 2:9, Revelation 11:6, Ezekiel 38:20-22.

60 Rev. 17:5.

61 Obadiah 1:18, Ezekiel 24:14, Jeremiah 49:2, Zephaniah 2:8, Isaiah 11:13-14, Zech-ariah 12:5-6 and elsewhere.

62 Ezekiel 38:18-39:6

63 *Northern Storm Rising* – Russia, Iran, And the Emerging End-Times Military Coalition Against Israel - Page 159 under "The Burial of Enemy Bodies for Seven Months (Ezekiel 39:11-12,14-16) Published by Harvest House 1- Copyright 2008. Authored by Dr. Ron Rhodes.

64 New King James Version; with emphasis added.

65 New King James Version; with emphasis added.

66 2 Thess. 2:9-12.

67   Isaiah 46:9-10 and John 1:1, and 14.

68   The Coming Global Transformation Amazon web links are below.

     Written version: https://www.amazon.com/Coming-Global-Transformation-Times-Presentation-ebook/dp/B01KYDPCMI/ref=sr_1_2?ie=UTF8&qid=-1480788292&sr=8-2&keywords=the+coming+global+transformation

     Audio version: https://www.amazon.com/Coming-Global-Transformation-Times-Presentation/dp/099822281X/ref=sr_1_3?ie=UTF8&qid=1480788292&sr=8-3&keywords=the+coming+global+transformation

69   2 Thess. 2:9-10

70   Acts 4:8-12, John 3:16, Romans 10:9-11

71   Arnold Fruchtenbaum, The Footsteps of the Messiah: A Study of the Sequence of Prophetic Events (San Antonio: Ariel Press, 1982), p. 176.

72   https://timlahaye.com/Home/Content/527

73   Pew research information was taken on 9/8/16 from this website: https://en.wikipedia.org/wiki/Religion_in_the_United_States

74   World army rankings were taken on 9/8/16 from this website: http://www.globalfirepower.com/countries-listing.asp

75   British Isle statement was taken from this website: https://en.wikipedia.org/wiki/British_Isles on 12/15/15.

76   Dr. Mark Hitchcock quote taken from this website: http://www.lamblion.us/2010/02/hitchcock-discusses-us-in-ezekiel-38-39.html on 12/15/15.

77   Dr. J. R. Church quote taken from page 220. The Guardian of the Grail book is in reprint and available for purchase at www.prophecyinthenews.com

78   You can watch this entire Hocking and Salus event at this website: https://vimeo.com/26460214

79   Cornwall information taken from this website heraldofhope.org.au/wp-content/uploads/2013/12/Tarshish-Britain-or-Spain.pdf on 12/18/15

80   Comment taken from this website article: http://heraldofhope.org.au/wp-content/uploads/2013/12/Tarshish-Britain-or-Spain.pdf

81   Quote taken from Wikipedia website at this link: https://en.wikipedia.org/wiki/British_Empire on 12/16/15.

82   World army rankings taken from the Global Firepower website linked here: http://www.globalfirepower.com/countries-listing.asp

83   The Temple Institutes website is: http://www.templeinstitute.org/

84   This event has not yet occurred, almost 2000 years after. That centuries have passed since the destruction of the

     Jewish genealogical records further evidence the supernatural orchestration of the emergence of these pure-bred Jewish witnesses. Only a God, who knows the beginning from the end, would be able to trace their tribal origins.

85   Regarding the mystery: Romans 11:25, Ephesians 3:3-6. Regarding the grafting in: Romans 11:17-24

86   John 1:29, 36 refers to Christ as the sacrificial Lamb of God.

87   Holman Bible Dictionary.

88   Thomas Nelson Publishers, Inc Nashville, Tennessee 2010 page 2371

89   Jamieson-Fausset-Brown Bible Commentary at this website: http://biblehub.com/commentaries/jfb/revelation/14.htm

90   John Gill's exposition of the Bible at this website: http://www.biblestudytools.com/commentaries/gills-exposition-of-the-bible/revelation-14-4.html

91   Matthew Poole's Commentary at this website: http://biblehub.com/commentaries/poole/revelation/14.htm

92   Direct apparition messages are available to read on these Internet sites:

     http://www.world-prayer-for-life.org/pg051.html

     http://en.wikipilipinas.org/index.php/1986_Apparition_-_Manila,_Philippines

93   History of the Rosary quote was taken from this website link: http://www.theholy-rosary.org/rosaryhistory

94   The Fifteen Promises of the Rosary can be all read at this website: http://www.theholyrosary.org/rosarybenefits

95   The Fallible Assumption of Mary is also on the Internet at this site: http://www.prophecydepotministries.net/2011/the-fallible-assumption-of-mary/

96   Mary apparition quotes taken from the Internet on 9/19/16 at this link: http://www.medjugorje.eu/amsterdam/

97 Rapture verses are in 1 Corinthians 15:51-52 and 1 Thessalonians 4:15-18. The Catholic position on the Rapture is taken from this Internet link on 9/21/16: http://www.catholiceducation.org/en/religion-and-philosophy/apologetics/are-we-living-in-the-last-days.html

98 The Chosen People quote is taken from the Internet at this site on 9/23/16: http://novusordowatch.org/2015/11/pius-xi-jews-friends-israel/

99 Amillennialism quote taken from this Catholic forums website on 9/22/16: http://forums.catholic.com/showthread.php?t=97141

100 Concerning the consecration of the world to Mary on October 8, 2000. http://www.theholyrosary.org/fatimaapparitions

101 World Peace and consecration to the Immaculate Heart of Mary are mentioned on this website: http://www.ewtn.com/library/MARY/FIRSTSAT.htm

102 Petrisko quote taken from his book, "Call of the Ages." Queenship Publishing Santa Barbara, California, 1995, pages 197-198.

103 Isabel Bettwy quote taken from her book called, "I Am The Guardian of the Faith: Reported Apparitions of the Mother of God in Ecuador." The visionary quoted is Patricia (Pachi) Talbot. Franciscan University Press Steubenville, Ohio, 1991, page 63.

104 Encyclopedia Britannica quote was taken on 9/22/16 from this website link: https://www.britannica.com/place/Seven-Hills-of-Rome

105 J. C. Ryle, Light from Old Times - Volume 1, Charles Nolan Publishers, Moscow, ID, 1890, pages 54-55.

106 Paschal definition taken on 9/26/16 from this website: https://www.smp.org/dynamicmedia/files/6373199144c2b62a4a01b759411d98dd/TX001312_1-Background-Paschal_Mystery.pdf

107 Quote about the wine taken on 9/28/16 from this website: https://www.ewtn.com/library/Doctrine/EUCHAR10.HTM

108 John Walvoord book entitled, *Every Prophecy of the Bible*, on page 606.

109 Tim LaHaye book is entitled, *Revelation Illustrated and Made Plain*, page 285.

110 Barnes Notes on the New Testament by Albert Barnes... Revelation 17 commentary section.

111 Arno C. Gaebelein, The Revelation, New York, NY, "Our Hope," 1915, pp. 99, 101,102.

112 Pagan Rome and Papal Rome quote taken on 10/6/16 from this website: http://www.reformation.org/pope-constantine.pdf

113 Fish symbol explanation taken from this website: http://www.christianitytoday.com/history/2008/august/what-is-origin-of-christian-fish-symbol.html

114 Foxe's Christian Martyrs of the World, Uhrichsville, OH, Barbour & Company, Inc, pp.64 1990

115 Foxe's Christian Martyrs of the World, Uhrichsville, OH, Barbour & Company, Inc, pp.75-76 1990

116 Catechism of the Catholic Church, no. 891.

117 https://en.wikipedia.org/wiki/Council_of_Trent

118 These important notes from The Council of Trent were taken on 10/13/16 from this website: https://www.thegospelcoalition.org/article/9-things-you-should-know-about-the-council-of-trent

119 Sedevacantists information was taken from this website on 10/13/16: https://en.wikipedia.org/wiki/Traditionalist_Catholic

120 Zeitoun quote taken from this website: http://www.zeitun-eg.org/zeitoun1.htm

121 Queen of All: The Marian apparitions' plan to unite all religions under the Roman Catholic Church by Jim Tetlow, Roger Oakland and Brad Myers. Page 5, Eternal Productions 17 Harvest Road, Fairport, NY 14450. 2006. This book is available as a paperback and also as a Kindle book at Amazon.

122 Ibid., page 6

123 Quotes taken from two separate Internet sources on 10/20/16 at this website: http://www.therealpresence.org/eucharst/mir/english_pdf/Ferrara.pdf and http://www.christusrex.org/www1/apparitions/http:/pr00054.htm

124 Quotes taken on 10/20/16 at this website: http://www.therealpresence.org/eucharst/mir/english_pdf/Bordeaux.pdf

125 Voices, Visions, and Apparitions, authored by Michael Freze, OSV Publishing 1993, Page 52

126 Book called, "Eucharistic Miracles and Eucharistic Phenomena In The Lives Of The Saints," by Joan Carroll Cruz 1987 Tan Books and Publishers, Inc. Rockford, Illinois. Pages 251, 253.

127 Article accessed on 10/24/16 from this website: http://www.ncregister.com/dai-ly-news/truth-or-hoax-alleged-eucharistic-miracle-under-investigation-in-mexico

128 Quoted from this website: http://www.therealpresence.org/eucharst/mir/english_pdf/Regensburg.pdf

129 Quoted from this website: http://therealpresence.org/eucharst/mir/english_pdf/Lanciano1.pdf

130 "Why World Peace Depends on it is taken from this website: http://www.fatima.org/consecrussia/peacedepends.asp

131 Quoted from this website: http://www.fatima.org/consecrussia/peacedepends.asp

132 Quotes about Russia taken from this website: http://www.fatima.org/consecrussia/peacedepends.asp

133 Messages from Heaven Amazon link: https://www.amazon.com/Messages-Heav-en-Biblical-Examination-Heavens-ebook/dp/B01I4HGEBY/ref=sr_1_1?ie=UTF8&q-id=1480628891&sr=8-1&keywords=messages+from+heaven

   Another Jesus Amazon link: https://www.amazon.com/Another-Jesus-eucha-rist-christ-evangelization/dp/0979131529/ref=sr_1_1?ie=UTF8&qid=-1480629107&sr=8-1&keywords=another+jesus+roger+Oakland

134 Plague information was taken on 11/4/16 from this website, http://ancienthistory.about.com/od/epidemics/tp/10PlaguesEgypt.htm

135 The Revelation Record by Henry M. Morris, Tyndale House Publishers, Inc. Wheaton, Illinois; pages 193-194

136 Babylon and Jerusalem reference times taken from the New King James Version.

137 Jezebel and Harlot parallels were taken from the Queen of All book by Jim Tetlow, Roger Oakland and Brad Myers; pages 112-113

138 Twist of globalisation: All faiths come together article was taken from this website: http://expressindia.indianexpress.com/news/fullstory.php?newsid=35246

139 Quote taken from this website: http://spiralgoddess.com/Mary.html

140 Holman Bible Dictionary under the category of Asherah.

141 Quote taken from Wikipedia at this website: https://en.wikipedia.org/wiki/Asherah.

142 *nikaoô*, translated from the New American Standard Hebrew and Greek Dictionaries

143 Stephanos definition is from Strong's Concordance. It was taken from this website: http://biblehub.com/greek/4735.htm

144 Dr. Reagan book is published by Lamb & Lion Ministries; First edition (October 9, 2012). It is available at his website: www.lamblion.com.

145 Sinner's Prayer quote taken from Wikipedia over the Internet on 8/13/11 at this link: http://en.wikipedia.org/wiki/Sinner's_prayer

146 Sinner's prayer example was copied from the Internet on 8/13/11 at this website link: http://www.salvationprayer.info/prayer.html (slight emphasis was added in this appendix)

147 Quote welcoming those who prayed the sinner's prayer into the family of God copied over the Internet on 8/13/11 at this link: http://www.salvationprayer.info/prayer.html

148 The days will be shortened into seven years, which is commonly referred to by Christians as the "Tribulational Period," or "Daniel's Seventieth Week." Apparently, the continuance of the perilous events beyond seven years would ultimately lead to the destruction of mankind.

149 Fatima quote taken on 9/29/16 from this website: http://www.catholicapologetics.info/catholicteaching/privaterevelation/russia.htm

150 Consecration explanations taken on 9/29/16 from this website: http://www.catholicapologetics.info/catholicteaching/privaterevelation/russia.htm

151 Pope Benedict XV quote taken from this website: http://www.fatima.org/essentials/facts/PopeBenXV.asp

152 Pope John Paul II quote taken from this website: https://catholicstrength.com/2015/12/11/saint-john-paul-ii-and-devotion-to-our-lady-of-guadalupe/

153 Battle of Lepanto quote taken from this website: http://realmenpraytherosary.org/october-7th-feast-of-our-lady-of-the-rosary-battle-of-lepanto/

154 Prof. Plinio Corrêa de Oliveira quote taken from this website: http://www.tradition-inaction.org/SOD/j128sdHelpofChristians_4-24.htm

155 Tribulation Road, is the final book of the trilogy and has not been published as of the release of this book.

The NOW Prophecies

**Disaster in Iran
Destruction of Damascus
Decline of America
The Final Arab-Israeli War**

God's word to Noah was to prepare NOW for a world-wide flood. God's word to Joseph was to prepare Pharaoh and Egypt NOW for seven years of famine. God's word to Jeremiah was to prepare the Jews NOW for seventy years of exile into Babylon.

The key word in these historical examples was NOW! What does God's Word say for us to prepare for NOW? What are the tough decisions we need to make?

The NOW Prophecies book identifies the biblical prophecies that were written centuries ago for THIS GENERATION! These ancient inscriptions predict powerful events that will profoundly affect everyone.

This book makes it easy to understand how to get ready NOW for what to expect in the near future!

Bill Salus is a media personality that has appeared on major Christian TV networks like, TBN, CBN, Daystar and more. Additionally, he is a conference speaker and the bestselling author of Psalm 83, The Missing Prophecy Revealed, How Israel Becomes the Next Mideast Superpower. Visit Bill's website at www.prophecydepot. com

Nuclear Showdown
in Iran

Revealing the Ancient
Prophecy of Elam

Missiles cloud Mideast skies over the Persian Gulf. Iran shuts down the Strait of Hormuz. Arab oil is choked off to world markets. Hezbollah and Hamas launch scores of missiles into Israel. Terror cells initiate cycles of violence in America. Global economies begin to collapse. Radioactivity permeates the skies over Bushehr's nuclear reactor. Countless Iranian's hastily seek refuge into neighboring nations. The Arabian Gulf becomes a cesspool of contamination. Desalinization plants can't process the polluted waters. A humanitarian crisis burgeons out of control. A disaster of epic biblical proportion has finally arrived in the Middle East!

About 2600 years ago the Hebrew prophets Jeremiah and Ezekiel issued parallel end times prophecies concerning modern-day Iran.

Today the rogue country is becoming a nuclear nation and aggressively advancing its hegemony throughout the greater Middle East. Nuclear Showdown in Iran, Revealing the Ancient Prophecy of Elam is a non-fiction thriller taking the reader on a journey of discovery through the eyes of the prophets and the minds of today's key national players.

Can anything good come from the evil that is about to befall us?

The ancient prophecy of Elam will reveal what God has ordained, what the prophets saw and what you need to know and do now.

Psalm 83
The Missing Prophecy Revealed

An ancient prophecy written over 3000 years ago reveals that the Arab states and terrorist populations, which presently share common borders with Israel, will soon confederate in order to wipe Israel off of the map. These enemies of Israel are depicted on the red arrows upon the book cover image, and their mandate is clear:

> They have said, "Come, and let us cut them off from being a nation, That the name of Israel may be remembered no more." (Psalm 83:4).

Psalm 83 predicts a climactic, concluding Arab-Israeli war that has eluded the discernment of today's top Bible scholars, and yet, the Middle East stage appears to be set for the fulfillment of this prophecy. While many of today's top Bible experts are predicting that Russia, Iran, Turkey, Libya, and several other countries are going to invade Israel according a prophecy in Ezekiel 38, this timely book explains how Psalm 83 occurs prior. Discover how Israel defeats their ancient Arab enemies, and why Americans need to stand beside Israel in this coming war! Here are a few endorsements from the experts:

"Invaluable New Insights"

– Dr. David Reagan, the founder of Lamb and Lion
Ministries and host of Christ in Prophecy Television

"I wish I would have written it"

– Dr. David Hocking, the founder
of Hope for Today Ministries

"Groundbreaking"

– Dr. Thomas Horn, bestselling author
and founder of Raiders News Network.

Buy your copy of Psalm 83, the Missing Prophecy
Revealed at *http://www.prophecydepot.com*

Psalm 83: The Missing Prophecy Revealed, How Israel Becomes the Next Mideast Superpower

Table of Contents

Chapter 1 The Missing Prophetic Puzzle Piece

Chapter 2 Can the Future of the Middle East be Known? Overview of Psalm 83

Chapter 3 When Diplomacy Ends, War Begins

Chapter 4 The Mideast Stage is Set for the Apocalyptic Wars

Chapter 5 Psalm 83 or Ezekiel 38, What's the Next Middle East News Headline?

Chapter 6 Israel's Exceedingly Great Army

Chapter 7 My People Israel

Chapter 8 The Future for America in Bible Prophecy

Chapter 9 America's Role in Psalm 83

Chapter 10 Isralestine - God's Middle East Peace Plan

Chapter 11 Who-domites? Who Are the Edomites Today?

Chapter 12 The Ancient Arab Hatred of the Jews

Chapter 13 The Final Palestinian Farewell - The Reprisal of Edom

Chapter 14 Psalm 83 and the Prophets

Chapter 15 The Psalm 83 Report

Chapter 16 Obadiah's Mysterious Vision

Chapter 17 Psalm 83 - The Arab Confederacy

Chapter 18 The Ezekiel 35 – Psalm 83 Connection – the War Before Ezekiel 38

Chapter 19 The Three Judgments of Egypt

Chapter 20 Egypt's Desolation, Deportation, and Conversion

Chapter 21 Isaiah 17—The Destruction of Damascus

Chapter 22 The Destruction of Damascus Continued

Chapter 23 Ezekiel 38-39 Overview

Chapter 24 Iran's Double Jeopardy in the End Times – The prophecies of Elam and Persia

Chapter 25 Why Iran's Absent from Psalm 83

Chapter 26 Greater Israel - The Future Maps of Isralestine

Chapter 27 Preparing for Psalm 83

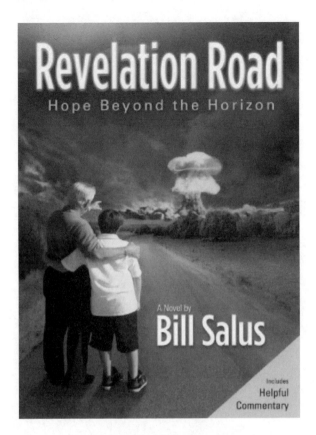

Revelation Road
Hope Beyond the Horizon

You are invited on a one-of-a-kind reading experience. Enjoy a novel and biblical commentary at the same time. This unique book is designed with appeal for both fiction and non-fiction audiences. George Thompson believes his grandson Tyler lives in the final generation. Lovingly, he prepares the lad for the treacherous road ahead. All young Tyler wanted was a chance to join his sister at East-side Middle School in the fall, but the Arab Spring led to an apocalyptic summer disrupting his plans. Middle East wars and nuclear terror in America quickly turned his world upside down. Join the Thompson's on their journey through the Bible prophecies of the end times, and discover how their gripping story uncovers the silver lining of hope against the backdrop of global gloom and doom. The commentary section explains how their story could soon become your reality!